D1083695

Criticism of Oral Rhetoric

Criticism of Oral Rhetoric

Carroll C. Arnold

The Pennsylvania State University

Charles E. Merrill Publishing Company
A Bell & Howell Company
Columbus, Ohio

Published by
Charles E. Merrill Publishing Co.
A Bell & Howell Company
Columbus, Ohio 43216

Copyright © 1974 by Bell & Howell Company. All rights reserved. No part of this book may be reproduced in any form, electronic or mechanical, including photocopy, recording, or any information storage and retrieval system, without permission in writing from the publisher.

ISBN: 0-675-08812-7

Library of Congress Catalog Card Number: 73-93006

2 3 4 5 6 7 8—79 78 77 76 75

Printed in the United States of America

To

A. Craig Baird who opened my eyes
to the nature of rhetorical
criticism;

The Pennsylvania State University
students who have taught me
through their criticisms;

Bie Arnold, candid, best critic.

Table of Contents

Preface

This book exists in part because when I was an undergraduate I could find no one in a group of excellent teachers who could explain to me why what I took to be a florid, platitudinous speech by Fisher Ames should have contributed to the implementation of the Jay Treaty of 1794-1795. Some historians have said Ames's "On the Treaty with Great Britain" (April 28, 1796) had that effect in the House of Representatives. Yet the principles of literary and logical criticism my teachers and I knew confirmed our own judgments that the speech was a poor thing indeed.

That literary, rhetorical, and speech criticism could and should be conceived as distinguishable processes using at least some distinctive data and norms, I first learned from A. Craig Baird. On reapproaching Ames's speech as rhetoric and as speech, I found it a personal act by an ailing legislator, done to remind a legislature lost in details that, whatever their faults, treaties are the bonds and sureties of nations. On such terms Ames's florid address achieves historical standing as a social action, though it may be a nullity as literature and logic. A major goal in writing this book has been to assist others, and myself, in making such distinctions in the criticism of verbal works.

There are two basic and probably never wholly answerable questions I invite readers to explore with me. They seem deceptively simple when phrased. They are: What happened when *A* spoke seriously to *B*? Did *A* achieve as much as was possible in rhetorical relationship with *B?* The chapters that follow suggest some ways of asking subquestions in the hope of securing partial answers to the basic questions.

I would be chagrined if anyone supposes I proffer *the* ways of describing, interpreting, and evaluating oral rhetoric. My aim is to present *some* ways of probing. The inquiries I propose have two concerns in common: discovering basic *phenomena* of rhetorical situations and rhetorical talk *and* interpreting those phenomena *socially*. Rhetorical speech is personalized action having social ends. Hence, I take it, the most fundamental problem in its criticism is to find ways of exploring it as social force. The critical processes suggested here tend to serve that purpose.

The nature of rhetoric that is oral and the nature of its criticism are treated in chapters I and II. Since talk symbolically communicates ideas, chapters III and IV deal with how obvious and less obvious ideas may be espied and interpreted. Chapter V explores some ways by which structure and form modify listeners' perceptions of verbalized thought and feeling, and chapters VI, VII, and VIII examine the further modifying potentialities of oral style. The little charted influence of nonverbal phenomena is the subject of chapter IX; and chapter X treats special problems which often, but not invariably, confront critics of rhetorical speech.

Unabridged texts of eight speeches appear in Appendixes A and B. Parts of each speech are examined as illustrative matter in chapters of this book, but each speech remains an inviting object for comprehensive criticism. Appendix B also contains two critiques in which critical methods suggested here have been applied. I trust these critiques will be read as the personal experiments in criticism which they are, and not as "models."

My deepest debts are acknowledged in the dedication of this volume, but I have other important accounts to acknowledge. Richard L. Johannesen read the next-to-final draft of this book; the final version would be far poorer, indeed, were it not for his extraordinarily helpful criticisms and suggestions. For encouragement, help, and prodding I am indebted to Mr. Denny Rea and Mr. Tom Hutchinson of Charles E. Merrill Publishing Company. And to all my colleagues in the Department of Speech at The Pennsylvania State University I am obligated for intellectual stimulation from which derives whatever I may have thought afresh.

C. C. A.
University Park, Pennsylvania

Criticism of Oral Rhetoric

Chapter I

Speech as Object of Criticism

No one wants to analyze all the speech around him or her. There is not time. More urgent demands have to be met. But at other times knowing what speech *did* or *is doing* is necessary if we are to understand the patterns of human events. Thucydides thought the ways of Athens could not be understood apart from understanding Pericles's powers of speech:

> ... Pericles attempted to stop the Athenians from being angry with him and to guide their thoughts in a direction away from their immediate sufferings. So far as public policy was concerned, they accepted his arguments, sending no more embassies to Sparta and showing increased energy in carrying on the war; yet as private individuals they still felt the weight of their misfortunes. ... In fact, the general ill feeling against Pericles persisted, and was not satisfied until they had condemned him to pay a fine. Not long afterwards, however, as is the way with crowds, they re-elected him to the generalship and put all their affairs into his hands. ... It was he who led them, rather than they who led him, and, since he never sought power from any wrong motive, he was under no necessity of flattering them: in fact he was so highly respected that he was able to speak angrily to them and to contradict them. Certainly when he saw that they were going too far

in a mood of over-confidence, he would bring back to them a sense of their dangers; and when they were discouraged for no good reason he would restore their confidence.[1]

When the qualities of men's talk chart cultural paths, the nature of that talk requires understanding. The standards of speech which Cicero set in Latin oratory and which Augustine set in Latin preaching were the rhetorical models of Europe for a thousand years after their own times. One cannot know the literary history of that era without knowledge of Cicero's orations and Augustine's homilies. English criminal law respecting insanity cannot be understood historically without some knowledge of the brief but skillful plea Lord Thomas Erskine made on behalf of the deranged James Hadfield at the beginning of the nineteenth century. Temple University in Philadelphia exists because Russell Conwell conceived an immensely popular, if platitudinous, lecture "Acres of Diamonds" and founded a college with the proceeds.

Especially in democratic societies history turns on the qualities of speech. Robert Oliver is probably right in saying:

> Americans and all others who "live" democracy as well as value it, talk out their mutual concerns. There is no substitute for face-to-face confrontation. . . . *Man speaking* is the prototype American democrat. How he speaks, why, and with what results, are matters worthy of our constant concern.[2]

Political speaking illustrates the point most easily. The Kennedy-Nixon debates of 1960 suggest how sharply the qualities of public speech can shape a democratic society's future. More than 101 million Americans watched and heard at least one of the four 1960 "debates" between the presidential aspirants, John F. Kennedy and Richard M. Nixon.[3] The election contest proved so close that the contestants' qualities of speaking may well have determined the outcome. Social scientists have concluded:

> . . . the data appear to show that: (1) Viewing the debates tended to shift opinion in favor of Kennedy. (2) The gain for Kennedy appeared to have come from the ranks of the undecided. (3) The average gain for Kennedy, in these data, was about 4 percentage points per debate. (4) On the whole, the debates did not cause Nixon to lose favor with those who favored him in the first place. Kennedy's advantage was his gain from the large reservoir of undecideds rather than a direct net gain from Nixon.[4]

In nonelectoral politics, too, speaking and reports of speaking create influence far beyond the forums occupied. Such disparate figures as Malcolm X, the Reverend Billy Graham, Israel's Abba Eban, and former Chief Justice of the Supreme Court Earl Warren have given currency to ideas far more through addressing specific audiences than through writing for multitudes. In short, we live constantly with the consequences of others' speech acts, but we often do not understand them well enough to understand our own situations.

Given these conditions of social life, it is strange that the nature of oral discourse has interested relatively few Western thinkers. How speech is created, how it functions, and how it is received and interpreted have been given only sporadic study. All nonfictional prose has suffered analytical and critical neglect; persuasive prose has drawn still less systematic attention; and spoken rhetoric has worked its powerful ways in most cultures with the least methodological analysis.

It is not yet clear why the post-Renaissance world displayed so little interest in what Charles Sears Baldwin called the movement of composition "primarily intellectual, a progress from idea to idea determined logically." [5] Neither is it clear why oral rhetoric has received even less attention. We cannot deny, however, that English-speaking peoples and others have suddenly passed from a world in which print set standards for general communication into a world where the aural-visual dimensions of rhetoric have probably more importance than at any time since the end of the Greco-Roman era.

New media of audio-visual communication give speech a new ubiquity and potency, but other factors have also hastened the change. Social mobility, rapid transportation, and changes in habits of personal association have given spoken communication importance to a degree unthought of even in the 1930s. Welfare clients and other "disadvantaged" persons are brought by hundreds to state and national capitals to speak with governmental officials; university professors speak, consult, and teach so frequently in distant places that students and boards of regents protest their absences from "home" classrooms. International forums for youth and a thousand other special groups make face-to-face, intercultural communication commonplace. Pre-campaign phases of seeking executive, legislative, and party leadership include speaking and consulting around the world as normal features. Indeed, the citizen who is not constantly exposed to the oral rhetoric of people normally far removed from him and the public figure who is not engaged in making such communication have come to be defined as victims—of "underdevelopment" on the one hand and of "underexposure" on the other. In these and many other ways changing social and communicative patterns are so structuring life that none of us can avoid exposure to public speech, and few can realize their goals without making increasing amounts of public speech.

To understand and profit from this strongly rhetorical part of our social environment we need the most reliable descriptions of speech events that are possible. A first step toward obtaining those descriptions is to distinguish the rhetorical portions of public speech from other familiar patterns of our communication. Much confusion comes from trying to describe one mode of communicating while using concepts appropriate chiefly to some other mode. This kind of confusion has occurred for centuries when Westerners have tried to discuss "literature," "rhetoric" in general, and "rhetoric" that is oral.

LITERATURE, RHETORIC, AND ORAL RHETORIC [6]

We usually use the term *literature* to refer either to (1) imaginative, enduring works or (2) bodies of writing that deal with particular topics of study (e.g., the "literature" on nuclear fission). The second is a fairly specialized usage; "literature" more often carries the first meaning. The phrase "literary criticism" refers almost invariably to the analysis and judgment of imaginative, linguistic works. But the question of where one applies or does not apply the principles of "literary criticism" has never had an obvious answer. A "literary critic" has no need to justify his function if he treats poetry, the texts of plays, prose fiction, traditional essays, or those few remnants of speaking that have earned such "literary" labels as "oratorical masterpieces." But if a person calling himself a "literary critic" were to turn his skills of "literary" analysis on Edward Gibbon or Thomas Babington Macaulay as writers of history, or on David Hume's persuasive, philosophical writing, or on the colorfulness of W. T. Stead's journalism, or on Benjamin Disraeli's parliamentary speaking, that critic would, indeed, need to defend the proposition that what he explored constituted "literature" and was a proper target for the methods of "literary criticism." It would be fairly contended against him that the norms by which "literature" is ordinarily judged do not reveal the essentials of history, philosophy, journalism, or public speaking. The critic might be justly asked whether he had other-than-literary competence that justified his "excursion" beyond the domain of imaginative, usually fictive writing. Implied in such a challenge is an accepted view of man's verbal works: some of them are *other than* "imaginative" in the "literary" sense. Then what are they?

Other-than-literary verbal materials often have been loosely labeled "rhetorical." This has raised such problems as: Are history, philosophy, and journalism alike in some way that justifies their bearing a *single* descriptive label? We need not enter debate on that question because our concern is not to decide where to attach the term *rhetoric* but to decide what we are saying if we attach that term to what is spoken. On this, we can be quite clear.

In Greece *rhetoric* was defined as "the faculty of observing in any given case the available means of persuasion." [7] Obviously, finding "means of persuasion" for a "given case" is not the same as finding the means of creating an imaginative, usually fictive communication. Imaginative and fictive works are seldom produced to persuade in a particular set of circumstances. Even if we use Donald C. Bryant's deliberately broader definition of what is "rhetorical," most imaginative, fictive works fall at least partly outside what Bryant calls "rhetoric." For Bryant, what is "rhetorical" has "the function of adjusting ideas to people and people to ideas," and "rhetoric" as an art is "the rationale of informative and suasory discourse." [8] Bryant means to imply that there may be "rhetoric" *in* "literature." But "adjusting" as an active process and "informative and suasory" as primary purposes cannot *fully* describe the character and purposes of most imaginative, fictive works. They may be "adjustive," but they are apt to be something more. They have "informative and suasory" purposes, but they almost invariably have aesthetic purposes too. "Rhetoric" as Bryant conceives it can sensibly refer to *some* aspects of *some* verbal works we are likely to call "literary," but "rhetoric" will not designate their full character.

What we see in Aristotle's and Bryant's definitions are attempts to point out that in some of what people do with words there is an obvious effort to change other people's views *in direct, deliberate ways*. Both definitions imply that there are also verbal works in which this practical intention is *not primary*. The implication is that some works have and some do not have the strongly practical, deliberate, suasory, or instructional qualities that are associated with the "rhetorical."

If there are such differences of purpose and character among verbal works, it is understandable that in Western culture there has often been an impulse to distinguish "literary" from "rhetorical" works. And, of course, those distinctions, if they exist, explain why we do not assume that a "literary critic" is automatically qualified to pass judgment on a parliamentary speech or that a "rhetorical critic" is automatically qualified to pass judgment on a novel or poem. The questions that identify and the standards by which we evaluate imaginative, fictive creations will not identify and allow full evaluation of practical, informative, and suasory creations. And what we need to say about a practical, persuasive speech in order to reveal its nature, as speech, will not help us much in explaining a novel, as novel. Some works of man invite interpretation and evaluation by one set of principles, and other works must be interpreted and evaluated by other principles. Therefore anyone thinking about criticism must specify *which* sets of critical questions he is going to apply to whatever he looks at. The terms "rhetorical" and "literary" are useful means of signaling whether one's questions and standards are those peculiarly appropriate to practical suasion and instruction or to imaginative, fictive works.

In this book I shall consider chiefly how we may better understand *rhetorical* forces when they are *oral*. For the sake of clear focus I propose to set aside other-than-rhetorical considerations in criticism. The choice is arbitrary. *Paradise Lost* is a poem with prominent rhetorical features that can only be completely understood if Milton's rhetorical methods are examined together with his literary methods. Many novels (e.g., Upton Sinclair's historic *The Jungle)* have rhetorical dimensions. They cannot be fully understood unless both their "literary" and "rhetorical" dimensions are studied. The same is true of much advertising and many filmic works. Informative and suasory intentions may be present, but nonrhetorical questions and questions about media other than speech must be raised if the full force of these works is to be understood. So, without challenging the proposition that many works of man are created to achieve "literary" *and* "rhetorical" functions, I choose to focus this book upon the "rhetorical" —the directly informative and suasory.

When one decides to explore the rhetorical aspects of human discourse, he still faces the question of whether the medium of presentation distinctively molds the objects of study. For reasons that will emerge, I take the position that when rhetorical communication is presented orally it differs in kind from rhetorical communication delivered in less personalized ways. Accordingly this book will treat the study of *speaking* in which informing and persuading are prominent and sustained goals. One reason for this rather arbitrary focus is that until relatively recent times commentators and critics have given the peculiar dimensions of oral rhetoric little attention.

Nearly fifty years ago Herbert A. Wichelns wrote:

> We have not much serious criticism of oratory. The reasons are patent. Oratory is intimately associated with statecraft; it is bound up with the things of the moment; its occasion, its terms, its background can often be understood only by the careful student of history. Again, the publication of orations as pamphlets leaves us free to regard any speech merely as an essay, as a literary effort deposited at the shrine of the muses in hope of being blessed with immortality.[9]

Wichelns wrote this comment after surveying a large body of eighteenth, nineteenth, and early twentieth century writing on literary criticism, biography, and history. In general, he found scant attention paid to the role of public speech in public life and culture. Since the 1920s perhaps two or three shelves of careful analyses of spoken rhetoric have been produced, and these have been prepared chiefly by scholars associated with the Speech Communication Association and its predecessors and affiliates.

One might expect that modern journalists would have attended to the growing powers of spoken rhetoric in the nations of the world, but they have not. Most journalists, even radio and television journalists, seem fixedly oriented toward writing and therefore unable to view oral communication as *action* rather than as "literary effort deposited at the shrine of the muses in hope of being blessed with immortality." In 1959, John F. Wilson surveyed more than a thousand journalistic commentaries on speeches and speakers in America. He was led to make the following description of what he found in books, magazines, and newspapers published in the first half of the twentieth century:

> Patterns occasionally . . . grow out of a chronological consideration of the speech or out of cause-effect relationships, but more often lay criticism is tossed off at random or organized around a series of topics arranged in a hierarchy revealing [the critic's] personal preference rather than systematic consideration. . . . The treatment of topic is chosen as fancifully as the method.
>
> . . .

While one may be sure that every commentator had some conscious or unconscious image in his own mind as to what constituted excellence, he only infrequently reveals that image to the reader. When he does so, it is many times almost an accident.[10]

It would be difficult to demonstrate that journalistic treatment of oral rhetoric has changed in the decade and a half since Wilson drew these conclusions.

The general neglect of oral rhetoric by historians, biographers, critics, and journalists can probably be traced to a conception of communicative behavior that has dominated much of Anglo-American literary thought since the eighteenth century. That view of how linguistic creativity occurs is described by René Wellek in these words:

> The process of creation, not being easily observable or measurable, was . . . conceived as something fundamentally irrational, a result of the subconscious forces of the human mind, a product of feeling and volition, even of enthusiasm, passion, and inspiration. Such a process of creation was considered ideal. . . .[11]

This view of verbal creativity is by no means dead, as a critic of modern prose indicates:

> Knowing that he cannot hope to interest, or even make himself fully intelligible to, the whole of the contemporary reading public, the twentieth-century novelist or historian does not even try: he writes for his own public, whatever that may be. The chances are that his public will be people more or less like himself, with a comparable range of interests and a similar outlook on life. Some such restriction may have been forced upon the twentieth-century author; but if, as often happens with the sensitive and intelligent young writer, he consciously addresses himself to some sort of Third Programme public, he is in danger of being led into preciosity and obscurity and a cult of the esoteric.[12]

In short, the *adaptive* aspects of communication have been considered minimally in literary theory for several centuries. As Edward P. J. Corbett has put it: "[The] merger of poetics with rhetoric helps to explain why the eighteenth century was the last great age of a serious academic interest in rhetoric."[13] What appears to have happened is that the image of poets as inspired creators of verbal forms became part of the image of ideal composers of prose, to the extent that rhetoric as an art of adapting ideas to people and people to ideas seemed at best uninteresting and at worst a set of schemes for prostituting "true" insight. This conceptualization emerged in rhetorical theories of the late eighteenth century and can still be perceived in the "managerial" or "invention-less" rhetorical theories and concepts of the twentieth century.

This is not the place to argue whether theories of literary art and criticism are inadequate if they fail to take into account problems of intellectual and verbal adaptation. The point is that *rhetorical* criticism and especially *speech* criticism must focus centrally upon how ideas are adapted to rhetorical situations, for this is the basic process of rhetorical behavior.

But the contention that rhetorical adaptation is beneath serious consideration dies hard. The thoughts of William Freke in 1693 are certain to appear somewhere in tomorrow's journalistic comment on political speaking:

> But indeed, after all, as I have said, no Rhetoric is like honesty, and no speech like reason, if we have truth on our side, that's all, and enough, if we take but care to illustrate that sufficiently; only this we ought to remember in prudence, to let our last words be most forcible, as they are likely to be the most lasting impression; and indeed, to leave the truth and follow colours too much, is like Aesop's dog, by catching at the shadow to lose the substance.[14]

There is enough of reality in this kind of statement to make the whole view plausible—if the full nature of rhetorical adaptation is not thought about carefully. How much the Freke-like analyses miss is suggested by the analysis of Harold Zyskind, a twentieth-century philosopher:

> The full rhetorician begins with the question, What shall I cause the issue to be so that I may adopt an advantageous position? In 1952 one remembers Adlai Stevenson saying that Communists in government was not the issue; but some Republicans made it so. In rhetoric issues and problems are made, not born. Nor is such making confined to local issues. It can swell up to the task of the times, as in 19th-century America it swelled to our manifest destiny to advance in the Pacific. Similarly, today, leaders of resistance movements in the ghettos, at the Pentagon, and in the universities may or may not have a theoretically defensible view of what are the issues of the time and what should be the priorities among them. But there can be little doubt that they have gone a long way towards determining what has been and is to be at the top of the national agenda. To the degree that rhetoric has thus centered history on our destiny or our social ills, it has begun, in the sense indicated, to generate the world (its subject matter).[15]

Professor Zyskind's point is a most important one. Rhetoric, including spoken rhetoric, *creates* issues which *become* what Freke thought of as the "truth on our side." Issues that were created by John F. Kennedy's presidential speaking or by Henry Kissinger's explanations of the "Nixon Doctrine" exist today partly because those speakers articulated data of the "real world" in their own unique ways. Ideas and phrases about "true believers" exist among us partly because Eric Hoffer in 1951 published a rhetorical book using that phrase in its title and then articulated thoughts on the same theme on national television networks in the 1960s. A number of conceptions about the roles of blacks and whites in American society bear the stamps of Malcolm X, Governor George Wallace, Dr. Martin Luther King, and the late President Lyndon B. Johnson. Many Americans' conceptions of Israel's rights and her role in the Middle East are the creations of Abba Eban's eloquent defenses of his country. One could cite hundreds of evidences, from every generation, for Zyskind's claim that rhetoric does "generate the world" in very many circumstances.

Perhaps these are reasons that since the Second World War there has gradually developed among rhetorical and philosophical scholars a recognition that social environments cannot be fully understood without understanding the rhetorical discourse contained within them—including the peculiarly personalized worlds created and demolished by acts of speaking. For these tasks at least some critical principles are available. Ancient ways of explaining speech as influence were recovered some time since, and additional strategies for understanding the social force of spoken communication have emerged.[16] Some of the most basic of these strategies will be discussed in later chapters, but the general nature and functions of criticism must be considered first.

THE NATURE AND FUNCTIONS OF CRITICISM

"Criticism" is almost as ambiguous a word as "literature" or "rhetoric." As the term will be used here it refers to a special application of a rather common kind of human activity. We are all "critics" at some time during almost any day. You go to a movie or a play with a friend, or you discover that your friend has visited the same arts and crafts exhibit that you visited. As soon as you both know you have shared one of these experiences, an attempt at "criticism" becomes natural in your next comments.

Moments together now seem incomplete until some descriptive-evaluative ideas have been exchanged. Often, "Did you like it?" or "What did you think of it?" need not be asked. Descriptive-evaluative statements come almost automatically. This is ordinary, everyday criticism. "It seemed so-and-so to me," or "I've seen better colors," and similar statements are virtually automatic comments when people discover they have common, sharable experience with places, things, works of art, other people's behaviors. This is *criticism-in-small*.

Consider what is the most satisfying kind of talk in such everyday critical exchanges. Most would agree that these conversational moments are most agreeable when what is said: (1) describes clear perceptions of what was actually there to be experienced, (2) lets a listener know what standards or norms are being applied to the experience under discussion, and (3) allows listeners to know what judgments the commentator has come to and how those conclusions grow out of the preceding descriptions and revelations of critical standards. "I thought it was an excellent movie because the characters were as true to life as the futuristic plot allowed" can be taken as a tiny paradigm of satisfying, discussable criticism of an everyday sort. One knows the judgment (excellent), the standard applied (true-to-life characters), and the reasoning (the standards were met as far as possible, given the constraints imposed by the plot). Why is such critical comment satisfying? Chiefly because clarifying discussion can grow *from* it. If anyone wants to explore details of the film further, he has been given leads. He can ask, "True to life in what ways?" or "What character problems did the plot present?" If the reasoning perplexes, the listener knows what to ask: "You think every movie has to have true-to-life characters? Why?" or "I don't understand how the plot affected the characterization. What do you mean?" In a single statement we see the movie rendered sharable, so discussable. Description is at least begun. At least one evaluative standard is revealed. The reason behind the evaluative conclusion is suggested. By contrast, "I loved it!" tells only something about the commentator. It says nothing about the thing observed or about the criteria used in judging. The judgment reported remains private. It identifies an undiscussable, unshared experience. The object of the comment remains hidden. No one's understanding is advanced, and no inviting directions of inquiry are revealed. Discussion is shut off, not opened.

The chapters which follow will expand the paradigm. They will deal with criticism that at least: (1) identifies significant qualities of the speaking commented on, (2) reveals criteria applied to those qualities, and so (3) offers a *reasoned* judgment of how fully the speaking achieved what was possible under the circumstances.

Unfortunately criticism of speaking frequently lacks some or all of the three characteristics just enumerated. There are reasons. Oral rhetoric is always a personalized request for adherence to some proposition or position.[17] Ordinary comment about this kind of communication is likely to be jumbled—mixing personal reactions to the personalization with information about the quality of the rhetoric as rhetoric. Or, one may get only, or mostly, personal reaction to the speaker as person. "John Kennedy has charisma and Richard Nixon doesn't" is at best equivocal and is probably a private report. "Charisma" is a very ambiguous term. The statement is private and undiscussable unless the reporter and someone else have previously agreed on a definition of "charisma." Moreover, since not one of the speakers' behaviors has been described in any way, one cannot discover whether the commentator's judgment is reasoned or not. It is usually the personalized character of speech that makes such "private reports" outnumber "critical reports" in ordinary responses to speaking.

All speaking communicates *both* the content of stated ideas and information about the speaker's attitudes. We hear what the speaker *says,* and we "read" his attitudes toward himself, his content, his situation, and his listeners. We judge and respond to the message on the basis of both kinds of information. So, ordinary response to speech is quite properly at least as much empathic as critical, in the sense in which "critical" is used here. What the speaker seems to *be* partly determines whether and why we want to accept his invitations to believe. But if we report empathic responses without critical data and reasoning, we will only reveal our condition as empathizers. In order to function critically, one needs to adopt what is at least partially a nonparticipatory stance, describing speaker, speaking, and self almost as though standing apart from the event. In this sense speech criticism requires a special degree of self-discipline that ordinary listening does not and need not.

What is meant by *describing* speech will become clear when we consider the aspects of speech that are most readily looked at in criticism. What it means to say criticism ought to be *reasoned* needs immediate consideration. To ask for or to promise reasoned critical judgments implies that there are criteria, or norms, or standards (the terms can be thought of as synonyms) that will legitimately test whatever is studied. And if we have norms that "test," the "tests" ought to yield conclusions that are reasoned rather than haphazard or impulsive. Where, then, do we get the norms from which all critical reasoning must emanate? From what we think we know about how the thing we criticize *ought* to "work" or "be."

The *theory* of an art or practice yields the norms according to which we judge how far an instance of the art achieved what was possible. Comparing a description of what-went-on with a theoretically derived image of what-was-possible, we reason that what-went-on worked well, indifferently, or ill. To offer a reasoned, critical judgment of anything one builds up a theoretical model of what full achievement would be and then compares the actual with the theoretically possible. The Dutch philosopher, Remy Kwant, makes the point thus:

> The musical critic who, after analyzing the performance of an orchestra comes to the conclusion that the concert was below par, can make this critical observation only because he has an idea of how the composition should have been executed. If he has not the slightest idea of this, he has no norm at his disposal which permits him to say that the performance was good or bad. Similarly, an examiner cannot give an examination if he has no norms. . . . All these examples indicate that no genuine critique can be exercised by anyone who has no idea of what a particular human achievement should be. In a word, the exercise of critique implies knowledge of a norm or norms governing that achievement or activity.[18]

Norms for criticism come from theoretical knowledge of what can be accomplished, given the principles that govern the work someone attempts. For virtually any art or practice—landscaping, boat building, painting, speaking—there is a body of generalizations that purports to define what can be achieved if the full resources of the method and the materials are used in the best way known. Whether his critique is of a game of billiards, a ballet, or some rhetorical speaking, a competent critic builds an "ideal" image of what could be and compares that image with what his descriptive data tell him *was* in the present case. He is then able to report to others how far the real event seemed to "live up to" the possibilities which the principles of the art suggest were present in the circumstances. That is criticism as I shall treat the subject in this book. The process renders intelligible and discussable (1) *what actually occurred, (2) the ways in which the occurrence did or did not live up to the "normative" possibilities, and* (3) *what the critic concludes in overall judgment given the findings of inquiries (1) and (2).* The final judgment is *reasoned* and discussable because, when communicated, the conclusions are openly related to the critical data and norms. Social, biographical, historical, psychological, or other kinds of investigation may be necessary to discover and understand "what actually occurred," but in the kind of criticism considered here, these lines of investigation are not ends in themselves but means of acquiring the "truest" bases for critical judgment.

The norms of criticism derive from theory, as has been said. The theory from which a speech critic draws his norms is a collection of generalizations sometimes called "rhetorical theory" and sometimes called "communication theory." These are generalizations purporting to say what works in practical communication and how. As theoretical statements they are essentially descriptions of communicative processes, but they can be looked at also as "predictions" about what can and cannot happen under this or that set of circumstances. The incomplete body of rhetorical theory [19] we possess alleges, for example, that people respond more willingly and efficiently to information they find orderly than to information in which they cannot see significant relationships. Converted into a prediction or *norm,* that theoretical statement becomes an assertion that speakers who *show* listeners how uttered ideas relate to one another are more likely to gain willing and efficient attention than speakers who do not. Using such a theory-based norm, a critic can investigate by all available means whether Speaker A helped his listeners to see relationships among his ideas and, on the basis of the findings, estimate how fully Speaker A exhausted the possibilities of satisfying the listeners' normal (or "normative") relations-seeking expectations. We do not arrive at "scientific measurements" by applying theory-based norms to speaking; we arrive at reasoned judgments that can be explained to others and "tested" against their conceptions of rhetorical theory and their perceptions of what was actually done and what could be done.

There is no logical reason why a book on speech criticism should not treat norms for blending rhetorical with poetic materials and goals, norms for achieving rhetorical goals through dramatic forms, or norms for achieving rhetorical ends in communication between two different cultural groups. The chapters to follow do not treat such extensions of rhetorical and speech criticism, however, because to treat only the basic principles and methods of the criticism of rhetorical speech leaves all too much before us. To consider how we can analyze and evaluate speaking done in English in circumstances typical of Western culture requires that we seek generalizations about how communication works in all representative types of Western rhetorical situations. Of course, no one has knowledge equal to that task; even so, what could usefully be said on the subject would require the space of several books. Therefore, another arbitrary limitation must be placed on what will be covered in this textbook. The chapters to follow treat *basic* critical processes useful in criticism of speaking that is prominently rhetorical and purportedly addressed to listeners who have knowledge and values generally associated with Western culture.

It would be a mistake to suppose that as we concentrate on matters about which we have most theoretical and commonsense knowledge we make it possible to produce rigorous causal inferences and scientific predictions. To establish firm causal relations or to make predictions in a scientific way, one must have causal *laws* from which to reason. But rhetorical theory only asserts possible and probable relations between rhetorical strategies and human choices. At most, a theoretical statement about rhetoric says, in effect: "*If* X were the only force impinging on the listener and *if* the listener allowed himself to be exposed to X, then X would yield response Y more often than not." A critic's norm in such a case would say, in effect: "*To the extent that* the listener willingly perceived X *there is a likelihood* that the listener experienced Y." All critical inferences are *probabilistic*. They cannot be stronger than that because the norms on which they are based are only statements about probable and possible consequences of strategies.

How, then, does a critic get close enough to realities to make his judgments worth his own or anyone else's time? He does so by reasoning—as an expert on rhetorical communication—about the relative weights that should be given to *all* applicable norms. Consider a simple example. It is well established that an idea uttered several times is more likely to be perceived and remembered than the same idea uttered once. This gives us one possibly applicable norm: repeating tends to increase the likelihood that listeners will notice and remember. But this norm is not the only one we would want to reason with if the message in question is the cry of "Fire!" shouted in a crowded room. Our norm about the probable consequences of repeating is not *ir*relevant in this case. It is simply not as relevant to our analysis as some other equally reliable norms. Knowledge of the conventions of our language will tell us that loudly shouting "Fire!" is a well-known way of warning people that there is danger. Moreover, the cry was uttered in a crowded room. Social knowledge tells us that fires in crowded places are normally thought of as especially dangerous. To the rhetorical expert this fact suggests another rhetorical norm: *threats* tend to seize attention and alter attitudes strongly if listeners believe their own interests are at stake. Already a critic begins to see how a set of strong probabilistic statements can be made about the rhetorical character of the cry "Fire!" Repetition of the cry would almost certainly have been a surer way of seizing attention and influencing behavior; but *if* the crowded room were small and *if* no hubbub drowned out the cry, linguistic conventions and the characteristics of human responses to threats would quite probably work to assure that the single cry would achieve the speaker's purpose. If the critic's canvass of the facts of the situation and his review of available, interrelated norms have been thorough, his critical judgment becomes one that is based on special information specially interpreted. By getting facts peculiarly relevant to the judgment he must make and by knowing the full array of pertinent norms, he qualifies as "expert" rather than layman, and his conclusions become *judgments,* not just opinions. This is a critic's entire basis for asking to be taken seriously.

It is implicit in what has just been said that conclusions which ask to be taken seriously because they are expert judgments will have to contain a good deal of explanation and argument. In an excellent essay entitled "The Anatomy of Critical Discourse" Lawrence W. Rosenfield rightly stresses the fact that rhetorical criticism is

> . . . an exercise in forensic reasoning. The critic's commentary is analogous to that of the trial lawyer who bases claims as to the proper verdict in a case on his interpretation of the facts in the light of some legal code. . . . We may . . . expect that reasons offered in critical discourse will lay claim to being the product of a "measurement" [comparison of descriptive data with the probabilities specified by normative standards].[20]

At another point in his analysis Rosenfield restates:

> To answer what features of criticism distinguish it from other types of reason-giving discourse, we have . . . maintained that the term "criticism" is most sensibly reserved for that assertive discourse produced by expert-spectators whose judgments as to the execution of . . . rhetorical phenomena are supported by forensic arguments.[21]

As Rosenfield contends, criticism is always argument if it can claim to be more than opinion giving. It is argument that (1) defends its own accuracy as it reports what happened, (2) identifies and defends the critic's choices among relevant norms and his way of applying them *in these circumstances,* and (3) shows how and why the judgments offered spring logically from application of norms to data.

Such critical argument allows intelligent sharing of experience; more importantly, it can enlarge human understanding. One critic observes and reasons, then defends his judgments before others. A second critic (or the first one at some other time) engages in the same enterprise, perhaps drawing on the perceptions and reasonings in the first criticism. The second criticism has the prospect of building upon and beyond the first critic's insights. It is therefore apt to be more complete or richer than the first. A third attempt may go beyond the first two, adding still more to available understanding. By such processes of mutual correction and successive enrichments, knowledge and understanding are enlarged across generations. The fact that we so sketchily understand the power and functioning of rhetorical speech today is at least partly due to the limited amount of speech criticism that has been attempted in modern times. With only a small amount of such criticism in our heritage, a good many serious questions about why people speak as they do, when they do, are only superficially answered in what passes for rhetorical theory. Why, for example, do the ceremonies of civilized societies always seem to require that speaking shall occur? Perhaps if dedicatory speeches had been as thoroughly studied for content, form, style, and presentation as sonnets, we would understand better than we do why every generation insists on dedicatory speeches and what it expects of them.

Two examples can illustrate some of the ways understanding can be expanded in consequence of speech criticism. First, a "scholarly" instance. Here is a brief excerpt from a recent book on the rhetoric of the Puritans:

> Despite the attractiveness of Ramus's teaching, the Puritans were not the thoroughgoing Ramists that Perry Miller and Wilbur Howell have contended. In their academic training in rhetoric and logic, the English Puritans studied principally from texts in the neo-classical tradition. Therefore, they were exposed to an integrated and functional system of training in oral communication. The structure and development of the speech, as well as the communicative act itself, were recognized as integrative processes.[22]

Here Professor White states very briefly a major, new judgment about Puritan preaching and theology. Elsewhere he presents his grounds for it. This judgment is based on years of studying Puritans' preaching and their religious-psychological-social theories of rhetorical communication. His knowledge of their studies and their habits of thinking has allowed him to understand their preaching in a new way. Their sermons now seem to have developed out of a *blend* of "Ramism, Aristotelianism, and neo-Ciceronianism" which they combined "with their concepts of the psychological nature of man and the morphology of conversion." [23] White's fully argued case contends that Puritan sermons reflect in their substance, form, style, and presentation this complicated integration of several streams of thought to which they were exposed. This argument adds important dimensions to scholars' understanding of what Puritan preaching "really was" and why. Previously two leading scholars (Perry Miller and Wilbur Samuel Howell) had argued, on evidence they had collected, that the Puritans' sermons were as they were primarily because the preachers borrowed "rules" of speech from what were called "Ramistic rhetorics." The explanations stopped there. White took their data and conclusions and reexamined them together with his new evidence on how the preachers actually perceived their tasks and their listeners. He came to see the sermons as responses to unique conceptions of sermonic task, communication, and "rules." White contends the sermons were *psychologically* designed in a way that made Ramistic "rules" usable.

The important point here is that all three critics (Miller, Howell, and White) contributed to historical understanding. But if the first two had not pointed up a connection between the sermons and the Ramistic rhetorical tradition, the third critic would have been less likely to concentrate on the Puritans in just the way he did. Possibly he would not have offered his richer understanding of the sermons at all. Both the history of American culture and the history of public speaking are more intelligible because Miller and Howell built up explanations to which White in his turn could add, and in adding "correct" by broadening. This is the way careful, well-argued, scholarly criticism advances general knowledge. Each critic uses past criticism (if there is any) and supplies planks for a platform of knowledge that all can share.

But the values of criticism are not confined to scholars. Any careful criticism of contemporary speaking enhances understanding of contemporary events. Especially when controversial communication occurs, careful criticism becomes essential. Most casual responses will be opinionated and probably will prevent rather than help understanding of actual events. A modern instance that still has reverberations was former Vice President Spiro T. Agnew's televised address, delivered on November 13, 1969, in which he criticized the television networks' coverage of news. The speech was delivered from Des Moines, Iowa. A text of it is printed on pp. 367–375, together with a student's critical examination of the rhetorical event.

Agnew's speech instantly became the object of diverse, often self-serving, descriptions and judgments. On its subject—the relations between government and journalism—one can hardly claim to be informed today without knowing what happened on November 13, 1969, and immediately after. Nonetheless, many of the reports and pronouncements by public figures confused rather than "put the matter straight." The President of the National Broadcasting Company said the speech was an "unprecedented appeal to prejudice." The President of the Mutual Radio Network said the speech was a "call for fairness, balance, responsibility, and accuracy in news presentation." [24] It is difficult to believe the two broadcasters had heard and read the same speech, but the difference between their descriptive evaluations fairly illustrates the divided interpretations one could find in the media of communication and on local streets following the speech.

In such circumstances how is an intelligent citizen to understand the episodes that affect his life? Where rhetorical speaking is the episode, he can only do his own criticism. The alternative is to choose some "authority" blindly from the welter of conflicting reports. Joyce Williamson's critique of Agnew's speech (pp. 356–366) is one woman's personal resolution of the question, "What shall *I* think happened?" She made her critical study three years after the event because Mr. Agnew's act of speaking was still a political and journalistic issue. For like reasons another student at another university created his own criticism of the speech two years after the event. His critical methods were different from those Ms. Williamson used, and his judgments were both like and different from hers. Jack Orr of Temple University wrote:

> ... [in this event] the traditional distinction between persuasion and coercion breaks down. Agnew is reasonable and artistic as he dialogues with the silent majority. However, the overheard effect of this dialogue is coercive to the television network newsmen. Being persuasive to one group, Agnew is implicitly inflicting coercion on the other.[25]

Williamson and Orr asked themselves slightly different questions about the speech as a public occurrence. Williamson sought to understand what forces in the speech and situation evoked approval from about three-fourths of all Americans who knew about it. Orr, on the other hand, wanted to understand why the speech evoked opinions so sharply divided. Each critic clarified a part of what happened. Those of us who have the benefit of both students' findings can understand the whole event better than either critic did alone. From Williamson we find out about the internal character of Agnew's "reasonableness," as seen by so many listeners and readers. From Orr's analysis we see why an NBC President heard "an appeal to prejudice." The event of 1969 and the continuing controversy over it have become increasingly intelligible and, strangely enough, no one appears to have been wholly "irrational" in the event or concerning it.

Both scholars and citizens need to know the basic methods of speech criticism if they are to think for themselves and for each other in an increasingly oral world. An alert citizen or scholar need not produce systematic critiques of all the speech heard or made. It is at those points and places where speech achieves special importance relative to public and private life that systematic criticism is needed. Then, one must know how to make independent assessments of what is going on or turn the management of personal judgment over to other people. In general, speech criticism is simply the search for logical and psychological explanations of the speech-related events that are important to our daily lives.

A CRITICAL STANCE

The chapters to follow make no pretense of presenting all the ways one can profitably think about spoken rhetoric. There are several tested approaches to the criticism of rhetoric, and no avenue to an understanding of human communicative behaviors ought to be rejected out of hand. However, this book is confined to discussion of aspects of oral rhetoric with which virtually every critic must inevitably cope if orality of discourse is to be taken into account. In concluding this introductory chapter, I therefore wish to point briefly to some other vantage points from which rhetoric is currently being examined and to indicate the extent to which the rudimentary considerations discussed in the following chapters can and cannot accommodate or contribute to them.

Thonssen, Baird, and Braden have outlined an encompassing, neo-Ciceronian approach to analysis of formal speeches.[26] These authors demonstrate by extended examples that asking traditional questions about speakers' backgrounds, their modes of proof, the make up of their audiences, and the measurable effects of their rhetorical efforts can give us valuable understanding of speaking as a social-political force. I hope not to disregard such questions in the following chapters, though I may suggest that they be posed in untraditional ways.

Quite different ways of synthesizing data from descriptions of rhetorical behavior are suggested in the works of the literary critic, Kenneth Burke. A number of speech critics have drawn on his insights. Their "dramatistic" searches for "identifications" and "images" reflected or generated by rhetoric involve inquiries into the *states of mind* that rhetoric may reflect or produce or both. Theirs might be called quasi-clinical, or at other times analogical, investigation of the causes for rhetoric's production, acceptance, or rejection. This approach to the study of rhetoric has produced a variety of stimulating studies,[27] but because I shall deal with the more obvious phenomena of rhetoric and especially with implications of orality, I shall pursue Burkean lines of thought very little. However, much of what will be said can be useful in "clearing the way for" Burkean interpretations.

Edwin Black's *Rhetorical Criticism*[28] urged critics to give special attention to the long-ranged influences of rhetorical acts—influences on the makers of the rhetoric as well as on those who later come under such rhetoric's broadening influences.[29] Black also pointed to the desirability of recognizing heretofore unaccounted for forms of rhetoric such as "exhortation." Somewhat in contrast, I shall treat classification of types of speaking very little.

Ross W. Winterowd would have rhetorical critics give greater emphasis to style as form and proof.[30] Some elemental aspects of this critical stance will be adopted in later chapters dealing with criticism of oral style.

Chaim Perelman has argued that critics should concentrate on the detailed methods by which people "seek adherence to a thesis."[31] Readers will find this point emphasized throughout this book. They will also find influences of the English logician, Stephen E. Toulmin, in subsequent discussion of the *logos* of speech.[32]

As editor, critic, and lecturer, Marie Hochmuth Nichols has proposed and illustrated ways by which critics of oral rhetoric can add to historical knowledge. She has also elucidated Kenneth Burke's critical concepts and urged increased attention to the functions of language in oral rhetoric.[33] In chapters VI, VII, and VIII more than usual attention will be given to ways of criticizing oral style. It is surely a major, though not an exclusive, goal of all rhetorical criticism to refine historical studies by reconstructing the ways in which speech and other rhetorical processes created the issues and world views that history records.

The contributions rhetorical criticism can make to literary criticism have been admirably illustrated by Wayne C. Booth in his *The Rhetoric of Fiction*[34] and by Donald C. Bryant in a number of essays.[35] For reasons already indicated these considerations will enter our discussions only indirectly—the focus here is on criticism of practical, oral rhetoric. Nonetheless, it appears that some critical strategies proposed for oral rhetoric can have use in elucidating the rhetorical qualities of literature.

Perhaps the leading exponent of analyzing and judging political and ethical dimensions of rhetoric *as a function of rhetorical criticism itself* was the late Richard M. Weaver. His *The Ethics of Rhetoric*[36] and his essay "Language Is Sermonic"[37] illustrate his point of view and critical method. For purposes of this book, the problems of ethical criticism will be deferred for consideration in the final chapter (pp. 239–285). Since the norms of rhetorical communication and the norms of ethics derive from different philosophical systems, I shall try to avoid mingling the two types of considerations.

A recent volume of criticism suggests and illustrates the wide variety of methods by which useful critical data and judgments can be extracted and formed. In *Explorations in Rhetorical Criticism*[38] twelve scholars describe as many different approaches to rhetorical works and use their methods in criticism of appropriate bodies of rhetoric. Some, but by no means all, of these productive lines of inquiry are considered in the present volume.

Others among these methods address specialized critical problems and do not fall within my consideration of basic critical issues.

None of the thrusts in criticism just summarized has failed to illumine what happens when people deal rhetorically with one another. Neither do these ways of inquiring critically—or any other way—tell all. But apart from the ways we *might* inquire to understand oral rhetoric, there are some very basic matters about which we *must* inquire if only to discover whether a given answer would be pertinent to a full description of the speaking studied. These are the kinds of inquiries that the remainder of this book attempts to suggest, explain, and illustrate. Many other interesting and valuable questions might be raised about any rhetorical event, but first, such questions as these might be addressed whenever rhetoric is oral:

1. What is peculiarly "said" by the fact that a message is *spoken* with rhetorical intent?
2. What are the main ways in which conscious meanings—what the Greeks called *logos*—are conveyed in spoken rhetoric?
3. What constitute the structure and the form of a spoken rhetorical message, and how is meaning derived from such structures and forms?
4. What are the most obvious ways that language makes for clarity and suasion?
5. What meanings do aspects of physical presentation have in spoken messages?

Whoever could answer these five questions would have the most profound body of normative information about speaking that the world has yet possessed. He would know the primary principles by which to reason toward profoundly weighty judgments about the intimate and public affairs of human beings. No one can give full answer to even one of these questions, but one can find partial answers to each. Criticism that enlightens can therefore begin. To know what *can* be said in rational answer to these questions is to possess more than ordinary understanding of the pervasive world of rhetorical speech.

NOTES

[1] Thucydides, *The Peloponnesian War,* trans. Rex Warner (Baltimore: Penguin Books, 1954), pp. 134–135.

[2] Robert T. Oliver, *History of Public Speaking in America* (Boston: Allyn and Bacon, Inc., 1965), p. xviii.

[3] Frank Stanton, "A CBS View," in *The Great Debates,* ed. Sidney Kraus (Bloomington: Indiana University Press, 1962), p. 66. Stanton's estimate is conservative; other estimates range from 85 million to 120 million.

[4] Saul Ben-Zeev and Irving S. White, "Effects and Implications," in *The Great Debates,* ed. Sidney Kraus (Bloomington: Indiana University Press, 1962), p. 334. The election was decided by a margin of 118,550 in a total vote of 68,335,642.

[5] Charles S. Baldwin, *Ancient Rhetoric and Poetic* (New York: The Macmillan Company, 1924); reprint ed. (Gloucester, Mass: Peter Smith, 1959), p. 3.

[6] Propositions set forth in this section are discussed in greater depth in my "Oral Rhetoric, Rhetoric, and Literature," *Philosophy and Rhetoric* 1 (Fall 1968):191–210.

[7] Aristotle, *Rhetoric,* translated by W. Rhys Roberts, from *The Oxford Translation of Aristotle* edited by W. D. Ross (Oxford: The Clarendon Press, 1925), Vol. 11, 1325 [b], by permission of The Clarendon Press, Oxford. Or see the same translation in *Aristotle's Rhetoric and Poetics* (New York: Random House, Inc., Modern Library Series, 1954), p. 24.

[8] Donald C. Bryant, "Rhetoric: Its Functions and Its Scope," *Quarterly Journal of Speech* 39 (December 1953): 413 and 404 respectively.

[9] Herbert A. Wichelns, "The Literary Criticism of Oratory," in *Studies in Rhetoric and Public Speaking in Honor of James Albert Winans* (New York: Russell & Russell, Inc., 1962), p. 182. Originally published in 1925 by The Century Company, New York.

[10] John F. Wilson, "Fifty Years of Rhetorical Criticism by Laymen," in *Reestablishing the Speech Profession,* Robert T. Oliver and Marvin G. Bauer eds. (University Park, Pa.: The Speech Association of the Eastern States, 1959), pp. 10–11.

[11] René Wellek, *The Rise of English Literary History* (New York: McGraw-Hill Book Company, 1966), pp. 49–50. Welleck's immediate reference is to the popular theory of poetic creativity, but the same view was taken of prose writing and finished speaking.

[12] James R. Sutherland, *On English Prose* (Toronto: University of Toronto Press, 1957), p. 84.

[13] Edward P. J. Corbett, *Classical Rhetoric for the Modern Student* (New York: Oxford University Press, 1965), p. 560.

[14] From Freke's *Select Essays Tending to the Universal Reformation of Learning.* Quoted in John M. Lothian, "Introduction" to Adam Smith; *Lectures on Rhetoric and Belles Lettres* (Carbondale: Southern Illinois University Press, 1971), p. xxxi.

[15] Harold Zyskind, "Some Philosophical Strands in Popular Rhetoric." Reprinted from *Perspectives in Education, Religion, and the Arts,* edited by Howard E. Kiefer and Milton K. Munitz, p. 390, by permission of State University of New York Press. © 1970 The Research Foundation of State University of New York. All rights reserved.

[16] Two federally funded conferences exploring the behavioral aspects of "spoken interactive communication" and "the relevance of rhetorical studies in the late twentieth century" have published proceedings which are well worth study in connection with this statement. See Robert J. Kibler and Larry L. Barker eds., *Conceptual Frontiers in Speech-Communication* (New York: Speech Communication Association, 1969) and Lloyd F. Bitzer and Edwin Black eds., *The Prospect of Rhetoric* (Englewood Cliffs: Prentice-Hall, Inc., 1971).

[17] My definition here is derived from that used by Ch. Perelman and L. Olbrechts-Tyteca in *The New Rhetoric* (Notre Dame: Notre Dame University Press, 1969).

[18] Remy C. Kwant, *Critique: Its Nature and Function* (Pittsburgh: The Duquesne University Press, 1967), pp. 18–19.

[19] I shall use the term "rhetorical theory" rather than "communication theory" henceforth because I conceive "communication theory" as treating all "rhetorical theory" and considerably more; e.g., generalizations about acoustics, symbolic systems that are not commonly used in human speech, ways of processing communicative information, etc.

[20] Lawrence W. Rosenfield, "The Anatomy of Critical Discourse," *Speech Monographs* 35 (March 1968): 55–56.

[21] *Ibid.*, p. 57. Rosenfield is not, of course, using the term "forensic" in a sense that should imply the *total* absence of praise which Aristotle might have called epideictic or of advice which Aristotle might have called deliberative discourse.

[22] Eugene E. White, *Puritan Rhetoric: The Issue of Emotion in Religion* (Carbondale: Southern Illinois University Press, 1972), p. 17.

[23] *Ibid.*, p. 18.

[24] Both statements appeared in an Associated Press "roundup" of comments made immediately after Agnew spoke. *Centre Daily Times,* November 14, 1969.

[25] Jack Orr, "Agnew at Des Moines: A Dramatistic Analysis," unpublished paper presented at the annual convention of the Pennsylvania Speech Communication Association, Pittsburgh, October 15, 1971. Orr's paper contained extensive description and argument too long to be quoted here.

[26] Lester Thonssen, A. Craig Baird, and Waldo W. Braden, *Speech Criticism* (New York: The Ronald Press Company, 1970).

[27] One of the earliest critical studies influenced by this strain of thought and devoted exclusively to a speech maker was Martin Maloney's "Clarence Darrow," in *A History and Criticism of American Public Address,* Marie K. Hochmuth ed. (New York: Longmans, Green and Co., 1955), III, 262–312. One of the subtlest studies incorporating Burkean and other critical viewpoints is Richard B. Gregg's "The Ego-Function of the Rhetoric of Protest," *Philosophy and Rhetoric* 4 (Spring 1971): 71–91. Criticism of the sort I refer to here is specially indebted to Burke's *The Philosophy of Literary Form* available in a revised edition (New York: Vintage Books, 1957) and *A Rhetoric of Motives* which has been reissued several times since its original publication (Englewood Cliffs: Prentice-Hall, Inc., 1952).

[29] The continuing influences of Agnew's rhetoric of 1969 are examples of the kinds of long-ranged forces Black wishes to have analyzed. Criticism would then extend beyond consideration of immediate influences such as those Williamson and Orr explored.

[30] See for example his *Rhetoric: A Synthesis* (New York: Holt, Rinehart and Winston, Inc., 1968) and his "Beyond Style," *Philosophy and Rhetoric* 5 (Spring 1972): 88–110.

[31] Perelman and Olbrechts-Tyteca, *The New Rhetoric.*

[32] In later chapters I shall draw especially from his *The Uses of Argument* (Cambridge: At the University Press, 1958).

[33] Marie Hochmuth Nichols's published lectures, *Rhetoric and Criticism* (Baton Rouge: Louisiana State University Press, 1963) treat all of these considerations.

[34] Wayne C. Booth, *The Rhetoric of Fiction* (Chicago: University of Chicago Press, 1961).

[35] One of the most significant of these has already been referred to: "Rhetoric: Its Functions and Its Scope." *Rhetoric and Poetic* (Iowa City: University

of Iowa Press, 1965) was edited by Bryant and contains a number of essays by him, Black, and others, most stressing the role of rhetoric in literature.

[36] Richard M. Weaver, *The Ethics of Rhetoric* (Chicago: Henry Regnery Company, 1953).

[37] First published in Roger E. Nebergall ed., *Dimensions of Rhetorical Scholarship* (Norman: Department of Speech, University of Oklahoma, 1963).

[38] G. P. Mohrmann, Charles J. Stewart, and Donovan J. Ochs eds. *Explorations in Rhetorical Criticism* (University Park: The Pennsylvania State University Press, 1973).

Chapter II

Rhetorical Situations and Unspoken Contracts

Whether rhetorical speaking achieves its goals depends on how well it is adapted to those who hear it. Soliloquies are interesting clinically or as literature, but as social rhetoric they impress us little. Hamlet is interesting as a human being but not as a Danish statesman. Even Polonius's platitudinous counsels have more social significance than Hamlet's soliloquies. But if rhetoric is social, a major problem for its critics is how to get an understanding of the people it influences. A properly candid critic must admit that he hardly understands his own reactions to rhetoric, much less the reactions of, say, 300 people listening to an appeal for scholarship funds in a city miles away. How, then, can he understand the audience of a diplomat addressing the United Nations Assembly or the international audiences that hang on the words of presidents and premiers? At a glance, the task seems to make speech criticism either the labor of a lifetime or a foolhardy enterprise from the start. Yet before turning away from these prospects we ought to remind ourselves once more of what criticism is and what it is for.

Careful critics—of art, philosophy, speech, and so on—do not claim to present final versions of the objects they study. They admit that not everything about these objects can be gathered in and interpreted by one mind. Critics know that when we think we are dealing with things we believe we can know finally, we do science and mathematics. They know that we do criticism when we believe the best that human beings can achieve are reasoned, informed interpretations that may expand but cannot complete understanding. They know, too, that criticism is best motivated by the simple wish to have a judgment instead of an opinion about something that "counts." The best critics, in all fields, approach their work with this kind of modesty, aspiring only to make helpful sense to themselves and to others.

Even the best critic of speaking does not expect to know *all* about all the people addressed through speech. He does, however, hope to *conceptualize* those people and their surroundings in ways he can defend as true to the knowable "facts." If he can do this and can understand the phenomena of the communications offered, he can apply the norms of rhetorical theory and arrive at judgments that may be helpful to him and to his peers. So, when thinking about situations in which speech occurs, our critic's concern is not to employ polling organizations or teams of psychiatrists to tell him about audiences; his initial step is to find some reasonable way of *conceptualizing* what an "audience" *is* and under what conditions it responds to speech.

SITUATIONAL ANALYSIS

A very useful way of conceptualizing the many circumstances in which response is given to rhetorical speech comes from an analysis proposed by Lloyd F. Bitzer in 1968 and widely discussed by rhetorical scholars ever since.[1] Bitzer's essay suggests that we may conceptualize rhetoric as discourse occurring in situations where "solutions" are wanted and where the needs or "exigences" of the situations *can* be altered by *discourse.* In situations that allow rhetoric to function socially, Bitzer advises us to seek out and define exigences or readinesses for change. This will require recognizing that the humanly responsive entities in each situation are the audience and the communicator, but we must see, too, that the situation *as a whole* will bring into force constraints (opportunities and limitations) within which and through which any rhetor must work to evoke change. These opportunities and limitations consist of (1) everything at the disposal of the rhetor for purposes of inducing change and (2) demands and readinesses that exist in the situation in any given moment. Approximately stated, this is Bitzer's way of conceiving the circumstances within which rhetoric has to function. The conceptualization can be expanded into a way of seeing speeches critically.

The text of a tiny speech delivered some years ago by Congressman George P. Miller of California appears in chapter III (see pp. 54–55). In later chapters we shall look repeatedly at that speech because it conveniently illustrates much that speech critics need to explore. It is therefore helpful to explore its rhetorical situation at this point.

If we followed Bitzer's leads, how would we conceptualize the rhetorical situation in which that short speech occurred? We would begin by collecting data about the audience. At this point poll data and many other kinds of descriptive information might be important. But our reason for collecting data would not be just to write about the audience; it would be to locate the opportunities and limitations of rhetoric—the exigences—created by the nature of that audience and moment. We would inspect the setting—the meeting of a convention delegation—to identify limitations and opportunities for rhetoric. In this manner we would process all information we could find, searching always for the exigences rhetoric must change and the constraints within which the changes, if any, must be effected.

Here is some situational information pertaining to Miller's speech. The place was the Cow Palace, a huge convention hall in San Francisco. The occasion was the National Convention of the Democratic Party in the summer of 1956. It was afternoon of the day the convention considered what it should say in its party platform. Behind the scenes a controversy was growing over what should be said about civil rights. Two years before, in 1954, the Supreme Court of the United States had struck down the separate-but-equal doctrine under which black people had for years been denied equality of opportunity. Though the decision was a momentous one, the platform committee of the Democratic Party proposed that the convention neither endorse nor complain of the decision. This issue would be debated on the floor of the convention in the evening of the day we are examining. The afternoon's convention deliberations had ceased, now, and the California delegation had gathered in a corner of the hall for a caucus. The delegation knew that liberals in the convention were preparing a platform statement endorsing the Court's 1954 decision. The purpose of the caucus was

to decide what California should say in the debate that would follow this proposal in the coming evening. Slightly more than forty
California delegates attended the caucus. Their chairman announced (using a hand microphone and a small public address
system) that a former National Chairman of the party, an advocate
of *not* endorsing the Court's decision, wanted to speak to the group.
After this, the chairman said, delegates might also speak. Then
the group would decide what their position would be in the evening debate on the party's civil rights plank.

The California delegation was "liberal" on civil rights. The
former National Chairman's advice that the delegation ought to
support the platform committee's noncommittal statement was
heard rather coolly. When he had spoken, the former National
Chairman left; then George P. Miller asked to be heard. Miller had
served several terms as a Congressman, was now in the state legislature, and would soon return to Congress. In this convention he
was a delegate and was serving as parliamentarian of the
convention.

The California delegation had allowed television equipment in
their corner of the hall, and their meeting was nationally televised
as it took place.

From a "list" of facts like this we cannot immediately say what
rhetoric was called for from Mr. Miller, who wanted the delegation
to support a vigorous, affirmative statement concerning the Supreme Court's decision. Even with so few data to deal with, a
critic needs a disciplining, conceptual scheme for organizing what
he knows. He must finally be able to say what the forty or so
Californians "really were" as *an* audience in *a* situation having
unique qualities. This is where Bitzer's suggestions can be of
help.

We can begin by asking whether our information tells us what
the exigence or exigences of the situation were. What was needed
or expected or wished for here? Which of these matters could *talk*
do anything about? Answers come easily in this case. The main
exigence or need was to form an agreement on how the delegation
would vote on the civil rights planks to be proposed during the
coming evening. Connected with this, and subordinate to it, there
was probably need to work out strategies by which to support
whatever the group decided should be their stand during the
evening. And there was surely need to articulate some kind of
response to the just completed talk by the former National Chairman. By asking what the *exigences* were, thought is directed away

from details for their own sakes and toward needs and their priorities. A hierarchy of exigences emerges: first, get a decision; second, settle ways of implementing the decision; third, hear some response to the former National Chairman. These bare statements declare a critical view of the rhetorical facts that existed as opportunities and limitations for *anyone* addressing this audience in this situation.

We have not yet considered *who* should enter this situation to present talk. We have stated what *any* speaker immediately following the former National Chairman ought to deal with if he intended to adjust to the psychology of the situation. We have made our first set of critical decisions: what the exigences were, their order of psychological importance, and that talk could alter the situation.

If we are content with this stage of our analysis, Bitzer's conception of rhetorical situations suggests that a next step should be to review our data once more. This time we ought to ask whether any information hints at how the exigences of the situation can or cannot be effectively altered. One item certainly does. The delegation is known to be "liberal" on civil rights. That implies that anyone wanting this group's support for a noncommittal or "soft" civil rights plank would have to enter the situation cautiously. That kind of rhetor would probably need to reveal his position and his arguments indirectly. A "soft plank" advocate would face an audience of doubters, but a Court-endorsing advocate would have an easy assignment if all he wanted was to have the delegation affirm an endorsing stand. He would need to do little more than assure the listeners that their predispositions were right and urge them to express those predispositions. He might need to be more original than this if he proposed strategies for the evening's debate. And almost any derogation of the former National Chairman's ideas would gratify the audience. Except in respect to strategies for the evening, an advocate of endorsing the Court's decision would chiefly need to *amplify* shared ideas; the need for argumentation would be minimal, for the salient conclusions already existed within the situation.

A critic does not always find it this easy to locate clues to the kinds of rhetoric different sorts of speakers need to apply to rhetorical situations. A way of inquiring that gets necessary information and a critical interpretation directly is to ask: What are the prevailing *attitudes* toward alternative ways speakers might try to change the exigences? In the case of the California delegation the answers come easily as soon as we spot the fact that they are all "liberals." In more complicated situations extensive explorations of historical, sociological, and psychological data may be needed to answer the basic question concerning attitudes existing within situations.

In our example we have a small, homogeneous audience. What of large, heterogeneous audiences? A practice used by public opinion analysts becomes useful. Many such analysts conceptualize large, diverse populations as "publics" or sub-audiences—mentally dividing the mass into groupings of persons who think alike and have similar values, allegiances, and interests. This sort of grouping is, of course, something the analysts create in their own minds. The people "out there" need not be aware that they are being seen as parts of this or that "response group" having, say, a "union orientation" or a "middle-American orientation" or other attitudinal characteristics the analyst has found it useful to isolate for convenience in thinking. The whole point of this way of thinking is to reduce to manageable numbers the psychological differences that must be thought about analytically.

The same way of thinking allows speech critics to comprehend heterogeneity in audiences. If we were to examine the rhetorical situation that existed on the evening of the 1956 Democratic Convention's debate on its civil rights plank, we would certainly need to conceptualize sub-audiences in order to think systematically about the situation. Research would soon tell us that there were at least three attitudinal patterns on the convention floor: there were "liberals" who felt passionately that the party must strongly endorse the 1954 Court decision or stand convicted of moral bankruptcy; there were delegates who discounted the "moral issue" and feared that the party would lose votes and perhaps spawn a third party if the plank were strong; and there were delegates, chiefly from Southern states, who intensely disliked the Court's decision and hoped to thwart its effects by any available political action. A concept of these three "audiences" would allow a critic to see clearly what Bitzer calls the constraints (special opportunities and limitations) that existed in this rhetorical situation. Obviously no position on civil rights could solve the exigences of the situation as the entire audience saw them. There were opportunities for speakers (1) to try to shift the "center" toward one of the other attitudinal positions, or (2) to shift people from one or the other of the "extreme" positions to the middle, "soft-comment" position recommended by the official platform committee. There the rhetorical options would end insofar as the goal of altering attitudes was concerned. A critic seeing this much would have begun to formulate his theoretical criteria for distinguishing rhetorical "mistakes" from "judicious" rhetoric.

Conceptualizing heterogeneous audiences as audiences made up of "publics" or "sub-audiences" defined by their attitudinal homogeneity is not simply a convenience in rhetorical criticism. It is a way of thinking that is consistent with the nature of rhetoric itself. Aristotle pointed out long ago that:

> . . . individual cases are so infinitely various that no systematic knowledge of them is possible. In the same way the theory of rhetoric is concerned not with what seems probable to a given individual like Socrates or Hippias, but with what seems probable to men of a given type. . . .[2]

Data about audiences usually need to be restructured into data about *types* of listeners. If we can distinguish attitudinal group-ings, we have located a way of applying theoretical information to mixed audiences without having to know about every person listening.

Sometimes a critic will know most of what he needs to know about attitudes because he watched the situation develop at firsthand. In other circumstances he may have to collect informa-tion from historians, from organizations that measure public opinion, from election records, from census figures and journalistic reports, from personal interviews and surveys. The range of pos-sible sources is striking. One critic studying the rhetoric of con-sumers' complaints found he had to interview a systematic sample of retail merchants and complaint-office managers in order to discover the attitudes of complainants' listeners. A series of little books called *The Parliamentary Companion,* edited by Charles R. Dod and published after the elections of several nineteenth-century Parliaments, gives the economic and political interests of each parliamentarian's electoral district. Inferences about parliamen-tary groupings can be made from such data. Much can be inferred about the attitudes of Jonathan Smith's Massachusetts audience (see pp. 376–386) from reading county histories, old diaries that have been saved, and the speeches that were made at the Conven-tion he addressed. The description of George Miller's audience given above came from consulting *The World Almanac,* reading back issues of California newspapers, and from old notes made while watching the telecast from which the speech text was drawn.

A critic seeking to understand the pro-independence rhetoric in Philadelphia between 1765 and 1776 found most of his information about the Philadelphia audience in existing historical research, but he found he needed to interpret the information by considering the "schools" of historiography the historians adhered to. One cannot predict where information on audiences will be found, but a critic can know in advance the general *kinds* of information that will prove of most value.

Some kinds of questions are worth more than others in searching out information about audiences' attitudes. The lines of inquiry below almost always yield useful information if the questions can be answered at all.

 Are there significant numbers of listeners who share allegiances that bear on solving the exigences?

Are there significant numbers of listeners who share stereotypes of people who could be involved in solving the exigences?

Are there significant numbers of listeners who share beliefs about "who is to blame" for the exigences?

Are there significant numbers of listeners who share conceptions of "who can solve" the exigences?

Are there significant numbers of listeners who share ideas on *how* the exigences ought to be solved?

Do significant numbers of listeners share pertinent attitudes based on age, sex, socioeconomic class, level of education, general intelligence, or the like?

Do significant numbers of listeners differ from others in the *intensity* with which they hold attitudes pertinent to the exigences?

Are there senses of polarity—extreme difference—that set some listeners apart from others on matters pertinent to the exigences?

Do ambitions to dominate in solving the exigences differentiate significant numbers of listeners from others?

Do significant numbers of listeners' *priorities* among the exigences differentiate them from others?

Do significant numbers of listeners sense conflicts (e.g., between allegiances and ways of solving exigences, between solutions and people involved) that set them apart from others?

Does inclination or "drift" toward or away from particular solutions separate significant numbers of listeners?

This is not an inclusive list of questions to ask about audiences, nor is there any magic in any or all of the questions. They merely suggest how a critic needs to think when looking for significant information about audiences. Each question aims at two kinds of information: (1) information about attitudes relevant to solutions of the exigences, and (2) evidence about how attitudes *pattern* to show that the audience is either a homogeneous one or one comprised of rhetorically significant sub-audiences. Questions of this type save a critic from spending time producing historical, sociological, biographical, or other information that will prove of little value in rhetorical criticism per se.[3]

An analysis of pertinent attitudinal patterns refines a critic's definitions of the "targets" rhetoric needs to reach. If we decide the two *main* exigences in Congressman George Miller's situation were to form a decision on how to vote in the forthcoming civil rights debate and to settle on strategies for giving effect to those decisions and if we know the audience was a homogeneous one that supported endorsement of the Supreme Court's decisions, we shall have brought to light the primary constraints within which any speaker must work in addressing that audience. The same knowledge enables us to infer what the situation did *not* invite. It did not invite rhetoric devoted to proving that civil rights were desirable. That was already agreed to. The situation did not invite rhetoric counseling procrastination. This was a special caucus called to get a clear, prompt decision. The situation did not invite rhetoric dealing with civil or human rights considered apart from politics. After all, this was a *political* convention. The list of uninvited kinds of rhetoric could be extended, but the immediate point is that by identifying the relevant attitudes of the audience we not only identify what is rhetorically possible in a situation but also what is rhetorically ill advised.

Not all the opportunities and limitations of a rhetorical situation arise from the attitudes of audiences. What has been traditionally called the "occasion" or the "setting" also creates opportunities and imposes limitations for "fitting" rhetoric. This is part of what Professor Bitzer means when he says that rhetorical situations may prove to be "highly structured or loosely structured." As examples of "highly structured" situations Bitzer cites courtroom situations:

The jury is not a random and scattered audience but a selected and concentrated one; it knows its relation to judge, law, defendant, counsels; it is instructed in what to observe and what to disregard. The judge is located and prepared; he knows exactly his relation to jury, law, counsels, defendant. The counsels know the ultimate object of their case; they know what they must prove; they know the audience and can easily reach it. This situation will be even more highly structured if the issue of the case is sharp, the evidence decisive, and the law clear.[4]

The illustration is excellent for it reminds us of forces beyond the attitudes of audiences which can establish "rules of the game" and define rhetorical targets. A critic cannot be fully clear about what speech can and cannot do in a rhetorical situation unless constraints imposed by occasion and setting have been explored.

On February 12 of any year, some allusion to Lincoln is virtually mandatory in a political speech. The act of dedication structures rhetorical situations so that themes of progress and human worth—relative to whatever is being dedicated—are almost inviolably ordered. If something affecting the future must be discussed, its practical usefulness must be treated or an inherent demand of the situation will have been ignored. The presence of dignitaries forces acknowledgment of their presence; the presence of policy makers suggests discussion of policies; the presence of production workers suggests discussion of how policies affect practices. The location of the rhetorical situation also imposes options and limitations. The history of the place may demand notice; special facilities may need to be referred to; the mood of discourse may be controlled at least partially by decor and space relations. In short, full understanding of a rhetorical situation requires that it be canvassed to see whether special "rules" are imposed and opportunities offered by circumstances that override the general attitudes of the audience. The critic's question is simple: What *else* limits and gives opportunity to the maker of oral rheotric?

When exigences, attitudes of listeners, and structural options and limitations have been identified, a speech critic has the resources from which to synthesize his full conception of a rhetorical situation. To be genuinely useful, the synthesis must be more than a review of features. What is needed is an integrated image of how those features interrelate to form the situation into a unique working-place for attempts at rhetorical influence. Put differently, the critic tries to conceive of each situation as a receiving-system that will operate in certain ways if fed rhetoric with one set of specifications but function differently if fed rhetoric having other specifications. Even the working-place and receiving-system analogies are somewhat inadequate for describing the full conceptualization a critic needs, for each can imply a *fixed* set of allowances, whereas rhetorical situations always begin to change as soon as rhetoric begins to influence their elements. What a critic needs to conceive of is a working-place or receiving-system that is *awaiting* rhetoric's influence, beginning to alter favorably or unfavorably to a speaker's purposes as soon as rhetoric begins to affect it.

We can illustrate this kind of thinking by turning again to George Miller's rhetorical situation. Stating what all our evidence means, we could say that as Miller entered it this was a situation *inviting talk,* provided the talk would hasten action toward committing the California delegation to support a strong civil rights statement and, perhaps, set forth a parliamentary strategy for the evening. Rhetoric having other purposes would have to alter the existing elements of the situation before it could be heard with full willingness. We might add, too, that the informal, corner-of-the-hall, after-session character of the caucus plus its small size encouraged swift, direct, and relatively informal communication.

These few words express in summary the rhetorical meanings contained in the miscellaneous information we have about the entire occasion. The statements tell as concisely as possible what the allowances and limitations of the situation were. To state this much is the whole goal of studying rhetorical situations in criticism. When dealing with a more complex situation, our synthesizing statements would, of course, have to be more extensive but still sharply focused.

A synthesis of information concerning the evening session of the 1956 Democratic Convention (relative to the civil rights debate) would state that three sub-audiences agreed on the major, practical exigence: taking a vote on the party's civil rights position. No rhetoric would be satisfactory to all three sub-audiences. The occasion was formal and the hall huge, so all rhetoric would have to fit the prescriptions of the convention's parliamentary rules and be presented in "set speeches." Any rhetoric seeking to create a majority for any position would need to try to: win "speak softly" delegates to the "liberal" side favoring endorsement of the Court's decision, instill a cautious spirit in "liberal" delegates, arouse enthusiasm in cautious delegates, or encourage a spirit of compromise in certain Southern delegates. The most important sub-

audience would be the politically cautious one which could either
move in the "liberal" direction or, standing fast with the Southern
sub-audience, defeat the "liberals." To move the middle, vote-
conscious subgroup, "liberal" rhetoric would need to minimize
fears of lost votes and of third-party movements; rhetoric from the
"center" and from the Southern group would need to maximize
those fears. Many delegates would be attitudinally in conflict. The
liberal tradition of their party since the New Deal would give them
attitudes favorable to the liberal position on civil rights, but dependence on Southern electoral votes would create countering
attitudes favorable to a "soft" platform statement. Attitudes spring-
ing from idealism and from interest in practical politics would be
the key elements in the receiving-system.

Other critics might state their syntheses differently, giving
different weights to the several constraining and allowing elements
of the rhetorical working-place. But whoever distills a concise
statement of potentialities along the lines illustrated will be in
a position to explain clearly what he or she believes rhetoric could
and could not do in the civil rights debate at the 1956 Democratic
Convention. That critic will also have composed, more or less
implicitly, sketches of the thematic options rhetors from all sides
had available to them. Furthermore, should anyone doubt this
critic's analysis, there will be clear and open grounds for intelligent discussion of alternative interpretations. From such discussions, too, something might be learned about this convention as
a rhetorical situation.

By such processes critics can conceptualize rhetorical situations as places or receiving-systems *awaiting* rhetoric adapted
to specific allowances and limitations of exigences determined
by the attitudinal patterns of the listeners and by the further
modifying forces of surrounding circumstances. Such images of
rhetorical situations are, of course, only conceptualizations, but
they are conceptualizations critics need in order to organize
descriptive data in interpretive, critical ways. The critic says, in
effect, "I understand the circumstances thus. Here are my reasons
for this interpretation. Here is the resulting synthesis of what
the psychological and sociological forces of the moment invited
and disallowed." [5]

UNSPOKEN CONTRACTS OF SPEAKING

To analyze and synthesize judgments about a rhetorical situation
is to spell out a series of contractual terms under which rhetors

function in order to alter the situation as they intend. But our concern is with situations in which speaking—not just any kind of rhetoric—takes place. The fact that speaking is a special kind of human action brings into play additional contractual terms at which we have not yet looked.

Though it is almost never said in words, anyone who tries to influence another through speaking indicates by those actions that *change* is wanted in the other. A speaker also implies that he wants the change *now*. Speakers have long-ranged goals reaching beyond their immediate situations, but they cannot step into rhetorical situations with other living, breathing people without announcing by that act that they want something *immediately*. What is the immediate demand of all rhetorical speech? Change inside the bodies of the listeners. Listeners know this, and that is why they watch their speakers closely, actively, sometimes defensively, emitting streams of "Yes's" and "No's" inside themselves as they listen.

By coming to speak, each speaker announces that *this* particular audience in *this* particular situation holds a key to some fulfillment of his goals and desires. Why else would he have appeared? Instead of putting his message in writing and distributing it impersonally or producing a documentary film containing his ideas or sending someone to speak for him, he has chosen to engage *personally* with the people who are a part of a rhetorical situation. He has decided to communicate through a direct, self-exposing relationship. This involves some risks. He must create "fitting" person-to-person relationships within a set of constraints not of his making, and he must maintain and guide those relationships moment-by-moment through a period of time. Whatever motivated him to communicate is now risked on his capacity to generate "right" responses within a particular segment of humanity with whom he has locked himself in time and space. Even if his medium is radio, television, or telephone, he makes similar undertakings—sometimes running even greater risks, as when his controls are only his voice and perhaps a mechanically produced image of himself. Thus, because to speak is to act in a highly personal way, each speaker communicates by the act of speaking that he is dependent on *these* hearers. He also communicates that in his dependence, he is relying on his own capacities to maintain effective human relationships in hopes of achieving immediate goals. All this he tells by coming to speak.

To clarify the contractual implications of speaking it is helpful to consider how understandings implicit in speech situations differ from those of other rhetorical engagements. In any and all rhetorical engagements we will find one or more of the following understandings, but in all rhetorical engagements involving speaking and listening all of the understandings just below will be present at all times.

1. There is an understanding that the communicator is extending an attempt to influence toward all who will accept the role of respondents, and he is doing this calculatingly in the interests of his goals. (This need not be true if I read a British editorial, but it must be the case if the editorialist makes the same points in public speech or serious dialogue.)

2. Because the rhetor is admittedly trying to influence, it is understood that haphazard, unpurposeful behaviors by him are inappropriate for the duration of the rhetorical engagement. In Bitzer's terms the rhetor promises a "fitting" response to a rhetorical (informative or suasory) situation. Haphazard responses will deny that the situation is *rhetorical*—one needing melioration. (Whether a writer is really trying to influence a rhetorical situation is often moot; by entering a live situation that is rhetorical, a speaker commits himself to it.)

3. It is understood that the perceptions, motivations, and experience of the respondents are the ultimate forces through which the rhetor must gain whatever influence he seeks. His perceptions and motivations hold the status of "guests" in the house of his audience's awarenesses. (This is true of any rhetorical situation according to the definitions I have adopted.)

4. As long as they agree to be the rhetor's "hosts," audiences tacitly accept as legitimate the rhetor's attempts to influence, but they do not promise they will finally judge his purposes and propositions favorably. (A reader may choose to be "host" to a writer as rhetor or as literary artist or both—as when the reader reads a "message play"; but a listener hearing a speaker in a rhetorical situation has no choice but to accept speech as a legitimate attempt to influence, whether effectively or ineffectively.)

Each of these understandings may exist in *any* engagement involving rhetorical messages, and I believe the third understanding is inevitable in any communicative situation where influence of any sort is exerted. However, all four kinds of understandings seem invariably implicit if a speaker comes into a rhetorical situation to *stand with* his message in personalized, space-time relationship with listeners. It is all but impossible for speakers and listeners not to relate to one another if speaking-listening is going on at all; and if circumstances have made the situation a rhetorical one, any speaker will seem to "welch" on his part of the four agreements if he *seems* not to observe them.

In addition, at least two other implicit understandings are unique parts of communications involving oral rhetoric, but they are not characteristic of rhetorical engagements that are not oral. These are:

5. By engaging as speaker and listeners, participants accept it as proper that listeners' interpretations of the speaker's *personality* may be counted as genuine parts of the contents of the message. (As readers we are inclined to put qualities of personhood aside even if we know such qualities, though we do look for evidence of attitudes toward subject matter. In most cases, however, we do not know the personalities of our rhetorical writers.)

6. Engaged as speakers and listeners, participants tacitly agree that there is no appeal—for the time being—from the listeners' immediate estimates of what is "true" and of what are "sufficient reasons." (Since listeners will rarely recur to a record of the engagement as readers might, speakers must influence through listeners' *immediate* perceptions and responses, even for the purpose of enforcing a lasting mental record which the listeners can later reexamine and reflect upon.)

In oral rhetoric speakers make special concessions. Listeners grant them only limited privileges. Speakers may have purposes relative to listeners. They may *try* to achieve those purposes through shaping listeners' experiences. They may even try to exercise influence through their personalities. But little else is conceded to speakers. They forgo modes of influence other than indirect, verbal-gestural behaviors.* By implicit concession they confine their efforts to those *this* audience conditioned by *this* situation is willing to call "appropriate." They place even their ultimate goals under the mediation and jurisdiction of their listeners' immediate judgments.

---

* They may, of course, introduce all manner of nonverbal stimuli as well (graphs, film strips, bloody togas, etc.) but as Aristotle noted, these "inartistic proofs" are not inherent resources of the manner of communication adopted; they are accessories to it.

All rhetorical situations involve an imbalance of privileges between audience and rhetor, but the harsh character of speakers' concessions is an important fact to remember in speech criticism. Whose standards "go"? The listeners', not the critic's, and for the most part not the speaker's. In the essay cited earlier Herbert A. Wichelns said,

> . . . poetry always is free to fulfill its own law, but the writer of rhetorical discourse is, in a sense, perpetually in bondage to the occasion and the audience; and in that fact we find the line of cleavage between rhetoric and poetic.

With reference to the further imbalance of privileges in oral rhetoric, Wichelns had said earlier in his essay:

> If now we turn to rhetorical criticism [of speeches] as we found it exemplified . . . , we find that its point of view is patently single. It is not concerned with permanence, nor yet with beauty. It is concerned with effect. It regards a speech as a communication to a specific audience, and holds its business to be the analysis and appreciation of the orator's method of imparting his ideas to his hearers.[6]

Wichelns might have qualified "imparting his ideas to his hearers" by adding: within the framework of special concessions already extracted by the orality of the rhetorical situation.

We can sum up the pattern of situational concessions peculiarly imposed when rhetoric is oral by composing the special "compact" a speaker actually agrees to by the act of trying to speak influentially. Put in his terms, the "compact" runs like this:

> For reasons of my own I have decided to stake some of my hopes on *you* and the judgments *you* will form in this situation, at this time. I have chosen to speak because I have concluded that I cannot have all of what I want unless you will be influenced by me. I therefore ask you to let me into your thoughts and feelings for a time. I recognize you will insist that I adjust myself, my thoughts, and my purposes to the attitudes you already have. I will try to do this if you will let me expose some of my own thoughts and feelings as I seek the endorsement I need from you.
>
> I concede that *you* shall be the judge of me, of my thoughts, and of whatever feelings I *seem* to express. I concede that the primary thing that will count between us is the satisfaction you can find in the relationship I evolve with you in the coming minutes. I know that what I seem to *be* will count as much or more in our relationship than the

words I *say*. I accept personal responsibility for all I say and do and
for my ways, and I concede that you have a right to judge me *as a
person* according to what you think of my sayings and doings.

We all know that I came here to manage you somewhat. I know that
you grant me that privilege very tentatively. I recognize that you can,
and have a right to, reject me at any moment of our relationship To
the extent that this makes me uneasy, I ask you to make what allowances you can for ways in which my unease may affect what I say and
do. It is because I need something from you that I have come to stand
with my visible and audible thoughts and feelings. I shall try to give
you some immediate rewards for allowing me to try to change you;
but if I don't succeed in that, I know you will judge *me* the failure, not
simply my ideas and strategies.

On these terms please let me try to change you. I say. . . .

CONSTRAINTS AS CONTENT

Few unselfconscious listeners fail to sense that what they hear is
communication appealing to, from, and through the constraints of
situation and orality. Consider the unspoken, situational, and
personal content that emerged beyond and between the words of
the third, fourth, and fifth paragraphs of Stokely Carmichael's
"Speech at Morgan State College" (p. 343). Could any student
or faculty member have missed his judgment that the merit of
"Black Power" as an idea was *not* the exigence in this place and
moment? Is there any doubt that the presence of press representatives required recognition or that Carmichael was trying to exclude the press from the operative rhetorical situation he was
hastening to shape to his own preference? Who would miss the
implication that now, since Carmichael and the audience were
face-to-face at last, their personal relations required special attention? Whether Carmichael made his adjustments and used his
opportunities well or ill is not the issue here. My point is simply
that forces and resources grew out of the situation at Morgan
State College on January 16, 1967, and those forces were data
Carmichael had to recognize, had to use or be used by, and had
to speak *through* to his listeners. What the listeners heard and saw
was speech mingled with the meanings of situation and the act of
speaking. Because this is usually the case, criticism must take all
constraints and their consequences into account if there are to be
description, reasoning, and evaluation relative to oral rhetoric.

Because they view speech with some detachment, critics are
likely to neglect communicated content not found in the obvious

places: words and gestures. A forewarning instance appears in one of the many studies made of the Kennedy-Nixon debates of 1960. A Canadian team of social scientists expressed surprise and some disappointment at the following finding:

> . . . the questions we asked here were carefully worded so as to allow respondents to talk either about what the candidates said or about the two men themselves and how they performed. . . . The fact that so little comment was directed at the subject matter of the debate or at any of the arguments involved, and so much more at the candidates themselves and the general quality of their respective performances as debaters, would seem to confirm what some commentators have already suggested. This is that a television debate of this kind, which focuses attention so sharply on the contestants themselves, leaves a mass audience with . . . some very distinct impressions of the capabilities of the two men as debaters and as persons, but (as our results suggest) with very little idea of what the debate was all about.[7]

A speech critic remembering that speakers speak very personally to, from, and through the constraints of a rhetorical situation involving orality might have expected precisely this finding and these implications. There was little difference between the basic political positions the two candidates expressed. What, then, was there to learn from? How each man handled himself in this unique rhetorical situation. A viewer could judge each man's skill in choosing and handling ideas and making them "fit" the format of the program and the audience's expectations. There was language. Was it "appropriate" to a speaker who sought to be President of the United States and was presumably "demonstrating his wares" this evening? There was the behavior of each speaker toward the other, toward the questioners on the program, toward the machinery of television, and toward the audience "out there." All this was speech content to be "read" and interpreted by those who chose to. The research data show that Canadian listeners did indeed take in these kinds of content. But the professional analysts failed to think about the opportunities and restraints of situations and of speaking. They worried because the listeners drew little from the largely similar ideas the speakers uttered. The analysts functioned as conventional critics too often do; the content *said* was deemed of paramount importance. Undoubtedly such content is important, but a *speech* critic must recognize that possibly a speaker's use of his options, his management of situational constraints, and his exhibited relationships with others are more significant, as message, than the words he utters.

It has been the argument of this chapter that to criticize any speech fully one must identify the dimensions of the rhetorical situation, noting especially what it allows and what the orality of communication allows. It is in relation to the constraints of situation and orality that words, concepts, "logic," a speaker's movements, etc. have significance. A critic who remembers this will feel no sense of contradiction in granting that as logic or literature Bryan's "Cross of Gold" speech is pitiful; whereas, as personalized, time-bound, situation-bound instigation for change in an immediately present audience it could be and was a mighty event at a political convention decades ago. A critic sensitive to the potentialities of rhetorical situations and orality will recognize that in the heat of revolutionary ferment even blemishes need not be rhetorical flaws. "You know not the power of my ugliness," confided the French orator, Mirabeau.

Just to keep history straight, speaking as action must be distinguished from the after-images of that speaking. When the historian Allan Nevins pronounced William H. Seward's "Irrepressible Conflict" speech of 1858 "a characteristic piece of impetuosity," [8] he made a mistake. Only criticism focused on speech as action within rhetorical situations could correct the error. Studying Seward as *speaker,* Robert T. Oliver revealed the vast difference between the significance of the speech and of what happened to the text of it. Says Oliver:

> The speech meant little either to Seward or his listeners. The two Rochester newspapers ignored it, and the country would have known nothing of it—except that, two days later, Seward bethought himself of his usual practice to send the manuscript copies of his speeches to Albany for publication in Thurlow Weed's *Evening Journal.* Thereby was launched the ruination of his career, smashed by a phrase the South and the anti-abolitionist North emblazoned into a slogan of defiance: *the irrepressible conflict!* [9]

Here, speech criticism with due attention to situation and the character of speech as action emended history. Not Seward speaking in Corinthian Hall, but Seward mailing the text of his address was the act that probably cost him his party's nomination for the presidency. And was the "piece of impetuosity" really Seward's or the act of his journalist friend who chose to print?

The only critical perspective that can soundly accommodate oral rhetoric is one that accepts speeches as mediative actions intended to regulate the experience of specific audiences by means of, in spite of, and because of conditions and privileges conferred by situations and orality. The apparatus of literary criticism or of philosophical criticism will not reveal speeches as they were or as they come into being. The first contents of speech are the contents exigences, audiences, and special features of situations insert into them and allow them. The second contents are those the human relationship of speaking-listening creates and allows. It is when these contents have been surveyed and their meanings found that a critic of oral rhetoric is ready to turn to things communicated in more obvious ways.

None of this is to say speaking may not have historical, philosophical, or moral origins of significance. The aftermath of speech, too, may have significance. There is great merit in exploring these dimensions of oral rhetoric. But to keep realities in view, direct knowledge of the intricate event that had the foreshadow and the after-image must provide the foundation of even broadly ranging criticism, if the criticism has a base in the originating rhetoric at all.

NOTES

[1] Bitzer's "The Rhetorical Situation" was first published in *Philosophy and Rhetoric* 1 (January 1968): 1–14 and has been reprinted in several anthologies of essays on rhetoric. In this chapter I shall draw heavily from this paper, from unpublished writings by Professor Bitzer, from discussions I have had with him concerning "the rhetorical situation," and from Richard E. Vatz's "The Myth of the Rhetorical Situation," *Philosophy and Rhetoric* 6 (Summer 1973): 154–161. Since I shall adapt these authors' ideas rather freely, neither is responsible for what I shall say, and the interpretations that follow should not be taken as representing their views exactly.

[2] Aristotle, *Rhetoric,* trans. W. Rhys Roberts, 1356^b, by permission of The Clarendon Press, Oxford; Random House ed., p. 27.

[3] A number of writers have criticized speech critics for reporting large amounts of historical and other data that they cannot, in the end, use in interpreting the *rhetorical* aspects of the events they study. It may be interesting that the average annual income of an audience is $17,153, but that figure is not useful unless it tells something about the audience's attitudes toward subjects discussed rhetorically.

[4] Bitzer, "The Rhetorical Situation," p. 12.

[5] For such a situational analysis see Joyce Williamson's critique of Agnew's speech, pp. 356–366.

[6] Wichelns, "The Literary Criticism of Oratory," pp. 212 and 209 respectively.

[7] Elihu Katz and Jacob J. Feldman provide the quotation as coming from a study of Canadian audiences' responses. The study was made by the Research Division of the Canadian Broadcasting Corporation. No more detailed citation is given. See "The Debates in the Light of Research: A Survey of Surveys," in Kraus ed., *The Great Debates,* p. 200.

[8] Allan Nevins, *The Emergence of Lincoln,* 2 vols. (New York: Charles Scribner's Sons, 1951), I, 411.

[9] Robert T. Oliver, *History of Public Speaking in America,* p. 295. A fuller discussion of the speech is in Oliver's "William H. Seward on the 'Irrepressible Conflict,' " J. Jeffery Auer ed., *Antislavery and Disunion* (New York: Harper & Row, Publishers, 1963), pp. 29–50.

Chapter III

Explicitly "Argued" Content

Practical effects, immediate or long-ranged or both, are rhetoric's reasons for being. A rhetorical speaker *instigates,* as Donald C. Bryant has expressed it. His listeners perceive patterns in his instigations and react to their own interpretations of them. More often than not a speaker reacts, in turn, to his listeners' responses and instigates further and perhaps in new ways. The events of communicative speaking proceed as a dynamic, interactional process.

Critical description of oral rhetoric must concentrate on process —the interplay of instigations and effects. And the nature of rhetorical effects needs to be understood comprehensively. Rhetorical effects are not described by a tally-clerk's announcement of listeners' votes or by other records of behaviors that occurred after speaking ended. The effects of rhetorical speaking are ongoing, adhering-nonadhering experiences that listeners have as they continuously transform a speaker, his instigations, and other contents of a rhetorical situation into a steadily changing series of interpreted messages. Even the verbal parts of spoken messages must be seen as stimuli continuously received and processed through the duration of speaking and, in retrospect, afterward.

From this point of view oral rhetoric appears substantially persuasive. The messages emerge as sequenced claims or allegations. Some are explicitly evident; others are only implicitly revealed.[1]

From a listener's vantage point a rhetorical message is a series of interrelated, assertive forces offered for *his* interpretation and evaluation. It is the listener's processing of stimuli that should be of primary interest to a critic of oral rhetoric. It is the form of the message "out there" that he needs to know about, but this is the hardest part of communication to grasp and examine. A critic cannot see into the listener's mind or follow the processing of speech behaviors observed. Yet he must try. He will be tempted to study messages as *things* rather than as instigations conceived to direct and control behaviors "out there." But then he will describe only "documents"—the dead records of the verbal parts of what were once series of stimuli let loose within rhetorical situations. Are there ways of looking at speaking that can protect critics against this sort of mistake? To conceive of the verbal contents of speech as stimuli that make *claims* can help.

THE CLAIMS OF ORAL MESSAGES

In approaching what the Greeks called *logos,* the content of speech borne by words, I think one can do no better than to adopt the image of discourse offered by Stephen E. Toulmin in his *The Uses of Argument:*

> A man who makes an assertion puts forward a claim—a claim on our attention and to our belief. Unlike one who speaks frivolously, jokingly or only hypothetically (under the rubric 'let us suppose'), . . . a man who asserts something intends his statement to be taken seriously: and, if his statement is understood as an assertion, it will be so taken. Just how seriously it will be taken depends, of course, on many circumstances—on the sort of man he is, for instance, and his general credit.
>
> . . .
>
> The claim implicit in an assertion is like a claim to a right or to a title. As with a claim to a right, though it may in the event be conceded without argument, its merits depend on the merits of the argument which could be produced in its support. Whatever the nature of the particular assertion may be—whether it is a meteorologist predicting rain for tomorrow, an injured workman alleging negligence on

the part of his employer, a historian defending the character of the Emperor Tiberius, a doctor diagnosing measles, a business-man questioning the honesty of a client, or an art critic commending the painting of Piero della Francesca—in each case we can challenge the assertion, and demand to have our attention drawn to the grounds (backing, data, facts, evidence, considerations, features) on which the merits of the assertion are to depend. We can, that is, demand an argument; and a claim need be conceded only if the argument which *can be* produced in its support proves to be up to standard.[2]

Professor Toulmin was not writing specifically about rhetoric, but the passage just quoted does treat discourse as an *event* in which there is dynamic, intellectual relationship between communicator and respondent. The instigator has serious, affective intentions toward a respondent. The respondent perceives the utterance as one *meant* to modify his experience. He knows he has the right to challenge if the grounds for claims seem perplexing or insufficient. He functions as judge on questions of relevance, significance, and sufficiency. The instigator knows, or ought to know, that his respondent can and will exercise these rights of judgment. The basic problem from the communicator's position is to do *enough* of the "right" things to make his claims credible. To this extent, at least, Toulmin's conception of an "argument" is a description of rhetorical communication. This is precisely the view a speech critic needs when approaching the verbal content of speech, and a number of critics have demonstrated that they can make realistic and useful descriptions by viewing *logos* in substantially the way Toulmin proposes.

To use this viewpoint in speech criticism we need to expand it slightly in order to see that in oral rhetoric personal as well as conceptual and linguistic elements are legitimate parts of the claim-making process. Reputation, what the speaker seems to be doing, even his person, may function as claim, data, warrant, backing for warrants, rebuttal, and qualification—just as truly as verbally symbolized concepts. In speech both casual and calculated behaviors can imply and qualify claims. Anything visible or audible can be perceived by a listener as "backing, data, facts, evidence, considerations, features" and even as claims themselves.[3]

When a critic has identified the exigences and constraints of a rhetorical situation and has conceptualized the unspoken contracts governing it, his next interest is apt to be with the verbal elements of communication—the *logos*. He must, of course, explore these elements in the light of what he has learned about unverbalized controls in the situation. The remainder of this chapter deals with first steps in that direction, and adaptations of Toulmin's concepts will be valuable for that purpose.

It is useful, though not imperative, to begin by examining what was claimed in the most explicit, verbal ways. This is not to forget that very important claims are also made implicitly, but a critic who looks first at the most explicit claims and afterward at subtler claims will end by glimpsing the interactive force that these kinds of claiming have on one another. A special reservation needs to be entered, however. By proposing that one distinguish explicit claims of discourse, I do not suggest differentiating among contents on linguistic principles or principles of traditional, formal logic.[4]

Generally speaking, if you apply the tests of formal logic to rhetorical materials, you will derive only two kinds of information about any series of explicit statements:

1) Your analysis will show that the conclusion asserted is not *necessarily* so.
2) You will be able to report that the explicit statements either do or do not have a *form* that *resembles* the forms you can find described in a book on formal logic.

Neither of these two kinds of information sheds much light on the adherence-nonadherence activities the statements would generate in the minds of listeners. One reason so little can be discovered about rhetoric through this kind of logical analysis is that rhetorical statements seldom deal with matters that are related to one another with firmly predictable regularity. Rhetorical discourse tends only to *allege* and *argue* that ideas fit together logically or "follow" logically. This has been recognized since Aristotle pointed to it as his primary reason for distinguishing rhetoric from demonstration (rigorous syllogistic and inductive reasoning).[5] The second difficulty in applying formal logic to rhetorical claims and their supports has been emphasized by Henry W. Johnstone, Jr.: "The very attempt to set up a philosophical argument in such a way as to make it possible to ascertain whether it is formally valid or not seems inevitably to result in a misrepresentation of the argument." [6]

Brockriede and Ehninger first called attention to the usefulness of Toulmin's "Layout of Arguments" as an answer to these problems. They said:

Toulmin's analysis and terminology are important to the rhetorician for two different but related reasons. First, they provide an appropriate structural model by means of which rhetorical arguments may be laid out for analysis and criticism; and, second, they suggest a system for classifying . . . proofs which employs argument as a central and unifying construct.[7]

At a later point in their essay Brockriede and Ehninger added:

. . . Toulmin by emphasizing *movement* from data, through warrant, to claim produces a conception of argument as dynamic. From his structural model [of claim making] we derive a picture of arguments "working" to establish and certify claims, and as a result of his functional terminology we are able to understand the role each part of an argument plays in this process.[8]

The "work" claim making does or does not do for a listener is, of course, a fundamental part of the processes speech critics need to identify, describe, and evaluate by comparison with what was rhetorically possible.

A further feature of Toulmin's analysis is that it avoids the confusion that comes from supposing what one person sees as "an argument" will be seen in the same way by others. Toulmin focuses on the *pathways* people's minds are likely to follow *if* they discern a cluster of statements as "arguing" for or against something. This allows a critic to estimate from what he knows of the situation whether an explicit bit of claim making is likely to be noticed "out there." If he believes the unit would be so noticed, he has found it explicit and can ask whether what was provided as "argument" would seem sufficient to the listeners.

To Toulmin there appear to be six possible elements of any *complete* "argument." These he diagrammatically represents thus:

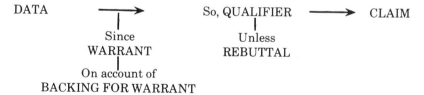

A CLAIM is any assertion to which a communicator appears to have committed himself by seriously offering it as "true." At the simplest level of interpretation any proposition or declaration can seem a CLAIM. Further inspection is likely to show that only *some* propositions are actually contended for by having supportive assertions associated with them. DATA are whatever information is, or could be, supplied in answer to a question such as: "What have you got to go on?" To the CLAIM, "Someone is trying to call me," the datum, "My phone is ringing," might be added, if needed, in order to invite a "movement" of thought from the *sound* to a conclusion that some message awaits the owner of the telephone.

Toulmin defines WARRANTS as "hypothetical, bridge-like statements" which "register explicitly the legitimacy of the step involved" in moving from the DATA to the CLAIM. As with any other element of argument, a persuader may or may not supply WARRANTS in words. In any case, such statements are those that answer questions like, *"How* do you get from your DATA to your CLAIM?" A statement like, "That sound was devised as a signal that someone wants to speak with me" could warrant the CLAIM "Someone is trying to call me." The vertical line connecting the movement from DATA to CLAIM with the WARRANT indicates that the WARRANT *justifies*—gives authority for—the step from DATA to acceptance of CLAIM.

A QUALIFIER, if offered, is an "explicit reference to the degree of force which our data confer on our claim in virtue of our WARRANT." Any indication of the limits of a CLAIM, such as "probably," "presumably," "in most cases," "almost certainly" would constitute a QUALIFIER. Such qualifications are always outgrowths of some expressed or unexpressed "conditions of exception or rebuttal." If stated, these conditions specify "circumstances in which the general authority of the warrant would have to be set aside." The vertical line connecting REBUTTAL with QUALIFIER indicates the connection between QUALIFIERS that need to be attached to CLAIMS and the "conditions which might be capable of defeating or rebutting the warranted conclusion." In our telephone example, the fact that one does get "wrong numbers" might force qualification of the CLAIM that "Someone is trying to call me."

BACKING FOR WARRANT stands for any information that shows the WARRANT is really applicable to the D $\longrightarrow$ So,C movement. Information of this sort forestalls or answers doubts about whether a WARRANT really justifies drawing *this* claim from *those* DATA.

Toulmin's description of what a *fully* developed argument can contain is not in any way an assertion that arguments must be full ones in order to function effectively. All that the description attempts to do is identify the basic features an "argument" *may* have or *may* lack.[9] Since a speech critic's task is to identify what supports were needed *in the situation,* the fact that Toulmin's framework is descriptive rather than prescriptive or evaluative fits the requirements very well. Indeed, Professor Toulmin is insistent on descriptions and evaluations that weigh the adequacy of any "argument" against the demands of situations:

> . . . utterances are made at particular times and in particular situations, and they have to be understood and assessed with one eye on this context. The same . . . is true of the relations holding between statements, at any rate in the majority of practical arguments. The exercise of the rational judgment is itself an activity carried out in a particular context and essentially dependent on it: the arguments we encounter are set out at a given time and in a given situation, and when we come to assess them they have to be judged against this background. So the practical critic of arguments, as of morals, is in no position to adopt the mathematician's Olympian posture.[10]

Amplifying these observations, Toulmin points to the absurdity of demanding more supportive detail from a predictor than he could know at the time of predicting, or of claiming subsequent events as grounds for challenging the predictor's original reasonableness. The warning is all too needful for critics of rhetorical discourse. One observes with deplorable frequency charges that a particular bit of political speaking must have been ill-grounded or inadequately reasoned because predictions of war or peace were unfulfilled by history. Likewise, criticism of political rhetoric is replete with assurances that this or that statesman spoke the more brilliantly because policies he advocated were adopted a generation after his death. Toulmin makes the wholesome point that it is *available* knowledge that must be canvassed in the first instance and wisdom *at the time of speaking* that deserves attention in the second instance.

Toulmin's view of arguments is useful because what listeners perceive as "arguments" are likely to be the fuller, more explicit, claim-making processes in what they hear. A critic can look for (1) claim making that is verbally obvious and for that reason likely to appear as "argument" to listeners, and (2) less obvious claim making which listeners are likely to "take seriously" because of their own patterns of attitudes, the character of the situation, or the pertinence of the topic to the situation's exigences.

Having identified these verbal structures, he can reason from all the information he has to conclusions about whether the listeners were likely to find these explicit claims clear enough, complete enough, and appealing enough to be believed. If he remembers he is a critic of rhetoric and not of formal logic, he will not, in Toulmin's phrase, condemn "an ape for not being a man or a pig for not being a porcupine." [11] He will not have much use for concepts of logical validity unless he can show the audience(s) used them.

Insofar as "validity" can have any meaning in rhetorical situations, it is a critic's estimate of the psychological credibility of "Argument A," as its "judges"—the listeners—probably viewed the matter. The *rhetorical* validity of explicit arguments depends on whether there was enough defense of the claims to satisfy the people addressed. "How likely is it that there would be challenges from the listeners?" is another way to put the test. If the audience would apply rigorous logical tests to the claim making, a critic must also, or he cannot tell what happened. If little or no argumentative rigor would be demanded, the critic must accept that as the situational standard or mislead himself about the event as it was.

EXPLORING EXPLICIT CLAIMS

The more a speaker *says* about a claim, the more likely it is that his listeners will notice what he is doing. When they notice, they will begin to function in the manner of Toulmin's challenger of arguments—unless, of course, they so thoroughly accept the claims that they need no further suasion. Since it is usually wise in studying anything to study the clearest cases first, it is a sensible critical strategy to begin examining content for obvious kinds of claim making.

How this can be done will be seen if we experiment by looking at the claims delegate George Miller most explicitly made and developed. In chapter II we reviewed Miller's rhetorical situation. To what was said there we need only add that the speech appears to have been premeditated little and that an authentic tape recording of what Miller said is available. The text has been seen by Congressman Miller and is printed with his permission.

Miller addressed his fellow Californians as follows:

1   So far in this convention I have been acting as the lawyer or the
2   parliamentarian for the Chairman—a sort of a political eunuch. But

3   after hearing some of the words that I heard here tonight, I want
4   strongly to express myself.
5   I'm not very much impressed with the information that was just given
6   us by the former Chairman of the National Committee. |Cheers. | Any
7   more than I was impressed two years ago when the same kind of
8   information cost me a Congressman in my district. |Cheers.| And I'm
9   also filled up with hearing all this stuff about, "This plank will get ya
10   so many votes and this plank'll get ya that many votes, and this will
11   alienate these and this will alienate that."
12   There's only one issue involved, and it's a moral issue. And I'm
13   tired of hearing it referred to in terms of international politics or in vote
14   getting for either party. The issue involved here is a moral issue. It
15   stems from whether or not you believe in the Fatherhood of God and
16   the Brotherhood of Man. And if you do, you believe that |Cheers.|
17   all men are equal, and you're gonna do everything that you can
18   to create and implement the day when we'll see that equality as a living
19   thing!
20   That's all I have to say. |Cheers.|

Following the strategy just proposed, let us interest ourselves
only in the points at which Miller adduced "proof" or otherwise
associated ideas in ways that might make someone feel, "That's
arguing." Because the speech is short, we can do this most easily by
listing each claim Miller made and then seeing whether some claims
are explicitly supported. (Were we dealing with a long segment of
rhetoric, this way of working would prove unduly laborious.)

Examining the text shows that at least fourteen clear, declarative
statements were uttered. Each *could* be taken as a CLAIM, hence
all are listed below in order of their utterance. Anything I have
added to Miller's words appears within brackets.

Assertion Number	Lines of Text	Assertion
1	1–2	So far in this convention I have been acting as the lawyer or the parliamentarian for the Chairman.
2	2	[I have been] a sort of a political eunuch.
3	3–4	I want strongly to express myself.
4	5–6	I'm not very much impressed with the information that was just given us by the former Chairman of the National Committee.
5	7–8	[Two years ago] the same kind of information cost me a Congressman in my district.

6	8–11	I'm also filled up with hearing all this stuff about, "This . . . that."
7	12	There's only one issue involved.
8	12	It's a moral issue.
9	12–14	I'm tired of hearing it referred to in terms of international politics or in vote getting for either party.
10	14	The issue involved here is a moral issue.
11	14–16	It stems from whether or not you believe in the Fatherhood of God and the Brotherhood of Man.
12	16–17	. . . if you do [believe], you believe that all men are equal.
13	16–19	. . . if you do [believe] . . . you're gonna do everything that you can to create and implement the day when we'll see that equality as a living thing.
14	20	That's all I have to say.

Almost at a glance, one sees that twice Mr. Miller framed statements in a way that expressed and supported claims so that they sounded *"necessarily* true." These are very strong and very explicit claims. Statements 11, 12, and 13 involve the rhetorical structure: "If A, then B." This is a standard, "logical" form in Western culture. Any listener who heard and understood these statements was likely to have the sense that Miller was telling him something in a "strong" way; the "then B" parts of the two lines of thought could scarcely be perceived as other than insisted upon, if the phrasings were perceived at all. We may suppose that those who heard and understood the statements perceived something like:

DATA: you believe in the ⟶ So, CLAIM: You believe that all
    Fatherhood of God and the   men are equal.
    Brotherhood of Man

DATA: you believe that all ⟶ So,Q: "if" [unless you don't believe]
    men are equal   CLAIM: you're gonna do every-
        thing that you can to create
        and implement the day when
        we'll see that equality as
        a living thing.

We cannot know, of course, that Miller's listeners attended closely enough to preceive these "argumentative" relationships. Nonetheless, explicit verbal structures that interrelated ideas were present as potential stimuli. Therefore, what happened is worth describing clearly. Miller explicitly spoke of DATA about what the listeners allegedly believed. CLAIMS about what were necessary consequences were asserted. The word "if" gave a degree of QUALIFICATION to the second DATA ⟶ So, CLAIM movement. No WARRANTS were supplied. If any listener was moved to ask "How does the belief (DATA) *force* the conclusion (CLAIM)?" he had to answer his own question. He could do that by supplying some such WARRANTS as "Shared fatherhood and brotherhood imply equality" or "Belief in equality demands its implementation." Or, a listener could reject Miller's CLAIMS because he could not see how to get from DATA to CLAIM. Or, he could hesitate to believe the CLAIMS because Miller gave no BACKING for the WARRANTS. Or, a listener could reject the DATA as untrue for him (as one who doubts the Fatherhood of God or disbelieves that all men are equal). The possible responses to Miller's structured assertions can be quickly spelled out when we see what is present and not present in his explicit, argumentative structures.

The relatively simple process of identifying the present and absent details of claim making allows us to describe *how,* if at all, asserted relationships among ideas might be responded to. But identifying the constituents of Miller's little "arguments" does not end our critical possibilities. We could ask also whether these bits of claim making are unusual in any way. That might draw attention to the fact that these two clusters of statements are the points at which Miller was most insistent. Nowhere else in the speech did he contend for a CLAIM with such absolutism. If we suppose he was acting rationally, we have to infer that he thought beliefs in brotherhood and equality were such strong moral commitments in this audience that he could claim action was *absolutely* dictated. He supplied no WARRANTS, a thing safe to do when one thinks his hearers will jump automatically from DATA to CLAIM. He even recognized (by his "if") that if the DATA (beliefs) were not there in the listeners, then his CLAIM that action was a "must" was pointless. If he knew what he was doing, he must have been confident of the moral commitments of his listeners. If he did not know what he was doing but the listeners had the necessary moral beliefs, his "argument" was still powerful.

This is a point at which a critic goes back again to what he knows about the attitudes of the audience. We know Miller's audience was concerned enough about equality and civil rights that they wanted a liberal statement about the Court in the platform. Miller's "arguments" could work! They could work unless some listener was against joining his endorsement of equal rights to the theistic concept, "the Fatherhood of God." Would very many delegates be so insistently atheistic that they would refuse to act on their own beliefs because Miller sounded theistic? It seems unlikely in a group of politically active people. Our best, reasoned judgment must be that these two little "arguments" could have significant persuasive power with this audience; they could impel action toward making "equality a living thing."

Before leaving any "argued" segment of a speech it ought to be asked whether the speaker's prestige was likely to add to or detract from the "argument's" force. This is especially important where "arguments" lack stated WARRANTS. In our example, a little research would show that George Miller's relations with other members of his party had been and continued to be good. There is no reason to believe that his status as a political leader would do other than further reinforce the propriety of his claim that the delegation must act on behalf of equal rights.

Having inspected in detail the two most explicitly supported CLAIMS, we ought now to look for other, perhaps less obvious, "arguings." We shall find no other points at which ideas are as forcefully connected as in the cases we have just looked at, but a few other statements *might* be perceived as CLAIMS-contended-for.

Estimating the potential effects of loosely connected statements is a subjective enterprise. It is best not to try to see connections that are tenuous or subtle. This, too, is a troublesome temptation for critics. Mr. Miller's speech was a speech; the listeners heard it only once, in a corner of a huge hall. For a critic to try to spy out every imaginable CLAIM-support possibility—as one might properly do in *literary* criticism—only produces observations that are unrepresentative of what could have been perceived in *speech*. "Critics" with greater love for possibilities than probabilities have assured me that the "argument" illustrated on p. 59 was present in Miller's first words.

One cannot complain of these analysts' imagination, but to suppose that statements 1 and 2 of Miller's speech would be perceived as a serious D $\longrightarrow$ So, C movement presupposes a whole set of "iffy" conditions in Miller, in the convention, and in the listeners.

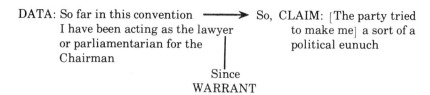

DATA: So far in this convention ⟶ So, CLAIM: [The party tried
     I have been acting as the lawyer   to make me] a sort of a
     or parliamentarian for the   political eunuch
     Chairman

                    Since
               WARRANT

       [This is the kind of job they
       give people to keep them from
       having their say.]

None is comfirmable from what Miller explicitly said nor from
what can be readily discovered about the 1956 Democratic Convention. Worse, the D ⟶ So, C movement and the assumed
WARRANT are in political life more likely *not* to be true than
true.

This example of "criticism gone wrong" illustrates more than
undue enthusiasm for reading "between the lines." It illustrates
unfortunate innocence of situational data and excessive skepticism.
Not knowing the duties of parliamentarians or how they are chosen
for large and serious meetings, the students who proposed this
interpretation had no "facts of life" on which to make normative
judgments. And having undiscriminatingly skeptical—if not
paranoid—views of the world or of politics, they were led into a
critical absurdity.

Restraint, realism, and regard for the *probabilities* of life and
rhetorical situations ought to control judgments of rhetorical
speaking. Study of content is best when it is a search for structures
and meanings *most* listeners probably would *not* miss. Miller's
speech consumed less than sixty seconds. Under these circumstances
only prominently interconnected statements were likely to be
heard as intentionally related to one another. If we look with these
cautions for additional explicit claim making, we shall not find
much not already identified. Probably *some* listeners perceived
statements 7, 8, and 9 in one of the following ways:

DATA: There's only one is-⟶ So, CLAIM: I'm tired of hearing it re-
sue involved and it's a moral issue.   ferred to in terms of international
                       politics or in vote getting for either
                | party.

              Since
          WARRANT

       [Pragmatic considerations
       do not apply in decisions
       like this.]

It is more likely that an inference might be perceived in statements 4 and 5:

DATA: Two years ago . . . ———▶ So, CLAIM: I'm not very much impressed
the same kind of information   with the information that was just
[as was offered by the former   given us by the former Chairman of
Chairman of the National Com-   the National Committee
mittee] cost me a Congressman
in my district. |

                          Since
                        WARRANT

                  [The situations are like
                  enough to justify comparison.]

It is plausible, however, that these same statements might be perceived by other listeners as having a different relationship:

DATA: Two years ago [I ———▶ So, CLAIM: [You should follow my lead
lost] . . . a Congressman in my   in being] not very much impressed
district | with the information that was just
                                             given us by the former Chairman of
                                             the National Committee

                          Since
                        WARRANT

                  The same kind of imformation
                  [will yield the same kind of
                  results].

   It is difficult to see other verbal structures likely to be perceived as explicit "arguments," and we cannot be sure the claim making we have inspected would actually be heard as "arguments." But the important thing is that all our observations confirm a single view of how Mr. Miller's "reasonings" worked. WARRANTS by which listeners could move in thought from DATA to CLAIMS were generally *not* stated; if people perceived "arguments," they had to justify their logic to themselves. This they could do if they believed strongly that equality was a moral matter. They could do it if they thought losing Congressmen was unfortunate. Evidence about the situation tells us that most listeners would have no trouble following Miller in either case. They were active liberals on equality, and they were practicing party politicians. They probably possessed the necessary patterns of attitudes to accept all the statements we have looked at *either* as "arguments" *or* as unconnected utterances of "truth."

Another thing is noticeable about these "arguments": only once did Miller rest a conclusion on DATA that were objectively verifiable—his loss of a Congressman. Elsewhere DATA had to preexist as belief in his listeners. If those beliefs were *strongly* held—and we have reason to believe they were—then most listeners probably assented to Miller's explicit CLAIMS with a good deal of emotion as well as with a sense of reason. Indeed, all of our observations indicate that Mr. Miller's most explicit CLAIMS did not really depend for their force on being formally linked together but on listeners' beliefs. His "arguments" were really just helps toward self-persuasion. They could not shake the convictions of doubters who challenged the CLAIMS, but they were verbal shapes that agreeing listeners could fill out and endow with rationality and feeling as they processed Miller's instigations. Whatever powers Miller's speaking may have had in its rhetorical situation cannot be attributed to logical rigor.

In discussing explicit argumentation I have avoided much traditional language: e.g., logical proofs, deduction, induction, causal argument. I have done so out of regard for the nature of rhetoric itself. Standard terms of logical analysis refer to verbal structures as though argument-as-influence exists *in* the symbols one uses. This may be so in logic and science, but it is not so in rhetoric. Argument in rhetoric is realized in the minds of receivers, or it is not realized at all. It is part of a rhetorical critic's task to conceptualize what words, as *logos,* can *cause* to happen "argumentatively" *in receivers.* The message that ultimately affects life "out there" is an idea-pattern occurring in a listener's experience because language was seen as structure that *seemed* "logical." One way *logos* influences is by having "logical" form.[12]

If words seem to show that certain things fit together "logically," that may add to the credibility of whatever is being claimed. Listeners' habits of thought may be engaged influentially. For example, Westerners habitually look for causes to explain things as effects, and they look for effects because they believe there are causes. They also look for similarities that authorize comparative conclusions and for examples that allow generalizations. When we hear connection-asserting, conclusion-authorizing relationships explicitly offered as reasons, we do not just put labels on them— "causal," "analogical," "inductive," etc.—nor do we analyze them for technical validity. If we respond to such reason giving by reasoning, we follow in thought along the "logical" pathway the speaker proposed (or some other), but we do so for *our* reasons, not for the sake of the "logical" form the *logos* had.

Rhetoric is not experienced as formal logic. To experience rhetoric in a "logical" way is to

> . . . *discover and complete emerging patterns.* There is no a priori set of conditions defining the sorts of relations which constitute a pattern; and accordingly, the way is open in processes of observation and experience for the discovery and testing of new modes of relation as bases for probabilistic inference.[13]

A critic of spoken rhetoric must do whatever he can to discover the patterned relationships that were likely to have been perceived in the speaker's *logos;* then he must try to calculate what force of "proof" they may have had in *this* rhetorical situation. He asks and answers as informedly as he can (1) whether the assertions of allegedly significant relationship were likely to be perceived by the listeners and (2) whether the listeners were specially invited to agree to CLAIMS because the interrelationships were alleged in the ways they were. One part of criticism's descriptive and evaluative work is completed when this is done. It will be done best if the critic inspects any and all relationships explicitly alleged, not just the types familiar in logic books. As Professor Zyskind points out, we do not fully understand all the emergent patterns that can be taken as "logical proof" in rhetoric. In speech criticism we had best not close our eyes to any pattern a speaker asserts as having the force of "proof."

Speaking can, of course, have major social effects even though minimal attention is given to verbalizing formal, relational patterns in support of CLAIMS. One will, for example, find few explicitly "argued" CLAIMS in Spiro T. Agnew's address on televised news (pp. 367–375). On the other hand, Leon Zellner's "What Can We Prove about God?" (pp. 337–340) depends very heavily on whether listeners understand and accept what Zellner explicitly asserts are the significant relationships among ideas. Churchill's "Address to the Congress of the United States" (pp. 301–308) mingles a few "arguments" with other kinds of "proving." Explicitly argued *logos* can give force to rhetorical speech, but it is by no means the sole or even a necessary source of persuasion. But about any oral rhetoric a critic ought to ask: "*Is* there 'arguing'?" If there is, he asks, "What could that 'arguing' achieve with the specific listeners who responded?" With even speculative answers to those questions he knows something useful about the character of the message.

There is a further way Toulmin's concept of argument can be critically useful. In addition to analyzing interrelated statements, as we have done with Miller's speech, a part of a speech or a whole speech can be conceptualized as "an argument" in order to see what DATA-WARRANT-CLAIM functions the larger units carry out. For example, it is interesting to see what Churchill was doing in the thought unit comprising paragraphs 13 through 15 (pp. 304–305). He made a claim at the beginning of paragraph 13: "Not all the tidings will be evil." Then he recited a series of events which were, from the Allied point of view, encouraging. But to make it unmistakable that he was *supporting* his CLAIM, he said at paragraph 15 that these instances were "proof": "I am so glad to be able to place before you . . . proof that with proper weapons and proper organization we are able to beat the life out of the savage Nazi." Clearly he put the credibility of this entire CLAIM-unit on the strength of the instances (DATA). We could diagram what he did thus:

DATA: Instances of Allied ⟶ So, CLAIM: "With proper weapons and
successes and improved   proper organization, we are able to
positions.   beat . . . the Nazi."

Since
WARRANT

[The DATA are sufficient instances of success through weaponry and organization.]

Interestingly, Churchill turned his CLAIM from a prophecy to a claim *of fact* in his restatement of it. A critic could ask about this broad unit of "argument" the same sorts of questions as we have asked concerning Miller's "If A, then B" claimings. The question would be whether the American Congressmen and the other Americans and British who listened by radio would make the intellectual movement from Churchill's DATA to either his prophetic CLAIM or his CLAIM-of-established-fact or both.

"Arguments" are of varying magnitudes. It is possible to conceive of an entire speech as a single, broad argument. Agnew's speech can be so conceptualized:

DATA: Instances of network ⟶ So, CLAIM: Networks need to monitor
newsmen acting in allegedly   their news functions and correct un-
unfair or inaccurate ways.   fairness and inaccuracy.

Since
WARRANT
The networks have enormous
power which must be used
fairly.

All three functions of this overall argument were filled in explicitly during the speech. Capsulized as a structure, the form and
substance of the speech show exactly where the controversial part
of it is. Where would a challenger be most likely to attack? On the
adequacy and choice of DATA and on the allegation that the instances were instances of unfairness and inaccuracy. Who would
deny the WARRANT? Everyone is for fairness. Who would deny
the CLAIM? Even newsmen would agree there ought to be regular
monitoring to assure fairness and accuracy. The quarrel, if any,
was bound to be over Agnew's DATA. And as this is written, after
Agnew's resignation, Agnew's data of 1969 are still being debated.
To frame the pith of an entire speech as a major argument or
series of arguments often shows what listeners had to accept in
order to accede to or challenge the speaker's general message.

There are, then, several ways that investigations of what is
explicitly "argued" can yield significant critical information. But
one must not assume that rhetorical power is proportionate to the
amount of "argumentation" in speaking. Speech is not *il*logical
because it "argues" little; situations demand different degrees of
explicit argument. Some audiences in some situations will demand that virtually all CLAIMS be defended explicitly with
pertinent DATA, with WARRANTS well backed, and with careful
QUALIFICATIONS. But the same audiences in other situations
may require little explicitly argued content on other subjects from
other speakers.

When dealing with oral rhetoric, it is a fallacy to expect uniform amounts of argumentation. The unspoken contract of speaking decrees that the *listeners* are the measurers of sufficiency, not
the critics, nor the speaker, nor any other listeners save those
listening *now*. Criticism undertakes to estimate whether what a
speaker chooses to "argue" could move listeners along the mental
pathways the speaker told them to follow, toward justifications
for his CLAIMS.

NOTES

[1] I am not arguing whether it is pedagogically useful to classify rhetoric as, say, description, narration, exposition, and argument. I do contend that these conceptualizations are not useful as *critical* categories. The difficulties into which they lead are succinctly but unintentionally shown in C. S. Baldwin's *Writing and Speaking* (New York: Longmans, Green, and Company, 1911). Following and continuing a long tradition, Baldwin firmly recommended these concepts as valuable for *both* teaching and criticism. But in the end he was forced to write: "Just as exposition is closely related to argument, so description to narration. Indeed, it is even less easy to keep the latter apart. . . . pure description unmixed with narration is neither very common nor very easy" (pp. 152–153). My contention is that such subtly intermixed concepts are not helpful in criticism.

[2] Stephen E. Toulmin, *The Uses of Argument* (New York: Cambridge University Press, 1958), pp. 11–12. My italics.

[3] *Ibid.,* p. 11. Toulmin seems to recognize these possibilities when he points to "the sort of man he is" as one of the circumstances that may determine "how seriously it [an assertion] will be taken."

[4] Most linguists do not claim to study the psychological significance of the linguistic forms they identify. Thus W. Nelson Francis observed in *The Structure of American English* (New York: The Ronald Press Co., 1958), p. 409: "What may be called the grammar of continuous discourse remains to be worked out." Later, John B. Carroll wrote: "Even though linguists have often written about the desirability of making an analysis of the content system of a language, their scant progress in doing so is probably an indication that such an analysis would be impossible without drawing on information about the *use* of a linguistic system by the speakers of a language." John B. Carroll, *Language and Thought,* 1964, p. 26. By permission of Prentice-Hall, Inc., Englewood Cliffs, N.J. A decade after Carroll's statement, the situation is substantially as he described it.

Logic as science concerns itself with symbolic forms but not with their contents as such. Leo Apostel in his "Assertion Logic and Theory of Argumentation," *Philosophy and Rhetoric* 4 (Spring 1971): 92–110; suggests that an "assertion logic" can be developed; it has not been worked out and would in any case be quite different from traditional, formal logic.

[5] Aristotle, *Rhetoric,* W. Rhys Roberts trans., 1356[a]–1357[b], by permission of The Clarendon Press, Oxford;Random House ed., pp. 26–28.

[6] Henry W. Johnstone, Jr., *Philosophy and Argument* (University Park: The Pennsylvania State University Press, 1959), p. 60. Johnstone's point is that even in philosophical arguments, argument does not proceed by formal, syllogistic or inductive steps; so, to apply formal, logical tests of validity, the arguments must be *reconstructed*. But the reconstruction will no longer be precisely what was argued because the terms and the forms have been changed.

[7] Wayne Brockriede and Douglas Ehninger, "Toulmin on Argument: An Interpretation and Application," *Quarterly Journal of Speech* 46 (February 1960): 44. In their *Decision by Debate* (New York: Dodd, Mead & Co., 1963) these authors make clear that *argument, dispute,* and *debate* are, for them, essentially synonymous terms explainable outside the framework of traditional logic.

[8] Brockriede and Ehninger, "Toulmin on Argument," p. 46.

[9] Toulmin does not explain his construct thus, but this seems to me a fair extrapolation from his general treatment of an "argument." "Arguments," for Toulmin, are structures *in defense of* claims; that full defense is needed or expected in all circumstances and on all subjects, he specifically denies.

¹⁰ Toulmin, *Uses of Argument,* pp. 182–183. All other language taken
directly from Toulmin in the explanations just preceding this quotation are
identified by quotation marks. They come from Toulmin's chapter III, "The
Layout of Arguments."

¹¹ *Ibid.,* p. 256.

¹² Some implications of this fact are discussed in Rodney B. Douglass and
Carroll C. Arnold, "An Analysis of *Logos:* A Methodological Inquiry," *Quarterly Journal of Speech* 56 (February 1970): 22–32.

¹³ Harold Zyskind, "Some Philosophical Strands in Popular Rhetoric." Reprinted from *Perspectives in Education, Religion, and the Arts,* edited by
Howard E. Kiefer and Milton K. Munitz, p. 387, by permission of State University of New York Press. © 1970 The Research Foundation of State University of New York. All rights reserved. Italics in the original.

Chapter IV

Implicit Content

We have looked at clusters of statements in Miller's speech, but only at those that seemed explicitly to invite listeners to make inferences of a logical sort. There remain a number of remarks in the speech that are unaccounted for. These do not seem related to one another in any "argumentative" way, yet they, too, assert things. They allege. There would be statements of this sort in any speaking, and ways must be found to account for their influence in rhetorical situations. There is a way of thinking that can help us to move critically from the explicit to the implicit or suggestive.

The ways people put words together in rhetoric seem to differ in the rigor with which they insist on how receivers shall think in response to the words. George Miller's unqualified, "argued" statements seem to assert that listeners *must* follow exactly the logical paths Miller prescribes. If they believe in the brotherhood of man, they *must* agree that there is *no* alternative to doing "all you can," etc. The words seem to say there is no other conclusion that is at all "logical." But other of Miller's statements are very much less insistent. Some statements, like the first one, seem to invite listeners to toy, to play for amusement, with the ideas expressed. Miller has been "sort of a political eunuch." My guess is that Miller did not care how much fun his listeners had with this metaphorical notion—provided they got the message that until this moment he had been feeling somewhat impotent in the convention's policy making.

A psycholinguist has suggested that we shall understand verbalization better if we think of it as an attempt to program receivers' responses in different ways and degrees. Said he:

> A sentence can be likened to a computer program; in fact that is precisely what it is: a set of directions for the human thinking machine. The hearer or the reader . . . constructs its meaning by following the "directions" it provides in terms of the concepts and conceptual relationships it evokes, also utilizing whatever further information he may have concerning the situation in which he hears it. This process may be called *interpretation*. . . . The speaker's intention in creating a sentence is not necessarily correlated with the situational meaning the sentence has for the hearer. The speaker may not be fully successful in creating a sentence that will be interpreted as he intends it to be. . . .[1]

Looking at Miller's speech from this position, we seem to have statements that "program" or "direct" hearers' thoughts with varying degrees of firmness. Some, like statements 11, 12, and 13, seem to "program" for systematic conclusion drawing. Others, like statements 4 and 5 or 7, 8, and 9 seem to urge reasoned conclusions, but less forcibly. And many, like most statements we have not yet discussed, make CLAIMS but seem to leave listeners free to couple these assertions to anything in the rest of the speech, to things in the situation, or to the listeners' private experiences. We are, it seems, dealing with bits of speech that aim at different degrees of control over thoughts. To think of speech this way is simply to recognize that all *logos* in rhetoric represents someone's attempt to exercise varying degrees of control over listeners' responses. Some portions of the *logos* are attempts to "program" directly, as when reasoning is obvious; some portions are looser, less insistent, more suggestive attempts. And, of course, as Carroll says, there is no necessary correlation between what the speaker seems to have attempted and what actually happened in the listener's interpretation. Yet different gradations of attempted directiveness are present, and critics should take note of the distinctions.

Hereafter I shall use the words "suggestive" and "implicit" as terms by which to refer to bits of communication that seem to invite listeners to *associate* what is said with other parts of the speech or aspects of the situation or with private experience. Using these terms, I shall consider in this chapter how critics can reason about the meanings and effects of units of language that do not seem to attempt programming with the rigor of "logical" structures. We are all familiar with this kind of language and experience. We know that hearing words like *red* can set off many different kinds of response. *Red* may cause one hearer to run through a "program" about a red dress, another to think of "Red China," another to associate the term with "Red Barn" eating establishments. Behind each program of association there is some bit of experience and some systematic thinking (perhaps done long ago) that causes the hearer to set the term in whatever context he does. In such moments we respond *through* what Carroll calls interpretation and, if we are listeners, our interpretations are always created out of what a speaker makes us perceive (through his programming) *modified by whatever from our past experiences we associate with it.*

This is not a sophisticated description of response behavior, but it indicates the justice of three important critical premises from which to reason about all oral rhetoric and especially about that in which directiveness or programming is implicit or suggestive.

1. Whatever the consequences of a speaker's utterance, those consequences always occur within the *listener's* world of awareness, and they occur under the "rules" his past experiences have given him.
2. The concepts that determine a listener's reactions may *or may not* closely resemble the concepts symbolically offered through acts of speech.
3. As they interpret, listeners *always* add to or take away from the intended meanings of what they hear.

These three premises all support a most important generalization about rhetorical experience and criticism: A critic will mislead himself if he supposes there can be any one-to-one identity between what the *logos* says and what is actually responded to "out there."

Such propositions make it clear that critics will be able to make only rough estimates of what instigative statements are likely to "set off" inside listeners, but informed criticism is not impossible because of this. We cannot tell whether "equal angles" will evoke pictorial images of triangles or abstract thoughts of geometric principles. But we can be confident that the words "equal angles" are very likely to "set off" something having to do with geometric forms if the words are heard at all. This kind of assurance about phrases and general ideas is enough to allow critical thinking about implicit meanings of speech. It is, as we said, the responsive tendencies of people characterized as "types," "classes," and "publics" that critics seek to estimate, and this they can do with sound knowledge of rhetorical situations and of the potentialities of speech behavior.

To get at the suggestive potentialities of things said, a critic needs some probing questions that, if answered, tend to uncover what discourse does or does not have the power to do. The following inquiries have worked well for this purpose when my students and I have worked with them, and several scholar-critics have also found them worth employing.[2]

1. What are the simplest interpretations listeners could put upon this unit of what was said?
2. What solutions (if any) does this unit of speech offer for listeners' problems and anxieties?
3. Does the context in which any statement or group of statements appears give it special claim on a listener's attention; if so, what are likely responses listeners might make in this rhetorical situation?
4. Are the claims and inferences suggested by the units compatible with each other and with the CLAIMS in which prominent arguments culminate?
5. Which of the following classes of judgment are encouraged or directly asked for by the units under study:
    a. *Factual:* judgments accepting or rejecting the alleged existence, form, capacities, etc. of something;
    b. *Optative:* evaluative judgments endorsing or rejecting something on the basis of general personal or social preferences;
    c. *Adjudicative:* judgments on the conformity that exists or is lacking between things or events and *formally agreed upon* codes or standards;
    d. *Predictive of desirability:* evaluative judgments endorsing things on the basis of their desirability, feasibility, potency, and so forth for the future?
6. To what extent do the units (considered individually and

good

collectively) suggest anything about the motives the speaker had for entering this rhetorical situation? [3]

All that is claimed for these six lines of inquiry is that when pursued in approximately the sequence listed here, the inquiries often reveal information about implied meanings that might have remained hidden if the questions had not been asked or if they had been asked in random order. No answer to any one question is likely to be significant in itself. What a critic seeks in using these questions are *patterns of answers* that allow him to generalize about the suggestive potentialities of what was said.

To see what information can be extracted if we approach speech in these ways, let us return to the fourteen statements extracted from Congressman Miller's speech (pp. 54–55). We have already identified four possibly "argumentative" structures, but even these may have contained implicit as well as explicit meanings. So, we shall need to look at all fourteen statements for implicit potentialities.

Because Miller's speech is so short, we can take individual statements as "units" of speech; but if our total body of oral rhetoric were larger, we would probably want to study larger "units." We might explore the suggestive potentialities of: an "argument," a main idea plus its supporting and amplifying materials, "pieces" of a dialogue or press conference, or any other block of communication that constituted a fully rounded segment of thought. The point is that each of the six questions we are about to use as critical tools can be asked about *any* "unit" of speech from a single word to the total communication. Statements as well as larger blocks of meaning will be looked at in the explanations that follow because Miller's speech is short enough to allow us to treat it both microscopically and macroscopically.

In chapter III it was suggested that speech critics ought to look for the obvious, not the subtly possible. We want to know what hurried listeners *probably* caught from the speaking that flowed around them. Hence the general question: *What are the simplest interpretations listeners could put upon this unit of what was said?* Scanning the fourteen statements Miller offered, one can notice that several convey the impression that Miller was rather emotional about speaking and about his subject.[4] It is plain that statements 1, 2, 3, 5, and portions of 4 and 9 (perhaps 14 also) tell about Miller's state of feeling:

> So far in this convention I have been . . . a sort of a political eunuch.
> I want strongly to express myself. I'm not very impressed. . . . I'm all
> filled up with hearing all this stuff. . . . That's all I have to say.

It is unlikely that any listener would consciously notice every one
of these scattered statements, yet anyone who noticed even two or
three of them would tend to interpret their utterance as indications that Mr. Miller was a bit "worked up." Moreover, if we change
the "unit" we look at and consider the entire speech as a unit, we
will have to say that listeners must have sensed that the speech
built up to an emotional climax, further inviting the interpretation that Miller was somewhat excited. From any point of view,
Miller's speech had material in it that signaled the presence of
strong emotion.[5]

We could pursue inquiry into "simple interpretations" further,
noting that "political eunuch," "I want strongly to express myself,"
and "I'm filled up" might generate the response: "George has been
frustrated." One who *heard* Miller utter the line, "That's all I have
to say," would be likely to translate it into, "And I feel better
now, too!" There are, in short, several ways in which a sense that
Miller spoke for *self*-expression could have been generated as an
interpretation of his talk.

Now, a negative possibility arises. Taking the time of an audience
in order to gratify one's own needs for self-expression tends to
breach the unspoken contract of oral rhetoric. Communication
for listeners is expected. We ought to note the possibility that
Miller's revealed emotionality could count against him—unless
we find out, as we shall, that the audience in this situation would
convert Miller's self-expressiveness into something agreeable
to *their* attitudes.

If we shift our "unit" of analysis again, we shall see other,
probable, "simple interpretations." The speech really had two sections: lines 5–8 invite the interpretation that *not* taking a clear
stand on the Supreme Court's decision will cost votes; lines 8 to
the end assert that it is *wrong* not to take a strong position. If a
listener heard the speech "in parts," he might interpret it: "The
Chairman's advice is immoral and impractical, too." It is easy to
believe that liberal, Northern Democrats in 1956 would be moved
in the direction Miller wished by this perception.

Trying still another kind of "unit" to see what happens, we can
ask about "simple interpretations" of the "arguments" we isolated in chapter III. They could have implicit as well as explicit
effects, but when we examine them we must preserve their natural

structure, for to reshape them would be to misrepresent what the listeners actually experienced.

The argumentative units of the speech occurred in these segments of the talk:

> I'm not very impressed with the information that was just given us by the former Chairman of the National Committee. Anymore than I was impressed two years ago when the same kind of information cost me a Congressman in my district.
>
> . . .
>
> There's only one issue involved, and it's a moral issue. And I'm tired of hearing it referred to in terms of international politics or in vote getting for either party. It stems from whether or not you believe in the Fatherhood of God and the Brotherhood of Man. And if you do, you believe that all men are equal, and you're gonna do everything that you can to create and implement the day when we'll see that equality as a living thing!

Here are two natural segments of Miller's talk which, whether heard as "arguments" or not, were capable of creating general impressions not directly associated with their argumentative qualities.

Miller's listeners were politically oriented. Some probably heard the first set of statements as: "That's poor politics," or "The idea isn't good for the party," or "That's a good reason for not being impressed," or "We could lose in lots of places if we aren't careful." No critic can say precisely what associations Miller's allusion to the lost election would evoke, but anyone ought confidently to suppose that most politically attuned hearers would be in some degree distressed at the prospects of the loss which Miller clearly emphasized. We see, then, that this unit had implicit power to evoke motivations toward actions—either as argument or as a set of words not heard as argumentative. The "logic" of Miller's movement from DATA to CLAIM contributed one force to which listeners might respond, and the citation of a political loss contributed an additional force. *Logos* and *pathos* were present together as potentialities for influence. This kind of interplay between "logical" forces and "feeling" is present in all rhetoric; therefore it is imperative that critics explore the suggestive overlay of arguments as well as their logical structures. Only so can critics describe and evaluate the full potentialities of argumentation.

Looking at the second cluster of "arguing" statements in the same way, we come upon another fact of importance. It also concerns the interrelationship of suggestive and argumentative content in rhetoric.

An attentive listener would probably get from Miller's second "argument" some such interpretation as: "He thinks belief without action is wrong," or "He thinks only disbelief in God could justify inaction here," or "He insists that action is the real proof of moral belief." Whoever followed Miller's remarks and formed such interpretations reflectively would have to fill a gap between "you believe" and "you will do everything you can." When we said in chapter III that a WARRANT must be supplied here, we were saying that *associative* processes are *one* source from which warranting can come. A warranting *statement* fitting the "logic" of the "argument" could be produced in a listener's mind. However, there is a nonlogical (but not *il*logical) way the gap could be closed. A listener could trust Miller so fully that the trust would constitute a WARRANT. The converse also would be possible; a listener could distrust Miller and find alleged want of integrity sufficient grounds for denying Miller's CLAIM. In each case, the WARRANT comes from outside the message because Miller provides no formal WARRANT. So, we get a general principle of criticism: Whenever WARRANTS are missing in argumentative structures, a critic must investigate what both reflection *and* free association could supply to fill the gaps.[6]

This last bit of analysis has led us to ask in a new way whether Miller's "arguments" were adequate, and for whom. By asking about the associative as well as the logical or reflective power of arguments, we get a psychological confirmation of what we found "logically" in the previous chapter. Not only as argument but as suggestion, too, Miller's CLAIMS in this unit had excellent prospects of being accepted. How do we know that? Because we know that the audience and situation were favorable. As political liberals the listeners were likely to (1) reason their way to WARRANTS that would fill the gaps, or (2) get from DATA to CLAIM by free association of ideas, or (3) so fully believe the CLAIMS or so fully trust George Miller that they would need neither DATA nor WARRANT in order to agree. From the situational evidence we have, there is no reason to think that any of the forty-some Californians would fail to assent to Miller's CLAIMS on one or another of these "logical" and psychological grounds.

Now, let us recapitulate. Taken altogether, what do we now know about Miller's speech? We know he furnished no explicit WARRANTS for DATA ⟶ So, CLAIM movements, and he gave no BACKING FOR WARRANTS. All of his argumentation required listeners who could fill "gaps" for themselves. We know also that his nonargumentative statements suggested, among other things, that Miller spoke under pressure of strong feeling, probably including frustration at not being able to participate in floor debates and certainly at the idea of ignoring the Supreme Court's decision on civil rights.

The only passage at which we have looked which does not seem to require some preexisting acceptance of Miller's moral-egalitarian assumptions occurs at lines 5–8, in statements 4 and 5. Whether that unit was heard as "argument" lacking a WARRANT or as mere implication that political loss was the price of accepting the former Chairman's advice, we can easily believe that California's political delegates would take Miller's threat seriously.

These are the technical facts we have uncovered thus far. We have now to do what the late R. P. Blackmur said was the task of all criticism once the technical data are found: "The rest of the labor is in the effort to find understandable terms to fit the composition of the facts." [7] "To find understandable terms to fit the composition of the facts" always requires that we join knowledge of the technical features of rhetoric to knowledge of the immediate rhetorical situation. When we compare what Miller said with what a delegation like his would want to hear at a caucus on whether to praise or not praise a Supreme Court decision favorable to civil rights, the "fit" of Miller's rhetoric to situation seems excellent. The explicit and implicit potentialities of what Miller said suited listeners who agreed with his ideas, feelings, and views about how to solve the exigence of taking a position on civil rights. Our data on the situation say this was precisely the kind of situation and audience Miller faced.

The analyses we have now completed on Miller's speech are the most crucial ones a critic carries out in evaluating rhetoric. Whether a critic is looking at Miller's brief speech or the outpourings of an Edmund Burke or a Fidel Castro, the core of his work is done when he can declare he has investigated the obviously explicit arguments and the simple interpretations people might make of the main suggestive units of the speaking. If in these respects he has clearly and informedly tested the explicit and implicit potentialities of oral rhetoric against the allowances of immediate rhetorical situations, a critic will usually have "broken open" the rhetorical engagement being studied. Further inquiries need to be made, but for the most part they will yield confirmations, qualifications, and extensions of the initial study of explicit arguments and obvious interpretations.

To see how this works in practice we shall go on to raise further questions about the implicit character of what George Miller said. We shall now ask: *What solutions (if any) does this unit of speech offer for listeners' problems and anxieties?* Again, we shall identify "units" of speech in various ways to learn as much as possible about the speech.

Not all speakers need to or wish to dissipate their listeners' problems and anxieties, but anyone who says needs exist or who intensifies listeners' anxieties creates expectations that he will also reveal "ways out." This has been recognized ever since Aristotle observed: "Now the political or deliberative orator's aim is utility: deliberation seeks to determine not ends but the means to ends, i.e. *what it is most useful to do.*" [8] It is not, of course, just in advisory speaking that it is important to manage hearers' tensions carefully. Almost any contemporary discussion of conditioning, drive reduction, tension release, dissonance, congruity, or, for that matter, "neuroses" experimentally induced in animals provides psychological reason for thinking that *not* releasing tensions generates frustrations. From all points of view [9] to create or expose anxieties and then to provide no avenue for their easement is psychologically penalizing. But that can be a sensible rhetorical purpose in some cases. Sideshow barkers, campaign organizers, athletic coaches, and many preachers and reformers direct virtually all their efforts toward intensifying people's concerns in order to motivate them to choose release mechanisms at hand but *outside* the rhetoric itself—enter the sideshow, contribute money or time, play harder, make a deeper religious or other commitment. Because different situations and purposes require that tensions and anxieties be managed differently, all speaking needs to be inspected for the presence or absence of solution-offering content or context.

If a critic studying Pericles's "Funeral Oration" failed to notice that Pericles *reassured* by pointing to the Athenian way of life as a release for the private anguish of the mourners, he would miss one of the basic strategies that makes this speech a masterpiece of its kind. A critic who failed to notice that in his speeches on the League of Nations Woodrow Wilson neglected to talk about what *Americans* would *gain* from joining the League would miss what may have been a historic mistake. On the other hand, to introduce "solutions" would have destroyed the affecting power of such great declarations of faith as Socrates's "Apology," William Faulkner's "The Writer's Duty" (on receiving the Nobel Prize in 1950), or Senator Mike Mansfield's eulogy at the casket of John F. Kennedy.

It is important, therefore, to note the encouragement and reduction of listeners' tensions in rhetorical speech and to relate these facts to the rhetorical situation.

George Miller's management of tensions can be described simply. He seeks to intensify political and moral concerns. But he offers only a single, ambiguous statement about how those concerns are to be released: "Do everything you can to create and implement the day when we'll see that equality as a living thing!" Did he, like Wilson, mistakenly neglect to show his audience what satisfactions were attainable through following his advice? Unless a tension-releasing "solution" was present in the situation, we ought to believe that Miller frustrated his hearers somewhat. But, of course, the "solution" was present and fully known to the California delegates. The releasing action was: Support a strong statement endorsing the Supreme Court's decision, then go to the convention floor in the evening and make that support effective. Miller's strategy was entirely sound—to motivate the audience toward the "solution" by building up their sense of concern. Then, the releasing actions would more certainly follow.

We are dealing here with some rhetorical principles we can generalize. They might be put thus: To the degree that problems are vivified and anxieties intensified, tension-releasing solutions must come *from somewhere,* else communication ends in producing unfocused feeling and/or general frustration. Generally speaking, failure to give clear directions for releasing tensions is a faulty rhetorical practice. Only where situational or other data assure a critic that frustration or vague euphoria was aimed at, or that tension release mechanisms were clearly known to the listeners, should he suppose nonreleasing rhetoric fulfilled its aims. In Miller's case we have the necessary situational information to justify us in saying Miller's intensifying strategies were sound. His listeners knew what to do; he did not have to tell them either explicitly or implicitly.

Sometimes it is possible to judge the wisdom of a speaker's management of tensions from evidence in the speaking itself. This is not the case with Miller's speech, but we need know nothing of Athens in the Periclean age to see that Pericles offered a number of realistic alternatives to several different sorts of mourners. It is also clear that Edmund Burke completed the normal movement of arousing and then releasing feeling when he said:

> Proceed in what you do, whatever you do, from policy, and not from rancour. Let us act like men, let us act like statesmen. Let us hold some

sort of consistent conduct. It is agreed that a revenue is not to be had
in America. If we lose the profit, let us get rid of the odium.[10]

It is absence of or ambiguity of solutions for problems that should
make a critic suspicious and send him to data about the situation
to discover whether the exceptional rhetorical practice could
achieve effects the speaker presumably wanted.

Our third question about implicit rhetorical content is really a
question about emphasis and a correlated one about probable
effects of whatever strategy is discovered. As initially stated the
question is: *Does the context in which any statement or group of
statements appears give it special claim on a listener's attention;
if so, what are likely responses listeners might make in this rhetorical situation?* Before applying this question in criticism, one
ought to reflect a little on the nature of human perception. There
are conflicting claims about how people perceive, but two broad
generalizations are almost unanimously agreed to. In the language
of Berelson and Steiner, (a) "people respond neither to discrete
elements one at a time nor to the sum total of discrete elements,
they respond to the relationships between them"; and (b) "perception imposes the task of interpretation, of deciding what objects
or events the sensory pattern actually does represent. Such interpretation is not usually a matter of conscious thinking-through but
an instantaneous perceptual response."[11] If these are the ways
people perceive, then the rhetorical procedures that frame or otherwise direct relational interpretations ought to be explored in all
speech criticism.

In most circumstances we all rely on four types of clues to tell
us what relational significances are asserted in communication.

First, we tend to feel that *proximate* things are likely to be related; we take the nearness of symbolic units as a sign that still
more subtle relationships may exist among the ideas. Second, when
things seem *similar,* we tend to suspect that they are further related
or that they belong together for a complex of reasons; so, things
said alike, implicitly claim to *be* alike. Third, when we find
things plainly *joined,* we tend to suppose they are parts of some
larger whole. When we see subconnections, we expect them to "add
up" to something or to continue their connectings until they amount
to some *thing.* For example, a series of uninterrupted statements
is expected to build up to the kind of unit we call *"a* speech."
Fourth, when we think we see a *part* of a familiar scheme or
framework, we promptly try to supply missing parts in hopes of

discovering the *whole* scheme or framework. Thus, when a speaker tells us about something we see as an "effect," we wonder about its "cause," for cause *and* effect seem necessary to complete the mental structure we are used to.

A speaker can aid or interfere with these perceptual tendencies. That which he does can be observed with some ease.[12] We have already considered one rhetorical procedure that can direct perception, hence interpretation: patterning statements in ways that encourage listeners to perceive them as arguments. There are, however, at least four other rhetorical operations that can direct perception suggestively, and they have only been hinted at in our analyses.

PLACING IDEAS IN JUXTAPOSITION

When statements occur near one another, the effect may be to suggest that they *belong* together. Ideas in the same "neighborhood" can seem to form a relational unit. Miller's speech contains a segment which illustrates what can happen. Statements 8 and 9 are not verbally related except by the coordinate conjunction *and*. Grammatical convention suggests that *and* asserts that the statements are independent—related only by sequence and general relevance to a larger frame of thought. But we saw in chapter III that it is not beyond reason to think that one of these statements is a *reason* for the other. "It's a moral issue" could seem the reason Miller is "tired of hearing it referred to. . . ." Yet to perceive what was said in this way, one has to do two interesting things: ignore the usual meaning of *and* and interpret the proximity of the statements as equivalent to something like, "That's why." Both things could easily be done by a perceiver. He has only to interpret *adjacency* as a sign of causal relation (which it often is), then suppress the grammatical meaning of *and*. Now, everything fits together into a causal frame.

By looking for additional influences of juxtapositions, one might be led to notice that statements 4 and 5 stand next to one another; that might suggest a special relationship. Again, the two are grammatically coordinate. Miller is "not impressed . . . *anymore than* I was impressed. . . ." Would it not be within reason to hear these words as asserting an analogy: the kind of advice that was costly two years ago will be costly again? That the hearer is to *compare* is not said in so many words, but the proximity of the statements could seem more important than their grammar, satisfying a listener that Miller was arguing, not just asserting.

A different kind of understanding could grow out of the juxtaposition of statements 1, 2, and 3. As we have noticed, each assertion suggests that Miller was emotional and frustrated. Could not
the fact that these statements would be heard together in uninterrupted sequence, as Miller's *first* utterances, emphasize the idea
that Miller was a bit emotional? If what we are told about human
perception is reliable, Miller's emotionality seems even more likely
to have entered listeners' awarenesses than our earlier observations suggested.

To summarize, if we want to know the meanings rhetoric can
have, something is often learned by looking behind the obvious
meanings of language to see what the "neighborhoods" of thoughts
could do to affect perceptions of their relationships.

Introducing Readily Noticed Similarities

Things that are alike in one respect are apt to be thought alike in
other respects. Expert speakers often use this psychological fact,
and critics should be alert to their strategies. Such rhetorical
processes as cumulating and piling up evidence become especially
effective if listeners believe the similarities among the cumulated
items indicate special interrelations among them. With listeners
only too ready to interpret one set of similarities as an indication
that other sets of similarities exist, speakers can often achieve the
impact of analogical reasoning by simply suggesting that items are
alike. Then, human psychology goes to work for them: "Elements
in experience are automatically and almost irresistibly grouped—
other things being equal—according to proximity, similarity, and
continuity." [13]

What a critic may discover by looking for suggested similarities
can be illustrated from Miller's statements 4 and 5. An *analogy*
is suggested by the mere juxtaposition of the statements, as we have
seen. More than this, the similarity between the information of
two years ago and the information just heard is directly asserted:
". . . the same kind of information cost me. . . ." Any listener who
noticed the assertion of similarity would think he was *directed* to
reason analogically: same ideas, same results.

Many analogies used in speeches are given their proof-power by
subtler ways of emphasizing similarity. Consider this passage from
George William Curtis's "The Public Duty of Educated Men":

> Our safety lies not in our institutions, but in ourselves. It was under
> the forms of the republic that Julius Caesar made himself emperor of

Rome. It was while professing reverence for the national traditions that James II was destroying religious liberty in England.[14]

The language of formal argument is missing, but the nearness of "our safety lies not in our institutions" to Curtis's mention of Caesar and James II makes it reasonable to suppose that Curtis meant Caesar's and James II's behaviors to be taken as DATA supporting the CLAIM he offered in the first sentence of the passage. Notice, too, that Curtis further invited this kind of understanding by using the same word forms to introduce each: "It was . . ." begins both sentences, and a "that" clause ends each of the last two sentences. Since Curtis gave these clues to how he wanted his words understood, our critical judgment ought to be that the records of Caesar and James II were probably perceived by listeners as "proofs" that "our safety lies not in our institutions but in ourselves." We should return to the kinds of analysis discussed in chapter III to weigh how this implicit "argument" would probably be received.

Suggesting Continuity of Thought

The chief function of transitions and summaries in communication is to emphasize the unity of relationships, directly or indirectly. Words, phrases, sentences, or larger units that function as bridges or summaries allege that there was or will be *continuity* in what is being said: that which has gone before is related to what will be said; what seemed discrete detail at first was in fact part of a continuity or development. Other, less formal strategies also evoke a sense of continuity: refrains, repetitions, restatements, and such language as "moreover," "from these data we can draw these conclusions," "next in time," "consequently." All such verbal formulations guide the connection-seeking activities of listeners. They stress system, unity, continuity in what is said; they help to show how ideas are supposed to fit together. Given the difficulties of oral communication, it is especially pertinent for speech critics to ask how, if at all, listeners' attempts to "follow" speakers were assisted, obstructed, or left unassisted.

If we ask this kind of question about George Miller's speech, a new discovery emerges. There is but one point at which Miller said something to emphasize that his statements were parts of an unfolding pattern of integrated thought. Line 16 contains the phrase, "And if you do." This clause signals that what will immediately follow is contingent on what just preceded. There is no other direct effort to point out how ideas relate to one another. Connective words are few and generally assert coordinate relations: "but," "and," and "any more than" are the conjunctive terms one finds.

Asking how Miller furthered continuity of thought leads us to see that he very nearly disregarded this rhetorical resource. We see that his statements and clusters of statements stood in series, not as interlocked thought. If listeners found what he said more intricately organized than a string of beads, the explanation lies outside the language of the speech.

Applying the same test to a fragment from Lincoln's reply to Judge Stephen A. Douglas at Jonesboro, Illinois yields a very different conclusion. Lincoln and Douglas met at Jonesboro on September 15, 1858, in the third of their famous public debates. Douglas spoke first. In his reply Lincoln chose to rebuke Douglas for statements made a few days before, when Douglas spoke alone at Joliet, Illinois. Contrast Lincoln's methods of keeping his allegations systematically before his listeners with Miller's neglect of such opportunities.

> If he was in his right mind, I cannot conceive how he would have risked disgusting the four or five thousand of his own friends who stood there, and knew, as to my having been carried from the platform, that there was not a word of truth in it.
>   JUDGE DOUGLAS: Didn't they carry you off?
>   There; *that question illustrates the character of this man Douglas exactly. He smiles now* and says, "Didn't they carry you off?" *But he said then,* "He had to be carried off "; and he said it to convince the country that he had so completely broken me down by his speech that I had to be carried away. *Now he seeks to dodge it,* and asks, "Didn't they carry you off?" Yes, they did. *But,* Judge Douglas, why didn't you tell the truth? I would like to know why you didn't tell the truth about it. *And then again,* "He laid up seven days." He puts this in print for the people of the country to read as a serious document. I think *if he had been in his sober senses* he would not have risked that barefacedness in the presence of thousands of his own friends, who knew that I made speeches within six of the seven days. . . . *Now, I say there is no charitable way to look at that statement, except to conclude that he is actually crazy.* There is another thing in that statement. . . .[15]

The issue was trivial, the challenge picayune, and the moment far from a great one; but Lincoln left no listener in doubt about what charge he was developing or how his successive statements were supposed to "build up" a basic challenge to Douglas's integrity.

Twice repeating his hyperbolic allegation that Douglas must have lost his senses, Lincoln kept Douglas's alleged shiftiness in the fore with blunt, unmistakable phrases and clauses: "He smiles *now* . . . but he said *then*"; "*Now* he seeks to dodge. . . ." None of these continuity-maintaining procedures is found in Congressman Miller's speech. Even the newspaper reports of Lincoln's debate tell that the audience's responses *built* as Lincoln sustained the continuity of his attack. Such response could not have happened in the same way during Miller's speech; in fact, the cheers are sometimes quite misplaced!

George Miller is not proved an incompetent speaker or Abraham Lincoln a great one because one gave a disconnected short speech and the other a serious, sustained charge against his opponent. But because he did maintain his attack as rhetorical strategy allows, Lincoln had *a* strength which Miller lacked. That much deserves some weight in any overall judgment on either man's speaking.

AIDING FIGURE-GROUND DISCRIMINATION

A final way contexts give ideas meaning and shape is through management of the figure-ground perceptions listeners are likely to have. Human beings are selective in determining what they will respond to. They perceive frames as well as pictures, but they usually choose to respond to the pictures. They hear traffic noises, but when they want to they can attend to companions' speech and shut out the noises. From one point of view listening is a continuous process of separating *figure* items from *ground* items during a flow of sound, action, and ideas that envelops awareness. A listener's problem is what to understand as *figure* and what to relegate to the lesser status of *ground*.[16]

Among the ways listeners solve figure-ground problems are taking juxtaposition, similarity, and special verbal signals as clues to how the sorting-out process is supposed to be done. These options were just discussed, but other clues also guide. Almost any resource of speech can signal, "This is important" or "This is an aside." One cannot enumerate all the ways speakers can signal how they want listeners to distinguish *figure* from *ground*;[17] however, phenomena that ought to interest speech critics can be illustrated.

Miller's statements 7 and 8 illustrate two clear methods by which speakers invite figure-ground discriminations. For one thing, Miller is abrupt. "There's only one issue involved, and it's a moral issue" comes suddenly, virtually "jerking" thought away from lost elections. It strongly invites a listener to conclude: "Everything said until now was peripheral." Also, the words "only one" insist on the centrality of *this* idea; others are to drop into the background. Abruptness combines with explicitness to stress that this is the *figure* Miller wants focused on.

Lincoln's Jonesboro remarks were equally forceful for like reasons. "There; that question illustrates the character of this man Douglas exactly" is an outburst that unmistakably points to *character* as the *figure* in this portion of talk. Repeated allusions to Douglas's alleged irregularities with "the truth" maintain the judge's character in the foreground. It is interesting to contrast these sharp, figure-ground delineations with the much more intricate processes Lincoln developed in his "Gettysburg Address":

> The brave men, living and dead, who struggled here, have consecrated it, far above our poor power to add or detract. . . . It is for us the living, rather, to be dedicated to that unfinished work. . . .

At Gettysburg Lincoln seems to have tried to set apart two *figures,* each with a different situation as its *ground.* The "brave men" must be *figure* and "we" the *ground* as long as thought is focused on Gettysburg Cemetery, but "our" dedication seems *figure* and the cemetery *ground* when thought is moved toward "our" obligations. Minor signals such as repetition of "here," the term "rather" in the second statement, and the contrast between "living and dead" and "us the living" differentiate the complex figure-ground patterns respondents are to keep track of. But a critic of oral discourse should understand that cues so subtle are not apt to impinge sharply on the consciousnesses of hurried listeners. And just here, critics of spoken and of written rhetoric might well part company in their critical judgments. The speech critic would applaud the unmistakable figure-ground management of Lincoln at Jonesboro and the critic of writing applaud Lincoln at Gettysburg. Each according to his responsibility would be right, for admirable subtleties are disturbers of figure-ground perceptions in speech, but the same subtleties can prod an unhurried, admiring reader toward reflections of considerable depth.

From examining speakers' management of figure-ground controls a critic achieves a review of all other contextual claims upon attention. Surveying figure-ground patterns, one has opportunity to notice previously unseen, difficult-to-classify methods by which communicators assist perception of the more and the less significant. "What is made to stand out?" and "What is allowed to fall into the supporting background?" are, in a sense, summary questions that encourage synthesis of previous findings and at the same time draw attention to special context setting that is not rhetorically routine.

Our next question about implicit content draws attention to a matter not often discussed in connection with rhetorical criticism. It is entirely possible for the arguments of a speech to have one persuasive quality and the suggestive elements to supply quite different qualities to the total message. Implicit content may compensate (or fail to compensate) for weaknesses in explicit content, or the opposite may be the case. To understand what forces actually did the "work" of a speech, it is often of great importance to ask: *Are the claims and inferences suggested by the units compatible with each other and with the CLAIMS in which prominent arguments culminate?*

Miller's speech contains an internal conflict which, had his listeners been skeptical, might have destroyed his overall effectiveness. Whether statements 4 and 5 are interpreted as explicit argument or as implicit suggestion, they unquestionably assert that following the former Chairman's advice is likely to cost votes in the next election. But to worry about losing votes is not wholly consistent with believing that, "There's only one issue involved, and it's a moral issue." To worry about losing votes is flatly inconsistent with Miller's assertion that he is "tired of hearing it referred to in terms of international politics or in vote getting for either party." From any technical view the two parts of Miller's speech are inconsistent with each other. But we must remember that we are dealing with rhetoric and a live audience. The critic's concern is not with whether Miller was consistent, but with whether his listeners would perceive the conflict or would be likely to treat the two parts as *compatible* elements when they interpreted what they heard.

If Miller had had a skeptical audience, we would have to suppose that he made trouble for himself. When "it's a moral issue" was thrust forth so strongly, a skeptic might wonder, "Then, why did you make a big thing of losing a Congressman?" A skeptic might see Miller as a man willing to plead in *any* direction to win support, but we know Miller's actual audience was friendly and generally shared his views. There are ample ways by which they could interpret the two thrusts of the speech as compatible. A reasonable, liberal Democrat could accept both parts of Miller's case without a sense of conflict. He could relegate the voting theme to *ground* and the moral dimensions of civil rights to *figure* as Miller moved into the final part of his speech. Or he could just forget about the first point while thinking of the other. Or he could perceive Miller as offering two *independent* justifications for rejecting the former National Chairman's advice. Any of these patterns of thought would allow a California delegate to see Miller's speech as internally coherent and "consistent." But the important point is that Miller's explicit and implicit CLAIMS were compatible *only* if his listeners were *both* pragmatic and idealistic about the civil rights plank. Had he had idealists or people who genuinely wished to find him at fault as listeners, they could just as reasonably have judged him self-contradictory. The critical issue is whether a speaker's CLAIMS will be *seen* as compatible in the specific rhetorical situation.

A quite different kind of play between explicit argumentation and implicit suggestion existed in one of Winston Churchill's famous speeches, his first wartime radio address as Prime Minister of England.[18] German forces had broken through on the European front. The British and their allies were suffering catastrophic losses, and the vaunted Maginot line had been breached. How serious the situation was, the new Minister dared not fully reveal. Encouraging arguments were difficult to construct, yet the situation called for a major address by the Minister who had just taken leadership; and unless he counseled surrender, he must encourage. Churchill contrived for this situation a speech that millions perceived as candid, internally consistent, and encouraging. Below is a list of his "argued" CLAIMS and the CLAIMS he simply asserted or suggested.

Explicitly Supported CLAIMS	CLAIMS Asserted or Implicitly Suggested
Both sides are in danger since each is behind the other's lines.	The time is solemn and dangerous.
A "sudden transformation" of the battle positions may occur.	The size of the German attack makes the military position very dangerous.
We may look with confidence for stabilization on the French front.	There is ground for hope.

There is imperious need for vital ammunition.

This is one of our sublimely historic moments.

"Arm yourselves and be ye men of valor."

Our military advantages will produce effects shortly.

The French Army is famous for its dependability.

The military situation is by no means finally settled.

Military *action* is what the Allies most need; they have been too defensive in their thinking.

The RAF is scoring heavily against very great odds.

The next phase of war will involve direct attack on England.

When we are attacked, civilians will have their greatest opportunities for wartime achievement.

The attack will mark the gravest stage of the war for Britain.

The forthcoming attack will demand most from people at home.

War interests over-ride all other public and all private interests.

The French are steady in their resolve.

The British Government has now united and is determined.

Almost alone the British and French advance "the rescue not only of Europe but mankind from the foulest and most soul-destroying tyranny that has ever darkened and stained the pages of history."

The present call to determined resistance is the same religiously inspired call to which Englishmen responded "centuries ago."

It goes without saying that most of the "work" of this speech was accomplished through unsupported assertions and implicit suggestions, promises, and threats. Churchill admitted in later writings that at this time he could find few factual grounds for predicting ultimate success for the Allies. Probably that is why he offered but three "arguments" for optimism, and they were woefully weak in any formally logical sense: the battle lines were confused, so both sides shared the dangers of encirclement; the masses of allied troops had not yet engaged the Germans, so a "transformation" was possible; in history the French and British armies always recovered well, so "stabilization" of the French front was possible. Any even moderately skeptical listener could fairly have said to himself that Churchill's DATA were so weak in each case that the opposite of his CLAIM could be easily warranted. However, the implicit suggestions of ultimate success and the assertions of encouraging possibilities were clearly *figure* in the speech and, as it were, they carried the weak "arguments" toward credibility. Churchill's English-speaking listeners certainly wanted the arguments to be "true." This fact doubtless encouraged them to see strength rather than weakness in the arguments and that would make the arguments compatible rather than incompatible with the encouraging thrust of most of the speech. Because it was desirable and easy for listeners to endow the arguments with strength which really flowed from Churchill's highly suggestive optimism and determination, the speech seemed more reasonable than it really was. But how this was possible would not be fully noticed unless a critic asked in what senses Churchill's argumentation was compatible—or could *seem* compatible—with his other claiming and suggesting.

Churchill's "Address to the Congress" (pp. 301–308) was made more than a year and a half later. There, you will find stronger arguments; for example, look at paragraphs 13 through 19. Again, assertion and suggestion are the main supports for the optimistic tone of the speech. Once more, to ask about the interrelation and compatibility of explicit and implicit content lets us see where the "power" lay in the speech.

This kind of critical question draws attention to the sometimes consonant, sometimes ill-assorted forces speakers loose. But in asking it, it is important to remember that *perceptions* are more at issue than factuality or rules of logic. Susanne K. Langer's description of how people perceive gives a valuable view of what goes on in listeners:

> The abstraction inherent in perception as such results (if our current theories are right) from the elimination of countless possible stimuli; so the simplification is effected as in a lithograph, by eliminating everything but the features that will be left to function. It is not a process of emphasizing anything, but essentially of simplifying,

lightening the load before its impact on the nervous system has gone very far. This process is not usually felt. The emotive act, on the other hand, is really an act of emphasizing the exciting features, and is an act that is felt . . . ; it may enhance the original simplification or make a new one, even several new ones by turns, and yield the well-known phenomena of changing gestalt. In this process the irrelevant material is not filtered out, but eclipsed by the intensification of the great lines. Consequently the form seems to emerge from a rich background of vaguer details that may attain varying degrees of importance, and it may be their fluctuation which makes the stable lines strong by contrast.[19]

A critic's task is to estimate as reasonably as possible how specific listeners in specific rhetorical situations would have simplified, emphasized "exciting features," and "eclipsed" others in order to evolve from ongoing speech an interpreted, *whole* view of what they had heard. The critical question we are dealing with just now is whether the whole view would be of compatible elements or incompatible ones. Mr. Miller's audience can be counted on to find his speech a coherent appeal for "proper" actions. Churchill's listeners would surely abstract, simplify, and intensify in ways favorable to his overall optimism—both when he first spoke as Prime Minister and when he addressed the Congress. But had any of these audiences not *wanted* to believe, they could have found some of the speakers' arguments incompatible with the main thrusts of implicit content.

We come next to a subset of questions of special value. These questions often identify basic differences among speeches.[20] An overall question can be put thus: *Which of the following classes of judgments are encouraged or directly asked for by the speech units under study: factual, optative, adjudicative, predictive of desirability?* The point of making this inquiry concerning any unit of speech is to discover whether the content actually invited the kinds of response the speaker needed, given his purpose and the rhetorical situation. The ways of making this kind of inquiry derive from classical conceptions of how listeners make judgments in response to rhetoric. Aristotle observed:

> . . . of the three elements in speech-making—speaker, subject, and person addressed—it is the last one, the hearer, that determines the speech's end and object. The hearer must be either a judge, with a decision to make about things past or future, or an observer. A member of the assembly decides about future events, a juryman about past events; while those who merely decide on the orator's skill are observers.[21]

Aristotle was thinking of the kinds of judgments citizens of Athens made in their different listening roles. For the situations he chose to examine, his classification of judgments and his analysis of associated kinds of speaking were astute, but some judgments modern listeners make cannot be fitted easily into his tripartite analysis.

One must take notice that listeners often sit in judgment on matters of "simple fact." They decide whether water mains are or are not strong enough to carry required pressures, whether unidentified flying objects are in fact extraterrestrial, and so on. Scientists address scientists, scientists address citizens and political leaders, political leaders address each other and the citizenry, and citizens speak to each other—all with a view toward settling "the facts" of one circumstance or another. Policy discussions often cannot begin until fact-settling decisions have been made. Thus, as soon as one draws his thoughts away from the formal institutions of a Greek city-state, he must recognize that in many rhetorical situations judgments-on-the-facts are those asked for.

Merely by adding "factual judgments" to liberalized interpretations of Aristotle's other three kinds of judgments, we can characterize inclusively the things listeners are asked to *do* in responding to rhetoric. And if a critic has a full set of categories by which to describe responses to rhetoric, he is in a position to discuss the *power* a piece of rhetoric does or does not have. He can say what it *encourages* as response and what it does *not* encourage. He then has a way of estimating whether a speech is actually what Bitzer calls a "fitting response to the rhetorical situation." He can ask himself: Do the kinds of responses asked for in this speech lead to a resolution of the exigences that existed in the situation?

Some rhetorical situations contain exigences that can be fully removed if the rhetor can extract straightforward agreement on matters of fact. In our technological, pedagogical age there is much rhetoric which properly asks for judgments of facts and no more. It is also true, however, that one sometimes hears speakers on policy questions make the rhetorical error of instigating factual judgments only. Instead of advancing listeners' thoughts beyond facts and toward thoughts that will motivate them to choose among courses of action, these speakers mistakenly stop when they have only achieved agreement on data. It is therefore always pertinent to ask whether a speaker dealing with facts can *afford* to invite factual judgments alone. Sometimes this is enough; sometimes not. A competent critic will at least try to find out.

A second kind of judgment rhetoric can encourage was called *optative* above. Aristotle saw some Greek listeners functioning as "observers," merely applauding speakers' sentiments, skills, or both. But if we draw away from Athenian ceremonies and contests to gain broader perspective, we shall recognize that there are many occasions where listeners render other kinds of *preferential* judgments, participating in rhetorical situations as more than mere "observers." For example, when matters of taste come under discussion, this is the case. Are nineteenth-century Romantic poets to be preferred over moderns? What is the ideal female silhouette? To respond to rhetoric on these matters and many others, listeners consult "standards" that are very loose and of a personal sort. They choose preferred points along scales of "worth" ranging from "worst" through "indifferent" to "best." Lincoln's "Second Inaugural" and John F. Kennedy's "Inaugural Address" essentially asked listeners to *prefer* particular kinds of political outlooks for the next four years. Verifiable truth-to-fact was not primarily at stake. The judgments chiefly asked for were based on general cultural, personal, communal preferences. In other kinds of situations listeners are asked to respond by assigning degrees of nobility, honor, beauty, or rightness. Neither the precision of judgments-of-facts nor the exactness of measuring by *formally agreed upon* "rules" is asked for.

I have chosen to call these loose, preferential kinds of judgments *optative,* borrowing the anglicized name of a Greek verb mood which had among its functions the expression of a *wish.* By using that term I seek to emphasize that some responses sought by rhetoric arise from loosely anchored wishes, desires, or general preferences—that listeners are sometimes left to judge according to their own choices and to exercise their own options among standards.

The value of discriminating optative judgments from others that rhetoric can encourage is easily illustrated by exploring Theodore Roosevelt's "The Man with the Muck-Rake" (pp. 290–297). This speech was a criticism of indiscriminate journalistic attacks on persons and organizations. Roosevelt did not discuss whether muck-raking truly existed nor did he try to *prove* it had significant influence. He did not urge any formal action by listeners or government. He asked for fairness, decency, and equability in public discussion of individuals and groups. He asked neither unmitigated approval for those he defended nor unmitigated disapproval for muck-rakers. To the extent that he asked for action at all, he sought a whole society's endorsement of fairness. Such, at least, was the character of his rhetoric. He spent little time on the literal truth of what he said about muck-rakers; he held up no formal rule by which to judge their acts; he pointed to no specific decision about the future. He furnished speech calculated to generate general judgments about proprieties.[22]

Richard Murphy has said of Roosevelt's speaking that its "tone . . . was consistently hortatory." [23] The phrase happily suggests the urgency and intensity with which Roosevelt pressed for responses. In the main he asked for *optative* responses in the "Muck-Rake" speech. His probable impact on listeners can be identified by saying that if he received the responses he usually seemed to ask for, he would alter few people's perceptions of "the facts," and he would arouse enthusiasm for no particular course of action. "The Man with the Muck-Rake" consisted of rhetoric that asked for judgments less incisive than judgments of facticity, less confined in their grounding than judgments based on formal codes, and of less long-range consequence than judgments based on probable consequences of actions. Roosevelt invited personal judgments based on personal and social values and standards.

Identifying the kinds of judgments chiefly invited helps a critic to specify the powers and limits of rhetoric. If all Roosevelt wanted and needed were expressions of personal and social preference, it was no flaw that he furnished no arguments to "prove" muck-raking was fearsomely widespread and few arguments and suggestions to indicate just how much danger these journalists represented and what should be done about them. In fact, if Lucas is right that, "In essence, the President was asking the nation to give more attention to genuine reform and less to 'hysterical excitement,' " then he needed no other kinds of judgments than he asked for. But having seen the limits of his invitations, we know also some of the limits of his rhetoric. If we imagine he wanted specific actions, now, we could say with confidence that his rhetoric was unlikely to get them.

A third kind of response that speakers seek was called *adjudicative* in the question above. When ancient rhetoricians referred to this sort of judgment, they usually thought of decisions that convicted, acquitted, acceded, or denied. A less confined view allows us to see that there are many institutions besides courts where conformity between facts and formally agreed upon codes is judged. If a student argues that he has fulfilled the formal requirements for graduation or an American Indian contends that a treaty with his tribe was broken, facts and events are being compared to and measured by formal "rules."

It is even true that some rhetoric sets up "rules" and thereafter asks for judgments based on those rules. A speaker may give a definition, then argue that certain facts or events do or do not fit that definition. Or, he may cite a rule, law, or commandment and then ask listeners to judge what conforms and does not conform to the code. Theodore Roosevelt does this at paragraph 18 of "The Man with the Muck-Rake" (pp. 295–96). He cites the eighth commandment (Thou shalt not steal.) and then contends that people must accept the fact that to cheat or unfairly take wealth from a corporation is to "steal" as surely as when a corporation takes wealth unfairly. It is consistent with our earlier judgment about this speech, however, that one can find few such instances of requests for rule-bound judgments in "The Man with the Muck-Rake." United Nations debates, however, are often entirely about whether this or that nation's actions are really "self-defence" or "aggression" or "genocide," or some other kind of behavior which, the debaters allege, can be formally defined and therefore are open to adjudicative rather than moral (optative) judgment.

There are, then, many rhetorical situations in which speakers ask for judgments based on the prescriptions of actually or allegedly agreed upon codes. The codes may be laws, building codes, a book on etiquette, stipulative definitions, the inspection standards of the American Automobile Association, or the authorized doctrines of a church or a political group. In any case, the judgment asked for goes beyond mere factual judgment. It not only accepts or rejects claims to facticity; it goes on to *measure* alleged facts. Such judgments are at once more rigorous and more confined than optative judgments. Agreement about the codes restricts the deciders' freedom. And it is especially significant that giving an adjudicative judgment does not commit the decider to any further behavior. The juror is dismissed after rendering his judgment; he does not execute the law nor change it. By contrast, whoever renders a worst-indifferent-best judgment commits himself to a value system, for he *freely* chose and used the standards he applied. But rules, whether of etiquette, law, or doctrine, are impersonal and originate outside the judge. One need not like the standards to apply them. I express no personal preference and place at risk only my competence as a judge of relevancies and relationships if I consent to Thomas Huxley's statement in his "The Method of Scientific Investigation":

... you say, "All hard and green apples are sour; this apple is hard and green, therefore this apple is sour." That train of reasoning is what logicians call a syllogism, and has all its various parts and terms—its major premise, its minor premise, and its conclusion.[24]

Logicians are responsible for what they designate as legitimate syllogisms. If I assent to Huxley's claim that his example meets all necessary specifications, I have made no commitment to the wisdom or desirability of logicians and their syllogisms. But if I agree that it is *best* to reason syllogistically, I risk *my* standards rather than the logicians', and at a future time you may hold me responsible for my avowed affection for syllogizing. There is, then, a quality of impersonality and noninvolvement associated with giving adjudicative judgments. This sometimes makes them easier to secure than optative or predictive judgments.

For the fourth kind of judgment rhetoric commonly invites I have used the name *predictive of desirability* rather than the more widely favored term *deliberative*. "Deliberative" implies to many people that the judgments referred to are "deliberate" or take place in "deliberative assemblies." "Predictive of desirability" expresses what it is that is weighed when one gives this kind of response. Listeners weigh "the expediency or the harmfulness of a proposed course of action." [25] Responses that involve such estimates of desirability have been described by John Dewey:

Deliberation is not calculation of indeterminate future results. The present, not the future, is ours. No shrewdness, no store of information will make it ours. But by constant watchfulness concerning the tendency of acts, by noting disparities between former judgments and actual outcomes, and tracing that part of the disparity that was due to deficiency and excess in disposition, we come to know the meaning of present acts, and to guide them in the light of that meaning. ... Every attempt to forecast the future is subject in the end to the auditing of present concrete impulse and habit.

Somewhat later in the same section of his *Human Nature and Conduct* Dewey added,

The future situation involved in deliberation is of necessity marked by contingency. What it will be in fact remains dependent upon conditions that escape our foresight and power of regulation. But foresight which draws liberally upon the lessons of past experience reveals the tendency, the meaning, of present action. ...[26]

Speaking that seeks to elicit predictions of desirability invites listeners to find agreement between (1) what the speaking urges and (2) the "good" or "bad" promises for the future which their past and present experiences enable them to think of.

Recognizing the differing judgments that rhetoric can ask for gives a critic additional norms by which he can judge the fitness of speech to situations. He can note what a speaker asks of his listeners, in a part of a speech or in the whole. He can consider whether, if that pattern of judgments were granted, the speaker's purpose and the situation's exigences would be served. We can illustrate how estimates of this sort can be made if we turn once more to Congressman Miller's speech.

I would expect that an attentive, generally favorable audience might respond to Miller's invitations to give judgments in something like the following manner.

Statement Number	Kind of Judgment Encouraged	Probable Response of Generally Accepting Listeners
1–2–3	optative	Sympathy for speaker and readiness to hear him.
4–5	predictive and optative	Rejection of Chairman's advice on practical grounds and as "unworthy."
6	optative	Sympathy with speaker and rejection of political calculation as a "proper" basis for taking positions on civil rights.
7–8	factual and optative	Some degree of agreement, that it *is* a "moral" issue, plus intensified feeling against the "soft plank" proposal.
9	optative	Sympathy with speaker and further rejection of "playing politics" with civil rights.
10–11	factual	Some degree of agreement that it *is* a moral issue, and/or association of the issue with religious truths.
12	adjudicative or factual	Either: the conclusion follows by the rules of logic, or "of course, all men *are* equal."

| 13 | predictive | Unless we act as he says, we will be convicted of inconsistency or hypocrisy. |
| 14 | optative | He's right; we ought to act. |

If Miller had addressed a less friendly audience the probable responses of listeners would of course be different, but the classes of responses *invited* would remain substantially the same. In either case it becomes clear that Miller was chiefly asking listeners to respond to him with general, optative judgments based on their preferences.

Some analysts would interpret the characteristics of Miller's requests for responses somewhat differently, perhaps, but repeated experiments with this way of analyzing this short speech have shown that a large majority of all interpreters find it heavily loaded with requests for optative judgments. Almost unanimously students of speech criticism agree that for the most part Miller asked for judgments of importance, rightness, morality, and appropriateness. But what does this way of analyzing oral rhetoric add to our understanding of Miller's speech?

The analysis above clinches judgments that have been suggested by our other critical probes. Miller's was rhetoric that could intensify *existing* beliefs and feelings about civil rights and the Supreme Court's decision; but being so dependent on optative judgments, it could not generate *new* beliefs or feelings or help listeners choose among alternative courses of action. If could, however, "key up" listeners to act—if they already knew what could be done.

The same kind of analysis of Winston Churchill's "A Solemn Hour" shows a fairly even balance between requests for factual judgments (about the wartime situation) and judgments that predicted desirability (especially of determined resistance). These were, of course, precisely the kinds of judgments Churchill wanted to evoke among the beleaguered Britons. If we were to make similar analyses of pleas by such great defense lawyers as Lord Thomas Erskine and Clarence Darrow, we would find their speeches abounding in carefully devised demands for factual and adjudicative judgments (as one would expect). But each lawyer was also prone to break out of the theoretical restraints of the courtroom to offer arguments and suggestions that invited jurors and judges to weigh the *desirabilities* of their verdicts. By these means each attorney urged the listeners to *make* law rather than merely to judge *by* it. Looking at speeches made by rhetors who shared formal doctrines with their listeners, Roderick P. Hart, Jr. found two-fifths of all main arguments invited assent on adjudicative grounds but:

> Probably because they could not depend on their listeners' knowledge of and regard for formal codes, speakers facing non-doctrinal, uncommitted, or hostile audiences characteristically urged assent on factual and optative bases.[27]

Whether a critic examines speaking statement-by-statement or looks at larger units of communication to discover the types of responses invited, the inquiry gives insight into the speaker's adaptations to his listeners' attitudes and to the exigences of the situation. But it is perhaps even more valuable that this kind of analysis yields fairly objective evidence concerning what the speaking could achieve and what it could not. We secured especially clear knowledge of this kind from our experiments with Miller's and Roosevelt's speeches.

The final question proposed in this chapter re-alerts a critic to the importance of the unspoken contracts of speech situations: *To what extent do the units (considered individually and collectively) suggest anything about the motives the speaker had for entering this rhetorical situation?* This question probes for implicit evidence about the speaker's probable *ethos*—his credibility with his listeners.

If we ask this question about Congressman Miller's speech, we shall find that answers lie in information we have already extracted in earlier stages of criticism. There is direct evidence that he spoke at least partly to release his own tensions. It is certainly implicit in the speech that he felt strongly that his listeners were *obliged* to act firmly on the civil rights issue. From what we know of the rhetorical situation, it appears that none of these revelations would be thought to violate the tacit commitments of oral rhetoric because Miller's audience seems likely to have shared his views and feelings. They could perhaps even share his wish "to express myself." In fact, a few *did* make brief, self-expressive statements after Miller's remarks; then, they quickly agreed on their position for the evening debate. On the other hand, let us suppose Miller had given the same speech in the same way to a less favorable audience. Then, his revelations of self-expressive purposes might easily have been interpreted as inappropriate, for such an audience would expect the full deference of the unspoken contract between speaker and audience. Excitement and self-expressiveness on the dubious side of a question clearly break the contract between speaker and courted listener.

Asking the same question about Lincoln's "Gettysburg Address" helps to explain some unique historical facts about that speech. Most statements in it seem directed toward establishing facts about the situation and the audience's obligations in the light of them. To a considerable degree the speech asks that "facts" be accepted as true and that listeners accept Lincoln's adjudications of their duties. Contrastingly, Churchill and Roosevelt gave clear evidence in the speeches we have been discussing that they, as speakers, participated eagerly in their listeners' optative choices. Thereby, Churchill and Roosevelt appeared to be fulfilling the entire obligations of the speaker-listener contract. At Gettysburg Lincoln seemed to fill the obligations less clearly. Could that not be a reason why his speech was not enthusiastically received at the Gettysburg Cemetery but became famous only after being *printed* some days after the event?

As has been said before, answers to any one critical question never provide complete criticism, but asking what speaking tells about *why* the speakers are speaking can help us collect grounds for a final judgment. Answering the question tells us that some things George Miller said and implied would tend to set him apart from his listeners—unless they, too, were emotionally involved with the subject of civil rights. What Lincoln said suggested that he was more engaged with the Gettysburg Cemetery than with the immediate audience. Churchill and Theodore Roosevelt spoke as though *their* optative judgments and understandings of facts were naturally their listeners' also. In short, Churchill and Roosevelt seemed to try to articulate their listeners' own aspirations and judgments, identifying with their audiences; Miller and Lincoln identified themselves with their *own* judgments. For Miller this appears to have created no problem since the audience was prepared to identify with *him*. Lincoln's situation at Gettsyburg may not have been equally fortunate.

Whether information concerning why a speaker seems to have chosen to speak will count heavily in the final balance of criticism can only be decided when all critical describing has been completed. *Ethos* is a powerful communicative force, and it is affected markedly by the ways a speaker seems to involve *himself* with the subject, his listeners, and their situation. This is the point of raising our final question concerning the implicit content of speech.[28]

CONCLUSION

The test of whether it is worthwhile to make the inquiries proposed in chapters II, III, and IV is whether we understand speaking better after making the probes. We have been inspecting Miller's speech at each stage of discussion. What have we now learned about it? An interim critical statement might run something like the following.

Miller made a speech occupying less than a minute's time. What his words said could not have converted anyone who doubted the worth of supporting the Supreme Court's decision on civil rights. Nevertheless, his *logos* had the content necessary to intensify feeling and generate a will to act. Given the liberal Democratic character of his immediate audience, we have every reason to believe that Miller did strengthen in them a will to act in the way he hoped. The reasons for this judgment follow.

Miller "argued" little. When he did, he left his listeners to supply their own WARRANTS and any needed BACKING FOR WARRANTS. But the liberal Democrats would have usable WARRANTS within themselves: "morality is more important than expediency in matters of civil rights," "brotherhood implies equality," "we are obligated to act when we have moral convictions." These and like "articles of faith" could warrant all that Miller "argued." Indifferent or skeptical listeners would not have responded thus. They might well have formulated CONDITIONS OF REBUTTAL to challenge Miller's unqualified claims. But unless the former National Chairman made a deeper impression than we know of, there was nothing in this rhetorical situation to encourage skepticism or indifference in the audience Miller addressed.

The speech contained possibly incompatible lines of thought; however, there is more reason to believe that the conflict went unnoticed than that it weakened Miller's effectiveness. An already favorable audience of practical politicians was more likely to see the themes of political loss and moral commitment as independent themes than as logically conflictive.

The concepts most strongly promulgated, explicitly and implicitly, were that Miller spoke out of great feeling, including a sense of frustration, and that moral considerations were of first importance in making a decision about what the party's platform should say. By abruptness, by the unqualified character of claims, and by evincing high feeling Miller gave the status of *figure* to the moral dimensions of the civil rights issue. He did not prescribe the action he called for, though taking action was a main exigence of the rhetorical situation: (1) to take a stand concerning the party's platform, (2) to devise strategy, and (3) to make a response to the former Chairman's remarks. To address the first of these exigences Miller needed only to render action important. He did. He also responded firmly to the former National Chairman. He said nothing of strategy for the evening. However, to address the prime exigence his repeated invitations for optative responses were sufficient because the tension-releasing action of voting quickly was known and agreeable to all.

That Miller did little to give listeners a clear sense of continuity and unity in his speech was probably counteracted by the fact that his emotion mounted through the speech and established the moral issue as *figure* for the whole.

For his action-oriented audience, friendly to him and his values, Miller produced content easily capable of achieving the goal he appears to have sought.

By balancing and weaving critical findings into a systematic image of actual speaking and comparing that image with the possibilities in a rhetorical situation, one can produce coherent, reasoned evaluations of the sort just illustrated. When only situation and content have been considered, the result will not be a full account of a rhetorical event, but it will usually constitute the foundation for a full account.

What remains to be discovered? As yet we know little of how structure, details of language, and presentation may have modified the force of the communication we have so far studied only for its content. But since the other aspects of rhetorical art qualify content, comprehensive criticism usually needs to begin with analysis of situation and explicit and implicit content.

NOTES

[1] John B. Carroll, *Language and Thought,* © 1964, pp. 41–42. By permission of Prentice-Hall, Inc., Englewood Cliffs, N.J.

[2] These lines of questioning focus on *messages* and what they tend to suggest. Some promising lines of inquiry oriented toward, *"Why* did the speaker do what he did in the speaking situation?" have been proposed by Ruth M. Gonchar and Dan F. Hahn in *The Speech Teacher* 22 (January 1973): 48–53. The thrust of Gonchar and Hahn's methodology is clearly suggested by the title of their essay: "Rhetorical Biography: A Methodology for the Citizen-Critic." The methods suggested are promising supplements to the *what*-oriented criticism discussed in this book. Gonchar and Hahn propose ways of inquiring into a speaker's "(1) personality orientation; (2) views of leadership; (3) personal and political ideology; (4) epistemology; and (5) hierarchy value structure."

[3] At this point, especially, exploring what is suggested about personality influences, leadership intentions, ideology, epistemological influences, and hierarchies of value can help one see how *what* a speaker does suggests *who* he seems to be and *why* he has related himself to his audience through

speech. So to inquire would be to extend the methods of this book into the methods suggested by Gonchar and Hahn.

[4] Canvassing the suggestive potentialities of words and phrases will be discussed in the chapters on criticism of oral style.

[5] Unfortunately the evidence cannot be presented in a book, but in my opinion Miller's vocal patterns and physical delivery strongly reinforced the likelihood that one, major, simple interpretation would be that Miller was "really excited."

[6] One would arrive at substantially the same principle by reasoning deductively from postulates of Gestalt psychology or by presupposing that, faced with problems, we search for answers by means of "search models," as some research on creative and problem-solving thought argues.

[7] "A Critic's Job of Work," quoted from Blackmur's *The Double Agent, Essays in Craft and Elucidation* (1935) in Morton D. Zabel ed., *Literary Opionion in America,* 2 vols. (New York: Harper & Row, Publishers, 1962), 3rd ed., II, 789.

[8] Aristotle, *Rhetoric,* trans. W. Rhys Roberts, 1362 [a], by permission of The Clarendon Press, Oxford Random;House ed., p. 42. My italics.

[9] On this topic and many others related to rhetorical criticism I find J. A. C. Brown's *Techniques of Persuasion: From Propaganda to Brainwashing* (Baltimore: Penguin Books, Inc., 1963) especially clear, comprehensive, and always focused on the pertinence of modern psychological knowledge to the processes of producing and receiving communication. On factors relating to the role of suggestion in persuasion, including the roles of frustration, see pp. 75–81. On the dangers of drawing *direct* analogies between inducement and treatment of animal neuroses and human neuroses, see pp. 215–222.

[10] "On American Taxation," April 19, 1774, *The Works of the Right Honourable Edmund Burke,* 9 vols. (London: Henry G. Bohn, 1846), I, 494.

[11] Bernard Berelson and Gary A. Steiner, *Human Behavior: An Inventory of Scientific Findings* (New York: Harcourt, Brace & World, Inc., 1964), p. 112.

[12] Discussion in this chapter concerns only contextual cues which suggest the probable impact of statements. Contextual forces affecting the impact of larger units of discourse will be discussed in chapter V, and forces affecting the impact of units smaller than statements will be considered in subsequent chapters on style.

[13] Berelson and Steiner, *Human Behavior,* p. 106.

[14] The full text may be found in W. M. Parrish and Marie Hochmuth, *American Speeches* (New York: Longmans, Green and Co., 1954), pp. 365–380.

[15] *The Illinois Political Campaign of 1858* (Washington, D.C.: The Library of Congress, n.d.), p. 137. This volume is a facsimile of an edition of his debates with Douglas, prepared by Lincoln. Original italics replaced by italics to identify continuity-emphasizing elements.

[16] Berelson and Steiner observe: "The tendency . . . to organize . . . perceptions into figure-ground is apparently innate." *Human Behavior,* p. 106.

[17] Whether one uses constructs from Gestalt psychology, as I am doing, or adopts such alternative constructs as preparation, set, discrimination, the proposition that an end of speech is to regulate others' organizings cannot be avoided.

[18] Winston Churchill, "A Solemn Hour," delivered May 19, 1940. A validated text of this speech can be found in Donald C. Bryant et al., *Notable British Addresses* (New York: The Ronald Press Co., 1967), pp. 534–536.

[19] "Emotion and Abstraction" in Susanne K. Langer, *Philosophical Sketches* (Baltimore: The Johns Hopkins Press, 1962), pp. 77–78.

[20] For examples of their use in published research see Rodney B. Douglass and Carroll C. Arnold, "An Analysis of *Logos:* A Methodological Inquiry," *Quarterly Journal of Speech* 56 (November 1971): 22–32, and Roderick P.

Hart, Jr. "The Rhetoric of the True Believer," *Speech Monographs* 38 (November 1971): 249–261.

[21] *Oxford Translation of Aristotle,* 1358[a]–1358[b], by permission of the Clarendon Press, Oxford; or see *Aristotle's Rhetoric and Poetics,* pp. 31–32.

[22] For a different but not necessarily conflicting interpretation of Roosevelt's purposes see Stephen E. Lucas, "Theodore Roosevelt's 'The Man with the Muck-Rake': A Reinterpretation," *Quarterly Journal of Speech,* in press.

[23] Richard Murphy, "Theodore Roosevelt." Speech Association of America. *A History and Criticism of American Public Address* Vol. III, Edited by Marie Kathryn Hochmuth [Copyright 1955] New York: Russell & Russell, 1965, p. 347.

[24] Huxley delivered his lecture for the first time in 1866, and texts remain widely available. A text and partial criticism may be found in C. C. Arnold, D. Ehninger, and J. C. Gerber, *The Speaker's Resource Book,* 2nd ed. (Chicago: Scott, Foresman and Co., 1966), pp. 264–269.

[25] Aristotle, *Rhetoric* trans. W. Rhys Roberts, 1358[b] by permission of The Clarendon Press, Oxford;Random House ed., p. 33.

[26] John Dewey, *Human Nature and Conduct* (New York: The Modern Library, 1922), pp. 207–208.

[27] Roderick P. Hart, Jr., "The Rhetoric of the True Believer," p. 256.

[28] Professor Richard L. Johannesen has pointed out to me that to raise a question concerning a speaker's implicitly revealed attitudes toward his unspoken contract with listeners and toward his subject is akin to I. A. Richards's suggestion that all communicators convey "feeling," an attitude toward subject matter, and "tone," an attitude toward the audience as revealed through the communication. (See Richards, *Practical Criticism* (New York: Harcourt, Brace & World, Inc., n.d.), esp. Part III, Chapter 1, pp. 175–176.) Some of the many ways in which "feeling" and "tone" are conveyed uniquely in speech, as contrasted to writing, are suggested to a critic by holding in memory the terms of what I have called the "unspoken contract" of speaker and listener.

Chapter V

Structure and Form

One may hear it said today that, "What talk (or other artistic expression) *says* is more important than its form," but such an observation ignores the fact that we all speak *through* structures and forms. Most comment denying the significance of formal structure is actually comment asserting that some different form would be better in whatever event is under discussion. For example, Emerson was criticized by nineteenth- and twentieth-century commentators as a writer and speaker who failed to observe the standard structuring of "good" communication. The criticisms were, in effect, contentions that Emerson should have structured what he wrote and said differently. On the other hand, a recent critic wrote the following sentence: "Emerson's rhetoric gives off intimations of order, which the reader seeks to follow up without withering them into formulae." [1] If I understand the statement, the author is alleging that there is important structure and form in Emerson's essay-speech and that reader-hearers can respond to it, though they do not perceive the structures as obvious ones. This observation, too, implies that communication occurs *through* structures.

Even in social comment we see insistence on the importance of structure and form. A feature article in *Ms.* magazine recently began:

> The heart of the great change happening to women is not an organization or a book, not some political race or a few well-known women or a magazine. The real centers of change would continue, whether or not these more visible symbols existed. They are the brave women all over the country who are working to change their own lives, the lives of their sisters, and the world around them.[2]

Again, one vision of structure and form in life is rejected by asserting that another, more meaningful pattern exists and is to be looked for and learned from.

The human search for structures and forms that *mean* seems never ending and without limit as to subject. Quakers find meaning in structured silence, "new Christians" in rituals of baptism and biblical speech, liberals in focusing discourse upon the enumerations of the Declaration of Independence, conservatives on the obligatory sections of the Constitution, and teen-agers on styles of speech and dress and music. Even of understanding language itself the linguist, Noam Chomsky, writes:

> The process of coming to understand a presented utterance can be quite naturally described, in part, as a process of constructing an internal representation . . . of its full structural description. . . . It would not be surprising to find that what the hearer . . . perceives is an ideal pattern, not incompatible with the signal that actually reaches his ears, that is projected by the phonological component of his grammar from the syntactic description he has assigned to this signal.[3]

A critic of rhetorical speech must try to deal with still more complex aspects of linguistic behavior:

> . . . its ability to communicate information of different levels. For example, a message can be grasped purely and simply on the lowest and most practical level as a request for something. But to someone who knows how to interpret this request in all its complexity, it may be a polite euphemism for an order, or it may be a request for something not really desired as a pretext to begin a conversation about another subject, or the request may have been made to break an embarrassing silence, or be the outcome of a psychological need to talk— or a hundred other things.[4]

In short, structures, forms, and styles *mean;* exactly how, we do not know very well. A linguist like Chomsky can only presume that perceiving and recreating structures have something to do with understanding language. Aranguren can only say that if we know the structure, form, and circumstances of the things said, we may discover that these conditioning concepts mean more or less than the verbalized content. There are, we must confess, more mysteries than rules about how structures and forms modify explicit contents of discourse.

In the face of these mysteries rhetorical theorists and critics tend to turn the *problems* of structure and form into *obligations*. These they formulate, multiply, and thrust upon rhetors as critical demands. But these demands emerge from the heads of the theorists and critics, not from the expectations of actual listeners to actual discourse. The extended discussions of the *parts* of a speech which developed in post-Aristotelian Greece and Rome and in the "managerial" rhetorics [5] of the eighteenth and nineteenth centuries are examples of this tendency (though George Campbell proved less fascinated with structure for its own sake than most of his earlier and later peers). Even twentieth-century empiricists have expended much research effort on manipulating "arguments" and other "units" of speeches in the hope of finding fixed correlations between the structures of talk and responses to talk. All such efforts neglect the points made by Chomsky and Aranguren. The structures that count are the structures that occur in the minds of perceivers; as observers or critics we shall understand little of the meanings of structures and forms unless we also take into account the situational constraints that permit structural meanings to emerge.

On authority and evidence already cited, a critic's safe assumptions about the roles of structure and form in rhetoric seem to be these. People structure what they perceive. They simplify details by finding in them or imposing on them patterns which, in this chapter, I shall call *forms*. Such strategies as placing ideas in sequence, devoting different amounts of time to different ideas, or indicating coordinate and subordinate relationships among ideas will influence listeners' efforts to *find* structures that help them to comprehend.[6] It is the assumption of most contemporary psychologists that receivers try to pattern what they receive in order to create "wholes," overall *forms*, out of the detailed stimuli that flow around them. When they cannot find or create forms, they are frustrated.

We have little empirical evidence to tell us which structural behaviors listeners are most likely to seize upon as they search for satisfying structures and forms. We are left, in the main, to reason our way to critical norms—hypotheses—by which to judge speakers' structural strategies. In the reasoning to follow, I propose to use the word *structure* to refer to whatever *relatings of ideas are apparent* in speaking, and I shall reserve the term *form* as one by which to designate *the psychological consequences* of structures— the effects of structures on listeners. Both concepts are needed to analyze the processes represented in rhetorical theory by the Latin word *dispositio:* "disposing (in the sense of using) the materials invented for a speech" in the hope of "effecting the end intended by the speaker in . . . [a] given situation." [7]

A speech critic needs to know as far as possible: what dispositional options were open to a speaker, what dispositional strategies were used, what their potential influences probably were, and—if it is possible—how listeners' perceptions of *units* (including the whole) of the message were affected by the structural strategies. Pursuing this sort of understanding is not merely a matter of isolating "main points" or labeling the parts of a communication or evaluating by applying a priori rules for "well-made speeches." It is to the *functions* of structure that critics of oral rhetoric must attend. So let us turn to the nature of structure in oral communication and to ways of estimating its potential influence.

STRUCTURE

How listeners perceive structural elements in speech is not deeply understood, but research by Ernest C. Thompson and others has produced findings that can be valuable to critics. Here is a summary statement of Thompson's findings:

> [This study] replicated parts of a previous study with strikingly similar results. The relationships among sentences and among subjects' abilities to organize [as measured by the Goyer "Organization of Ideas" test] have been demonstrated to affect comprehension of a "message." The joint effect of structure and . . . [listeners'] ability to organize is additive in the sense that the better the message structure *and* the subject's ability to organize, the higher the comprehension score is likely to be. The findings clearly support established rhetorical theory regarding the value of a coherent message and established learning theory regarding the importance of individual differences.
>
> Of equal significance is the fact that the findings of this study are consistent with . . . earlier findings. . . . *Addition of statements to highlight relationships among units in a speech can enhance com-*

prehension. The value of transitions in oral communication has
been supported empirically on two occasions.

. . .

We can . . . accept with some confidence the strong indications here
reported that *relationships between structural units of discourse*
[sentences] do contribute to the coherence of a message and interact
directly with the listeners' abilities to organize, both factors affecting
comprehension in the expected direction.[8]

Shifting the orders of "attention step," "need step," and
"satisfaction step" in a standard speech had marked influence
on listeners' abilities to recall important information in another
investigation that also explored effects of functional segments of
speech. Those who heard a "normally" ordered speech (attention,
need, satisfaction) remembered more than those who heard a "less
well organized" version of the same speech (need, attention, satisfaction). But those who heard a "less well organized" version
remembered more than those who heard a "disorganized" version
(satisfaction, need, attention).[9]

In these and other experiments in which the conceptual relations
of segments of speech have been altered there has been consistent
evidence that asserting emphatic, "reasonable" relations among
ideas correlates with improved acquisition and retention of information. On the other hand, experiments which have manip-
ulated arbitrarily defined "units" or "sections" of speeches have
produced equivocal and contradictory findings. Critics can infer
that when listeners are *told* how to understand the relationships
among ideas, they are likely to understand better; when they are
left to create structures and forms without direct guidance, they
learn less. Strategies that help listeners to "see" relationships seem
to work as Kenneth Burke said: "Form is the creation of an appetite in the mind of the auditor, and the adequate satisfying of that
appetite." [10]

Conservative interpretation of traditional theory and evidence
from empirical research suggests that critics of speeches may use
at least the following as normative propositions about the effects
of structural patterns in rhetorical speech.

1. What listeners perceive early in a communication tends to
   "index" or "provide an anchor for" their perceptions and
   interpretations of what they afterward hear. The precise
   nature of influences flowing from this "indexing" process

is not clear. A critic can, nonetheless, reason that whatever attitudes and beliefs speakers encourage *early* will qualify all else—unless other kinds of influences are generated to counteract this tendency.

2. Probably because of the "indexing" process, ideas that are agreeable to listeners are "safer" opening materials than unappealing ones. In other words, the familiar strategies of establishing "identification" or "common ground" early in communication are psychologically sound, and speech which lacks or violates the principle behind these strategies ought to be viewed with some suspicion in criticism.

3. Other things being equal, speakers who put ideas favorable to their own positions *before* discussions of countering views are functioning in a way that is likely to enhance their prospects of having the influence they intend. Again, reversal of this structural pattern deserves to be viewed skeptically by critics.

4. Psychologically considered, the overall *form* of satisfying communication runs from fair and favorable attention to themes pertinent to the speaker's purpose, through some sense of need or concern with the subject matter, to a release from tensions.[11]

5. Listeners distinguish between randomly ordered statements and statements that follow relation-building, coherent sequences. Whatever verbal or other strategies help listeners to see relations among statements are likely to improve their understanding of what was meant. It does *not* follow, however, that when speakers do not provide special assistance, listeners will create no intelligible structures for themselves. They will at least try to. Critics ought to note and credit whatever structural help speakers give. They should also consider whether factors in the rhetorical situation and in listeners' experiences make perceiving the "right" structure easier or harder for them.

6. Since whether structural assistance is "sufficient" depends partly on the natural organizing abilities of the listeners, critics ought to adopt the general norm that evident orderliness is always a rhetorical virtue because it will help even the poor organizers to acquire and retain information.

These are rather restricted grounds on which to evaluate structure and form in oral rhetoric. However, there are other grounds.

Some come from what is generally understood about perception. For example, there is reason to believe people *hunt* for connections and relationships in whatever they perceive. Hochberg contends:

> Whether by early perceptual learning or by inborn arrangement, our nervous systems seem to choose those ways of seeing the world that keep perceived surfaces and objects as simple and constant as possible. . . .[12]

We simplify by "abstracting," a process referred to in chapter IV where Suzanne Langer's interpretation was cited (pp. 88–89). D. E. Berlyne is especially succinct about the process. He sees it as

> . . . making overt behavior depend on certain properties of a stimulus pattern while disregarding other properties. It means forming what logicians and mathematicians call an "equivalence class" of situations, which share some characteristics but are distinct in other respects, and performing the same response to all members of the class.[13]

We may at least hypothesize that one reason comprehension and satisfaction are associated with structural clarity is that clear relations among ideas make it easier for listeners to simplify and classify behaviors. What makes their connection seeking easier also directs particular kinds of classifying. It says, in effect, "This goes with that, but not with something else."

From such reasoning we get a critical question that can lead us to descriptive data about any speaking: *What aids to simplifying, classifying, and patterning were present in the rhetoric?* A critic can identify these aids (or their absence), open them to discussion, and reason about whether they were likely to advance a speaker's apparent purposes.

There is another, more speculative norm of structure which has long been a part of rhetorical theory. It has not so far been called into question by any empirical evidence. It is that orderliness is taken by most listeners as evidence of intelligence on the part of a speaker. On this supposition it would be defensible to reason that where we find structural clarity, we have a characteristic of rhetoric that contributes to credibility as well as to comprehension and retention of information.

In any rhetorical situation, factors other than the structural may prove more significant than what we learn about aids to simplifying, classifying, and patterning; but structure does need to be examined and evaluated if criticism is to be complete. That it can be done, we have already seen when we noted the absence of explicit language emphasizing structure in Miller's speech, its obvious presence in Lincoln's Jonesboro remarks, and the complexity of this kind of structural assistance in the "Gettysburg Address."

In 1968, Professor Franklyn Haiman presented an interesting paper in which, among other things, he asked whether unstructured communication might not become normative or at least a normal type of rhetoric in American culture.[14] It appears that the "subtle but unmistakable shift from . . . 'proper' modes of arrangement . . . to formless or stream-of-consciousness patterns" was a "trendy" phenomenon of the 1960s. Yet the formlessness which Haiman noted may in some cases have actually been a recognition that structure and form in speech need not be the same as the spatial structure and form of writing. In any case, it is self-evident but constantly ignored in criticism that only by means of visual aids (including gestures) can structures be spatially exhibited in speech. We are habituated to *spatial* orders in communication. Print exists in space, so paragraphing and other spatial signals can assist readers' connection seeking. But paragraphing, outlining, setting chapters apart, and the like have no counterparts in the flow of speech unless the substantive ideas are "cut" or "interrupted" by utterances that *announce* units, divisions, and so on. These announcements must be *inserted* into the time sequencing of "real" content. Even physical movements, special pauses, and inflectional signals of structural relationships are "interruptions" in this sense. We need not involve ourselves with the cultural ramifications of differences between writing and speaking, reading and listening in order to see that giving structure to speech involves creating patterns *in time* and verbalizing nonsubstantive "markers" to signal that those time-bound patterns are being evolved. It follows that a critic of speech must lay aside spatially oriented conceptions of structure and adopt different conceptions oriented to temporal organization. What are these?

In speech, statements follow one another in series as seconds and minutes pass. It requires words, phrases, statements, vocal and gestural signals to point back, point forward, or announce other kinds of relations among linguistic events that succeed one another through time. This kind of assistance to listeners can take many forms; whether they assist or not depends on the *conventions of marking* which listeners can recognize. In the highly literate parts of Western culture certain markings of time-bound structural relationships have become conventional, and it is to these that the next pages are devoted. It may well be, however, that when studying speech situations, critics will have to learn listeners' *unique* marking systems in order to understand the speaking as listeners did.[15] But for the time being let us concentrate on Anglo-American conventions.

Grammar is a system for declaring relationships—between subjects and predicates and among other linguistic elements. (These possibilities will be considered later with other aspects of stylistics.) We have seen some ways in which inserted statements, words, and phrases assert things about structure. Above the level of grammar and brief assertions, a speaker can also create a block of obviously interrelated statements and then place that block in a noticeable relation with other blocks. And, as was said, behaviors in delivery can signify special relationships among ideas.

A few ways of building basic units of thought in speech were noted in examples studied in chapters III and IV, but it was not then pointed out that those structure-marking words "cut" the flow of substantive information. In order to help listeners to simplify and classify, structure-marking terms have to interrupt to say something different. A statement like, "And the next point I call attention to" signals that a "point" has *been* made while it is signaling that a new "point" is *about to begin.* But the remark does not purvey substance; it speaks of relation, of order, therefore of structure. This is the character of all transitional and reca-pitulatory language—and of some emphatic language. The function is to tell the listeners to make "equivalence classes" out of the substantive content; listeners are told to *create* this or that mental structure.

Whether or not such verbal helps to listeners are present in speech is an elementary observation anyone can make. The opening of a fairly long speech by Susan B. Anthony, delivered in 1873, illustrates how few such verbal cues one sometimes finds in speech that is, nonetheless, highly insistent about how listeners are to pattern their thoughts. At the beginning of her speech Miss Anthony addressed a court trying her for having voted, as follows:

Friends and Fellow-Citizens:—I stand before you under indictment for the alleged crime of having voted at the last presidential election, without having a lawful right to vote. It shall be my work this evening to prove to you that in thus doing, I not only committed no crime, but instead simply exercised my citizen's right, guaranteed to me and all United States citizens by the National Constitution beyond the power of any State to deny.

Our democratic-republican government is based on the idea of the natural right of every individual member thereof to a voice and a vote in making and executing the laws. We assert the province of government to be to secure the people in the enjoyment of their inalienable rights. We throw to the winds the old dogma that government can give rights. No one denies that before governments were organized each individual possessed the right to protect his own life, liberty and property. When 100 or 1,000,000 people enter into a free government, they do not barter away their natural rights; they simply pledge themselves to protect each other in the enjoyment of them through prescribed judicial and legislative tribunals. They agree to abandon the methods of brute force in the adjustment of their differences and adopt those of civilization. Nor can you find a word in any of the grand documents left us by the fathers which assumes for government the power to create or to confer rights. The Declaration of Independence, the United States Constitution, the constitutions of the several States and the organic laws of the Territories, all alike propose to *protect* the people in the exercise of their God-given rights. Not one of them pretends to bestow rights.

> All men are created equal, and endowed by the Creator with certain inalienable rights. Among these are life, liberty and the pursuit of happiness. To secure these, governments are instituted among men, deriving their just powers from the consent of the governed.

Here is no shadow of government authority over rights, or exclusion of any class from their full and equal enjoyment. Here is pronounced the right of all men, and "consequently," as the Quaker preacher said, "of all women," to a voice in the government. And here, in this first paragraph of the Declaration, is the assertion of the natural right of all to the ballot; for how can "the consent of the governed" be given, if the right to vote be denied? [16]

An exceptionally clear statement of her purpose and the notable "piling up" of her evidence do most of the directorial work in this excerpt. Only *here,* repeated in the last lines, *directs* thought by means of transitional and summative language.

A fragment of speech phonographically recorded by Theodore Roosevelt in 1904 exhibits similar features. I no longer know where or from what source I taped this recording, but this is the whole of what was on a very old phonograph record I once had access to:

1   Our aim is to control business not to strangle it. And above all not to
2   continue the policy of make-believe strangling of big concerns that do
3   evil and constant menace toward big and little concerns that do well.
4   Our aim is to promote prosperity and then to see that prosperity is
5   passed around. But there is a proper decision of prosperity. We wish
6   to control big business, among other reasons, so it may secure good
7   wages for the wage workers as well as reasonable prices for the con-
8   sumer. We will not submit to the prosperity that is obtained by lowering
9   the wages of working men and charging excessive prices to the con-
10   sumer, nor to that other kind of prosperity that is obtained by swindling
11   investors or by getting unfair advantage over smaller business rivals.

Again, few verbal interruptions draw special attention to structural relationships. Perhaps *but* and *so* signaled connections, but there are no other such aids to simplifying and classifying.

Of speaking like that represented in these two examples a critic must say that listeners were not given much help by utterance of conventional pointing-words. Whether that was serious or not is a matter of speculation. About all one can do is try to take the place of the actual listeners and try to "hear" the speech critically, asking whether there is difficulty in grasping how the speaker wants thought to move.

As I try to "listen" to Miss Anthony and to Mr. Roosevelt, Miss Anthony seems entirely clear and Roosevelt considerably less so. True, Miss Anthony's opening "comes over" as a *series* of rather undifferentiated "pieces" of "proof," but the unmistakable purpose, stated at the outset, and the summative and interpretive functions of her repeated use of *here* seem to leave me no escape from the response: "Yes, indeed, you do have proofs that voting is your right as a female citizen." Legal evidence and interpretations are clearly the *figure* in this unit of speaking. They seem to function as focused proofs.

I find much more difficulty in catching "the point" of Roosevelt's remarks. I can grasp the individual statements, but I do not know how to fit them together to form a structured, whole unit of thought. It seems to me Roosevelt needed more connecting, pointing words to help listeners interrelate thoughts.

Some of Richard Nixon's verbal habits gave difficulty in a different way in the early years of his national prominence. For example, he so often used the phrase, "I want to make this perfectly clear" that it became a key element in mimics' imitations of him. This and a number of other overused phrases were later suppressed by Nixon and his speech writers. The general problems of using too many verbal clues to structure are illustrated in the following excerpt from the second Kennedy-Nixon debate, October 7, 1960.

Mr. Nixon replied to a question concerning governmental action to combat unemployment.[17]

1   *To combat unemployment we first must concentrate* on the very areas
2   to which you refer—the so-called depressed areas. Now in the last
3   Congress—the special session of the Congress—there was a bill: one
4   by the President, one by Senator Kennedy and members of his party.
5   Now the bill that the President had submitted would have provided
6   more aid for those areas that really need it—areas like Scranton and
7   Wilkes-Barre and the areas of West Virginia—than the ones that
8   Senator Kennedy was supporting. On the other hand we found that the
9   bill got into the legislative difficulties and consequently no action was
10   taken. *So point one, at the highest priority,* we must get a bill for
11   depressed areas through the next Congress. I have made recommendations
12   on that and I have discussed them previously, and I will spell them out
13   further in the campaign. *Second, as we consider this problem of*
14   *unemployment,* we have to realize where it is. In analyzing the figures
15   we will find that our unemployment exists among the older citizens; it
16   exists also among those who are inadequately trained; that is, those who
17   do not have an adequate opportunity for education. It also exists among
18   minority groups. *If we're going to combat unemployment, then,* we have
19   to do a better job in these areas. That's why I have a program for
20   education, a program in the case of equal job opportunities, and one
21   that would also deal with our older citizens. *Now finally, with regard*
22   *to the whole problem of combating recession,* as you call it, we must use
23   the full resources of the government in these respects: *one,* we must
24   see to it that credit is expanded as we go into any recessionary period—
25   and understand, I do not believe we're going into a recession. I believe
26   this economy is sound and that we're going to move up. *But second,*
27   *in addition to that,* if we do get into a recessionary period we should
28   move . . . . on that part of the economy which is represented by the
29   private sector (and I mean stimulate that part of the economy that can
30   create jobs—the private sector of the economy). *This means* tax reform
31   and if necessary tax cuts that will stimulate more jobs. I favor that,
32   rather than massive federal spending programs which will come into
33   effect usually long after you've passed through the recessionary pe-
34   riod. *So we must use all of these weapons for the purpose of combating*
35   *recession if it should come.* But I do not expect it to come.[18]

Mr. Nixon's verbal signalings about relationships are so plentiful that they call attention to themselves and draw attention away from his substantive points and their true relationships. The principle for critics to note is that indications of divisions and relationships are not, in and of themselves, rhetorical virtues. Another superior speaker, former Governor William W. Scranton of Pennsylvania, made this point when he urged members of the Pennsylvania Speech Communication Association to avoid undue stress on the *mechanics* of organization when teaching rhetoric. Rigid habits of structuring tend to get in the way of effective personal communication, he said as he accepted his hosts' "Speaker of the Year" award for 1966.[19] When looking at verbal and other clues to relationships, the thing to be studied in criticism is not conformity to a priori strictures but whether the clues could assist listeners to carry on their simplifying and classifying tasks.

It is in the same spirit that a critic ought to inspect introductions, statements of purpose, and conclusions. These conventional parts of spoken rhetoric can indicate the relationships speakers want to emphasize, or they can interfere with understanding. Their sheer presence, absence, brevity, or length are not in themselves rhetorical strengths or weaknesses. The critical issue is: Given the audience's needs and conventions, did the necessary introductory, purpose-stating, and concluding work get done?

The chief outcome of centuries of discussion about "partitioning" in rhetoric has been to demonstrate the wisdom of Aristotle's early observations. He insisted that "parts" of communications must *function* significantly in rhetorical situations or they are unimportant:

> A speech has two parts. You must state your case, and you must prove it. You cannot either state your case and omit to prove it, or prove it without having first stated it; since any proof must be a proof of something, and the only use of a preliminary statement is the proof that follows it.... The current division is absurd. For "narration" surely is part of a forensic speech only: how in a political speech or display can there be "narration" in the technical sense? or a reply to a forensic opponent? or an epilogue in closely-reasoned speeches? Again, introduction, comparison of conflicting arguments, and recapitulation are only found in political speeches when there is a struggle between two policies. They *may* occur then; so may even accusation and defence . . .; but they form no essential part of a political speech. Even forensic speeches do not always need epilogues; not, for instance, a short speech, nor one in which the facts are easy to remember, the effect of an epilogue being always a reduction in the apparent length. It follows, then, that the only necessary parts of a speech are the Statement and the Argument. These are the essential features of a speech; and it cannot in any case have more than Introduction, Statement, Argument, and Epilogue.[20]

One might quarrel with Aristotle on some details, but to avoid stultifying formalism critics need to adopt his position about the "parts" of speeches. What is worth doing by way of introducing, stating one's position or purpose, developing a position, and concluding is determined by a speaker's relation to his subject, his listeners, and the overall speaking situation. It is true that circumstances in which introductions are rhetorically unnecessary are rare, but they do exist. When one speaker follows another and speaks briefly to his predecessor's point, there is often no need for systematic introductory remarks. Circumstances requiring no specifically concluding remarks are also rare but not unknown. For example, George Miller might have suffered little diminished effect had he suppressed his one-sentence "conclusion." On the other hand, it would be difficult to argue that he lost impact by saying, "That's all I have to say." The line served the useful purpose of giving a convenient signal to listeners that Miller was now finished. In a sense even Aristotle's assertion that one must state his thesis or case in order to prove it is mistaken for the modern world. Implicative, insinuative, rhetorical development, where theses are not asserted at all or are revealed very late, is familiar to us, though it was not common in ancient Greece.

A critic's concern with the formal structure of discourse ought, then, to be with what *work* needed to be accomplished. What always needs to be accomplished by some means in initiating talk comprises no long list.

1. Attention (as favorable as possible) needs to be focused on the speaker's subject matter.
2. The audience needs to be placed in a favorable frame of mind toward the speaker and his purpose (insofar as purpose ought to be initially revealed). This may imply that background information concerning the subject needs to be supplied; whether this is so depends on the initial state of listeners' knowledge and attitudes.
3. Some sense of what is supposed to happen in the speaking to follow will be needed so that listeners will not anticipate confusion; but formal previews, like full revelations of purposes, are matters of adaptation and not of rule-bound obligation.

Each of these functions of introducing can be carried out in a variety of ways. What critics should look for is whether the events included *something* that fulfilled these normative requirements. The remarkable differences among Bernstein's introductory method, using music (p. 320), Roosevelt's historical-allegorical opening (p. 291), and Zellner's use of previously shared experience (p. 337) amply illustrate the range of strategies and the variety of methods which may be effective in carrying out the functions of introducing rhetorical messages. And, as Aristotle suggested, circumstances themselves may take care of introductory functions, rendering verbalization by the speaker unnecessary. A critic's task is to survey the total rhetorical situation, asking whether and how the indispensable communicative functions were cared for—by whatever means.

Some thesis, purpose, or subpurpose will need to be in evidence if listeners' connection-seeking propensities are to be satisfied in any moment. As speech flows on, what listeners take to be a speaker's purpose at a given moment will constitute an anchor to which details will be attached, forming the most intelligible patterns each of the listeners can form. A critic ought to watch closely what speakers give hearers as apparent purposes at each stage of speaking. When John F. Kennedy began successive thought units with the preposition "to" (pp. 312–313, paragraphs 6 through 10), he signaled that these thought units were coordinate and that listeners were to expect a *series* of items which would continue until the "to" phrases ceased. He had not forecast this series of addresses to special "audiences," nor did he need to; parallelism in language would be signal enough of this uncomplicated pattern— a series. Leon Zellner previewed the broad shape of his speech at the beginning (p. 337, paragraphs 1 and 2), then he went through his argumentation, and in an interim summing-up (paragraphs 10 and 11) he tried again to reinforce the basic structure of his whole communication thus far. I suggest that Zellner needed to give this kind of help in order to keep his listeners "on track" because his talk was heavily argumentative, and listeners must be aware of "right" anchors at all times. By contrast, Kennedy's simple series of addresses to special "audiences" probably needed no preliminary forecast and no concluding summary. His purpose in that segment of the speech quickly became self-evident.

These illustrations should show that critics need to inspect speakers' overall handling of previewing, proving, and reinforcing. The important question is: Where and how did the speaker force forward his major structural schemes? If in introducing, that should be noted; if in interim summaries, that should be noted; if in conclusion, that should be noted; if not at all, that. Then, consider what the difficulty of the content and the nature of the rhetorical situation made desirable. With such information no critic would be at a loss to say how the speeches of Susan Anthony, Theodore Roosevelt, Richard Nixon, Leon Zellner, and John Kennedy differed in providing clear, consistent focus for listeners' patterning behaviors. No one would be at a loss to say why Kennedy could keep hearers focused as he wanted without any introductory previewing, whereas Roosevelt, at least, needed to do something more to give his listeners a "track" to follow.

Critical evaluations of the functions commonly associated with concluding remarks will be well based if one simply asks: Is it likely that the listeners were finally clear and as favorable as possible toward the speaker and his message? If recapitulation was necessary to insure clarity (as it doubtless was in Zellner's case), then there ought to be recapitulation. If a final working upon attitudes and feelings could have disposed the audiences more favorably, then magnification and excitation were needed. If lingering doubts and hostilities might have been softened by final reconciliation or refutation, then these ought to have been offered. All these strategies are simply options. They need not always be exercised. Surely George Miller needed to say no more than he did to conclude. On the other hand, paragraphs 25–30 (pp. 307–308) of Churchill's address to Congress carry out an unusual concluding function. Is he not adding a new and different theme? Concluding remarks are not always as textbooks say they should be. There are good reasons why a British Prime Minister addressing an American Congress upon their entry into a war might achieve his military, political, and global purposes by ending his remarks with consideration of prospects and possibilities far in the future! How mundane—even offensive—an orthodox recapitulation of paragraphs 1 through 24 would have been!

When Aristotle said that introductory and concluding functions in rhetoric are always situationally determined, he also insisted that the clarifying and proving functions are the *essence* of rhetoric. These functions, like all others, must be adapted to rhetorical situations, but giving proofs for the "right" structures and forms does not leave the rhetorician as free to choose among structures as when he is handling introductory and concluding materials. First, he cannot *omit* to clarify and to try to prove. If he does, he simply fails to make rhetoric at all. Second, data and ideas are not wholly malleable. The raw materials of proof never submit totally to a rhetor's hopes or to listeners' preferences. The population of the United States is what it is, however I may wish it were smaller or larger and however I may adjust my statements about it. If I choose to use this datum at all, I must accept its substance and form as it is—a statistic, not changeable according to my wish or my listeners' understandings. How I *treat* it is open to my rhetorical choice. This is my range of freedom. On p. 175 Leon Zellner's attempts to ease difficulties presented by inherently abstract ideas are discussed. He could not change their abstractness, but he could and did illustrate the abstractions by reference to a snowfall and a flower. In these ways he could give listeners an easier understanding. Take another instance. The concept of a triune God exists in the world. If I want to talk about the concept, I shall find it cannot in itself be adjusted to my limited theological views or my listeners'. To mention it at all, I must accept both the existence of the notion and its intricacy. I must create means of adjusting myself and my listeners to the concept's intransigent nature.

In short, how any speaker handles ideas will be constrained by the nature of the ideas, but in other ways the ideas will be open to control if the rhetor is himself adjustable and creative. One of a speaker's creative ways of adapting ideas to his needs is by building them into structures and forms. He can regulate *how* these ideas will be seen. For example, though minutiae cannot be given much magnitude individually, they can be fitted together to form an aggregate or collection that has special importance. Again, a statistic can be amplified by connecting it with other kinds of data so that the number becomes an "indicator," perhaps of a "trend" or of the gross magnitude of something. Here, the job of criticism is to note and judge speakers' constraints, including constraints imposed by materials, and then to observe what the speakers achieve through exercising their freedom to create structural relationships.

One must think seriously about how forms evolve in listeners' minds, as they listen. Listeners start with some ideas and feelings about whatever is discussed. These conditions acquire focus from what happens early in communication. By gradual changes of view the listeners arrive, later, at somewhat different sets of ideas and feelings. The changes may result from the rhetor's content, from relations he has displayed, or, more likely, from the relations of both of these to the listeners' experiences. If changes of these kinds occur in audiences, there is usually some intelligible pattern in the movements from first to final understandings. A speaker's challenge is to regulate these changes so that they are favorable to his purposes; this regulation is the basic function of structuring what one says.

In general, rhetorical theory posits that the following things work to give speakers control over listeners' structured experience:

1. It is better to display data and ideas according to some familiar, logical, or psychological pattern than to put them into a strange pattern or no readily discernible pattern at all; i.e., it is better to observe conventions.
2. The amount of time spent on an idea influences its prominence and perceived importance within any patterned framework. (Of course, undue talk about a point can bore and so destroy emphasis on the point and on the pattern as pattern.)
3. Certain rhetorical procedures such as repetition, special verbal comment, imagery, and other processes of associating data and ideas with more interesting things will cause materials so treated to be perceived as having special significance.
4. Placement of ideas in relation to one another affects the importance those ideas will have for listeners, the first and final places in any sequence being those of most significance.

For each of these normative statements there is at least some confirming empirical evidence, and none of the statements is denied by evidence available. On the other hand, each statement must be qualified by the troublesome preface, "other things being equal." Since things are never equal between any two rhetorical communications, a speech critic can accept these norms *but only when he finds no countervailing forces within the rhetorical situation.*

What do these normative statements say about the processes, possibilities, and limitations that govern what speakers can and cannot do in handling data and ideas? For one thing, to give pattern to ideas is to help listeners; but to pattern anything is also to exclude or suppress some features of ideas and to emphasize others. So, whoever organizes material necessarily changes its meaning. He makes some perceptions easier and others more difficult. A critic must therefore have a sense of what different kinds of rhetorical patterns *do* to meaning.

Common sense takes us a considerable distance toward evaluating the wisdom of a given structural pattern, and a bit of thinking about how standard patterns alter meaning, force, and general interest can further equip us to make reasoned judgments about speakers' structural choices.

Ten or eleven structural systems recur again and again in rhetorical discourse. All have different rhetorical potentialities because they emphasize and suppress different aspects of data and ideas. One way of enumerating these patterns is to say there are:

1. chronological sequences,
2. spatial patterns,
3. patterns that present ideas in ascending or descending order,
4. patterns that emphasize causal relations,
5. problem-solution or "disease-remedy" structures,
6. indirect or "withheld proposal" sequences,
7. direct or "open-proposal" sequences,
8. reflective or "inductive" sequences,
9. patterns of elimination,
10. the "motivated sequence" described by Alan Monroe,
11. so-called "topical" sequences.

So that speakers' choices among these structures can be judged, we need to examine what is highlighted and what is suppressed by these ways of systematizing thought.[21]

Chronological patterns place time relationships in the foreground. This fact allows certain special perceptual forms to be created: climaxes may be built and suspense developed. No other structural system equally allows for these possibilities except, perhaps, the "withheld proposal" structure to be discussed later. But if one emphasizes temporal relationships as chronology does, he tends to suppress notice of causality, desirability, special topics of importance or interest. To narrate effectively will require excluding whatever has significance outside "the story." Leaving out such material may cause a speaker to de-emphasize important matters. I suggest that former Vice President Spiro T. Agnew's narrative of commentators' treatment of President Nixon's address (pp. 367–368, paragraphs 2–7) made his *criteria* for appropriate critical comment obscure. Partly because he chose to tell "the story" of the speech and the "instant criticism" that followed, Mr. Agnew's entire point came to seem something like: "They spoke too soon; they should have waited." A doubter could, and many did, ask *"How* long after a president speaks is a commentator *supposed* to wait?" Agnew's data could, in different format, have been used to argue that the commentators made *prepared* "refutations," but his narrative structure suppressed the stronger issue of preparation and, by its time orientation, made speed of reply the main idea conveyed.

Where movements of events through time form the pattern of communication, questions for critics to ask are: (1) Was movement-in-time truly the most important phenomenon for listeners to perceive? and (2) Were any important aspects of the data and ideas suppressed by this structure? If one can answer the first question affirmatively and the second negatively, he has good ground for saying the speaker chose wisely in casting ideas into chronological form.

Parts are often related to one another or to the whole by emphasizing their *spatial* relations. If spatial relations are crucial to a speaker's meaning, there is no better structural system for conveying what is meant. This is the fundamental method that produces description. But emphasizing spatial relations suppresses time relations, causality, desirability, and other possibly significant aspects of a subject. Also, once a few spaces are accounted for, expectations that *all* spaces will be explained are built up. It is important, then, that those who use spatial structures avoid promising more detail than they want or need to provide.

Basic questions for evaluating any instance of spatial structuring are: (1) Are enough but no more than enough spatial data provided? and (2) Are spatial relationships in fact those most pertinent for getting the judgments being sought from listeners?

Ideas are sometimes clarified or persuasively presented when aspects, types, or qualities of things are sequenced according to their increasing or decreasing importance, familiarity, complexity, etc. Because such arrangements emphasize increasing or decreasing qualities, patterns of *ascending or descending order* put the relativeness of things in the foreground. When such "rises" or "descents" are what listeners need most to see, this structure is very helpful communicatively. A small substructure of John F. Kennedy's inaugural address illustrates this pattern in effective use. Paragraphs 8, 9, and 10 (p. 313) form a small unit of thought saying, in effect, "We address the undeveloped nations, nations in our hemisphere, and the United Nations." To arrange these points in the opposite or "descending" order would seem strange, and to talk successively of the hemisphere, underdeveloped nations, and

United Nations would deprive the ideas of any intelligible inter-connection.

As do all structural systems, ascending and descending orders impose burdens. Once either is begun, *all* familiar stages of descent or ascent must be accounted for, or listeners will think there is something wrong with the speaker's understanding. The critical questions to be asked are: (1) Was the relative importance, size, or other quality contrasted really important for understanding what the speaker meant to say? (2) Was advantage gained from the climactic-anticlimactic "movement" which this structure gives? (3) Was each stage of ascent or descent important enough to justify its inclusion in this unit of talk? (4) Were all *necessary* stages accounted for?

Causality is a basic mode of logical analysis. It is, therefore, a common way of displaying patterned relationships. Western listeners are entirely familiar with several variations of this sort of patterning: cause-to-effect, effect-to-cause, effect-to-cause-to-antecedent-cause. Because thinking causally is so commonplace, any way of setting forth a set of conditions as cause for another set of conditions finds listeners ready to look for causes when they learn of effects and to look for effects when they learn of causative forces. Critics need to evaluate how clearly *listeners* will see alleged causes and how reasonable these causes will seem to them. They also need to consider whether the causal relations speakers try to stress are really important to the achievement of their goals.

Perhaps because causal relations are so familiar, even speakers of fame sometimes use this pattern carelessly, as they probably would not in writing. Adlai E. Stevenson, though much admired as a speaker, did so on September 3, 1956, in Cadillac Square, Detroit. At about midpoint in a campaign speech he began developing what he plainly signaled was a new "unit" of discourse, and he strongly implied the ideas he touched on were supposed to be understood *causally*. The segment of speech ran thus:

1   But the basic protection against unemployment must be to make our
2   economy stronger in all its parts and to make even more stable the
3   consumer purchasing power upon which full employment must depend.
4   *This is why* the Democratic party is pledged to raise the minimum
5   wage. Yet government guarantees of minimum wages and unemploy-
6   ment benefits will never be the real answer either. In this rich land,
7   and in the American tradition of free enterprise, it should be
8   through private channels that we find our way toward the new America.
9   *This is why* it is so important to repeal and replace the Taft-Hartley

10   Act with a new law which will strengthen and equalize the essential
11   processes of free collective bargaining. There is no disagreement about
12   the public interest in holding unions and employers alike to the
13   standards of responsible bargaining. But it is an offense to the standards
14   of fairness to load our labor laws with prohibitions on traditional types
15   of union security—by the misnamed right-to-work laws—and to pack
16   the National Labor Relations Board with representatives of
17   management.[22]

Having so spoken, Mr. Stevenson turned to another point.

This segment of talk was clearly marked off as a discrete unit of thought development.[23] Within the unit there were two familiar, verbal signals that what was being said should be understood *causally:* "This is why" twice connected antecedent and subsequent matters.

If one asks whether causality clearly binds together the conditions associated by the "this is why" formula, the answer must be that the relationships are *not* clear. The belief identified in lines 1–3 can be seen as cause for the party's pledge, identified in lines 4–5. But the significance of this causation is immediately minimized in lines 5–6. If this is noticed, the qualification will call into question the genuineness of the alleged cause; if it is not noticed as a qualification, the statement in lines 5–6 can only weaken the "cause" as cause. The second causal connection is also confusing. A cause stated in lines 6–8 "is why" the Taft-Hartley Act must be replaced. What connection there is between use of "private channels" and repeal of the act is not made clear. It is hard to think listeners would understand these interconnections.

At best the causalities allegedly binding together the ideas of this segment are less than ably clarified. That does not mean that listeners at a political rally challenged the causations. Ardent Democrats would doubtless suppress the assertions of causality, especially in the second instance, since in 1956 Democrats generally opposed the Taft-Hartley Act, and opponents of the Act were chiefly Democrats. On the other hand, if one asks whether Stevenson's assertions of causal connections were helpful, the answer must be negative. Simply to experiment with other ways of structuring this segment of talk shows that injecting the causal assertions was unprofitable. If we delete "this is why," lines 1–8 stand as independent assurances from a party leader. If we delete "this is why" and "so" from line 9, lines 9–17 can stand as a series of independent assurances that Stevenson is on the "right side" for his labor-oriented, Detroit audience. A critic's conclusion must be that Stevenson's remarks would have been stronger had he not tossed in phrases alleging causal relationships. He had no need to do this; his listeners would not challenge his statements in any case, and the allegation of causal connections would convince no doubter.

The critical questions always at issue where speakers align their ideas causally are: (1) Is it clear that causality does interrelate the ideas in ways that are significant and credible to listeners? (2) Does the causal relation asserted seem likely to convince the listeners that the ideas spoken of are not really separable? and (3) Given the rhetorical situation, was it useful to put causal relations rather than some other relations into the foreground? As a critic, I would argue that in Mr. Stevenson's case the causalities he asserted were not important to his listeners; therefore, what he said would have had even better impact without any of the "this is why" phrases. Other critics may differ from this view, but they must then argue the three questions above.

Problem-solution or "disease-remedy" structures are especially common when speakers are asking acceptance of courses of action. Then, talk typically sets forth a problem and recommends some means for its solution. Often something also is said about the feasibility and desirability of the suggested remedy. This kind of structuring has a strong psychological basis. People feel ill at ease in the presence of unsolved "problems," so a problem-solution sequence follows out the pattern of human desires for answers: (1) What *is* our "problem"? and (2) Where is the "answer"? Where problems are well known, speakers ought only remind listeners of them and spend most effort on developing the feasibility, desirability, and other aspects of solutions. Where problems are not yet understood, emphasis needs to be reversed and solutions only sketched or hinted at as something the listeners should look toward once they see the problems clearly. We shall see that this same structure can even serve as a kind of "cover" for an indictment—if discussion of an "evil" (problem) heavily overweighs discussion of the "remedy" (solution).

The primary thing to consider in evaluating problem-solution structures is whether the rhetorical efforts expended on problem and solution are proportionate to the knowledge and anxieties of the listeners. It is wasteful rhetorical effort to develop the importance of eating a balanced diet when people are hungry and carbohydrates are visible! It is foolish to expound solutions for problems people do not yet fully understand. So, the first critical question to raise about any problem-solution structure is: (1) Has the speaker balanced his treatments of "problem" and "solution" in ways that fit the actual exigences of the rhetorical situation?

Another critical determination is sometimes pertinent: (2) Did the materials of the unit of speech actually lend themselves to this kind of structure? Nothing is gained and some reputation for good sense may be lost by forcing talk about "Are there men on Mars?" into a problem-solution mold. A crude fit is possible. One could say that (a) evidence on the matter is frequently misunderstood ("problem") and (b) the best answer is that life as we know it cannot exist on Mars ("solution"). But a perceptive critic may want to say that these materials would have been more intelligible and the speaker's reputation for good sense probably would have been enhanced if he had put his ideas and data into a *reflective* or *eliminative* pattern. The "problem" about Mars is what to believe "true" and what to believe "false." Issues of fact are not conventionally discussed as "problems" of decision making.

Problem-solution patterns are perceived as natural when policies and courses of action come under discussion. Their use with other kinds of issues should make critics wonder whether other available structures might not have served the speakers' purposes better.

Indirect sequences, of which withholding one's proposal is a form, have many variations. Perhaps the basic example of the strategy is the salesman's "yes-response" pattern. There, ideas and appeals are so patterned that the listener's final assent is not clearly foreseeable until he has given so many preliminary assents that he is virtually committed to the final one. Some variation of this strategy is often the only means by which speakers can win full hearings from doubting or hostile listeners. Shakespeare's Mark Antony, speaking over the body of Caesar, makes a speech that exemplifies what subtle indirection can do to influence indifferent and hostile audiences. That short speech can also be read as a model of the precision with which listeners' minds must be controlled by speakers who try to proceed by indirection.

Masterful indirection in rhetoric can achieve poetic art, as at Shakespeare's hands or in Browning's *The Ring and the Book,* but the strategy is difficult to use with full effectiveness. First, to be indirect without seeming equivocal is difficult, and serious listeners have low tolerance for equivocation. Hence, rhetorical critics need to be alert to credit indirection that achieves the incisiveness that Shakespeare's Mark Antony does or that Stokely

Carmichael (pp. 343–355) does at some points. A critic should note, too, that many attempts at indirection achieve only pointlessness. An interesting instance occurred in a speech by civil defense lawyer, William Kunstler, in an address at The Pennsylvania State University on April 18, 1970.

Mr. Kunstler told at one point in his speech the story of William Penn's legal hearing for inciting to riot in seventeenth-century England. As Kunstler told the story, he indirectly emphasized similarities between Penn's hearing and the trial of the "Chicago Seven" in which Kunstler had participated as a defense attorney. Telling the story of Penn, with allusions to the Chicago trial, occupied about four and a half minutes of the speech, yet no auditor interviewed by members of a speech criticism class could afterward report "the point" of the "story about William Penn." And though there was applause at some points during the story, there was none at its conclusion. Mr. Kunstler was not at all unclear as to his point, and though readers of the speech text see the point immediately, Kunstler's indirection (and perhaps the power of narrative to overwhelm "side comment") appears to have cost him communication with a large audience. Yet he was speaking in the state founded by and named for the put-upon William Penn!

In evaluating indirect rhetorical structures a critic's basic question ought to be: Does the speaker closely control listeners' thoughts, moving them through stages of judgment inevitably culminating in intended conclusions? And speech critics have to guard against making this judgment on the basis of close study. As in Kunstler's case, thought movements that are clear to the eye are not always followed closely by those who *hear*.

Direct or "open-proposal" patterns are the reverse of the indirect structures just discussed. In a loose sense open-proposal patterns are deductive, and indirect structures are inductive. The advantages and disadvantages of these structures are, accordingly, radically different.

Aristotle's charge to speakers that they state their cases and then prove them was a counsel in favor of open-proposal patterning. Obviously we would want to qualify that counsel today, but no structural system is more clear and forthright than direct presentation. If listeners know a speaker's subject and are either open-minded or favorable toward his position, the direct approach can lead them clearly and simply to his intended conclusion. But the virtues of clarity and simplicity are not unmitigated. What if the listeners have heard it all laid out this way before? Then, a critic will want to inquire whether the speaker took pains to enliven the openness of his method through using vivid language, through delivery, through injecting "new" details, and by varying the kinds of substructures used within his open-proposal discourse.

The basic critical question about direct presentations is: Was anything lost because of the lack of suspense and inherently interesting "movement"? If not, this clear structuring was almost surely a rhetorical asset.

A *reflective* sequence is a pattern almost exclusively useful for discourse that tries to build up active inquiry in the minds of listeners. Typically this kind of talk evolves in the following way: (1) listeners are oriented to a problem, (2) they are informed concerning characteristics of the problem, (3) they are shown criteria which a satisfactory solution ought to meet, (4) they are invited to join the speaker in exploring the available means of dissipating the problem, and, in some circumstances, speech continues by (5) revealing the speaker's preference among available solutions, and (6) probing for the probable consequences of adopting the preferred solution.

Criticism of speaking organized in this fashion ought to ask: (1) Was the pattern appropriate to the speaker's and the listeners' objectives and states of mind? and (2) Was the material developed in both a logically and psychologically satisfying way? The first of these questions probes whether the speaker had sound reasons for putting his discourse into this structure. He had good reasons if he was in a reflective mood himself and if he knew his listeners were or could be perplexed enough to think carefully. A speaker who is, himself, still searching for answers has virtually no choice but to pattern his remarks in something like the reflective sequence. If he is to communicate his exploratory experience and mood in orderly fashion, this is the only easily followed structure open to him. The same is true for speakers who are committed to engendering reflection rather than to *directing* the choices of listeners. Teachers, for example, frequently adopt this stance, withholding their own views for the purpose of stimulating inquiry by students.

The reflective structure bespeaks uncertainty or a willingness that others should decide. It approaches "answers" indirectly, claiming that the speaker is himself uncommitted. This is why attempts to "sell" ideas by adopting this pattern are often charged with being fraudulent. Persuasion in masquerade as inquiry goes forth at high risk. The problem-solution structure is the candid persuader's alternative to the reflective sequence.

If reflectively organized speech suits a speaker's and audience's needs, criticism should seek to determine whether vigorous mental activity was really generated in the audience. In reflection listeners are asked to suspend judgment pending analysis of the problem, discovery of criteria for judgment, and analysis of alternative solutions. People strongly motivated to study, to search, can find such dispassionate investigations exhilarating, but others do not. They wish for quick resolutions of problems. A critic therefore needs to ask about speech reflectively organized (1) whether listeners were sufficiently stimulated to participate in cautious, deliberate reflection. A second critical question is related to the first: (2) Did the speaker incorporate all available rhetorical methods to inject imagery, movement, and other means of sustaining interest and involvement in this inductive communication?

The method of *elimination* is also called the method of residues and the "this or nothing" method. When using it, a speaker considers all credible solutions to a problem, showing that only *one* of the available options is really acceptable. If both listeners and speaker agree that the several alternatives are *worth* examining, an eliminative structure is almost automatically dictated by the situation. Herein lies the basis for the leading critical judgment required when speech follows this pattern: Was extended treatment of the several eliminated alternatives really necessary in the view of the listeners? Unless listeners have or can be made to have interest in an alternative, it will be sheer busy-work to expound it. Another way of expressing the basic critical question about this structure is: Will the audience see the review of alternatives as valuable and not as a process of destroying "straw men"? Plainly one must know the rhetorical situation and its exigences before he can judge the wisdom of eliminative structures.

The *motivated sequence* is a comprehensive formula for organizing speeches, first discussed by Professor Alan H. Monroe. Speeches following this structure go through most or all of these steps: an Attention Step, a Need Step, a Satisfaction Step, a Visualization Step, and an Action Step.[24] When used for persuasive purposes this sequence is, of course, but an outline of the *psychological stages* that are advisable when using the problem-solution pattern.

The names Monroe attached to his "steps" suggest headings for evaluating almost any rhetoric because they identify *effects to be accomplished* at various stages of communication. As was said earlier, to ask whether enough was done to secure attention (not simply in introduction but everywhere) is always a relevant critical inquiry. To ask whether enough was done to create (and *sustain)* a sense of need to hear more is equally relevant. To ask whether listeners were satisfied—in some fashion released from anxiety and tension—is likewise universally pertinent, though not all speakers' purposes require that speaking provide releases of tension. If actions were asked of listeners, it is a further part of criticism to ask whether those listeners were made to envision the consequences of their choices and whether they were finally motivated to act as the speaker wished. Monroe's "sequence" can be used as a kind of "schedule" of psychologically oriented questions about what speakers accomplished motivationally and when they accomplished it. From the point of view of criticism, the inquiries Monroe's formulation suggests ought to be raised about any speaking, whether or not the speaking is formally patterned as Monroe suggested.

Much rhetorical speaking, formal and informal, follows one or another of the structural patterns we have just discussed, but there is also much speaking in which the overall structure is determined by the peculiarities of the subject or the situation. The *topics* around which details are ranged may derive from special ways people think about specific subjects. For example, economic, social, and political aspects of public questions sometimes need to be covered. The two "topics," aerodynamics and cost, may be the important headings to have treated in a discussion of aircraft design. To take another instance, the "topics," content, structure, style, and presentation, have for centuries been the standard headings under which rhetorical theory is discussed. The most important aspects of the subject can be subsumed under these topics and put in the order just given, the topics suggest the phases of composition through which people usually go when creating rhetorical compositions.

With many subjects, then, the ideal structure is an *ad hoc* organization derived from (1) customary ways of thinking about the subject, (2) a speaker's wish to focus attention, or (3) an audience's need to attend to *selected* aspects of the subject. The critical questions to ask about topically organized talk are usually two: (1) Do the "topics," taken together, give a sufficiently clear view of the subject? and (2) Will the coverage *seem* both reasonable and inclusive from the audience's point of view? Little else needs to be asked directly about topically structured speaking. The topics are subject-bound, situation-bound, or both, so most other critical judgments concerning the functional value of the structure will emerge during analysis of the explicit and implicit contents of the message.

FORM

The justification for any structural pattern in rhetoric is the structure's capacity to make listeners see aspects of a subject as the kind of "unit" or "whole" a speaker wants perceived. The long-ranged reason for preferring one structural pattern over another ought to be that the preferred method will best direct listeners toward the final position the speaker wants them to attain. Therefore, the ultimate reason a critic must study details of structure is to discover what listeners were probably made to perceive at the end, or in remembrance, of the total rhetorical message.

Criticism that moves from comment on structural features to consideration of consequent *form* and then to estimation of probable rhetorical effects is rarer in speech studies than in literary criticism. But it should not be. Hermann G. Stelzner's intensive examination of Franklin D. Roosevelt's "War Message" is one of the few published inquiries that probes systematically and in detail the ways by which *form*—shape that transcends pattern— evolves from major and minor structural and linguistic decisions.[25] Stelzner's essay deserves close study by anyone who wishes to see the ways choices among leading themes, ordering those themes, sequencing statements, arranging words within statements, and choices of words themselves can create holistic meanings that go quite beyond the logical or lexical meanings of articulated parts.[26]

Without attempting analysis as detailed as Stelzner's (which treats stylistic as well as structural choices), we can explore how forms emerge from details of structure. The sample of speaking I shall use for illustration is chosen also to show that the norms of structure and form we have been discussing operate, at least for decidedly literate people, across modern languages and subcultures. The example is a short speech made by Selim Sarper, Turkish delegate to the United Nations General Assembly in 1956. Though Mr. Sarper's English was exceptionally good, English was plainly not his first language. On November 4, 1956, he spoke in English to the Assembly on a resolution calling upon the Soviet Union to withdraw its troops from Hungary and allow the United Nations to send a commission to inspect political conditions in

Hungary. The speech was internationally broadcast by radio and telecast in the United States.

The methods of critically analyzing rhetorical structure and form work just as effectively on this Turkish delegate's speech to an international Assembly as they might on any speech prepared by a British or American citizen for an audience of fellow nationals. The text of Mr. Sarper's remarks follows.

1   Mr. President: When this question was being discussed in the Security
2   Council, on the 28th of October 1956, upon instructions from my Govern-
3   ment I presented to the Secretary General a letter whereby I said that,
4   "The Government of the Republic of Turkey fully endorses the action
5   initiated by the governments of France, United Kingdom, and United
6   States by bringing that matter to the attention of the Security Council."
7   And now, Sir, it is with an anguished heart that I come to this rostrum
8   to associate myself once again with my colleagues who have raised their
9   voice in defense of a people in agony, of the Hungarian people, whose
10 lament for liberty is being choked in blood and plague. What do the
11 Hungarian people want, after all? They say, "Leave us alone! Remove
12 this yoke from our neck and let us live our own way of life." And what
13 was the answer to this pathetic plea? Only yesterday we heard that
14 negotiations were about to start between Soviet military authorities
15 and the Hungarian government aiming at making arrangements for the
16 withdrawal of the forces of occupation. We know now that these rumors
17 about so-called negotiations were deliberately spread for the purpose,
18 actually, of gaining a few more hours to complete military preparation
19 and then deal the merciless blow which finally destroyed the last vestiges
20 of liberty and independence in Hungary. And, Mr. President, to give
21 the finishing touch of perfection to this hideous monument of cynicism,
22 last night the representative of the Soviet Union delivered from this
23 rostrum a speech in which he used words such as: "freedom," "indepen-
24 dence," *et cetera,* and this at the very moment when the forces of occu-
25 pation in Hungary were destroying these freedoms, liberties, and
26 independence of the Hungarian people. Mr. President, it will be realized
27 sooner or later by everybody including the Soviet Union, that what they
28 have done in Hungary is, to say the least, a political mistake—an
29 enormous mistake. It was, Sir, a mistake because it is far more profitable
30 to establish bonds of friendship with an entire people than with a puppet
31 government. The Soviet Union had a good chance of establishing first
32 normal, then friendly, relations with the Hungarian people by considering
33 with sympathy their yearning for freedom and independence. This
34 invaluable opportunity is lost. Now, hatred will take the place of eventual
35 affection in every Hungarian heart. And mutual distrust will render
36 co-operation impossible for a long time to come. Is it now too late to
37 redress this deplorable wrong? The key to that problem is in the hands
38 of the Soviet Union. Tanks and guns can open the gates of a city, but
39 they are powerless—quite powerless—when the question is to conquer
40 the hearts and the minds of human beings. I realize, Sir, perfectly well,
41 that ideas such as these are met with mockery in some quarters. But

42   the fact that tens of thousands of almost unarmed men and women—
43   workers and students—I say workers mind you—think of Soviet soldiers
44   opening fire upon simple workers—workers and students sacrificed
45   their lives for freedom. This fact—this fact—doesn't this mean anything
46   to those who think they can wipe out liberty from the face of this globe?
47   Now, Mr. President, as to this emergency special session of the General
48   Assembly. I think the least we can do—the very least, indeed—is to
49   adopt the resolution tabled by the United States delegation, with an
50   overwhelming majority, in the hope that the wave of world public
51   opinion might make itself felt to those who can put an end to the situation
52   if they want to. Thank you, Sir.[27]

We are interested in what holistic meanings this speech would probably leave with the Assembly and viewing public. First, however, we need to ask what a "sense of form" or of wholes is. The matter is in many ways mysterious, but the observations of a physiological scientist can give us some notion of how humans apprehend and interpret data of speech or of any other sort:

> ... our *general policy* is decided at the highest level of all, that of the cerebrum. There the pattern of activity is shaped by the incoming signals, *suitably edited,* reacting with the store of past experience laid down in the brain. We do not know exactly where or how it is laid down, but we are all aware that it plays an important part in directing our attention and our behavior. Many of the signals from the sense organs can reach the level of consciousness and cause a brief adjustment of our activity, but those that interest us and direct our thoughts have been reinforced by the habits and images formed by past experience. This gives the impulse message its full meaning and fits it into our mental picture of the outside world.[28]

What I have been calling *form* is substantially what Adrian conceives as a "general policy" or overall impression of anything perceived. It is the outcome of selecting stimuli, noting and perhaps "editing" their structures, and blending the information with experience to create a more or less holistic perception of "what it's all about." A rhetorical critic will remember that the structures of messages are perceived within rhetorical situations which, themselves, contribute parts of the "images formed by past experience." Paul I. Rosenthal writes that a full conception of the effect of a message upon a receiver

> ... requires an exposition of and a judgment about the conditions that affected the receiver's perception of the message, specifically, his image of the source, his knowledge of the context of the communication, and

his collateral view of the message [of which his sense of its structure or lack of it is part]. A critical analysis that addresses itself to these factors, as well as to the representational content of the message, may essay a more realistic answer to the question of how the communication "worked." [29]

Adrian's and Rosenthal's remarks give healthy emphasis to the fact that at every stage of critical analysis one ought to be looking "forward" toward judgment of the "general policy" or Gestalt that the message and all that surrounds it will finally leave. Once we know what structural assistance a speaker offered, the question becomes: What, then, was the *general* meaning—the final form—that was shaped by structural stimuli and the forces in the rhetorical situation? Mr. Sarper's speech is a striking instance of how much would not be understood if a critic failed to look beyond structure to emergent form. Mr. Sarper may or may not have known it, but the *form* of his speech loosed a special kind of force.

In Mr. Sarper's speech lines 1–10 consist of statements that assert, and by their adjacency imply, that there has been consistency and continuity in Turkey's long-standing position on "this question." The statements also imply that the speaker is concerned with the parliamentary situation and, presumably, with the rectitude of nations' conduct.

At line 10, this kind of observation stops, and attention is shifted abruptly by use of an interrogative to the conditions of the Hungarians. Lines 10–26 form a strikingly patterned unit. Two questions are asked and answers are given to them. By this arrangement the Hungarians' demands are set against the Russians' answers—first, their verbal answers, then their contrasting answers in deeds. The perfidious quality of the answers, taken together, is not only asserted by the language of lines 10–26, but the structured contrast of words and deeds, demands and responses, works also to give the entire section the *form* of an indictment.[30]

Lines 26–36 appear at first hearing (or glance) to promise a new line of thought—a consideration of events from Russia's own point of view. Again, a unit of thought would be either quickly or gradually sensed, though no words called attention to the structural shift.

The new line of thought is rather formally argued. If reordered, lines 26–31 constitute a loose syllogism with some accompanying proof for the premises:

It is far more profitable to establish bonds of friendship with an entire people than with a puppet government.
This invaluable opportunity [to establish friendship with the people] is lost.
What they have done in Hungary is, to say the least, a political mistake—an enormous mistake.

Lines 31–33 function as amplification and support for the minor premise and 34–36 as reinforcement for the conclusion. If the segment is described in Stephen Toulmin's, rather than in syllogistic, terms, we derive essentially the same sense of argumentative structuring. The conclusion identified above functions as CLAIM, the minor premise as DATA, the major premise as WARRANT, and the content of lines 31–33 and 34–36 respectively amplify the DATA and give BACKING for the WARRANT. The technical relationships of ideas in the argument might not be noticed by listeners, but the unit would surely be heard as "some reasons" for a conclusion: the U.S.S.R. lost a valuable opportunity. There is something like "logical force" here, and this could make listeners find Mr. Sarper's thoughts more credible and at the same time make the thoughts of lines 26–36 stand more or less independently of the previous units. To line 36, then, a critic could reason that attentive listeners would have sensed three rather discrete, coordinate "points" about the situations in Hungary and in the Assembly.

The question form which appears at line 36–37 would surely signal a fourth "point"—one intended to consider what ought to be done in light of the previous "points." Lines 37-38 answer the question with the pessimistic assertion that only the Soviet Union can do what is really required. Lines 38–46 abandon what-can-be-done in light of the previous "points." Lines 38–40 answer that the present course is unwise even from the Soviets' own interests. How would such talk be understood? Certainly not as the promised consideration of a course of action. Perhaps as a confusing cluster of words vaguely amplifying the major "points" made earlier.

As one "hears" the speech, lines 38–46 sound like a group of statements characterizing Soviet actions as "mockery," abusing the very classes the Russians pretend to value most—workers and students. The theme, repeated in several ways, echoes the part of the speech which treated the speciousness of Russia's words, judged by actions. A critical guess might be that listeners' thoughts would be thrown back to the theme of "perfidy" in ways that would suppress earlier thoughts of "regrettable error." It seems entirely possible that at this point in listening "perfidy" was beginning to emerge as the true *figure* in the speaking.

The words "Now, Mr. President, as to this emergency special session of the General Assembly" emphatically announced a new thematic shift. What followed was what Mr. Sarper had to say about the Assembly's actions-as-solution for the Hungarian situation. This "solution step" consists of a single, complex sentence asserting that the pending resolution ought to be passed overwhelmingly "in the hope" of influencing the U.S.S.R. The limitedness of the solution is verbalized. Would not the actual meaning of the sentence be something like: "We can't do less, but it isn't much because the Soviets must do anything that will really count"?

By reflecting on the probable *emergence* of patterns of forces here, we can see in retrospect that the main thrust or form of the body of the speech (the three major "units" following introductory remarks on Turkish consistency) has been a claim that what Russia was doing was wrong. It is admitted that the Assembly's solution cannot solve the problem except indirectly. What, then, shall we say is the *form* that evolved from the structural and suggestive features of the speech?

Mr. Sarper spent 5 minutes and 14 seconds delivering lines 1–46. All of this material treated the *quality* of Turkish positions and the contrasting positions of the Russians. Only 33 seconds were consumed in talking about what the Assembly should do! These allotments of time and the indicting nature of the three "main points" about Russia show that while the speech has a problem-solution structure, that fact is not what is significant psychologically. Psychologically the speech turns out to be a *sustained indictment* with *pro forma* remarks about parliamentary action. Everywhere the "problem" is discussed. The problem turns out to be Russian "perfidy," and the "solution" offered is twice admitted to be weak and indirect.

If we remember the "indexing" potentialities of first ideas, we have further reason to say that Russian perfidy—the first "point"—was likely to color perceptions of the rest of what Mr. Sarper said. Moreover a "mockery theme" closed the "problem section," and it echoed the "perfidy theme" with which the section had opened. Would not these opening and closing themes tend to reinforce each other, especially in a debate on an *anti*-Russian resolution?

All analyses of possible structural effects argue that as a *whole* this communication must have seemed a sustained condemnation in this rhetorical situation. Except for the confusing lines 36–40, the body of what was said was arranged to support a thesis something like: "Russia's behavior is viciously cynical." Mr. Sarper may not have done these things by design, nor need we suppose Assembly members from every culture understood the speech in exactly the same manner. What analysis allows us to do is argue that anyone conditioned by Western conventions of structure and form probably sensed he had heard an indictment. We can also argue that no one used to hearing problem-solution structures in policy debates would be mystified by Sarper's procedure. He gave them standard, Western, structural fare, technically appropriate for this rhetorical situation.

Mr. Sarper's speech illustrates how hard it sometimes is to come to an informative critical conclusion without going beyond the mere process of identifying details and kinds of structures. Frequently one must discover what structural details "add up to"— what *form* or *forms* they create for listeners' apprehensions. To say merely that Mr. Sarper's speech was a problem-solution speech would be to miss its persuasive form. The speech is not an exception. Probe in similar fashion the speeches in this book by Theodore Roosevelt, John F. Kennedy, and Stokely Carmichael. Each presents a unique structure-form problem in criticism.

What I have called *form* is always *emergent*. It emerges as an overall meaning, growing in receivers' minds because internal structures of speaking interrelate thoughts in broad, inclusive patterns of meaning. Even an obviously patterned speech with verbal signals that direct thoughts marches toward its past— to become a thing remembered. It is not the structural signalings or the systems of interrelating ideas that remain with hearers when speaking has ended. There remain *results* of structural strategies, further modified by the structures imposed by the listener as he listened. These are the shapes of the messages listeners possess as the sound of each uttered word dies away. The speakers' structural strategies contribute to the created structures in the listeners' minds, but the created structures live on as the speakers' structures die away. What remain are the listeners' partly borrowed, partly created frameworks of understanding. Listeners create significant meanings from or about elemental, residual shapes. The resulting interpretation is what I have been calling *form*.

No critic can ever be sure he is "right" about the forms that emerge in listeners in consequence of speech, but he can reason about what evident rhetorical structures had power to create. The structural strategies discernible in speaking become the material from which critical judgments about form develop. The critic tries to blend what he knows from observation of content and structure with what he has learned from theory about the rhetorical potentialities of content so structured. By doing this he can come to see, with considerable claim to rationality, that Selim Sarper created *more* than a prosaically structured policy speech, that George Miller created a self-expression as well as some counsel, and a sensitive critic will find the ways to see what John F. Kennedy created beyond observations about problems and their solution. Study of rhetorical structures *culminates* in reasoned estimates of the natures of communicated forms.

NOTES

[1] Lawrence I. Buell, "Reading Emerson for the Structures: The Coherence of the Essays," *Quarterly Journal of Speech* 58 (February 1972): 69.

[2] "Found Women," *Ms.* 1 (January 1973): 45.

[3] Noam Chomsky, *Current Issues in Linguistic Theory* (The Hague: Mouton & Company, 1966), p. 112.

[4] J. L. Aranguren, *Human Communication* (New York: McGraw-Hill Book Company, World University Library, 1967), pp. 88–89.

[5] Douglas Ehninger applies this term to the rhetorics of George Campbell, Joseph Priestley, and others in his "Introduction" to Richard Whately's *Elements of Rhetoric* (Carbondale: Southern Illinois University Press, 1963), p. xxvii.

[6] For example, Ralph L. Rosnow and Edward J. Robinson observe: "When incidents that are perceived as rewarding or satisfying are initiated close in time to a persuasive communication, opinions tend to change in the direction of the arguments closer to the rewarding incident. When an incident is dissatisfying, or punishing, opinions tend to change in the direction of the arguments farther in time from it." *Experiments in Persuasion* (New York: Academic Press, 1967), p. 102. Here is but one of many strategic considerations that govern what is the "best" order of ideas in a rhetorical situation containing rewarding and punishing constraints. When there has just been a disagreement, it seems rhetorically wise to change the subject and return to the topic of disagreement only at a later time; and so on.

[7] Russell H. Wagner, "The Meaning of *Dispositio,*" in *Studies in Speech and Drama in Honor of Alexander M. Drummond* (Ithaca: Cornell University Press, 1944), p. 293.

[8] Ernest C. Thompson, "Some Effects of Message Structure on Listeners' Comprehension," *Speech Monographs* 34 (March 1967): 56–57. Used by permission of author and publisher. My italics.

[9] Fred R. Miller, "An Experiment to Determine the Effect Organization Has on the Immediate and Delayed Recall of Information," unpublished M.A. thesis (Miami University, Ohio, 1966).

[10] Kenneth Burke, "Psychology and Form," in Morton D. Zabel ed., *Literary Opinion in America,* II, 668. Originally in Burke's *Counter—Statement* (New York: Harcourt, Brace and Co., 1931).

[11] Two important qualifications apply, however. As was pointed out in chapter IV, there are circumstances in which speakers want to and need to leave listeners in some state of frustration. Also, there are rhetorical situations in which attention is *already* focused on pertinent themes.

[12] Julian E. Hochberg, *Perception* (Englewood Cliffs, N.J.: Prentice-Hall, Inc., 1964), p. 99.

[13] D. E. Berlyne, *Structure and Direction in Thinking* (New York: John Wiley & Sons, 1965), p. 45.

[14] Franklyn Haiman, "The Rhetoric of 1968: A Farewell to Rational Discourse," originally printed in *The Ethics of Controversy: Politics and Protest* (Lawrence, Kansas: Speech Communication and Human Relations Division, 1968), pp. 123–142. The text is also available in Wil A. Linkugel, R. R. Allen, and Richard L. Johannesen eds., *Contemporary American Speeches,* 3rd ed. (Belmont: Wadsworth Publishing Company, Inc., 1972), pp. 133–147.

[15] I suggest, for example, that Stokely Carmichael's speech at Morgan State College is not without structure and form; relationships among ideas are often signaled by devices not discussed in this book. My impression is, also, that Latin American speakers rely on structural systems and signals that differ in many respects from those that are conventional to Anglo-Americans.

[16] From Miss Anthony's "Constitutional Argument," as published in Ida Husted Harper, *The Life and Work of Susan B. Anthony,* 3 vols. (Indianapolis: The Hollenbeck Press, 1898), II, 977. The full text of the speech appears on pp. 977–992.

[17] The passage is printed essentially as in Kraus ed., *The Great Debates,* pp. 379–380, but I have modified punctuation slightly after studying a sound recording of the debate. I have also placed in italics those words that seem obvious structural signals.

[18] Lines 26–30 were by no means as confusing when uttered as they are in print. Vocally, Mr. Nixon clearly signaled that "and I mean . . . jobs" was a parenthetical remark. I have tried to suggest this aspect of his structuring by introducing parentheses which do not appear in other texts of the debate. The dots inserted in line 28 indicate that here Nixon hesitated as though searching for the next words.

[19] The observations were part of Mr. Scranton's acceptance address to the Association at its twenty-seventh annual convention, Harrisburg, Pennsylvania, October 21, 1966.

[20] *Oxford Translation of Aristotle,* $1414^a–1414^b$, by permission of The Clarendon Press, Oxford; or see *Aristotle's Rhetoric and Poetics,* pp. 199–200.

[21] In what follows I lean heavily on the insights of my former colleague, John F. Wilson, whose consideration of familiar patterns of rhetorical organization is as inclusive as any I know. See John F. Wilson and Carroll C. Arnold, *Public Speaking as a Liberal Art* (Boston: Allyn and Bacon, Inc., 1968), 2nd ed., pp. 224–244.

[22] Excerpted from the full text as published in the New York *Times,* September 4, 1956. Italics added to indicate causally connective phrases. Paragraphing deleted.

[23] This is clear from the fact that the reporter or the editor of the text chose to use paragraph indentation at "But the basic . . . ," and by the fact that the *Times'* text indicated by paragraphing that a thought unit ended at line 17. I think reading the speech without regard to typographical indentations would still suggest that these seventeen lines constitute a thought unit.

[24] For full discussion of the structure see Alan H. Monroe and Douglas Ehninger, *Principles and Types of Speech,* 6th ed. (Glenview, Ill.: Scott, Foresman and Company, 1967), Chapter 16.

[25] Hermann G. Stelzner, " 'War Message,' December 8, 1941: An Approach to Language," *Speech Monographs* 33 (November 1966): 419–437.

[26] Laura Crowell's careful study, "The Building of the 'Four Freedoms' Speech," *Speech Monographs* 22 (November 1955): 266–283, is another critical study of speaking that reveals how structural choices are deliberately made in order to create ultimate forms and hence "direct" the impact of oral rhetoric.

[27] This text was transcribed from an electronic recording made from the telecast debate. Except for what seems appropriate punctuation, typographic suggestions concerning structure have been omitted.

[28] E. H. Adrian, "The Human Receiving System," in *The Languages of Science,* Granada Lectures of the British Association for the Advancement of Science (New York: Basic Books, Inc., 1963), p. 114. My italics.

[29] Paul I. Rosenthal, "The Concept of the Paramessage in Persuasive Communication," *Quarterly Journal of Speech* 58 (February 1972): 30.

[30] More will be said of the power of verbal forms to "argue" in the chapters on style which follow.

Chapter VI

Stylistic Conventions and Norms

When a critic of speaking is satisfied that he understands how content, structures, and emergent forms worked in response to a rhetorical situation, there remain questions about how verbal style and physical presentation modified the impact of what was said. In traditional discussions of style (selection and arrangement of words) and delivery (manner of presentation) the speaker's rather than the critic's concerns have usually been emphasized. Verbal style and nonverbal style are treated as presenting distinct sets of problems. This makes sense when advising composers of rhetoric, for in composing we often think separately about language and about how to present our finished messages. But separating verbal and nonverbal considerations is considerably less realistic when criticism rather than creation of oral rhetoric is in view.

If we examine our experiences as listeners, we will recognize that as long as speaking "goes well," we react in a total way to language, utterance, inflection, and action. We focus on language or on presentation separately only when we perceive something that seems unusual in one or the other. When all elements function conventionally, the languages of words, vocalizations, and actions form a blended flow of meanings. It is that total flow that critics ought ideally to describe, interpret, and evaluate. Unfortunately this is not always possible for at least two reasons: (1) no one knows how to describe these forces as *blended,* unified sources of rhetorical influence, and (2) the nature of our language does not allow us to conceptualize and talk easily about several forces at the same time. For both reasons I shall sometimes deal with verbal and presentational forces together and sometimes deal with them separately in this and the next three chapters. When it seems possible, I shall treat verbal and nonverbal forces together; when they must be written about separately, you, as reader, must remember that from the vantage points of listeners the separation is artificial.

STYLE AS RHETORICAL FORCE

If any verbal or nonverbal behavior works *rhetorically,* it functions as "proof" of something. Remy Kwant would exempt no speech behavior from this "proving" function, and even if we do not choose to go as far as he, his description of what he calls "expression" describes what we have been calling rhetorical speech. Kwant says:

> Because there are many words, our speaking is an analysis, and because these words are connected we make a synthesis. Speech is always both analysis and synthesis, or at least an attempt to analyze and synthesize. . . . One who listens to a complex of linguistic signs and does not succeed in recognizing in it a reference to reality does not have the feeling that he is listening to genuine speech. Speech is essentially intentional, it has to be concerned with something, and what it is concerned with must disclose itself in speech.[1]

The kind of rhetoric we have been discussing always "discloses" something about alleged "reality." That is the way it becomes "suasory." A maker of oral rhetoric chooses *some* words and *some* behaviors from all the words and all the ways of behaving and uses these instead of others because he believes *this* "mix" or set of patterns will achieve what he hopes to achieve with his listeners. He does not do all of this self-consciously, of course. Many of his choices are habitual, the results of conditioning experience. But *selection* is always present in verbal and nonverbal behaviors, else there is no *rhetoric* in the activities. By definition *rhetorical* behaviors purport to analyze reality, represent it purposively, and by that disclosure achieve influence on someone else.

Consider how a rhetorical speaker works, when he is conscious of what he is doing. He tries to create patterns of verbal and nonverbal behaviors that he believes listeners will not mistake. If he is trying to hide meaning, he still functions in the same way. When he tries to *mean* through the English language, he chooses English words and speech patterns and interrelates them according to the "rules" of English grammar and phonetics. Then he "speaks English." In Kwant's terms he "synthesizes" reality according to certain principles his own views and the "rules" of English allow him. But another set of principles guides him also if he speaks rhetorically. Those are the principles —the "rules"—he has extracted from studying his listeners' situational states in relation to his immediate rhetorical purposes. The constraints of the rhetorical situation have to be incorporated with his views and the "rules" of English speech in order to complete the guidelines within which he may "disclose" those aspects of reality which will, he hopes, adjust his ideas to people and people to his ideas. Because he cannot do any of these things randomly and still function rhetorically, *all* his constrained choices must be viewed, in criticism, as parts of the proving or adjusting process that rhetoric is.

A critic of oral rhetoric must try to see whatever he can in all the languages speakers use, and he must attempt to interpret the probable impacts of those choices. No critic will succeed fully in this undertaking, for we understand our uses of verbal and nonverbal languages only partially. No doubt any critic trying to cope with the mysterious influences of stylistic choices ought to be humble when there is so much he will not be able to understand, but no speech critic need be mute. There are limited lines of critical inquiry that will allow critics to produce *some* reasoned explanations of how speakers' stylistic choices probably functioned to influence listeners in specific ways. Some of the understandings and inferences critics can make grow out of the normative conventions that govern the uses of verbal and nonverbal codes.

CONVENTIONAL STRUCTURES IN CODE SYSTEMS

Through the conventions of language systems we communicate what Kwant calls our "analyses" and "syntheses" of reality. Susanne K. Langer has put it thus:

> How are relations expressed in language? . . . We name two items,
> and place the name of a relation between; this means that the relation
> holds the two items together. "Brutus killed Caesar" indicates that
> "killing" holds between Brutus and Caesar. Where the relation is not
> symmetrical, the word-order and the grammatical forms . . . of the
> words symbolize its direction. "Brutus killed Caesar" means some-
> thing different from "Caesar killed Brutus," and "Killed Caesar
> Brutus" is not a sentence at all. The word-order partly determines the
> sense of the structure.[2]

Some linguistic patterns, like the word order in "Brutus killed
Caesar," are utterly commonplace. They do little more than denote
the analysis that has been made. Other patterns are no less
conventional but convey special meanings. For example, a conventional but rare way of putting words together can give an idea
special significance with those who notice the structure. Why is
John F. Kennedy's "Ask not what your country can do for you—
ask what you can do for your country" still quoted? No doubt
because the thought is noble, but also because the verbal convention, "Ask not," is specially "reserved" in English. "Do not ask" and
"don't ask" *mean* differently. The "ask not" structure seems to be
saved for a special kind of *command* about asking. It says something like: "You are to make a special commitment when you
suppress your impulse to ask."

Speech influences through thousands of commonplace and
"reserved" verbal and nonverbal conventions; but unfortunately
for critics, study of these oral conventions is in its infancy. Among
the general statements critics can make about the effects of
distinctive verbal and nonverbal patterns, the following one has
empirical and common-sense support: *The commonest pattern
of verbal or nonverbal behavior an audience knows will convey
the least meaning over and beyond what the words or acts literally
denote.* The verbal or nonverbal pattern an audience finds unusual
or views as a "reserved" convention is the one that injects extra
meanings into a message.

One implication of this principle is that speakers will communicate special meanings if they use certain conventions more
frequently or less frequently than is typical in a given rhetorical
situation. "Unusualness" of this sort may be conscious or unconscious, but it will send out its special meanings in either case—
even subliminally. Below are three instances in which extra-
denotative meanings were communicated by the mere presence
or absence of commonplace verbal patterns.

In the first instance critical discovery of extra-denotative
meaning depends on the critic's recognition that most people use

many sensory images in talk. Even a little-educated speaker is apt to speak metaphorically of the weather as "chilly" or "scorching," of someone in a dilemma as "between a rock and a hard place," and so on. Rhetorical theory posits that such images evoke extra *feeling* because vicarious sensory experience is triggered. In the instance at which we shall look first, a critic noticed that the colorful British Prime Minister, Disraeli, used these ordinary, sensory images seldom. The critical argument runs that this habit of omission is one explanation for the fact that nineteenth-century listeners frequently said that Disraeli seemed "aloof," "cool," and "Oriental." On this point the critic wrote the following.

> When the author-statesman made use of figurative language, the intellectualism of his speech style was not relieved. Said one of his biographers, "He had not enough of nature in him, he lived too perpetually in abstract plans and schemes, to be able to distil a beautiful or poetic side from sensuous life."
>
> Disraeli's metaphors were weighted with subtle, intellectual connotations, skillfully planned and suggestively delivered. Manchester [the city] was "the fatal author of these pernicious principles," the support of whose doctrines was merely "mimetic" on the part of the Liberal Government. Peel was the sort of parliamentarian who "traces the steam-engine always back to the tea kettle. His precedents are generally tea-kettle precedents." A few moments later, the detractor found the Minister "a great Parliamentary middleman . . . [who] bamboozles one party and plunders the other. . . ."
>
> In an effort to determine to what extent sense perceptions and intellection were bases of Disraeli's metaphorical comparisons I have carefully examined eighty-four extended, metaphorical passages from seventeen speeches delivered between 1843 and 1850. Of these examples, seventy are exclusively based upon abstract comparatives. In ten examples the comparisons rest upon sense-perceived qualities, while in four instances the intellectual or abstract elements of comparison [are] . . . intermingled with sensuous elements. There seems, then, ample evidence to justify Brandes' generalization that Disraeli touched the abstract and the intellectual much more frequently than the sensuous.[3]

Here is another instance of critical inference based on a speaker's deviation from "ordinary" linguistic practices. Of a passage from Ralph Waldo Emerson's lecture-essay, "The American Scholar," W. Ross Winterowd wrote:

> Because of the dearth of relative clauses and the absence of subordinate clauses, he cannot qualify ideas through predication and he cannot employ the standard tool of argument, the enthymeme. (In fact, one

notes that Emerson's sentences tend to be maxims in the Aristotelian sense.) [4]

Most people use a good many modifiers and qualifying clauses in their talk. Extensively used, these conventions make talk seem cautious. (See the discussion of Theodore Roosevelt below, pp. 169–182). Winterowd noticed that Emerson seldom used these verbal patterns and asked himself what under-use of the patterns must have done to Emerson's overall communication. The effect is, says Winterowd, that Emerson could claim but he could scarcely argue in the usual sense.

Richard M. Ohmann drew critical inferences about George Bernard Shaw's written prose in ways easily applied to speakers. Ohmann found Shaw putting items in series and phrasing the series in parallel constructions. Ohmann asked himself what extra meanings these language habits would communicate and what they might "tell" about Shaw's habits of mind. Ohmann concluded:

> Even in . . . amorphous parallelism . . . *formal similarity pleads the cause of semantic similarity,* and witnesses a preference for discourse ordered through equivalence.
> The writer who builds a serial structure chooses each successive number with an eye trained on likenesses; he emphasizes the process of selection . . . by reiterating linguistic elements that are formally identical and close to each other in meaning. It hardly seems too much to conjecture that these parallelisms take form under an impulse toward similarity.[5]

By asking what commonplace linguistic conventions each speaker or writer used constantly and what conventions he used seldom, Arnold, Winterowd, and Ohmann believe they located special meanings that their communicators conveyed to audiences. What impelled these critics to look at communications in these ways? Arnold was seeking to explain listeners' known reactions to Disraeli's speaking, and a biographer's clue led him to study Disraeli's use of conventional kinds of images. Winterowd was professionally interested in the relations between grammar and rhetoric; that interest led him to look intensively at Emerson's grammatical constructions. His discovery allowed him to reason out how Emerson must have *seemed*, rhetorically. Ohmann worked in the opposite direction. He suspected Shaw was "a similarity seeker." [6] Following his "hunch," he found Shaw used series and parallel constructions more frequently than a number of his contemporaries. Ohmann then reasoned about what heavy use of these conventional structures (1) might signify about the way Shaw thought, and (2) might communicate specially to readers.

Any of these ways of thinking can be useful in stylistic-presentational criticism: look for explanations for listeners' known reactions, study patterns generally and then reason out their probable rhetorical consequences, or check up on hunches about "what's going on" by gathering evidence and reasoning out probable rhetorical consequences. Theory, records of listeners' responses, or hypotheses can help one toward explanations of the usual and the unusual in either verbal or nonverbal behaviors. For example, experimental evidence suggests that only what seems to listeners a trifle unusual will be interpreted as having special meaning. Apply that theoretical proposition to nonverbal behaviors. "Desk-thumping" is rare in contemporary American speaking. One may infer that a constant "desk-thumper" will be specially noticed. What interpretations are listeners likely to make about him? Certainly that something unusual is going on—perhaps reflecting "too much heat" but in any case distracting. Or consider another example. There is in general American speech a vocal pattern in which a statement begins at a moderately high pitch, but pitch lowers step-by-step to the end of the statement or series of statements. It is an inflectional pattern that tends to be associated with expression of reverence or other serious emotion. To its overuse our folklore has even given a nickname: "preacher's whine" or the variant, "stained-glass window whine." Apparently people unselfconsciously know this pattern is a conventional, vocal indication of special emotionality, and they have a sense of when the pattern "belongs" and when it does not. Some (perhaps church-goers?) seem to have invented a slang phrase by which to distinguish its "natural" use from the monotonous or pretentious. The process is, of course, precisely the kind of analytical process through which a speech critic goes in forming judgments on how nonverbal patterns *mean* specially. Whether one seeks to understand verbal, vocal, or gestural behaviors, the critical process is the same: (a) one tries to sense what is usual, hence not specially noticed; (b) one looks for the *prominent* and for the *conspicuously absent* features of the speech he is inspecting; (c) one tries to reason out what the prominent and conspicuously absent features might suggest to listeners in their rhetorical situation; and (d) one draws whatever inferences he can defend concerning the relations of these aspects of style to the speaker's overall meaning.

These steps sound abstract, but they are less so in practice. Using Kennedy's inaugural address as a critical object, you can soon establish your competence to work in the ways just suggested. The full text of the address appears on pages 312–315. Audio and audio-video recordings of the speech exist. If you can secure one of these, you can come closer to explaining why many people thought this President was a "charismatic" speaker.

As a first step in criticism, look carefully at paragraphs 22–27. You will see that certain verbal patterns occur again and again. Notice how often ideas are set in *paralleled* and *balanced* structures and how often there are *antitheses* and other contrastive forms like "not . . . but" and "this . . . or that." Reflect next on what these conventional, structural devices *say* about the items that are balanced. Refer to Ohmann's theory cited on p. 146. Now, consider antitheses and "this . . . or that" forms. What do the structures *say* about the items set in opposition? Reverse Ohmann's theory.

When you have thought about these theoretical possibilities, consider the rhetorical situation of a modern, inaugural address, and consider further what John F. Kennedy added to that kind of situation. Would any special meanings be suggested by the comparative and contrastive phrasings because they came to a national audience from a youngish President who had narrowly won election on such slogans as, "We can do better" and "Let's get this country moving again"?

If you can secure a recording of the speech, you will be able to consider the further, special meanings Kennedy gave his balances and contrasts by changing the intensity of his voice, by shifting pitches, and by varying the lengths of pauses. Ask yourself the same questions about these nonverbal behaviors. You will probably find yourself almost involuntarily going through the four phases of critical analysis and judgment that seemed remote when stated in the abstract. You are likely to arrive at judgments that provide a bit of explanation for words like "charisma" and "the Kennedy image," used during this President's time in office.

There are other aspects of "the Kennedy style" which you can discover for yourself by similar critical processes. One clue: The passage printed as paragraphs 22–27, pp. 314–315, has sometimes been compared to Lincoln's "Second Inaugural Address." There are good reasons. Most are nonverbal. Can you find them?

SOME NORMATIVE VERBAL PATTERNS

I have been implying that users of a language know and understand the language alike. This is only partly true. A great many symbols and rules must be shared, or a language cannot be one in which people can communicate; but it is also true that there are dialects of virtually all "standard" languages. Nonetheless, in criticism we first have to know something about what is "normal" for the language community we study. If we do not know the normative patterns, we can make no differentiations among behaviors that will be "easy," "difficult," "clear," "obscure," "appropriate," and "inappropriate" for the generality of those who use the language.

The most basic normative patterns of any language are those dictated by its grammar—its "rules of the language game." Thus, some guidelines for speech critics can be built up if we think about what makes spoken English "easy" or "difficult" for users of "standard" English.

GENERAL GRAMMATICAL PATTERNING

A way to put a critic's general question about overall grammatical structure in speech is this: *Does the grammatical structure tie ideas together tightly and clearly, or have we sprawling, complicated structure that will make it difficult for users of standard English to grasp relationships swiftly?* To distinguish the "tight and clear" from the "sprawling" and "complicated" we have to know what "simple" *is,* in the structure of English. That is not very hard to discover, for there are only a few basic structures that a "kernel statement" may have in our language.*

If a statement is declarative and in the active voice, it has this basic form:

Noun Phrase (NP)—Verb Phrase (VP)— Noun Phrase (NP) *or*
Predicate Modifier (PM)

Only a few variations from this structure are allowed by the rules of the language. This simplest, therefore clearest, structure may occur in these ways:

---

*I shall define a kernel statement as the subject-verb-object-or-modifier element of any main clause. This definition and several propositions to follow are not acceptable as linguistic science for they are too simplified and too little qualified to describe English accurately as a linguistic system. However, a critic of speaking is more interested in *impressions created* by structures than in the technical natures of those structures. The simplified explanations presented here deal with how language *seems* when heard; they do not purport to explain what English *is* as a system of vocabulary and rules.

NP   VP NP   NP VP PM   NP   VP PM
George hit Bob.   Susan is lovely.   The route is long.

 NP   VP   NP   NP   VP
The dog bit the man. The dog ran.

You probably encountered these variants of NP–VP–NP or PM
when you began to learn to read. You may have begun with: "I
see Jane. Jane sees me. Jane runs. Jane is well." Later, you learned
two commonplace alternatives to this basic form, one for asking
questions and the other for talking in the passive voice:

               VP NP   PM   PM VP NP
For questions: Is Jane here?   Where is Jane?

                    VP
                  /   \
                 NP   PM
               Are you coming now?

For the passive voice:

         NP   VP   NP   NP   VP
        Jane was bitten by the dog.   The house is built
         NP   VP
        The work has been done.

At its simplest, English goes: NP—VP or NP—VP—NP or NP—
VP—PM or in questioning some part of the Verb Phrase gets first
position in the utterance. One can complicate these simple structures and build around them in many ways, but the essential
point is that all additions and modifications that affect the basic
forms of kernel statements make understanding more difficult for
users of English. In this fact lies a speech critic's norm for
evaluating the probable clarity or difficulty of grammatical
patterning. If a critic of English speech believes talk was meant to
be clear, he should examine the kernel structures of what was
said, applying the norm that the closer those structures are to
their basic forms, the clearer the grammar is.

Clearest relations of ideas are conveyed when the four forms
identified above are not interrupted by having added language
inserted between the elements of the kernels. "George, who is a
friend of mine, came home" is harder to grasp than "George is
a friend of mine. He came home." But, of course, the Dick-and-Jane
forms become monotonous. And these forms can generate inac-

curacy because the things talked about may be much more complicated than Dick-and-Jane structures allow one to say. Also, sheer grammatical clarity is not the only ideal speech needs to fulfill. A critic must weigh the value of clarity against other values such as interestingness, accuracy, emphasis, humor—even a speaker's wish to be somewhat ambiguous, as in a press conference. The weighing of these values can be guided by this general principle: *Complications of kernel structures tend to obscure meanings; therefore, variations from basic grammatical structures ought to be justified by evidence that the resulting rhetorical gains are worth more than the clarity that was lost.* This is a harsh but fair principle, given the inefficiency of listening. "I see Jane. She sees me. Do you see her?" are the clearest ways we can say things. But it is possible to be clear enough and to say things more interestingly and, perhaps, more accurately, through modifying the basic forms. Our principle simply says that when speakers sacrifice grammatical clarity without injecting compensating elements of interest and accuracy, they compose their ideas less clearly than they might.

To get at the quality of grammatical clarity, a critic needs to analyze the language of speech in some detail, but ordinarily it is not necessary to analyze *all* statements. It is usually enough to make systematic samplings such as we shall illustrate in the next chapter when we apply grammatical and other norms in actual analysis.

CHOICE AND USE OF WORDS

Whatever his grammatical strategies, a speaker's choices of words can affect listeners' ease of understanding. We know that a speaker's level of vocabulary can affect intelligibility, but it is an awkward fact that we do not have very precise norms of listening ease as it is affected by word choice. Most research on vocabulary in relation to ease of understanding has focused on ease in *reading.* Norms of listening ease must therefore be inferred from what we know of reading ease.

Pioneering research on reading ease was done a quarter of a century ago by Dr. Rudolf Flesch. Most later investigations have focused on prose less comparable to oral rhetoric than the journalism which occupied Flesch's attention.[7] It therefore seems wisest to infer what we can from Flesch's work.

Flesch's analyses of journalistic writing were based on three suppositions about the relations between choice of words and clarity and interestingness. His suppositions were:

1. A unit of thought is easy to understand in inverse proportion to its length, measured in words.
2. The most easily intelligible part of any word is the etymological root; syllables added to that root modify its meaning and so increase the difficulty of understanding the word.
3. References to persons and to relationships people can have to one another increase interestingness; there is some positive relationship between the numbers of such references and the ease and interestingness that receivers will sense on being exposed to a message.[8]

If we apply the first of Flesch's suppositions to speech, we face the difficulty that it is harder to say what a "unit of thought" is in speech than in written, punctuated prose. A writer usually signals what his "units" of thought are by punctuating, indenting, and otherwise using space, color, type size, and so on. However, listeners must grasp "units" and "divisions" of meaning from subtler, more fleeting signals. They can infer what "thought units" are from grammatical constructions, distributions of pauses, vocal inflections, changes in vocal and physical intensity, and from gestural movements; but interpretation of these signals is subject to a good deal of error. Anyone who has tried to write out the "text" of tape-recorded speech knows that deciding what-goes-with-what is often arbitrary. Nevertheless, as listeners, we all *do* decide that "This is related to that and that to those." We have to, else we cannot understand or even *mis*understand what is said. No matter how subtle, fleeting, and ambiguous the aural signs of pattern may be, people use them as definers of "units" of meaning because they have no other choice.

There is no reason to think critics are less able to perceive aurally marked off thought units than ordinary listeners. The rule is not to try to be too subtle. A conscientious critic will try to respond to language as an observant but typical listener with an important difference. The difference will be that he will apply criteria like Flesch's first supposition. Flesch reasoned that the more ideas a reader or listener has to keep track of before finding out what they "add up to," the harder it will be for him to understand what was said. The concept is consistent with what has already been said about grammatical structures, for complicated grammatical constructions are usually longer than simple ones. So a critic can combine the two conceptions into a single criterion as he listens in his special way: *Length and/or complexity of thought units are likely to obstruct understanding.*

The second of Flesch's suppositions is a valuable refinement of cruder bits of rhetorical advice. "Stick to simple Anglo-Saxon words" and "Don't use 'big' words" are commonplace counsels, but their advice is only partly sound. *Bicycle* is a familiar word, and it's not a "big" word. It's not an Anglo-Saxon word either; it is a combination of French and Greek syllables! But one would hardly trouble an English-speaking listener by using the word, bicycle. On the other hand, *gammon* is one letter shorter than *bicycle,* and it derives from Old English. But what does it mean? The point is that neither length nor derivation per se makes words difficult. Words become "difficult" for subtler reasons, as Flesch explains:

> Language gadgets . . . are of two kinds: Words by themselves, like *against,* and parts of words (affixes), like *dis-.* The more harmful of the two for plain talk are the affixes, since the reader or hearer cannot understand what the gadget does to the sentence before he has disentangled it from the word it is attached to. Each affix burdens his mind with two jobs: first, he has to split up the word into its parts, and, second, he has to rebuild the sentence from these parts. To do this does not even take a split second, of course; but it adds up.[9]

I suggest that if increasing the numbers of modifying syllables attached to root meanings can make *written* material seem difficult, this must be even more true for hurried listeners. In listening there can be little "review" of words, so the reconstructions Flesch speaks of will be still more difficult. This does not mean that affixes are to be avoided; it simply means that as a speaker uses affixed words he ought to be sure what he gains in meaning outweighs whatever he loses in ease of understanding.* Or, he ought to compensate for the difficulty of his terms by adopting other rhetorical strategies that ease understanding in different ways: repetition, variations in vocal force, meaningful alterations of rate, parallel constructions, etc.

---

* I am using "affix" to mean any syllabic addition placed before or after a root to modify that root's meaning. This is substantially Flesch's definition, though in oral communication I would include elements of compound words as affixes. Such affixes as I am thinking of include: *ab*hor, *anti*climax, *ir*-resist*ible, sum*-total, *sup*pose, *super*sonic, *trust*buster, *universal,* with*out,* etc. Flesch apparently excluded elements of compound words on grounds that the eye sees them as *two* words (e.g., sum-total, sun bath). I argue that the ear would not distinguish run-together forms or hyphenated forms from typographically separated forms (sun bath); hence, any additions of meanings achieved in any way would, I think, be complicating for listeners. Unfortunately there is no research on this matter.

Flesch's third supposition applies to speech with little adaptation. He assumes that humans are uniquely interested in other humans and in the relationships animate beings can have toward one another. Flesch inferred from this premise that as references to people and human relationships increase in number, the interest potential of prose increases. His confirmations of this inference come chiefly from studies of writing and reading. IIe found that 10 personal references per 100 words of journalistic prose was characteristic of "fairly easy" language and was readily intelligible to about 80 percent of American readers. These calculations are not necessarily true for contemporary spoken prose, but they suggest a rough standard by which to discriminate "personalized" from "impersonal" discourse, insofar as those qualities depend on vocabulary alone.*

SUMMARY

This chapter has presented elemental ways of thinking critically about verbal and nonverbal languages as elements of rhetorical proof. Whether criticism focuses on verbal, nonverbal, or both kinds of patterns, the basic critical process remains the same. The critic:

1. Tries to identify the usual within the language system.
2. Identifies especially prominent and conspicuously absent features of a speaker's use of the language.
3. Attempts to discover what these prominences and absences probably communicated within the rhetorical situation.
4. Infers major relationships between specific communications of stylistic elements and overall meaning of the speaking.

---

* In measuring personalization Flesch counted proper names of people or animals, all personal pronouns referring to people or personalized things such as ships and countries, and all names identifying human beings' qualities and relationships to others; e.g., man, woman, child, girl, father, aunt, husband, parent, guy, kid, friend, dame, etc. For purposes of criticism it seems chiefly important to compare speakers according to identical lists of such terms, worrying less about the particular terms in the list than about observing the general principle that names and references to human relationships contribute communicative human interest and ease of understanding. As I shall show, comparisons of speakers' uses of personalizing strategies can and often do go beyond mere use of such terms as Flesch chose to consider.

Concerning verbal style it has been proposed that the following features deserve special consideration when a critic explores the rhetorical potentialities of verbal language:

1. Relative lengths of thought units.
2. Complexity of basic kernel structures.
3. Types of metaphors consistently present or absent.
4. Repetition or absence of serial, balanced, and antithetical constructions.
4. Presence or absence of sensory and/or intellectual images.
6. Presence of affixes modifying the meanings of "roots" of words.
7. Presence of terms referring to persons and relations of animate beings, especially humans.

In the next chapter I shall try to illustrate some of the significant descriptive and evaluative information about speaking which is revealed by investigating aspects of verbal style by these methods.

NOTES

[1] Remy C. Kwant, *Phenomenology of Expression,* trans. Henry J. Koren (Pittsburgh: Duquesne University Press, 1969), pp. 119–120.

[2] Susanne K. Langer, *Philosophy in a New Key* (New York: New American Library of World Literature, Inc., 1951), pp. 71–72.

[3] Carroll C. Arnold, "The Speech Style of Benjamin Disraeli," *Quarterly Journal of Speech* 33 (December 1947): 433–434. The biographer referred to is Georg Brandes, author of *Lord Beaconsfield.*

[4] W. Ross Winterowd, *Rhetoric: A Synthesis* (New York: Holt, Rinehart and Winston, Inc., 1968), p. 95.

[5] Richard M. Ohmann, *Shaw: The Style and the Man* (Middletown: The Wesleyan University Press, 1962), p. 13. Italics are mine.

[6] *Ibid.,* p. 4.

[7] Flesch's *The Art of Plain Talk* (New York: Harper and Brothers, 1946) remains available in current editions and is worth any writer's, speaker's, or critic's careful attention. His formulae for evaluating the clarity and interestingness of writing are still used, along with others, in communication research, but his caution is one every speech critic should follow: "What I hope for are readers who won't take the formula too seriously and won't expect from it more than a rough estimate." More important, wrote Flesch, are "the principles of plain English" (p. xii).

[8] Each of these statements is my interpretation of the theory upon which Flesch seems to have formulated his measures of "plain talk" (actually writing). Each supposition is supported by empirical research and by everyday experience. It must not be supposed, however, that ease and clarity are either the only virtues verbal style should have or that all situations demand that Flesch's principles *alone* be met.

[9] Flesch, *The Art of Plain Talk,* p. 42. Notice how carefully Flesch observes the implications of his three suppositions about how to be clear and "easy."

Chapter VII

Analysis of Verbal Style

In this chapter we shall make some critical experiments upon parts of three speech texts. The object will be to discover what we can learn about the speeches by applying the lines of criticism suggested in chapter VI. We shall look in detail at the first fifty thought units of Leonard Bernstein's "The World of Jazz," Theodore Roosevelt's "The Man with the Muck-Rake," and Leon Zellner's "What Can We Prove about God?" The full text of each speech is presented in Appendix A, offering you opportunity to develop your own analyses and evaluations of the total communications. As we apply the critical norms previously discussed, we shall find ourselves stimulated toward new kinds of inquiry which have not been formally raised in preceding chapters. This natural broadening of critical insights is experience that demonstrates the impossibility of doing creative criticism by "rule" and that alone.

The three speeches at which we shall look were made in different periods of modern American history, in different rhetorical situations, by very different kinds of people: a President of the United States, a distinguished musician, and a college student. The differences among the rhetorical situations addressed and the responsibilities of the speakers will give us opportunity to test the critical methods of chapter VI on what should be diverse kinds of oral rhetoric. To each we shall address the seven kinds of inquiry summarized at the close of chapter VI, trying to think always about what "normal" linguistic behavior would be, what is conspicuous about each speaker's linguistic behavior, what these behaviors might communicate to listeners, and how the behaviors might modify the major impact of each speaker's content and structure.

RELATIVE LENGTHS OF THOUGHT UNITS

The first task in looking at verbal style in oral rhetoric is to discover what the aural "thought units" were *as heard*. This involves subjective judgments. Not everyone would identify the aural thought units of any speaking in just the same ways, but this is not a grave matter. If a critic examines the same kinds of units in all oral rhetoric, his comparisons will be reasonably consistent and probably informative. To help me in making my decisions I have listened to phonographic recordings of short political speeches by Roosevelt (there is no sound recording of "The Man with the Muck-Rake") and listened to sound recordings of the other two speeches. In each case I have tried to conjecture (for Roosevelt) and perceive (for Bernstein and Zellner) how vocal and verbal signals defined what linguistic units "went together." A critic working without any auditory image of the speaking he studied would, of course, have to depend still more on speculation, but he would not be prevented from making *comparative* analyses of thought units suggested by speech texts.

As soon as a critic has identified what he believes were the aural thought units of a communication he can make swift, overall calculations about the relative lengths of those units, at different points in one communication or within separate communications he wants to compare. My calculation is that the first fifty thought units of Bernstein's, Roosevelt's, and Zellner's speeches contain the following numbers of words:

	Total No. of Words in First 50 Units
Bernstein	526
Zellner	734
Roosevelt	917

These totals, by themselves, suggest a tentative critical inference: Roosevelt *may* have been difficult for his listeners to understand. But mere length of thought units cannot tell a clear story. If Roosevelt was exceedingly careful about the grammatical structures of his longish units, he may not have strained his listeners seriously. If Bernstein consistently cluttered his relatively brief units, brevity may not have helped much.

COMPLEXITY OF GRAMMATICAL STRUCTURES

It is seldom necessary for speech critics to work as expert grammarians or linguists would. Exponents of generative grammar, stratificational grammar, structural grammar, and traditional grammar can give unique and useful analyses of prose or poetry, but speech critics are chiefly interested in how grammatical structures would *seem* to hurried listeners and how those structures were suited to the overall demands of the rhetorical situations in question. The simple, speech-oriented, grammatical analysis discussed in chapter VI is a way of making quick descriptions, but what norms ought to be applied in a given situation has to be decided by reflection. One can begin with this premise: Speakers do and should adopt different levels of grammatical complexity as they move from situation to situation.

Robert F. Terwilliger contends that listeners "set" themselves to take in different levels of grammatical subtlety and that what they are "set" for determines what kind of grammatical structuring will be clear and satisfying:

> Fries has indicated that a vocabulary of only a few hundred words would allow one to understand most of the telephone conversations which take place in normal circumstances. A further analysis would unquestionably show that the sentences of these conversations were quite short, and that they were grammatically simple. The use of subjunctive clauses, parenthetical remarks, and the like is quite rare in such conversations. If someone introduces a complex sentence into a situation such as that, one thing will almost invariably result— the listener will say, "What did you say?" The unexpected—in this case the grammatically unusual—is not understood and a repetition is required for the listener to comprehend it.
>
> In other situations, the style of language may be totally different. In professional speaking and writing, for instance, sentence complexity is not only usual, it is even "required." [1]

If one accepts Terwilliger's notion, investigation into grammatical clarity needs to be preceded by a decision on the question: "What does what I know about the rhetorical situation indicate about the level of grammatical sophistication for which most listeners would be 'set'?"

My judgment is that Bernstein, Zellner, and Roosevelt ought to have aimed for grammatical simplicity. Bernstein addressed a national television audience at a popular hour; Roosevelt spoke to a general audience at a dedication but expected his remarks to be printed in popular newspapers; Zellner addressed a small, academically mixed, college audience in a basic speech course. If any situation allowed more complexity than others, it was Zellner's. His listeners were in college and were used to hearing fairly complicated discussion in classrooms. Still, not even Zellner would err if he kept fairly close to the norms of conversational grammar: short statements, simply constructed. Applying such a situational analysis, the critical norm becomes: Simple structures were desirable; complexity was a stylistic fault.

Usually a critic need not study every grammatical structure in the rhetoric he is analyzing. He wants to know only whether the speaker *tended* to behave one way or another. Sampling is ordinarily an adequate way of gathering the information one needs. One could analyze every tenth thought unit or look at randomly selected units or choose a number of samples in some special way. I propose to use the special way of sampling. We want to know whether our speakers *compensated* for longish thought units. Accordingly, I propose to look at the five *longest* thought units in the first fifty units of each speech. If this does not give reasonable grounds for a critical judgment, the sample can be increased until a defensible conclusion is possible.

Experiments have established that statements are more difficult to understand if qualifying language occurs *between subjects and predicates*. For example, the form NP—qualifier—VP is the hardest of all kernel structures to understand. Not quite as much difficulty is created if qualifying language occurs between verb phrases and their objects or predicate modifiers (e.g., NP—VP—qualifier—NP or PM). But the complex construction that is easiest to understand is one in which qualifying language comes either before a tight kernel structure or after the completed kernel. These generalizations constitute criteria of "difficulty" to be used as we look at what each of our three speakers did.

Here are diagrams of the five longest among Leonard Bernstein's first fifty units of speech:

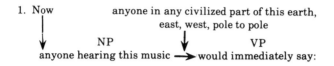

1. Now   anyone in any civilized part of this earth,
                                    east, west, pole to pole

            NP   VP
   anyone hearing this music ──→ would immediately say:

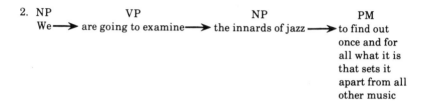

2. NP   VP   NP   PM
   We ──→ are going to examine ──→ the innards of jazz ──→ to find out
                                                           once and for
                                                           all what it is
                                                           that sets it
                                                           apart from all
                                                           other music

3.   PM

   ──→ all the way from the earliest Blues to Dixieland
       bands, to Charleston bands, to Swing bands, to
       Boogie-Woogie, to crazy bop, to Mambo—and much more.[2]

4. I suppose

        NP   VP   PM
        it ──→ is due ──→ to the fact that historically the
                          players of music seemed to lack the
                          dignity of the composers of
5. Perhaps   music
          NP   VP   PM
        this objection ──→ stems ──→ from the irremedial situation
                                     of what is after all a kind of
                                     brass band playing in a room
                                     too small for it

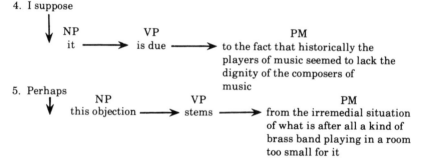

The diagrams show only *one* interruption of the basic NP—VP—NP or PM form. "Anyone in any civilized part of this earth, east, west, pole to pole" intervenes between the noun phrase functioning as subject ("anyone hearing this music") and the verb phrase ("would immediately say").[3] This long interruption presumably burdened listeners somewhat. In fact, it is the interruption that makes this one of the longest thought units in the early part of Bernstein's talk! But in units 2, 4, and 5 the simple, easy NP—VP—NP or PM form is followed. And the long modifying phrase identified as unit 3 was the end of a tight kernel statement:

NP	VP	NP	PM
it	covers	a multitude of sounds	all the way from. . . .

So, in four of Bernstein's five *longest* thought units the speaker gave his listeners the easiest grammar he could.

Though we cannot be certain our text for Roosevelt is perfect, let us assume it is accurate. We get a decidedly different picture upon analyzing Roosevelt's five longest thought units:

1. in the need for the housing of the Government

   but   of the way in which
   NP   VP   NP   the Nation has
   This growth → is → a proof   grown
                      and an example
                                                  and the sphere of
                                                  action of the Na-
                                                  tional Government
                                                  has grown

2. who never does anything else,   not a help to society,
   who never thinks or speaks or   not an incitement to good, but
   But   writes, save of his feats with
            the muckrake, speedily
      NP   VP   NP
      the man → becomes → one of the most potent
                          forces for evil

3. against those who make indiscriminate assault upon men in
   business or men in public life,

   NP   VP   NP
   One of the → is → that they invite a reaction which is
   chief counts   sure to tell powerfully in favor of the
                     unscrupulous scoundrel who really
                     ought to be attacked,

4. and, unfortunately,   instead of taking the form
                           of punishment of those guilty
                           of the excess,
               NP   VP   PM
               the reaction → is → very apt to take the form
                                   either of punishment of
                                   the unoffending or of giving
                                   immunity, and even
                                   strength, to offenders

5. As an instance   encountered in getting the
   in point, I may   right type of men to dig the
   mention that   Panama Canal

   ↓ one serious difficulty → is → the certainty that they
                                     will be exposed, both
                                     without, and, I am sorry
                                     to say, sometimes within,
                                     Congress, to utterly reck-
                                     less assaults on their
                                     character and capacity

One value of analyzing speakers' verbal patterns is that we sometimes discover probable reasons for the reactions we know other people had to the speaking. We saw this in the case of Disraeli. Here, our diagrams give a similar set of explanations. In the passage below Murphy explains what some reactions were to Roosevelt's speaking; our diagrams show how Roosevelt probably created some of those reactions, and Murphy's quotation from Roosevelt himself tells *why* he behaved linguistically as he did. Murphy says:

> Let us examine his use of the sentence, the phrase, and the word. He was a master of what Mark Sullivan called "the balanced and cushioned" sentence, the use of which Sullivan considered an "intellectual habit with him." The pattern consisted of a bold assertion, later so conditioned that the first force was curtailed or redirected. . . . "I see our President has been making another 'Yes, I guess not' speech on business, corporations, etc.," observed Grover Cleveland during one of Roosevelt's speaking tours. But it was Mr. Dooley who really took off Roosevelt's balanced sentence in a monologue:
>
>> "Th' thrusts," says he to himself, "are heejous monsthers built up be th' inlightened intherprise iv th' men that have done so much to advance progress in our beloved counthry," he says. "On wan hand I wud stamp thim undher fut; on th' other hand not so fast."
>
> The balanced structure was commonly regarded as a skillful device for advocating both sides at the same time. . . . But the designer of the form had his own explanation, which he once made to Lincoln Steffens:
>
>> I try to put the whole truth in each sentence; that is, if I propound a proposition I back hard against it all that conditions it. And the reason for this habit is that I've found out how one sentence quoted without context can be made to stab back and hurt me.[4]

The diagrams of the five longest thought units in Roosevelt's first fifty units show that Roosevelt did, indeed, "back hard" against his kernel structures "all that conditions" them. Of course, ease of understanding suffered and, as Murphy's citations show, this qualifying style opened Roosevelt to charges of evasiveness and self-contradiction. We cannot say that these prices were too high for protection against misquotation, but we can say what verbal habits made understanding difficult and opened an avenue of attack to his political critics. Because our analytical findings support and explain listeners' views, we also have a minor proof that our text is representative of Roosevelt's speaking.

An especially interesting side question about Roosevelt's style is this: Was there any way he could protect himself against misquotation and still maintain kernel structures as clear as Bernstein's? Or is it the case that a natural penalty of being clear in this way will always be that important qualifications become easily forgotten *ground* while the clear kernels of statements remain blunt *figures?*

When Zellner's five longest thought units are analyzed, the college student seems to stand between Bernstein and Roosevelt in grammatical clarity.

1. What I'm going to try to show is that

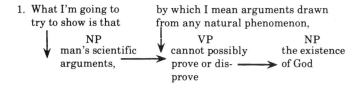

2. So, what I'm trying to show you is that

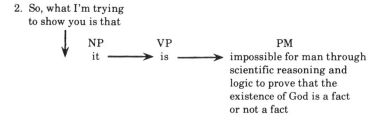

3. However, I'd like you to keep always in mind that

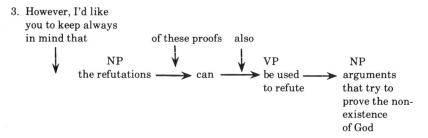

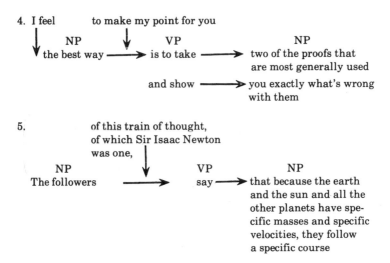

4. I feel   to make my point for you

         NP   VP   NP

the best way ⟶ is to take ⟶ two of the proofs that are most generally used

and show ⟶ you exactly what's wrong with them

5.

of this train of thought, of which Sir Isaac Newton was one,

   NP   VP   NP

The followers ⟶ say ⟶ that because the earth and the sun and all the other planets have specific masses and specific velocities, they follow a specific course

These diagrams show that Zellner interrupted the kernels in four of his five longest thought units. Twice (1 and 4) the verb phrases were slightly complicated by being double. In general it is difficult to see that Zellner gained anything by his kernel interruptions, but compared to Roosevelt's, Zellner's interruptions are not extreme.

The above experiments with simple grammatical analysis add justification to the conclusion hinted at when the numbers of words in fifty thought units were calculated (p. 157): Insofar as grammatical simplicity in long thought units can contribute to ease of understanding, Bernstein was markedly the "easiest" stylist of the three speakers. Roosevelt was decidedly most complex. He not only extended his thought units but further complicated them by difficult patterns of qualification. Zellner does, indeed, fall between Bernstein and Roosevelt on these criteria of simplicity.

METAPHORS, BALANCES, ANTITHESES, AND IMAGES

Mere quantitative information about numbers of metaphors, balances, antitheses, and images is not very helpful. We do not know much about a speaker's oral rhetoric if we know he used 17 metaphors, 10 balanced and 5 antithetical constructions, and 6 sensory images per 100 words. Such information tells us only that he probably would have been less interesting if he had used none of these. A critic needs to inspect such sources of interest for their quality and for what I can only call their "flavor." To do this, it is often helpful to pull these special stylistic forms out of their contexts so that they can be looked at as groups of terms. The qualities the terms share can be *seen* if we can look at them, and nothing else.

Use of this critical practice shows some significant things about the styles of Bernstein, Roosevelt, and Zellner. My own analyses of these features of the first fifty thought units of each speech come out thus.

Bernstein

Metaphors	*Balances* [5]	*Antitheses*
innards	(the series	pole . . . pole
robustness	enumerating	east . . . west
hard-boiled	types of	not through . . . but approaching
sticky	jazz)	robust . . . self-pitying
pain in it		gayest . . . pain
fools around		Haydn . . . dances
shadow of indignity		Verdi . . . fishermen
		jazz . . . Sousa marches
		loud . . . delicate
		improvisation . . . composition
		is not art . . . is art

Sensory Images [6]	*Intellectual Images*
this earth	historical approach
jazz (repeated)	expression (repeated)
innards	humor
sounds	entertainment
(types of jazz)	low-class (repeated)
sad	indignity-dignity (repeated)
happy	earthy
robustness	composition
hard-boiled	status
sticky-sentimental	delicate
self-pitying words	argument (repeated)
pain	art (repeated)
trumpet	
Brahms	
Bach	
tennis	
fools around with notes	
folk music	
minuet	
dances	

scherzos
aria
fishermen
shadow of
improvisation
Sousa marches
loud
brass band
room too small

Roosevelt

Metaphors

sphere of action
we war with
say a word
muckrake (repeated)
filth on the floor
body politic
sternest war
epidemic
mudslinging (repeated)
whitewashing (repeated)
Aristides is praised

Balances

vile and debasing (repeated)
never does . . . never thinks
not a help . . . not an incitement
there are . . . there is . . . there should
every evil . . . every evil . . . every writer . . . every
    man
liar . . . thief
untruthfully . . . untruth (repeated)
easy to twist . . . easy to affect
men . . . men
ought to be . . . ought to be . . . ought . . . to be
on stump . . . in newspaper . . . in book

Antitheses

carnal . . . spiritual
crown . . . rake
lofty . . . debasing
no good . . . great harm
scoundrel . . . honest man
mudslinging . . . whitewashing
Aristides . . . the unjust
punishment [of] unoffending
immunity [to] offenders
profit . . . destruction of
    character

Sensory Images

corner-stone
wooded wilderness
the Potomac
man with the muckrake
look . . . downward
muckrake in his hand
look up . . . regard the crown
rake to himself the filth on the floor
fixes his eyes
flinch
must be scraped up
mudslinging
whitewashing
dig the Panama Canal
put in the penitentiary

Intellectual Images

business of government   exposure and attack
sphere of action   benefactor

national government   mendacity
nation   premium
growth of population   hysterical exaggeration
growth of wealth   assail (repeated)
growth in complex interests assault (repeated)
natural problems   confusion of ideas
Washington's time   a reaction (repeated)
tendencies for good   unscrupulous scoundrel
carnal instead of spiritual things exposed (repeated)
aught that is lofty   excess (repeated)
that which is vile and debasing destruction of character
feats with the muckrake   public sentiment
help to society   deterrent
incitement to good   normal sensitiveness
potent forces for evil   the public service
body politic   right type
evils   character and capacity

Zellner

Metaphors

(none unless
possibly
"zenith")

Balances

earth around the sun . . .
   moon around the earth
to refute . . . to refute
earth and sun and all the
   planets
specific masses . . . specific
   velocities . . . specific
   courses
they argue . . . they say
these people argue . . .
   they say

Antitheses

proving . . . disproving
many people . . . I
not . . . but
existence . . . nonexistence

Sensory Images

eye
the retina
earth and the sun
[visual orbit drawn]
spiraled into the sun
gone straight out
[broken orbit drawn]

Intellectual Images

the existence of God (repeated)
scientific data
scientific arguments
natural phenomenon
God
Judeo-Christian faiths
supreme being
zenith
to demonstrate
fact
scientific reasoning
refutations
proofs (repeated)

argument from design (repeated)
natural mechanism (repeated)
Planner
the solar system (repeated)
protein molecule
life as we know it
logic (repeated)
masses and velocities
course
orbit
infinitely improbable (repeated)
parabolic or hyperbolic curve
predesigned (repeated)

You may not agree in all cases with my classifications of these terms and phrases, but unless our disagreements are very wide they are probably not crucial. The reason for pulling terms and phrases out of context and placing them in lists is to get an undistracted impression of whether key terms and phrases in a speaker's style have, or lack, any of the qualities we would expect in normal, interesting, varied, oral communication. The lists above show clearly that there are marked differences in the kinds of key terms our three speakers used. To decide whether those differences are significant, we need to isolate the norms by which we can judge the merits of metaphorical, balanced, antithetical, and sensory and intellectual language. The following statements have general, normative acceptance in rhetorical theory.

1. Unless metaphors are confusing or distasteful, their presence tends to make communication seem "interesting" and "colorful." Moreover, comparisons and metaphors always suggest "inherent" relationships and so can "argue" in favor of the interrelationships they assert.[7]
2. Balancing ideas by verbal means or putting them in series tends to make the ideas seem more likely to "belong together" and, as Ohmann suggests (p. 146), these groupings of ideas may make what is said seem sweepingly true and important.
3. Setting ideas against one another in antithetical constructions tends to arouse interest through the conflict of ideas it suggests. This stylistic form can also "argue" that the conflict or contrast it linguistically suggests is true in fact.
4. Sensory images tend to stimulate listeners to experience vicariously; to that extent the linguistic form invites them

to become experientially, hence feelingly, involved in what is said.

5. Intellectual images and implications tend to make listeners *work* to process and use the ideas referred to. This is more laborious than experiencing vicariously, and it may suggest that human concerns are not strongly valued by a speaker who leans heavily on intellectualization.

Only parts of these five sets of statements have been confirmed by scientific research, but none is denied by existing experimental studies. Each has long been accepted as reasonable in rhetorical and literary theory. If we accept these statements, we can interpret the different kinds of stylistic data we have extracted from the early thought units of our three speeches.

Using the five sets of statements as norms, we can make the following tentative inferences about what is probably meant by the classifications of linguistic forms we have completed.

1. Our data show that balanced constructions were much more frequent in Roosevelt's speech than in the speeches of Bernstein and Zellner—even when we take into consideration that Roosevelt used most words to make his first fifty statements. On the basis of the statements in 2 above, we should conclude that Roosevelt made his ideas seem "impressive," "sweeping," and "important" by these procedures.

2. Assuming the truth of the first set of normative statements, we would conclude that whereas Bernstein and Roosevelt may have increased listeners' interest and created an impression of colorfulness through moderately frequent use of metaphors, this was *not* a feature of Zellner's influence in the first part of his speech.

3. Bernstein evoked vicarious, sensory experience in listeners much more often than either of the other speakers. Assuming statement 4 above, we would conclude that Bernstein's hearers probably became more vitally and intimately involved in what he said than did listeners to Roosevelt or Zellner.

4. Roosevelt and Zellner seem to have communicated a great deal about abstractions. Assuming the truth of statements in 5 above, we are led to believe that Roosevelt's and Zellner's audiences had to *think* harder than Bernstein's

hearers. It does not follow that Roosevelt's or Zellner's hearers disliked the work they had to do, but we must infer that they had to *want* to understand more than Bernstein's listeners.

5. Bernstein seldom used the strategies of balancing ideas or of placing them in series, but he was as likely as Roosevelt and more likely than Zellner to introduce contrastive and conflictive effects through setting up antitheses. None of our five sets of norms purports to explain what would happen when Bernstein, an expositor, used these "argumentative" techniques more than two avowedly persuasive speakers.

Our five sets of norms allow good progress toward critical understanding of how the three speakers' verbal styles worked for or against them. But we have not exhausted the ways of finding out from the lists of words and phrases what may have happened. With sorted lists of verbal usages before him, a critic ought to take advantage of the process which experimenters and other scientists sometimes call "eyeballing the data." This is simply *looking* at the information, using one's observational abilities, and searching for any systematic characteristics that seem present. The practice is fruitful for getting special understandings of each of our three speakers.

Looking over an array of any speaker's metaphors, one can ask whether anything seems especially true of these allusions, taken together. To ask this might draw attention to the interesting fact that all but two of Bernstein's metaphors have something to do with *physiological* experiences, actions, or conditions. It is widely thought that ideas which touch on physical conditions of persons have especially basic or "vital" importance to hearers or readers. If we believe this, we ought to modify conclusion 2 above, adding that although Bernstein did use relatively few metaphors, most of them could have especially personal, vital meanings for listeners. We could even reason that a few such metaphors might do the work of many of other kinds in interesting listeners.

Roosevelt's metaphors turn out to be very different when one "eyeballs" them. Each is now, and was even in 1906, common to political talk. And "say a word" was even then a hackneyed circumlocution for "speak." A critic (or listener) who knew history would know that in ancient Greece Aristides was called "the just" and that his name has been a metaphor for "justness" ever since.

A critic who noticed these things about Roosevelt's metaphors would want to modify conclusion 2 still further. He would probably want to say that where Bernstein used especially vital metaphors, Roosevelt's were commonplace—probably losing nothing, but unlikely to give Roosevelt's language any special rhetorical force.

Balanced constructions can be looked at in much the same manner as metaphors. Bernstein used no balances that were not antitheses also. For the time being, this fact gives us no newly interpretable information. But the content of Roosevelt's balances is striking. All but two relate to right, wrong, good, bad, or to some aspect of morality! Only "men . . . men" and "on stump . . ." are, in themselves, without moralistic content. And when one looks at the contexts of these two balances he finds that the "men" were objects of "indiscriminate assault" and the "stump" etc. are the sources of "gross and reckless assaults." So *every* balanced construction in Roosevelt's first fifty thought units tends to give enlargement and impressiveness to *moral* judgments!

Several of Roosevelt's balances have another feature, if one notices it. In nearly half, the *final* element in the pair or series is in some way "bigger" or more important than the first element. We get "vile and *debasing*," "not a help . . . not an *incitement*," "liar . . . *thief*," and the like. It appears, then, that Roosevelt not only made ideas more impressive by placing them in balanced structures, but he frequently further emphasized his moralisms by arranging climaxes within those balances and series. Since it is clear from experience and experimental evidence that what comes last in a series often acquires special force, a critic would be reasonable if he amplified conclusion 1 above by adding that Roosevelt probably increased the force and interest of what he said by filling his balances and series with humanly significant and often *mounting* allusions to good and evil.

Zellner's balances also had unique content, as is evident from reviewing the terms contained in them. Every element of his balances had something to do with geophysics or with argumentation. Of course, these were his basic subject matters; he *had* to talk about these things. But why in balanced constructions? Perhaps because these are not inherently exciting topics Zellner tried to add interest by choosing verbal structures that *were* inherently interesting. We cannot know that he did this deliberately, but his pairs and his one series ("earth and sun and all the planets") come at points where balances and series are not imperative just to be clear. He achieved special force whether he planned it or not. Perhaps, indeed, he should have tried this kind of strategy more often to relieve the essential difficulty of his subject.

We can look at antitheses in much the same ways. Bernstein seems to have used antitheses to keep listeners interested. There is not much "argument" implied by his antitheses: the "gayest" jazz contains some "pain," "jazz" is not louder than "Sousa marches," and so on. His contrasts are descriptive and interesting because ideas are clarified by contrast; that is all. Only two antitheses make what might seem "argumentative" claims. "Not through the usual historical approach which has become all too familiar, but through approaching the music itself " is one of them. Here, both words ("all too familiar") and antithetical form "argue" in favor of Bernstein's approach and against the "historical approach." The other distinctive antithesis says people claim "that it [jazz] is not art; I think it *is* art." Here terse language and the contrastive force of antithesis emphasize the complete opposition of the two positions. Bernstein's own declaration thus becomes almost defiant.[8] Apparently this was a contrast he wanted listeners to understand as a complete conflict. In any case he combined words, grammatical structure, and vocal delivery in ways that would work simultaneously to underscore the conflicting nature of the two elements of the antithesis.

A critic ought to say that Bernstein used antitheses with special artfulness. When he needed stylistic contrasts to make ideas interesting, he created mild antitheses; when he wanted to argue subtly on behalf of his "approach," he did it with structure as well as with words; when he wanted to declare himself strongly, terseness, structure, words, and delivery were combined to make his point. Here was full, strategic use of the resources of speech.

The fact that Roosevelt's balances all had moral content ought to lead a critic to check antitheses for similar content. In fact, *all* his antitheses pit a "good" against a "bad" or a "bad" against something worse! Even the "crown . . . rake" structure is a metaphoric contrast of "good" pursuit of the constructive and "bad" pursuit of the destructive. So, moralistic content characterizes *both* his balanced and antithetical structures. We have a new, significant datum in this!

Zellner's few antitheses also seem to work like his balances—giving his abstract ideas greater interest and emphasis. "Proving . . . disproving," "not . . . but," and "existence . . . nonexistence" are prominently opposed in meaning and form. Yet the oppositions were not essential to what Zellner was saying. "Many people have made it their expressed purpose in life to argue about the existence of God" would have said substantially the same things Zellner put into the "proving . . . disproving" structure. But the antithetical way of saying these things was probably more likely to keep listeners attentive. There was also a point at which Zellner used antithesis to emphasize *his* position, much as Bernstein did. The "many people . . . I . . . neither" structure, as well as the words, focused on the important difference between Zellner's real rhetorical purpose and the purpose some listeners might have suspected he had.

From looking at what stylistic structures can say through structure *and* words it becomes clear that balances and antitheses can do more than create and sustain interest. They can also "argue." Antitheses can emphasize differences, as they so often did for Roosevelt. Balances can equate or establish hierarchies as they did for Roosevelt, or they can simply inject interest as they did for Zellner. It also emerges that all three of our speakers used balances and antitheses astutely, managing the reinforcing powers of these forms as their content and address to listeners required.

Speakers' stylistic images can be "eyeballed" with similarly enlightening results. An intriguing thing I believe I see in Bernstein's sensory images is that they *clustered,* as though to evoke particular kinds of feelings at different points in his speech. After the mixed set of references to earth, jazz, "innards," and sounds in general, there comes an enumeration of coordinate types of jazz. What could this concentrated series of names do within listeners? For those who knew jazz well the names could evoke momentary, aural remembrances of the different types of music; some might "feel" the differing melodies and rhythms of these jazz forms. Listeners who could not thus reconstruct the music could still feel that the series emphasized the inclusiveness of jazz as a genre of music. For either type of listener Bernstein's extended series would surely make the concept and the history of jazz seem greater, more impressive, and possibly more important in personal, sensory ways.

Closely connected with this series is another series that names various mood-qualities of jazz: sad, happy, robust, hard-boiled, sticky-sentimental, self-pitying, painful. Here is a second, unbroken flow of evocations to remember and to feel. I think it is plausible to believe that these two, closely associated, evocative series of terms worked together to arouse feelings toward jazz that would be especially favorable to Bernstein's "case" on behalf of jazz.

Later in his first fifty thought units, Bernstein introduced another series of terms. It, too, seems calculated to evoke attitudes and images in a systematic way, this time through antitheses. First, listeners' attitudes and images are associated with such classical musicians as Brahms and Bach; these are paired with attitudes and images associated with the highly disciplined game of tennis. Then, against this series of thoughts and feelings, Bernstein sets the (jazz) images of "fooling around with notes" and images associated with "folk music." The disciplined is set against the relaxed. Next, the formal minuet is juxtaposed to "rustic German dances." This is followed by mention of formal scherzos. Then, as though reproducing the same structural-emotional pattern with which the series began, the formal aria is paired off against the songs of simple fishermen. To me, at least, there is something akin to thematic play in music occurring in this passage; stern and formal images are played against relaxed images and associated attitudes. One cannot say either that Bernstein created this "play" consciously or that many of his listeners responded to it, but the alternation of types of music about which people have feelings could surely, for some listeners, have the effect of an antithesis-generated *argument* in favor of jazz as musical expression and experience.

What I am calling "movements" of sense images can be seen by simply reading down a sequenced list of Bernstein's sensory images. As a critic, I would argue that one "movement" evoked and sustained feelings about the diversity and inclusiveness (and satisfactions?) of jazz while another evoked attitudes and feelings affirming the significance of jazz. Still other of Bernstein's images seem to have done isolated bits of evocative work, enlivening ideas where needed.

Probing imagistic language in the ways just illustrated reveals new dimensions of what we called in chapter IV "suggestive content." Coming at that content through detailed study of verbal structures (and aspects of delivery) gives a critic added information about what happened suggestively when talk occurred. This point is reinforced if we undertake the same kind of inquiry into the character of Roosevelt's sensory images.

Of Roosevelt's sixteen sensory images, ten have to do with some sort of physical activity: *"look* . . . downward," *"look* up . . . *regard* the crown," *"rake* to himself," *"fixes* his eyes," *"flinch,"* "be *scraped* up," "mud*slinging,"* "white*washing,"* *"dig* the Panama Canal," and *"put* in the penitentiary." Each of these images suggests an action, and each has strong moral suggestiveness if seen in its context. The axiom of literary and rhetorical criticism that one stylistic quality can counterbalance another suggests we ought to infer that Roosevelt's *active* images may have counter-balanced the abstractness we previously noticed in his moral and political conceptualizations. And if we notice also the visual qualities of "corner-stone," "wooded wilderness," "the [nearby] Potomac," and the "man with the muck-rake," the inference that he *did* ease the "burden" of his abstractness and complicated grammar gains further support.

Zellner's modest use of sensory images illustrates a different kind of stylistic compensation. One can hardly talk of God, geo-physics, and logic without being abstract! What better way to counter this abstractness than to *picture* whatever can illustrate the abstract ideas? Zellner invites his hearers to picture the eye, the retina, the earth moving around the sun, a planet spiraling "into the sun," a planet breaking out of the elliptical orbit and going "straight out into nowhere." In addition, he drew on the blackboard the elliptical and the aberrant paths of the earth. Whether he was conscious of it or not, he effectively used visual imagery to help listeners experience crucial parts of his thought in *concrete* ways. As with Roosevelt, if Zellner's hearers were bothered by his somewhat complicated syntax and abstract con-tent, they were also given some relief through "seeing" elements of his thought.

Looking at the columns of "intellectual images" confirms the critical judgments we have been developing. Bernstein seems to have used abstract phrasings only when it was inevitable. Most of these images turn out to be subordinate to more strongly empha-sized, experiential aspects of music. This is scarcely surprising in speech about a sensory experience, music; but one can imagine a less astute speaker adopting "the historical approach" and emphasizing such abstract matters as melody, rhythm, and polyphony. The point is that Bernstein did not *have* to concretize his subject matter, but he *chose* to. His credit as stylist lies in that fact.

Given what we have already noticed about Roosevelt's moralistic tendencies, we should expect to find his intellectual images heavily concerned with morals and, perhaps, politics. We do. Of the 39 different concepts listed (several used more than once), 20 are associated with some moral value, 11 have political denotations or connotations, 4 have to do with aggressive action of some sort, and 4 others are of other kinds. If we combine this information with that derived from earlier inquiries, we have detailed explanation of Professor Murphy's overall description of Roosevelt's style: "He incessantly extolled some gospel, and in a manner distinctly homiletical." [9]

SIMPLICITY AND HUMAN INTEREST

To complete our illustrations of the seven lines of critical inquiry suggested in chapter VI, let us apply Flesch's criteria for "ease" and "human interest" to our samples of rhetorical speech. Below are the data I derive from each speaker's first fifty thought units. Affixes per 100 words and numbers of personal references per 100 words are based on two 100-word samples randomly chosen from the fifty thought units.

	Bernstein	*Roosevelt*	*Zellner*
Average no. of words, first 50 thought units	10.5	18.34	14.7
No. affixes/100 words in two samples from first 50 thought units			
Sample 1	29	45	29
Sample 2	27	47	44
Personal references in two samples from first 50 thought units			
Sample 1	3	3	9
Sample 2	5	5	4

Interpreting information of this sort reopens the question of how quantitative data ought to be used in criticism. The data above are valuable but certainly ought not be accepted as "proving" anything about our speakers unless other critical reasoning indicates this is justified. *Literal* interpretations of the quantitative data in our table would suggest some such conclusions as:

1. If length of thought units is a measure of "difficulty," Roosevelt was most difficult, Bernstein least, and Zellner midway between.
2. If number of affixes per 100 words is an indication of "difficulty" of vocabulary, Roosevelt was most difficult, Bernstein least, and Zellner midway between.
3. If number of personal references per 100 words is an indication of "ease" and "human interest," Bernstein and Roosevelt were equally easy and interesting and Zellner was still "easier" and more "interesting."

But none of these conclusions can be accepted at face value. Counter-weighing possibilities must be taken into account before inferences can be made from such data.

The first conclusion above can probably be accepted at face value, but not by virtue of its own authority. The conclusion can be believed only because it reconfirms what every other inquiry into structural "ease" and "difficulty" has suggested. The total words each speaker used to make fifty thought units and the grammatical constructions of their longest thought units *also* point to the conclusion that Roosevelt falls lowest in ease and clarity, Bernstein stands highest, and Zellner stands between them. Our quantitative data on thought units suggest the same thing. It is, then, not any *one* set of data but the *agreement* among three different kinds of data that enables us to accept the first conclusion with confidence.

We shall need a definition of what normative "clarity" and "ease" may be before we say that any of these speakers was genuinely "easy," not simply more "difficult" than Bernstein. Unfortunately most statistical norms available are based on "reading ease"; among these Flesch's scales come closest to what we want because his norms are based on journalistic prose. The standards of journalistic writing are not vastly different from the standards our speakers ought to have observed. Bernstein and Roosevelt spoke to popular audiences and expected their utterances to be read as well as heard. Zellner's situation was not a "popular" one, and he did not expect to have his speech published; he was making an assigned speech in a classroom, and his objectives appear to have been at least somewhat like those of journalist-expositors. For these reasons Flesch's norms can probably be used as *roughly* appropriate to the oral rhetoric with which we are dealing.[10]

Using a definition of a "sentence" much like that which I have used to identify "thought units," Flesch found that "standard" prose appearing in popular digests (e.g., *Reader's Digest*) contained "sentences" averaging 15–17 words each. Compared against this norm Roosevelt's and Zellner's prose seems unlikely to have presented any great difficulty to the audiences who heard these speeches. Bernstein's lecture must have seemed especially easy. Again, we ought to be cautious about inferring conclusions from any single kind of quantitative data about style; however, what we found when examining the speakers' grammatical constructions confirms what Flesch's norms tell us. In both length and complexity Bernstein was shown to be a simple, easy stylist, Zellner intelligible but more difficult than Bernstein, and Roosevelt genuinely complicated in *both* length of thought units and internal structure.

Drawing conclusions about the complexity of speakers' vocabularies presents another problem in finding suitable norms on which to base judgments. Given the kind of analysis I have used, there is no alternative to using Flesch's norms again.[11]

In the samples taken from Bernstein's speech there are about 28 affixes per 100 words. Flesch found 37 such affixes in 100-word samples of the "standard" written prose of popular digests. Bernstein's language falls so far below Flesch's definition of "standard" it is impossible to believe that in this respect he was other than easy to listen to. If there is doubt about so sweeping a critical inference, other lines of inquiry will justify the judgment. Comparison of Bernstein's vocabulary against standard lists of most-frequently-used English words will show that he also spoke very simply by this measure. Any subjective weighing of whether his technical concepts were simplified for nonexpert listeners will yield similar results.

But to jump with equal assurance to the conclusion that Zellner's vocabulary was "standard" because he averaged 36.5 affixes per 100 words in two samples would be unwarranted. There is great disparity between the numbers of affixes in the two samples, as there was not in the samples of Bernstein's prose. Peculiarities of this and any other kind ought to alert a critic to the likelihood that "something special" went on in speaking.

A good first move toward understanding the peculiarity in Zellner's style would be to take new samples to discover whether the speaker shifted in complexity erratically or systematically. As it happens, if you compare the numbers of affixes in any 100 words in Zellner's first three paragraphs with the numbers in any 100 words from paragraphs 4, 5, and 6, you will discover that the first sample contains markedly fewer affixes than the second. Further detailed study will show that there is some sort of mounting complexity in the vocabulary used through Zellner's first fifty thought units. Now, the task is to find out whether there was any good reason for this.

Thinking about how Zellner's *tasks* shifted through the fifty units will give an answer to the shifts in vocabulary. Zellner (1) tells his own motivations and introduces his subject in relation to the rhetorical situation, (2) explains the kind of reasoning he is going to deal with, (3) explains a specific, geophysical argument, and (4) refutes that argument by applying principles of formal logic. In short, his rhetorical tasks become progressively more complicated as the talk moves along. Actually, he used almost as few affixes as Bernstein in his opening; his language became more and more "difficult" as he moved toward his discussion of the New- tonian argument. As one critic, with this descriptive informa- tion before me, I have only admiration for the fact that with so complex a subject Zellner managed to stay *near* the average vo- cabulary level of popular writers.

There is little to say about Roosevelt's use of affixes except that he consistently adopted terms that tended toward the "difficult," as we are now measuring "difficulty." There is little reason to go deeper into the matter because the judgment that he tended toward the difficult in word choice is completely consistent with other observations we have made. Grammatically, too, he created avoid- able problems of complexity. On balance, one has to believe it would have been easy to say what Roosevelt said in simpler thought units, in simpler words, and with as much force and active imagery.

To apply Flesch's criteria of "human interest" to the same por- tions of the same speeches shows that although one can get a useful judgment from quantifying terms that refer to people and human relationships, there are also other means by which speakers personalize what they say. According to Flesch's measures, 6–9 personal-reference terms appeared in "standard" digest-prose. By that criterion Roosevelt and Bernstein were impersonal and Zellner about "standard." But surely most critics would have the intuitive impression that Bernstein, at least, was *not* "impersonal." And what- ever negative reactions Roosevelt stirred in his listeners, imper- sonality and aloofness are not among the attributions history records. The matter of personalization and humanization deserves further inquiry.

Inspect Roosevelt's first fifty thought units for humanizing elements, other than sheer *naming*. He creates a human figure whom he will use analogically: the man with the muckrake as pictured in Bunyan's *The Pilgrim's Progress*. With that image firmly implanted in listeners' minds Roosevelt makes reference after reference that will call up the image of that *man*, though the man is not named. Consider these words, within which possible humanizing meanings have been placed in brackets:

> There is filth on the floor [like the filth the *man* concentrated on] and there are times and places where this service is the most needed of all the services that can be performed [the *muckraker* does some good]. But the man who never does anything else [like the *man* in the story], who never thinks or speaks or writes save of his feats with the muckrake [like the *man* who wouldn't look up at the crown], speedily becomes, not a help to society, not an incitement to good, but one of the most potent forces for evil.

A human being is literally named only once in these statements ("the *man* who"), but there are at least four other points at which listeners were invited to *picture* the man with the muckrake. They were also invited to *feel* about him as though he had been identified by name. So, even though Roosevelt did not use many names and personal pronouns, a critic will be justified in saying that Roosevelt *did* humanize what he said—by means which Flesch's and other quantifying measures of style do not automatically reveal.

Bernstein, too, achieved humanizing effects in ways not measured by most quantifying techniques. From the beginning he talked of jazz as being able to *do* things *to* humans and *for* humans. Jazz even has human attributes. Jazz is happy, sad, robust, hard-boiled, sentimental, gay, wild, pained; it has and expresses humor, "fools around," "plays," has "fun." These are not "personal references" in the customary sense, but they certainly humanize thoughts about jazz.

The inadequacy of Flesch's formula for revealing all ways by which speakers humanize their talk does not mean Flesch's principle of watching for names of people and relationships is a useless principle. The *principle* is useful in all rhetorical criticism, but what need to be watched for are both *names* and other *evocations of humanized images*. Zellner's is a speech in which we can see both the naming and imaging processes at work to humanize rhetoric. His personal references through paragraphs 3–6 (the most difficult) consist of I, you, my, people, God, they, we, and

Sir Isaac Newton. No doubt these helped to humanize what was said, but Zellner went further. He framed what he said so that *people do* things. They "argue," and Zellner challenges "them." He puts other people and himself into conflictive relationship, creating the image of a personalized debate. A careful critic ought to credit Zellner with achieving personalization of a difficult subject *both* by injecting a "standard" number of direct, personalizing words and by creating an image of human conflict, precisely at the points where his ideas had to be most abstract and his vocabulary most complex.

The naming of persons and personal relationships is an important, readily available way speakers can give their rhetoric human appeal, but speakers find other artful ways of personalizing, too. A critic ought not be slavishly bound to standard "measures" of personalization or any other rhetorical attribute; standard measures like Flesch's are exceedingly helpful, but speakers often achieve standard effects in highly original ways. Critics must have the will and ingenuity to search them out.

These illustrative applications of seven ways of probing verbal style show that if imaginatively used, those lines of inquiry can contribute to development of balanced, critical judgments about style. What overall judgments about our three speakers do we now have? It is surely clear that none of our three speakers *failed* in the early portion of his speech. It is even more clear that Bernstein stands out as a superior stylist—relative to Zellner and Roosevelt and relative to all the normative standards we used respecting seven stylistic behaviors.

In grammar, vocabulary, and conciseness Bernstein made himself unusually easy to understand, though his subject was potentially a complex one. He achieved much liveliness by introducing a variety of inherently interesting verbal patterns and by achieving the concreteness that portrayals of action, appeals to the senses, and quick, functional contrasts can give to speech. Perhaps most important, he made his hearers participate *in* jazz by helping them to experience it vicariously and by inviting them to see jazz as having human-like attributes. In the respects we have been considering, Bernstein was a full rhetorical artist.

Zellner partially achieved what was open to him, given the unavoidable abstractness of his subject matter. There was unnecessary complexity in some of his verbal constructions. He achieved part of the color and activity that metaphors, balances, and sensory images could give. He attained impressive degrees of verbal simplicity and personalization, if we recognize that his subject was more abstract than either Roosevelt's or Bernstein's. His task was difficult and he met it with most of, though not all of, the available verbal resources.

Of Roosevelt we must say that his complexity not only made him difficult to understand at times, but it also opened him to charges of evasiveness and inconsistency. His strength of style lay in the force he generated through deploying images and attributions in verbal structures that *argued* for his claims. To a considerable degree he mitigated the relative abstractness of his subject matter by incorporating active and humanizing images that had potential both to interest and to persuade. He achieved emphasis and force by all available means except conciseness and grammatical simplicity, but he stands demonstrably below Bernstein and Zellner in clarity.

Such summary judgments as these have critical significance because behind each judgment there stands clear, discussable evidence. Not every critic will discover precisely the same evidence or interpret it exactly as I have, but because of the ways evidence was collected, the evidence is open to the evaluation of all. The verbal styles of Bernstein, Zellner, and Roosevelt have been rendered discussable, and critical judgments have been rendered correctable in case I have erred. Intuitive evaluations of verbal style are not this easily discussed and evaluated. This is the prime defense I make for such systematic analyses of verbal style as I have tried to illustrate.

Notes

[1] Robert F. Terwilliger, *Meaning and Mind: A Study in the Psychology of Language* (New York: Oxford University Press, 1968), pp. 216–217.

[2] Bernstein clearly set off this long predicate modifier as a special unit of meaning. He did so by pause and vocal inflection which detached it from its associated NP—VP elements. Ohmann (see p. 146) might argue that Bernstein thereby specially emphasized the *expansiveness* and *inclusiveness* of jazz, giving special importance to this long series of items by balanced and paralleled constructions within it.

[3] The statement after "say" seems a separate thought unit because it is a complete grammatical thought and because the speaker emphasized its separateness through delivery.

[4] Richard Murphy, "Theodore Roosevelt," pp. 352–353. Speech Association of America. *A History and Criticism of American Public Address* Vol. III, Edited by Marie Kathryn Hochmuth |Copyright 1955| New York: Russell & Russell, 1965.

[5] Antitheses are usually balanced in some way. Most of Bernstein's balanced constructions involve ideas that are markedly different or are opposed to one another. I have classified all of these as *antitheses*. Had he used such forms as "the robustness, the power, the vitality" or "beating rhythmically and swaying

happily," I would have called those forms *balances* and not antitheses. For reasons that will emerge, it is useful to differentiate forms which, like balances, pull ideas *together* from forms that insinuate conflictiveness among ideas, as antitheses do.

[6] I have tried to list all words and phrases that seem likely to make a listener think of anything feelable, hearable, tasteable, smellable, or visible. These I have called "sensory images." For example, "self-pitying words" could suggest phrases of lyrics a hearer could "hear" again; "sticky-sentimental" could do the same or could generate sensations of stickiness or cloyingness. Concepts which would be difficult to experience in ways that involve use of the senses have been listed as "intellectual images."

[7] Metaphors are technically defined as figures of speech in which a term or phrase is applied to something to which it is not literally applicable, in order to suggest a resemblance. Readers wishing to begin exploration of the very involved subject of how metaphors function in language would do well to begin by reading Michael M. Osborn and Douglas Ehninger, "The Metaphor in Public Address," *Speech Monographs* 29 (August 1962): 223–234. Lectures V and VI of I. A. Richards' *The Philosophy of Rhetoric* (New York: Oxford University Press, 1965) are also valuable sources on this subject.

[8] In a recording of the broadcast one can hear Bernstein emphasize these nuances vocally, stressing "not" but stressing "is" even more. In editing the lecture for print Bernstein or someone else chose to print "is" in italics.

[9] Richard Murphy, "Theodore Roosevelt," p. 347. Speech Association of America. *A History and Criticism of American Public Address* Vol. III, Edited by Marie Kathryn Hochmuth [Copyright 1955] New York: Russell & Russell, 1965.

[10] Flesch's norms would *not* be appropriate, however, if we were performing a critique on Stokely Carmichael's speech at Morgan State College (pp. 343–355) or on Jonathan Smith's eighteenth-century address to the Massachusetts Ratification Convention (pp. 385–387). There would be no reason to equate the standards of modern journalistic prose to standards operating in either of these circumstances.

[11] I chose to measure the difficulty of vocabulary by quantifying the affixes per 100 words. Only Flesch has worked out norms for this measure. Other kinds of analysis can serve, however. One could calculate scores based on the frequency with which words appearing in a speech also appear in frequency-of-use lists for popular English. But frequently-of-use scores would present the same interpretive difficulties that face a critic who uses Flesch's method of analysis—one would need to know the *kind* of English usage that was observed in assembling the frequency-of-use tables.

Chapter VIII

Nonstandard Styles
and Special Verbal Devices

Speakers of English do not possess just *one* set of stylistic norms, but this is a fact scarcely recognized in chapters VI and VII. There are many groups who share distinctive life styles, special ethnic identities, ages, professional commitments. Most such groups develop shared, linguistic norms that differ slightly or greatly from the norms of "general American speech." When critics encounter oral rhetoric that uses elements of these "nonstandard" styles, they must consider how far their own understandings of norms allow them to go in stylistic criticism. This chapter argues that sound knowledge of how words persuade reveals much of how any style influences.

Some have contended that critics must live the lives of the in-groups they study or they cannot evaluate in-group rhetoric with accuracy. In some detailed respects this is no doubt true, but the argument exaggerates the variance that usually exists between general and in-group rhetoric. Moreover, "outside" critics who carefully study in-group situations have certain special advantages because they can maintain critical distance between themselves and the rhetoric. They will miss some obvious meanings and many nuances of rhetoric they only observe at critical distance, but they will also see much that participants take for granted or view with passions that prevent incisive description. Critical neutrality and distance have disadvantages, but their disadvantages are probably not more serious than those of participative criticism.[1] Both participants in rhetorical processes and "outside" critics make distinctive contributions to our understanding of oral rhetoric.

In this chapter we shall suppose our critic is "outside" in-groups "looking in." This is the vantage point we have when we undertake criticism as a way of learning about people who differ from ourselves. It is also the vantage point which everyone doing rhetorical criticism has much of the time. Further, to discuss criticism from "inside" in-groups using "nonstandard" communicative styles would require an attempt to treat all the distinctive rhetorical patterns found in all the distinctive cultural groupings in our society, and this is a task impossible to attempt in this book.

FUNCTIONS OF THE NONSTANDARD

In the pages to follow we shall try to find some ways in which standard methods of stylistic criticism can help a critic interpret oral rhetoric that has attributes of "nonstandard" style. As critical objects we shall look at the oral styles of two speakers addressing ethnic in-group audiences. It happens the ethnic groups involved are American black people, but the critical approach to the rhetoric and rhetorical situations would be substantially the same if the in-group audiences were self-identifying professionals, teen-agers, Italian-Americans, or any other group which had developed elements of what I am calling "nonstandard style."

First, we shall examine an excerpt from Stokely Carmichael's "Speech at Morgan State College." (The full text appears on pp. 343–355.) The speech was delivered in Baltimore on January 16, 1967. At the time he spoke, Carmichael was National Chairman of the Student Nonviolent Coordinating Committee (SNCC) and was on a national lecture tour. His speech at Morgan State was the first of two speeches he would make in Baltimore that day. Mr. Carmichael was widely known as an activist leader in the civil rights movement and as the popularizer of the then controversial concept "Black Power." Even among black people some considered him a radical. Only two days before he spoke in Baltimore, Carmichael had announced that he would not be a candidate for Chairman of SNCC when his term expired in May of 1967 but, he said, he would remain active in the equal rights movement as a whole. At Morgan State College he addressed a predominantly black audience composed largely of undergraduate students. There are stylistic features in Carmichael's speech which only a critic fully conversant with the usages of Black English and of the equal rights movement in 1967 could explain, but there are other standard and "nonstandard" aspects of Carmichael's style which any informed critic can discover, interpret, and evaluate.

To deal with Carmichael's or any other speaker's in-group style, a critic needs to understand how "nonstandard" styles function for speakers who are not confined to a single set of stylistic norms. In the first place it is mistaken to suppose that there is a "black rhetorical style" or a "southern rhetorical style"; there are varied usages within each stylistic community. Nonetheless, in each such self-identifying group there are certain verbal, grammatical, phonetic, and even ideational and "logical" patterns that are means of communication which are not available in "standard American English." Some of these an outsider can recognize and interpret, though some are so "private" to the in-group that only those who understand the group thoroughly can perceive them.

To understand our excerpt from Stokely Carmichael's speech we need to know, as outsiders, that in 1967 Carmichael was a young (not yet thirty), civil rights leader of more aggressive inclinations than a number of others. For this reason he was "controversial" among blacks as well as whites. To some (apparently including Dr. Martin Luther King) Carmichael's "Black Power" slogan seemed impolitic in 1967. To others "Black Power" seemed the challenge of the future. It is pertinent, too, that Carmichael had attended and graduated from Howard University in Washington, D.C., not far from Baltimore, the seat of Morgan State College.

Those who have studied Stokely Carmichael's speaking know that he can observe the conventional norms of "standard" American English if he wishes to and needs to. At Morgan State he adopted some stylistic patterns characteristic of (1) the in-group language of the academic world, (2) the in-group verbal and vocal patterns characteristic of Black English as spoken in Northern urban centers, and (3) patterns characteristic of "general American speech" tinged with standard "Southern American speech." It is important to observe that *all* of these dialectal styles were appropriate to Carmichael and to the rhetorical situation in Baltimore. In a similar way, the speaker's metaphors, series, balances and antitheses, grammatical constructions, patternings of thought units, and vocabulary partook of *all three* styles. At Morgan State, then, Stokely Carmichael was not a one-style speaker. For him, as for many spokesmen of his stature who represent special groups with distinctive styles, the features of in-group language functioned as added stylistic options in communication. For such speakers in-group style is not what is sometimes referred to in sociolinguistics as a "restricted code" that confines what a speaker can perceive and communicate. The in-group styles function for versatile speakers as "elaborations," giving them a "code" that goes beyond the resources of standard English.

From observing Carmichael's varied stylistic resources we shall soon see that it is a compound style that must be analyzed and judged. The same is very often the case in other in-group situations. Carmichael's compound style is evident in the following excerpt which we shall explore in detail:

1 Property rights, property rights is what the United States Con-
2 stitution is based on. You should know that. Property rights. People
3 who didn't own property could not vote when this country was first
4 founded. Not until years afterwards such people were able to vote. So
5 the analysis is the question of property versus propertyless people.
6 That's what it's all about.
7 That's what those rebellions are about. Nothing else, nothing less.
8 And what appalls me about the black leaders is they do not have the
9 guts to condemn the grocery-store owner. Now I will say anytime a man
10 has been charging us all that money for fifteen years, his store should
11 have been bombed five years ago. Should have been out of the neighbor-
12 hood five years ago. And if nobody wants to do it, then you can't blame
13 people when they move to do it for themselves. If you want to stop re-
14 bellion, then eradicate the cause.
15 You are college students, you should think. Now then we want to talk
16 finally about the responsibility of youth. That's black students. It is
17 time for you to stop running away from being black. It is time for you to
18 begin to understand that you, as the growing intellectual, the black
19 intellectuals of this country, must begin to define beauty for black
20 people.
21 Beauty in this society is defined by someone with a narrow nose, thin
22 lips, white skin. You ain't got none of that. So now what you try to do
23 when you pick a homecoming queen, you look for the brightest thing that
24 looks light, bright, and damn near white. And you have your mothers
25 sending you up here. "Be sure to pick a nice-looking fellow with curly

26   hair when you get married, dear." Or if your lips are thick, bite them
27   in. Hold your nose; don't drink coffee because you are black.
28   Everyone knows black is bad. Can you begin to get the guts to develop
29   a criteria for beauty for black people? That your nose is boss; your lips
30   are thick, you are black, and you are beautiful? Can you begin to do it
31   so that you are not ashamed of your hair and you don't cut it to the
32   scalp so that naps won't show? Girls, are you ready? Obviously it is
33   your responsibility to begin to define the criteria for black people about
34   their beauty. Because you are running around with your Nadinola cream.
35   Your campus, the black campuses of this country, are becoming infested
36   with wigs and Mustangs and you are to blame for it. You are to blame
37   for it.

If one approaches this passage exactly as one might any other oral
rhetoric, certain unique features of Carmichael's style become apparent. His metaphors, balances, and antitheses are so interrelated
that it is not possible to point to the potential force of one without
commenting on how that force adds to, prepares the way for, or
derives from the force of interplaying structures. The repetition with
which the passage begins actually starts a *progression* of more and
more negatively weighted allusions to the concept, property:

> *Property rights, property rights* is. . . . *Property rights.* People who
> *didn't own property. . . .   . . . property versus propertyless people.*

The method here is not at all peculiar to black rhetoric. The
progression could be persuasive to any audience identifying itself
with the less propertied people of a society.

But Mr. Carmichael swiftly connects the antithesis of property
versus people to *black* people in urban centers: the ghetto riots and
rioters of immediately preceding months. Fifteen words containing two paralleled constructions *bind* the property-versus-people
issue to urban violence in general:

> *That's what* it's *all about. That's what* those rebellions *are about.*
> *Nothing* else, *nothing* less.

Parallel forms assert still further the connection the words assert
absolutely. Once more, the strategy might have occurred with any
audience feeling sympathy for the propertyless, but Carmichael
has inserted the cue word "rebellions." In his rhetorical situation
it can assure everyone that the property-versus-people antithesis
is really a property-versus-*black*-people antithesis. It is the character of *that* antithesis that lines 6–7 assert and interpret.

From this point on in the excerpt balances, antitheses, and metaphors are specially freighted with in-group meanings. In lines 11 and 12 "Should have been out of the neighborhood five years ago" not only parallels the preceding predicate but is a subject-less sentence, especially common in black usage. Moreover, getting white store owners "out of the neighborhood" had at least a quarter of a century of currency in urban, black rhetoric.[2] Thus in-group grammatical form and theme personalize Carmichael's charge of economic exploitation, as the charge is reinforced by repetition and parallelism.

Entering his final topic, Carmichael addresses his audience of college students injunctively rather than argumentatively or impartially. A balanced antithesis reinforces his commands: "It is time for you to stop . . ."; "It is time for you to begin. . . ." Antithesis becomes even more harsh in lines 21–22 as racial differences are bluntly asserted through denotation combined with antithesis in slang style:

Beauty in this society is defined by someone with *a narrow nose, thin lips, white skin. You ain't got none of that.*

The expected conjunction "and" between "lips" and "white skin" is omitted as is often done in Black English, but to any nonuser of that style the omission gives added force. These are, then, grammatical and verbal choices a black speaker addressing blacks could safely and effectively use.

Lighter, ironic, but no less insistent stylistic ploys follow in lines 22–27. Familiar (to the in-group) formulae bear Carmichael's criticism of collegiate blacks. Some criticisms are reinforced by rhythm and even rhyme. But virtually every aspect of the verbal style is such that only a black speaking to blacks *as part of their community of thought and language* could use it safely. "The brightest thing that looks light, bright, and damn near white," ". . . if your lips are thick, bite them in," "hold your nose," etc. are words and phrasings that have extensive metaphoric *and argumentative* connotations within the community to which the audience and Carmichael belonged. But, as though he feared his lighter touches might dilute his point, Carmichael resumes his blunt injunctions, giving them extra force by means of antithesis (lines 30–32) and sarcasm ("Nadinola cream," "wigs and Mustangs"). Every nuance of lines 28–37 has in-group meaning but means much less to people who are not black. The stylistic *formulae* are standard (balances, antitheses, metaphors, rhythm, rhyme), but all the "proving" force of the stylistic usages is special. Some terms are not fully intelligible to one not a member of the speaker's and listeners' special cultural and language community.

Any critic can learn a good deal that is useful and interesting from analyzing in-group rhetoric of Carmichael's sort. But as our experiment shows, some of what goes on is likely to be missed by any outsider. Standard criticism can discover rhetorical *methods,* but not always rhetorical *meanings* in in-group discourse. But all meaning does not elude standard criticism. By ordinary norms we would have to say that Stokely Carmichael's style was absolutistic. If we look for qualifying, temporizing, soliciting terms in our excerpt, we shall find none at all. All statements, balances, antitheses, and rhetorical questions assert or imply absolute and unqualified knowledge on the speaker's part. Carmichael's images also have this authoritative quality. Sensory and intellectual images seem about evenly distributed, but the speaker seems to demand specific, unqualified attitudes toward each imagistic concept: property, rebellion, white store owners, *the* neighborhood, beauty, noses, lips, skin, color, hair, Nadinola cream, wigs, Mustangs. Judgments of "good" and "evil" are demanded. One need not be a part of the in-group to catch this meaning; however, one would have to know a good deal about Morgan State students' initial attitudes toward SNCC and Stokely Carmichael to judge whether as a young black addressing young blacks Carmichael could secure adherence by speaking thus authoritatively. Once more, stylistic method and quality can be discovered by the outside observer, but to estimate effects requires knowledge that can only come from *within* the group that identifies itself as "special."

Using general norms, we would expect rhetoric of Carmichael's absolutistic sort to be relatively free of interrupted kernel statements. Qualifications and modifications usually produce stylistic complication. In fact, Carmichael rarely interrupts NP—VP—NP or PM thought movements. At lines 2–4, 18–19, and 35, where he does introduce interrupting qualifiers, the qualifications are virtually essential in the first two instances; in the third the qualification *broadens* the criticism of campus life.

The usual norms of criticism also suggest that authoritative, little qualified speech is more likely to be "easy" than "difficult," and Carmichael's prose was "easy." His thought units average about eight words in length—markedly shorter than the 17 Flesch found characteristic of digest-prose. Two, 100-word samples from our excerpt contain 26 and 24 affixes respectively—well below the 37 Flesch found "standard." The first 100 words of the excerpt contain 7 personal reference terms. The last 100 words contain 18 (mostly forms of "you"). On the average, Carmichael was well above the standard of six personal references per 100 words.

If we add these bits of information to what we have previously gathered, we have grounds to conclude that Stokely Carmichael at Morgan State was easy and interesting to follow, *provided* those who heard him tended to agree with his positions and/or to defer to him as an authority on the future of the black-rights movement.

What is perhaps the most important thing to be learned from an experiment in criticism of in-group rhetoric remains to be observed. Ordinary norms in rhetorical criticism imply that ideas need to be "developed" and "argued out" in language lest they be imperfectly understood. By these standards Carmichael was simplistic—asserting more than showing interconnections among property rights, votes, economics, self-respect, and the position of black people. But in-groups tend to share special patterns of values and to have consensus about "how things are" and "what goes with what." They also have special language by which to communicate about these shared notions. Astronauts have such understandings. So do teen-agers. An in-group member can "read" a special term as a reference to complex bodies of common knowledge. At a hint he can move quickly from DATA to CLAIM along paths that are standard for his group. Stokely Carmichael was functioning in this kind of rhetorical situation. Finished criticism of his oral style must explain in some degree how these special, enthymemic processes of interconnecting ideas worked.

By ordinary standards Carmichael seems to have spoken rather "choppily" and to have lacked amplification of ideas. However, many special concepts arising from the unique experiences of blacks were shared between him and his hearers. Also, his audience knew the "shorthand" language of "black consciousness"—cues that stood for entire lines of thought and judgment. The audience knew further that Carmichael represented the "Black Power," activist school of thought in the equal rights movement. In short, there was much about black experience, black power, and the civil rights movement past, present, and future which no black speaker needed to verbalize. "Reasoning" and "idea development" could

be cued *in predictable ways* because of the knowledge and attitudes Carmichael and his audience shared. What appear partial
expressions or developments of ideas could become cues for full
identifications and developments in the minds of listeners. *And
this is true wherever speakers and listeners share intricate bodies
of thought, doctrine, attitudes.*

Studies by Roderick P. Hart, Jr. have gone farthest to establish
this important point about the rhetoric of in-groups. On comparing
more than sixty speakers functioning under varying circumstances,
Hart concluded that as

> shared philosophical commitment of listeners and speakers in-
> creases. . . :
>   1) doctrinality will increase;
>   2) absolutism will increase;
>   3) philosophical concepts will be emphasized over the practical;
>   4) codes will become increasingly important;
>   5) more and more linguistic resources will be available;
>   6) the past will become more important;
>   7) specificity will decrease;
>   8) facticity will decrease;
>   9) detail will become less important;
>   10) assertiveness will increase;
>   11) rhetorically generated "tension" will increase;
>   12) the group will become increasingly valuable rhetorically.[3]

These are characteristics Hart found in the rhetoric of speakers
who spoke to audiences with whom they shared close allegiance to
a "doctrine." Hart defined a "doctrine" as a *written* statement of
belief: the *Book of Mormon,* the formal creed of a church, the Communist *Manifesto.* When speakers who adhered to one of these
"doctrines" addressed audiences who also adhered to the creed,
the speakers' rhetoric usually had the twelve characteristics listed
above. Hart's contention is that the same characteristics ought
to be expected wherever speakers and listeners share systematic
beliefs and know they share them. My contention is that Stokely
Carmichael's speech supports Hart's point. Hart's list of characteristics generally describes the excerpt at which we are looking,
and it describes the speech as a whole even more accurately.[4] The
"doctrines" of equality, independence, repressions of blacks by
whites, and the "old doctrines" of imitation and emulation are
constantly referred to. Philosophical supports of the "new doctrines" are cited, in-group code words abound, in-group language
supplements general language, past experience has a major place

in the speech as a whole, except by way of allusion specific facts of the moment are not prominent, virtually no thought is developed in detail, tension is certainly built up, the shared blackness of speaker and listener is a major rhetorical theme. And the absolutism suggested by unqualified assertions has already been noticed in our earlier analyses. It seems, then, an entirely fair inference to conclude that Carmichael's was the kind of speech we ought to expect where the speaker assumes that his listeners share his values and "doctrines" almost entirely.

We may learn more about how to understand nonstandard styles if we now look at an "outsider" trying to address a self-identifying group which possesses a body of in-group resources, some of which are available to the speaker and some of which are not. The segment of talk we shall examine comes from a speech by the then Mayor of New York, John V. Lindsay. He was speaking to about 125, mostly black, Democrats at a political meeting in Orlando, Florida during that state's 1972 presidential primary election campaign. Lindsay was one of about a dozen Democrats who were seeking party support for nomination as Democratic candidate for President.

The rhetorical situation gave Mayor Lindsay problems. At best it would be difficult for him to generate identification between himself and Florida voters, black or white. He shared with them allegiance to a party and its general political principles, he shared political experience, and he shared his general public interests and his humanity. That was about all. In style and in substance his task was to present himself as a potential leader interested in Florida's problems and in the problems of black people. He needed to seem a man who was clear headed and decisive enough to get things done if nominated. It was politics and the Democratic party in particular which gave Lindsay whatever in-group identification he could claim at Orlando. He did not cope in thought or in style with what the circumstances allowed him.

A political reporter friendly to Lindsay said of the Mayor's speaking during the early part of his Florida campaign:

> He is promising the voters here hard talk—and he's giving them rambling, sometimes incoherent rhetoric. He's promising the voters a tough fight—but he remains ethereal, almost bemused.[5]

Lindsay's audience at Orlando came to hear a "stranger" offer himself as a candidate for leadership. The only unusual thing about the Orlando meeting, as a political rally, was that most of the party members gathered were black and were likely to think of themselves as having, in 1972, political "clout" blacks had not had in the party in other years. Lindsay was probably known chiefly as the liberal mayor of the largest, most famous, and perhaps most notorious city in the nation. Under the circumstances, what the listeners needed was clear, easy-to-understand, personalized communication about their party, its future, the role of black people in it, and how Lindsay could further the interests of both as a national leader. Thoughts and inferences were needed to prove that Lindsay was politically intelligent in ways black Democrats from a relatively rural area could understand and admire.

Mayor Lindsay erred, in substance and style. He gave his listeners unclear substance couched in a nonstandard style—whether judged by the standards of ordinary political campaigning or by the standards of general American English. In a circumstance where he needed to prove himself, he was almost entirely assertive. He spoke chiefly about himself and his experiences, in which his hearers had not participated and could scarcely participate in vicariously. What he said was not oriented to action or couched in the language of confident leadership and party identification. Here is a portion of the speech.

```
 1      I suppose it really comes down in the end—uh, uh—to the frustration
 2   and outrage that I have over the failure of the American promise and
 3   the American dream and, uh, the feeling that I have inside of my gut
 4   when I test the streets of my city or almost any other major city of the
 5   United States you can point to and, indeed, in all throughout the
 6   land, because what I see and have to deal with on a daily and regular
 7   basis—uh—is the degradation of human life, the—uh, uh—exclusion of
 8   so many people from the mainstream of the country, and I'm not just
 9   talking about the minorities of the United States. I'm talking about
10   blacks and browns and the Indians of our country, all of whom I've
11   watched and, uh, shared with their experiences of trying to make it.
12   But I'm talking also about the average person and the average family—
13   working men—who find that the entire system is ganged up against
14   him—inequitable tax laws, powerful benefits and exemptions for those
15   who constantly seem to have a voice and an ear in Washington. I'm
16   talking about the growing number of elderly people on fixed incomes
17   who are victimized by the same system. Talking about women who
18   don't have a chance for promotion because they are women. I'm talk-
19   ing about students who are not listened to because they are students.
20      I call this the outsiders for the most part. I also think of myself—
21   though I don't enjoy it very much—as being an outsider because if you're
22   mayor of a central city area in the United States—even one that, uh,
23   has a budget as big, almost as big, as the top two or three largest
```

24   states put together in this country, and even though we have 300,000
25   employees in our city system, you know the deck begins by being stacked
26   against you, by malapportionment in the state legislatures, by mal-
27   apportionment in the United States Congress, and by all those forces
28   that traditionally—uh, uh—had sought to avoid the problem of urban
29   America where all of the headaches gathered.[6]

This is not a representative sample of Mayor Lindsay's campaign rhetoric, and it *looks* especially unfortunate stylistically because all vocal pauses are included; but with these stripped away as they would tend to be in the hearing, the style is still as Mr. Perry reported: "rambling, sometimes incoherent" and "almost bemused." It seems a highly personal, almost "private" style. Why?

For one thing, thought units are very long. They average about 19.5 words each. Listeners must follow the intricacies of grammatical patterns very carefully to understand what is asserted and how one concept is being connected with another. The difficulty does not come from interrupting kernel statements; it comes from Lindsay's habit of appending long, complex, modifying clauses to otherwise clear kernel structures. Sometimes so many thoughts follow NP—VP forms that it would be difficult for hearers to remember what the basic thought was. Here is one example from lines 9–11:

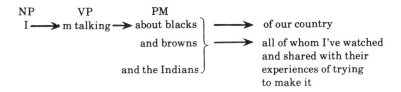

Mr. Lindsay interrupted his kernel structures no more than Leonard Bernstein or Stokely Carmichael. His problem was an eccentric habit of "tacking on" so many ideas that they obscured kernel notions. Another idiosyncrasy of his style was to frame qualifications and modifications in ways so unobservant of standard English structures as to render it difficult to extract a meaning. For example, consider lines 4–6: ". . . or almost any other major city of the United States you can point to and, indeed, in all throughout the land. . . ." From the standpoint of speech criticism it is irrelevant to say that "throughout" and "all" are redundant and so "incorrectly" combined. The issue is: What is the *meaning* of "and, indeed, in all throughout the land" *after* one has said, "almost any other major city of the United States you can point to"? Utterance and stylistic forms are taken by listeners as *meant*. A listener's question will be, "What does the addition *mean?*" Listeners will not weigh grammatical "correctness"; they will ask *why* Lindsay "added on" here. And there will be no answer. The stylistic mannerism is nonstandard, but the real problem is that no one possesses any standard by which to translate it systematically.

Carmichael's paragraph 5 (p. 343) is as grammatically "irregular" as the most obscure of Lindsay's verbal structures; but Carmichael had an audience that could make the "leaps" from idea to idea because they shared with him the formulae of the talk of the times and the idioms of Black English and Southern American speech. Mayor Lindsay's listeners did not have such clarifying resources by which to interpret him when he abandoned traditional grammatical and logical formulae.

None of Lindsay's metaphors and images had any special, suggestive power to make his ideas cohere as Carmichael's allusions to violence in Vietnam and violence in inner cities made his apparent *non sequiturs* cohere. No thematic unity is fostered by: "American dream," "inside my gut," "mainstream," "ganged up against," "blacks," "browns," "Indians," "voice and ear," "elderly people," "test the streets," "degradation of human life," "average people," "workman," "powerful benefits," and "malapportionment." These are disparate, scattered concepts that could at best communicate an intense but vague disillusionment.

A stranger facing a self-identifying in-group can involve them with himself by choosing language that places him in *their* conditions. It is true that Mayor Lindsay's language was "personal" by Flesch's standards (8–9 personal references per 100 words), but the Mayor's personalizing terms were mainly: "I," "my," and *"you," used in the sense of "if you were I"!* The visitor was emphasizing his individuality, not his identity with his Orlando listeners. In sum, he offered his Florida listeners an idiosyncratic, complicated, ruminative kind of discussion not at all held together by suggestive terms that could build an overall impression of meaning.

James Perry wrote that although Mayor Lindsay sought to appeal to the average and underprivileged men and women of Florida, "The irony is that he doesn't look or sound like such a man." [7] He also reported that the Mayor spoke at Orlando without once being interrupted by applause or other overt signs of his listeners' understanding and approval.

A speech critic might explain these facts by pointing out that Lindsay's style was "nonstandard" in that it matched neither general American standards of utterance nor the standards of "folksy" campaigning for votes in the South. The language did not reflect what he and his listeners shared conceptually and linguistically. Perhaps among his associates in New York City his rambling, ruminative style could have communicated qualities of compassionate reflectiveness, but at Orlando it could only seem an eccentric, private, perplexing mannerism. He needed to display himself as a visiting Democrat among Democrats residing in Florida, not in New York City. That was the only in-group tie he could claim and build upon. He did not. And as the reporter-observer implied, Lindsay's style was merely eccentric, so perplexing.

From our two examples of "nonstandard" styles an important critical principle emerges: *No stylistic behavior is rhetorically "nonstandard" if listeners possess "standards" and "rules" by which to "translate" it into a recognizable grammar and logic, but any stylistic behavior for which listeners do not have "guidelines for translation" will be disturbingly eccentric in that situation.* In the respects we have analyzed, Stokely Carmichael was a *conventional* stylist at Morgan State College in 1967. There, his deviations from general usage were not eccentric; they systematically reinforced his message. But John Lindsay's deviations from general norms at Orlando *were* eccentric and hence uncommunicative. None of his listeners had experience that equipped them to unravel his linguistic-ideational patterns. And a further point emerges: the ethnic, in-group structure of Lindsay's Orlando audience had little if anything to do with his failure. As a white Northerner, he could not in any circumstance incorporate the experience of Southern blacks into his style. The weaknesses of his oral style derived from failure to fit language and ideas to the norms of general political campaigning. His style was "nonstandard" in the sense that *no* group of Floridians had the necessary guidelines by which to "translate" it. "Nonstandard" styles, then, may, or they may not, fit the standards known in the situations in which they are used.

SPECIAL RHETORICAL MEANINGS OF VERBAL FORMS

How language *means* is something I shall not try to answer. The functionings of human symbolic processes are matters of perennial debate, and the debates to date have ended inconclusively. But some things about meaning seem relatively clear and of importance to speech critics. One is that the ways words are put together can *mean,* just as what words denote can mean. In attempting to summarize some ways language means, William K. Frankena has said:

> ... it seems possible to distinguish a number of factors, each of which may be and has been referred to as the meaning or part of the meaning of ... [an] utterance. These are:
>
> 1) The primary conceptual content symbolized, i.e., presented and evoked.
> 2) The propositional attitude (with regard to this) expressed and evoked.
> 3) The secondary conceptual content presented and evoked.
> 4) The propositional attitudes (regarding this) expressed and evoked.
> 5) The emotions and conative [goal oriented] attitudes expressed.
> 6) The emotional tone.
> 7) The emotions and attitudes revealed.
> 8) Other kinds of effects.
> 9) The purpose.[8]

Put less exactly, Frankena and his colleagues contend that anything said may offer ideas, assert that they are true, offer and invite an attitude toward what was said, imply something further, reveal goals or intent of the utterer, express feelings about content or the manner of its expression, reveal something about the utterer's general attitudinal profile, have an array of *effects,* and be a purposive *act* committed by the utterer. Any of these meanings of anything said could have special significance in a given rhetorical situation, and concerning these possibilities a critic would also want to notice what the speaker's ways of speaking imply about his attitudes toward his audience.

Frankena and his colleagues found it important to remember that utterances *present, express,* and *connote emotionally.* What a statement *presents* is what it says according to the terms and the grammar used. What it *expresses* is what it reveals about the speaker's attitudes toward what he is saying and toward his audience. What it *connotes emotionally* is what it further says *through* respondents' feelings.

To some extent we have already been observing and interpreting these three dimensions of rhetorical meaning. In earlier chapters we noticed that balances, antitheses, and metaphors can "say" things, express attitudes toward ideas, and evoke feelings toward ideas. These are frequently used verbal devices, but there are other standard ways of saying that also have potentialities for communicating more than one of these dimensions of meaning. In Frankena's language all such special structures "do something; they are among the powers of nature which an organism or group may employ [and respond to] ." [9]

Through the history of rhetorical theory balances, antitheses, metaphors, and other distinctive ways of verbalizing have been called "figures of speech." For the most part they have been studied as ways of ornamenting prose and poetry. The Belgian philosopher, Chaim Perelman, has reemphasized to modern critics Aristotle's potent notion that these verbal structures frequently *argue* rather than simply beautify.[10] Following Perelman's and Aristotle's views concerning the rhetorical significance of such phrasings, I shall refer to them as verbal *devices* in order to stress their practical significance.

Looked at as devices that can *mean* practically and argumentatively, most of the special devices speakers use fall into these classes:

1. Devices that can "argue" through repeating.
2. Devices that can "argue" through comparing.
3. Devices that can "argue" through enlarging the meanings of ideas that they associate together.
4. Devices that can "argue" through constraining possible meanings.
5. Devices that can "argue" through contrasting.

It is well established that people pay more attention to things repeated than to things heard but once. Up to some point we do not quite know, any verbal strategy that allows repetition of ideas "argues" that they have special importance and should be specially noted. All Western languages have a number of standard structures which do this kind of rhetorical work. Their names and the distinctions among them are less important to critics than the fact that special "argument" through repetition can be achieved by speakers in a number of ways.

Alliterations are repetitions of identical sounds in successive words. The repeated sound can draw special attention to whatever the alliterated words are presenting, expressing, and evoking. Winston Churchill's series, "excited, disturbed, self-centered atmosphere" repeats the "s" sound, and this is likely to claim added importance for the fact that he did *not* find these negative qualities in America. That, in turn, gives added importance to the "good" qualities for which he is praising Americans. If not too obvious, alliterations can subtly increase attention and argue for the alliterated ideas.

Antimetaboles are repetitions of words in successive clauses, but in reversed order. Perhaps the most famous antimetabole in contemporary rhetoric is Kennedy's "Ask not what your country can do for you—ask what you can do for your country." The "argument" of this form was discussed on p. 144.

Appositions are restatements of ideas previously referred to. The last seven words of "The boastful Mussolini . . . is now but a lackey and serf, *the merest utensil of his master's will*" not only say the basic idea a second time but strongly *express* Churchill's attitude toward Mussolini; and they doubtless *evoked* feelings toward Mussolini. In all three ways the apposition argued specially that Mussolini was a virtual nullity.

Climaxes are achieved through placing items in series in order of rising importance or emotional connotation. The device can not only argue that the items *are* of rising importance, but it also can sometimes evoke mounting feelings. Churchill was surely striving for these persuasive effects in "Hope has returned to scores of millions of men and women, and with that hope there burns a flame of anger against the brutal, corrupt invader, and still more fiercely burn the fires of hatred and contempt for the filthy Quislings. . . ."

Parallelisms are achieved by using the same words and patterns of words in successive phrases, clauses, or sentences. As we have seen, the devices argue that the paralleled items do, indeed, belong together and that these items are specially important. Kennedy accomplishes both lines of "argument" by combining parallelism and antithesis in: "Now the trumpet summons us again—not as a call to bear arms, though arms we need—not as in a call to battle, though embattled we are. . . ."

Polysyndetons and *asyndetons* are insertions of definite articles or conjunctions where they would not ordinarily be expected or omissions of them where they would be expected. The effect is to emphasize by jarring the expectations slightly. Carmichael gets the effect by omitting "and" before "white skin" in "Beauty in this society is defined by someone with a narrow nose, thin lips, white skin." Kennedy makes a series more impressive by adding "the" unexpectedly in "the energy, *the* faith, and *the* devotion." Roosevelt did the same with "and": ". . . but the forces of truth *and* love *and* courage *and* honesty *and* generosity *and* sympathy." Bernstein subtly argues that a series of items really *does* form a special mix when he omits an expected conjunction at the end: "Well, there you have it: melody, rhythm, tone color, form, harmony."

Each of these is a relatively common way to call attention by repeating something or not doing it where expected. Each is a standard *but not invariably used* device for announcing, "This is of special significance." Each *says,* of course, as all language does, and each *expresses* a special attitude the speaker has toward his idea and, perhaps, toward his audience. Each may add something to feelings *evoked* because of what the device (e.g., climax) automatically builds into the ideas. Much of the force achieved by Kennedy, Carmichael, Roosevelt, and Churchill would be missed if a critic failed to notice these speakers' constant uses of repetitive devices as strategies of argument.

Other familiar verbal devices *argue by comparison.* Again, all present or *say,* all *express* the user's attitudes, and all are likely to *evoke* feelings because feelings are likely to exist toward at least one element of any comparison. In the speeches used for illustrative purposes in this book significant claims are supported by the following comparative devices.

Analogy is sometimes thought of as a relatively formal structure of argument, but analogical claims are sometimes made by the simple practice of putting *potentially* comparable statements next to one another. We saw this in George Miller's treatment of the loss of a Congressman, and we can see it in Spiro Agnew's observations: ". . . this attack emanated from the privileged sanctuary of a network studio and therefore had the apparent dignity of an objective statement. The American people would rightly not

tolerate this concentration of power in Government." Is
not Agnew claiming that there is a logical analogy between
the regulation of powers in networks and in government?

Allegory occurs when, in a narrative, some events, characters,
or objects are given metaphorical meanings. We have
already observed that Theodore Roosevelt borrowed and
used John Bunyan's allegorical "man with the muck-rake."
This is the only instance of allegory in the speeches discussed in this book, but the form is sometimes used to argue
in modern sermons, and it was especially popular in early
Christian preaching. Wherever used, the special function
of the device is to transfer *feelings* associated with the
allegorical object to whatever that object is compared to.
Thus, Roosevelt implicitly claims that journalists are as
disagreeably interested in attacking others as the man
with the rake was in dirt on the floor.

Metaphor (or simile) is the application of a term or phrase to
something to which it is not literally applicable. We have
examined a number of instances of its use. Carmichael's
"Your campus . . . infested with wigs and Mustangs" has
special condemnatory force because "infested," "wigs,"
and "Mustangs" metaphorically stand for aspects of campus and black life of which Carmichael has previously
made it clear he is critical.

Metonymy is using the name of one thing as the name for
something else to which it has a *logical* relationship. This
way of comparing argues with special directness because
it implicitly asserts that the connection between compared
items is not *just* metaphorical. Bernstein says saxophone
tones are "in fact" imitative of *vocal* qualities when he
calls the sound: "breathy, a little hoarse, with a vibrato,
or tremor, in it." A genuine identity of qualities is argued
for by this comparison.

Onomatapoeia is using a word that imitates in *sound* something associated with the thing named. It is a device less
used in speech than in writing, but Agnew's "gaggle of
commentators" makes claims both metaphorically and
onomatapoetically. "Gaggle" suggests the sounds of geese,
and its use expresses Agnew's claim and attitude that
commentators deserve no great credit for wisdom.

Synecdoche is identifying something by naming a *part* of it
or identifying a part by naming the *whole* thing. Churchill

claims deliberate and conscious behavior makes Nazi Germany what it is when he refers to all of Germany as "the Nazi mind." Kennedy contends that the planned moonshot has enormous significance when he refers to it by the name of the "whole" enterprise: "explore the stars." By these devices each speaker makes a claim that something *is* as he says and, moreover, it deserves the attitudes and feelings that are implied by reference to the part (Churchill) or the whole (Kennedy).

It is imperative for speech critics to recognize that every comparative which is not purely ornamental is making a claim of considerable power. The listener who does not reject or stumble over Carmichael's "infested" or Agnew's "gaggle" or Kennedy's "explore the stars" has in fact "bought" an important claim about what the facts are; he has accepted the negativism or positivism which the speaker so swiftly expressed.[11]

It is also useful in criticism to take special notice of what is assigned "superiority" and "inferiority" by means of comparative forms. One does not see the full persuasive force of Agnew's speech without noticing that, in every comparative, network newsmen are assigned inferior qualities and status. With only slightly less consistency Roosevelt did the same with the journalists he talked about. It is further true that Agnew and Roosevelt sustained argument by comparative strategies to a greater extent than the other speakers we have used for illustrative analyses. A significant set of critical questions which you might explore as an exercise in criticism is: Did the other speakers whose speeches are in this book need more comparative devices to further their rhetorical goals? How do Bernstein's comparisons and analogies work differently from Agnew's and Roosevelt's? When comparative devices do not "argue" and yet are not mere "ornaments," what do they communicate above the level of denotation?

Devices which *enlarge* meaning were considered in our discussion of the styles of Bernstein, Roosevelt, and Zellner. These devices associate ideas together, thereby claiming the ideas *belong* together and expressing the speaker's belief that the ideas are related in the ways he implies. Roosevelt's balanced constructions and Kennedy's balances and serial constructions had this effect for reasons Ohmann has stated (see p. 205).

Among verbal devices that can have enlarging or expanding effects, the following ought to be regularly noticed by critics.

Allusions are incidental mentions of items which, by being mentioned, are alleged to be related to what one is otherwise saying. An allusion can suggest that whatever thoughts the allusion triggers "are relevant here, too." When Roosevelt alluded to Aristides, he invited listeners who knew the story of Aristides to bring all the issues of Aristides's disputed justness into Roosevelt's argument that too much praise *or* too much criticism can be unfair and unfruitful. In a different way Carmichael's quick allusions to DuBois, Richard Wright, A. J. Rogers, Claude McKay, and LeRoi Jones expanded his listeners' impression of how much black literature existed. Here, allusion and series worked together as enlarging devices.

Balanced or *paralleled* structures are formed by creating pairs or series of similarly phrased ideas, emphasizing their interrelations both by grouping them and by repeating similar or identical words and word orders. We have seen how these devices work in a number of instances. To take one more example, President Kennedy implied that American policy was *comprehensive* when he similarly phrased the series: ". . . we shall pay any price, bear any burden, meet any hardship, support any friend, oppose any foe in order to assure the survival and success of liberty."

Cumulation is "piling" together related items, sometimes incorporating *climax* but not invariably. The device can add "weight" to what is said because the listing seems to expand it and give it bulk. Churchill used the method in his speech to Congress. Beginning with "Not all the tidings will be evil," and ending with "All these tremendous facts . . ." he cumulated six successive kinds of "good news," implicitly asserting that the amount of "good news" was truly impressive and was justification for his and his listeners' optimism.

Oxymoron is a way of uttering a *seeming* contradiction. The "contradiction" can argue for an unspoken meaning, as it does when Bernstein says: "The real note is somewhere in there, in the crack between them [keys]." The assertion that it is there, but isn't, *expresses* though it does not *present* (in Frankena's terms) belief that the note exists whether it is on the piano or not. Carmichael concocts a bumbling oxymoron, puts it into the mouths of whites, and thus expresses his own belief in and attitude toward the hypocrisy (confessed by the contradiction) of whites: " 'We deplore the high prices they charge the Negro for rotten meat.' " [12]

Series may be constructed by placing three or more ideas in a group, making them seem to belong together. *Cumulation, climax,* and/or *parallelism* can intensify the persuasive force of a series, as we have seen in a number of instances.

The psychological potentialities of these enlarging structures have been expressed thus by Ohmann:

> A continuant of this sort invites the reader [or hearer] to extrapolate the class in the direction pointed by the given portion of the exten-sion, and in order to make his do-it-yourself projection he must first have understood, consciously or not, the *in*tension of the class. He must, that is, have grasped the rubric under which the members are *alike*.[13]

Ohmann was writing specifically about series, but his observations apply to all the devices just identified. It can be added that the oral *acts* of alluding, balancing, cumulating, building oxymorons, or constructing series will *express* any speaker's assertion that the "members are alike." Each such act can also *evoke* feelings toward the items' being alike. I believe, moreover, that when speakers stand *with* their enlarging devices before live listeners, the act of speaking itself adds a further insistence that the lis-teners must make the "projections" as the device and the speaker's personal use of it direct.

Verbal devices of a fourth kind direct or constrain meaning. They insist that listeners think no more and no less than the speaker specifies. They put limits on a listener's freedom to make his own interpretations. In this sense these devices are the con-verse of the enlarging devices just discussed. In one way or another each of the following strategies prescribes the range of listeners' thoughts.

All-or-nothing-terms are words which assign completeness or emptiness to whatever the terms modify. Carmichael uses such terms prominently. He speaks of *"any* Friday or Saturday night," "the *whole* damn National Guard comes," "ain't *nobody* going to love us," *"everybody* in our ghettos knows." These and such terms as *each, none, com-pletely,* assert fullness or emptiness in the class of things spoken of. Their use further expresses the speaker's belief in absolute fullness or emptiness. A major reason we can say that Stokely Carmichael talked in absolute terms at Morgan State is that he was prone to contend through all-or-nothing terms that there were no exceptions to the classes of things he discussed.

Quantifying terms are words which assign some specified degree of fullness or emptiness to classes of things spoken of. Where allness terms prescribe inclusiveness in meanings, quantifying terms like "some," "a fraction," "a minority" (or majority), "one out of three," prescribe limitedness in meaning. Bernstein attains precision and some credit for being careful when he says: "The popular song . . . has *certain* strict patterns. Popular songs are in *either two*-part or *three*-part form. *By far the most numerous* are in the *three*-part." Quantifying terms make claims precise, and they may express restrained and "objective" attitudes on the speaker's part.

Definitions are formal statements that isolate the not-meant from the meant, typically by specifying genus and species, giving examples, comparing, contrasting. As Perelman and Olbrechts-Tyteca point out, to give a definition is to claim something about its "rightness" because any definition "implies the possibility of several definitions . . . among which a choice must be made." [14] Stokely Carmichael speaks of the persuasive force of definitions in paragraphs 15–23 of his speech at Morgan State (pp. 346–348). He makes the point that the definitions people accept govern whole chains of related thinking. Both considerations are important in criticism. All of paragraph 2 of Kennedy's inaugural address is an attempt to get listeners to define-out some data about the world and the United States' relation to it and to define-in certain other data about the "world today." If Kennedy's definition of the world is accepted, the whole course of action suggested by his pledges becomes reasonable and even necessary. If the strategy works with the audience, Kennedy becomes "master" of their perceptions about American foreign policy. Bernstein said jazz was "an original kind of emotional expression, in that it is never wholly sad or wholly happy." By so defining he tells listeners precisely what they are to think of as the qualities of jazz. If his definition is accepted, as he claims it must be, entire chains of subsequent thinking become virtually predetermined.

Carmichael's, Kennedy's, and Bernstein's definitions all claim rightness for the specifications they give, express the speaker's belief in the boundaries he is setting, and potentially direct listeners' thoughts and attitudes into patterns predetermined by the definitions.

Dependent clauses are "subordinate words including a subject and predicate, but syntactically equivalent to a noun or adjective or adverb." [15] As Winterowd's observations indicate (see pp. 145–146), these clauses usually qualify. They assert that so much may be believed but no more. In Carmichael and Roosevelt we have strongly contrasting practices: Carmichael rarely introduces a dependent clause, but Roosevelt introduces them frequently. These are, of course, differences we would expect between "absolutistic" and highly qualified rhetoric, but the absence and presence of these verbal forms are the facts that convince us Carmichael does speak authoritatively and Roosevelt cautiously.

Elimination is a pattern of ordering statements or arguments so that choices are successively eliminated. We considered it as a pattern of general structuring, but the same method, applied to individual statements, can also argue that "the last is true because it is all that is left." The last four lines of Zellner's paragraph 10 illustrates: ". . . so what have I shown you? Have I shown that God does not exist? Certainly not. I have shown only. . . ." If he has not done the first, he must have done the other. The device asserts that this is true; Zellner's use of it asserts that he believes it is true. To deny it we would have to feel that Zellner did not know what he had tried to do or that he was deliberately lying for some reason.

Retraction, also called epanorthosis, is verbally canceling out something already said. Bernstein did this when he said: "By this time I've probably given you the impression that jazz is nothing but Blues. Not at all." Whether the device is planned as in this case or is an impulsive, "I shouldn't have put it that way," a retraction argues that the correction has special importance and that the idea being corrected has special weight. Here, it is the *attitude* implied by correcting one's self that persuades. The signal that the speaker is so concerned that he wants to retrace his steps becomes our "proof" of the idea's importance.

Rhetorical questions are commonly defined as questions "posed not for purposes of eliciting answers but for purposes of asserting or denying something." In reference to oral rhetoric it would be better to say rhetorical questions are posed for the purpose of *demanding a predictable, unverbalized answer.* The series of questions in paragraph 45 of Carmichael's speech illustrates. All but the first two questions must be answered, "No!" or Carmichael's use of the device fails. And the successive "Noes" must imply, as the last question is asked: "I must do something more useful for my people." If any of these predicted, unverbalized answers goes unmade, the strategy of the series falters because the successive answers were supposed to evoke self-persuasion. Much the same is true of a single rhetorical question. To ask, "Don't we agree?" is to assert, "We do agree." If a listener responds as the questioner predicted, the listener proves to himself what the questioner wanted; but if the response is "wrong," the "argument" fails.

In different ways all of the above devices are verbal attempts to direct and focus listeners' thoughts. They are attempts to keep attention under a speaker's tight control. In the speeches we have examined there are marked differences in the strategies used. Carmichael, Zellner, and Agnew used constraining verbal devices frequently. Churchill and Kennedy used them relatively seldom. It would be an enlightening project in criticism and in development of rhetorical theory to explore the extent to which speakers' purposes, their rhetorical situations, and their subjects encouraged them to use constraining verbal devices in different ways and degrees.

A final group of verbal devices consists of those which *argue through contrast.* As we have seen when examining the workings of antitheses, contrastive forms assert that conflict exists among elements contrasted. And emphasizing differences alleges that the differences are more significant than any similarities. Though chapters and books have been written about the nature of metaphor, one must go to older rhetoricians for adequate discussions of how contrastive forms of language work. One of the best statements comes from Richard Whately:

> Every thing is rendered more striking by contrast; and almost every kind of subject-matter affords *materials* for contrasted expressions. Truth is *opposed* to error; wise conduct to foolish; different causes often produce opposite effects; different circumstances dictate to prudence opposite conduct; opposite impressions may be made by the same

object, on different minds; and every extreme is opposed both to the
Mean, and to the other extreme. If, therefore, the language be so constructed as to contrast together these opposites, they throw light on
each other by a kind of mutual reflexion, and the view thus presented
will be the more striking.[16]

Contrastive forms specially energize, as Whately said, but every
contrast also claims: "These elements do *not* fit together." Each
asserts that the speaker finds and believes that the elements
are different in significant ways. The presented differences always
have at least the potentiality of evoking special feelings. Such
persuasive forces, in addition to stylistic energy, are conveyed by
the following devices.

> *Antithesis* is the most obvious and familiar of contrastive
> verbal structures. It is achieved by juxtaposing terms,
> phrases, clauses, statements, or other thought units whose
> contents are allegedly different. A criterion of effective use
> of this form is that the opposition of ideas must seem "nat-
> ural" to listeners. If the difference seems doubtful or forced
> or "too artful," the form cannot assert either the signifi-
> cance of the alleged differences or the speaker's belief in
> them. It has also been contended that frequent use of
> antitheses creates impressions of argumentativeness or
> even contentiousness. Why this can happen has been sug-
> gested by our earlier analyses of antitheses.
>
> *Hyperbole* is exaggerating obviously. The strategy invites
> listeners to take seriously the "realities" behind what is
> actually said but to allow feelings aroused by the exaggera-
> tion to "spill over" into responses toward the realities.
> Churchill did not expect the terms "lackey and serf, the
> merest utensil of his master's will" to be taken literally, but
> he doubtless did expect that Mussolini's obvious subordina-
> tion to Hitler would be recognized as significant, and he
> doubtless hoped that distaste for lackey-dom, serfdom, and
> utensil-dom would generate added contempt for Mussolini.
>
> *Irony* is saying something in a way that allows the real
> meaning to be recognizably opposite of the literal meaning.
> Former Vice President Agnew is a frequent user of irony.
> For example, he reports the topics of Harriman's commen-
> tary without a single evaluative adjective, but he does so
> after having used the signaling terms "trotted" and "re-
> cited." Therefore, listeners knew Agnew's "objective" re-

marks about what Harriman said really meant Harriman was partial. Single words can be used ironically. Agnew meant the opposite of the "perhaps" with which he prefaced his remarks about "credibility gap." In all cases, if listeners accept and endorse the true meanings behind the literal meanings of irony, persuasion can occur as the real assertion is believed and feelings are aroused by the conflict between the untrue literal and the actual meanings.

Understatement is saying less than is actually meant. This form is, of course, often ironical. Churchill's "They have certainly embarked upon a very considerable undertaking" said far less than he meant, and the remark was in some degree ironical because he had just finished saying the Axis Powers' timing had been very poor. Laughter from the audience signaled that both qualities had been seen and enjoyed—as argument against the Axis Powers and for the Allies' future prospects. His "I am sure they will approve very highly of my journey here" illustrates understatement also. It says much less than Britain's real relief that the United States had entered the war, and it also could constitute a kind of claim upon the Congress for all-out cooperation and coordination. Much more than irony, understatement tends to be playful and to argue delicately without strong evocation of feeling.

CONCLUSION

I have not fulfilled the aspiration expressed at the beginning of chapter VI: to treat verbal and nonverbal aspects of style as interplaying forces that organize patterns of experience. Readers of chapters VI, VII, and VIII will have recognized that *verbal* behaviors have been the main subjects of discussion. One reason, as I have said, is that we know somewhat more about verbalization than about nonverbal communication. Another reason is that it is very difficult to write of two things or two elements of a single process at the same time. Nonetheless, the reminder is in order that all speaking is a mix of gestural, vocal, and verbal actions. However discussed, style and delivery must finally be evaluated as suasory force with compound, not disjointed, impact.

There are moderately sophisticated premises from which critics may reason about the effects of verbal language. These have been used in proposing methods of stylistic criticism in this and the preceding two chapters. Additional inferences that can be made about nonverbal communication will be discussed in the next chapter. To summarize what has been said thus far is the purpose of the present conclusion.

The psycholinguist, George A. Miller, is fond of reminding his colleagues that, "There is no limit to the number of different sentences that can be produced in English by combining words in various grammatical fashions. . . ." [17]

There being no comprehensible limit to available verbal (and nonverbal) resources, it is obvious we can look for no universal, a priori guidelines for their criticism. However, empirical research has generated the following normative propositions about verbal style which is rhetorical and oral. The first five statements below relate to distinctions between oral and written English styles. They have been only indirectly discussed and used in the last three chapters.

1. Speakers will refer *to themselves* more often than writers usually do. Notice that this generalization implies that speech will normally have more "personal references" than the kind of writing from which Flesch induced his norms for "ease" and "human interest."

2. There are likely to be more "pseudoquantifying" terms (loose quantifiers like *much, many, a lot, very*) in speaking than in writing. Notice that this implies that "quantifying" terms may have less precision in speaking than in writing but that real, not pseudoquantifiers may give speech a special degree of precision in the views of hearers.

3. All-or-nothing terms tend to appear more often in speech than in writing. Notice that this generalization implies that the "absolutism" of a speaker like Stokely Carmichael may seem less "absolute" to a listener than to a reader.

4. Speaking is likely to contain more qualifying words *(however, but, except,* etc.) than writing. Notice that an implication is that "excessive" qualification such as Roosevelt's may have seemed less unusual to hearers than to readers.

5. Speakers are more likely than writers to use language that reveals they are passing judgments or otherwise involving themselves in evaluative processes. (This generalization should be considered in connection with propositions 6 and 7 below.) [18]

Propositions 6, 7, 8, and 9 constitute empirically supported premises from which critics can reason safely concerning the *expressive* and *evocative* potentialities of verbal devices.

6. Language revealing that a speaker has strong attitudes *against* what he discusses will not be received favorably by listeners who hold views different from his, but this kind of language will be liked by listeners who *share* the speaker's expressed views.

7. Language that does *not* reveal *(express,* in Frankena's terms) strong attitudes tends to be more persuasive than opinionated language *when audiences are doubtful or in disagreement* with the speaker.[19]

8. Among most persons tested (chiefly college students) there is a pronounced tendency to prefer evaluative language that is positive over negatively evaluative language *when a choice is offered.* Critics may thus suppose that at least for educated, young listeners "accenting the positive" in content and style is more attractive than negativism—if the listeners have a choice between the two styles.[20]

9. Satire (and probably irony) is not capable of producing marked *changes* of attitudes. It may be an excellent way of reinforcing existing attitudes.[21]

For these nine generalizations there is some empirical research evidence. In further search for general norms against which to weigh data about the verbal devices speakers use, critics must depend on judgments that derive from experience and tradition. Most of the remaining statements in this summary have been stated, explained, and used in preceding pages.

10. Listeners think most terminology and verbal structures they notice are intentionally used by speakers—unless the speakers deny this in some fashion. Speakers are thus "held" for what their verbal forms seem to say, express, and evoke.

11. Whatever listeners perceive as slightly or markedly unusual in form, terminology, or other usage can grasp their attention and hence function to emphasize and argue for or against the content associated with the unusual usage.

12. A listener's judgment of what is appropriate in style will be a judgment that takes into consideration the particular speaker and the role in which the listener has cast the speaker in the rhetorical situation—as the listener perceives that situation. This is true regardless of (a) the stylistic patterns the listener himself uses or (b) the specific rhetorical task the speaker seems to be assuming.[22]

13. Verbal structures do special "work" in oral rhetoric if they (a) lend variety to the style of utterance and (b) reinforce ideas strategically. Among the common, special effects of standard verbal patterns are these:

    a. Speech with noticeably few qualifying devices other than those which *exclude* (definitions, antitheses, allness terms, rhetorical questions, and eliminations) tends to be perceived as "authoritative" if agreed with and "absolutistic" or "extreme" if disagreed with. Such speech can reinforce, but it is minimally effective in persuading to new views.

    b. Speech involving repetitions, comparisons, or other equating devices can add meaning and degrees of importance to content because these structures seem to enlarge the classes of things referred to.

    c. Sensory images evoke and intensify feelings, especially when the images are capable of arousing vicarious physiological experience.[23]

    d. Intellectualization (use of abstract but not imprecise conceptualizations) places extra demands on listeners' perceptual efforts without the reward of emotive experience. Other features of content and style can compensate for this "drain," but it remains difficult to arouse strong feelings of identification between listener and speaker through intellectualization.

    e. Simple terms and uninterrupted kernel statements are characteristic of that speech which listeners find easiest to hear and to comprehend.

    f. Concepts can be personalized and humanized by introducing personal references, personifications, and other devices that assign animation to content. Such devices increase listeners' interest in and involvement with what is said and expressed.

g. Repetition of thematically identical or related concepts emphasizes the concepts, arguing for their importance and often implying special conclusions about them and the speaker's attitudes toward them.

h. Speakers' extensive use of some conventional types of "figures of speech" and infrequent use of others can generate impressions concerning the speakers' attitudes toward content and toward listeners, but critics must infer these effects for there are few if any norms by which to predict effects in relation to any quantitative balance among the "figures."

i. Comparisons of all sorts clarify and argue for the existence of significant commonalities in the things talked about. Contrasts of all sorts argue *against* the existence of significant commonalities.

14. In virtually all situations in which English is the basic language it is "safe" to observe the conventions of *general* American English. Exceptions occur when a speaker is so closely identified with a special language community that listeners expect him to signal his recognition of that identification through observing the linguistic patterns peculiar to the group.

15. Rhetorically speaking, no verbal behavior is "nonstandard" if the audience accepts it as "normal" and has "standards" for it.

16. The more nearly a speaker's stylistic qualities reflect the patterns characteristic of the language communities to which listeners *believe the speaker belongs,* the more appropriate they will find that style for *that* speaker.

17. Speakers addressing in-groups to which they, themselves, belong can successfully use in-group style as an additional verbal resource and can depend upon in-group knowledge as developmental content that may not need to be verbalized.

These basic "rules of thumb" for interpreting and evaluating speakers' verbal choices are consistent with what empirically supported rhetorical theory we have and with what is ordinarily referred to as traditional rhetorical theory. As premises for critical reasoning the guidelines do not exhaust the bases from which critics may reason about the probable impact of verbal features of rhetorical speech. They do, however, provide starting points for basic descriptions and interpretations of what goes on verbally (and sometimes nonverbally) in consequence of oral stylistics. I hope to have illustrated that even when one uses these premises alone, interesting and often significant responses can be made to the question: "What happened linguistically and nonverbally when A spoke seriously to B?"

NOTES

[1] As one of many available instances, I suggest that Richard B. Gregg's "The Ego-Function of the Rhetoric of Protest," *Philosophy and Rhetoric* 4 (Spring 1971): 71–91 is criticism by an outsider which penetrates the rhetoric of students, blacks, and feminists more deeply than participants in that rhetoric could do.

[2] Langston Hughes had touched the same theme on August 14, 1943, in his column, "Letter to White Shopkeepers," published in the *Chicago Defender* as a comment on inner-city riots. See Lucia S. Hawthorne, "A Rhetoric of Human Rights as Expressed in the 'Simple Columns' by Langston Hughes," unpublished Ph.D. dissertation (The Pennsylvania State University, June 1971), pp. 31–41.

[3] Roderick P. Hart, Jr., "Philosophical Commonality and Speech Types," unpublished Ph.D. dissertation (The Pennsylvania State University, 1970), p. 87. Hart's earlier study, "Doctrinally Oriented Speaking as a Rhetorical Genre," an unpublished M.A. thesis (The Pennsylvania State University, 1968), provides other data supporting his 1970 conclusions. See also Hart's essays, "The Rhetoric of the True Believer," *Speech Monographs* 38 (November 1971): 249–261, and "On Applying Toulmin: The Analysis of Practical Discourse," in G. P. Mohrmann, Charles J. Stewart, and Donovan J. Ochs eds., *Explorations in Rhetorical Criticism,* pp. 75–95.

[4] Considering the entire speech, one finds the past a prominent topic in the first 31 paragraphs and philosophical concepts are prominent topics in paragraphs 10–23. While he is decidedly specific about problems, Carmichael is anything but specific about solutions—another characteristic Hart found in a number of his "doctrinal" speakers.

[5] James M. Perry, "Lindsay Gropes for a Theme," *The National Observer,* February 5, 1972, p. 5. The excerpt from Lindsay's Orlando talk which appears below comes from Perry's report and was apparently tape recorded and transcribed by Perry.

[6] "Sampling Lindsay's Rhetoric," *The National Observer,* February 5, 1972, p. 5.

[7] Perry, "Lindsay Gropes for a Theme," p. 5.

[8] *Language, Thought & Culture,* Paul Henle ed. (Ann Arbor: University of Michigan Press, Ann Arbor Paperbacks, 1965), p. 138. The quotation is from Chapter 5, "Some Aspects of Language," written by Professor Frankena on the basis of extended, interdisciplinary discussions. At its level of abstraction, the analysis remains consistent with the findings of later studies.

[9] *Ibid.,* p. 141.

[10] This position is central to Perelman and Olbrechts-Tyteca's *The New Rhetoric* and is discussed in theoretical terms on pp. 149–163. The point is implicit in Aristotle's discussions of qualities of style, especially on metaphor: 1404^b–1405^a and elsewhere in Book III of the *Rhetoric.*

[11] Some important ramifications of this point are discussed in Perelman and Olbrechts-Tyteca, *The New Rhetoric,* pp. 242–247 and 371–410.

[12] What I have said expands the term *oxymoron* to make it cover contradictory phrases and clauses. These seem to me to yield the "pointed foolishness" which *oxymoron* literally means. Orthodox definitions tend to confine the term to smaller verbal units; e.g., *cruel kindness.*

[13] Richard M. Ohmann, *Shaw: The Style and the Man,* pp. 9–10.

[14] Perelman and Olbrechts-Tyteca, *The New Rhetoric,* p. 214.

[15] H. W. Fowler, *A Dictionary of Modern English Usage* (New York: Oxford University Press, 1965), 2nd ed., revised by Sir Ernest Gower, p. 90. This definition based on "traditional grammar" seems preferable to others because the modifying, limiting meanings of clauses are of most interest to rhetorical critics.

[16] Richard Whately, *The Elements of Rhetoric,* ed. Douglas Ehninger (Carbondale: Southern Illinois University Press, 1963), 7th ed., p. 323.

[17] George A. Miller, "Some Preliminaries to Psycholinguistics," *American Psychologist* 20 (1965). Reprinted in R. C. Oldfield and J. C. Marshall eds., *Language: Selected Readings* (Baltimore: Penguin Books, 1968), pp. 202–212. The line cited appears on p. 205. Miller has pressed this point repeatedly in his writing, emphasizing that the details of every use of language cannot be known.

[18] The first five propositions are supported by Joseph A. DeVito's comparisons of skilled communicators' behaviors in speaking and writing. See DeVito's "Psychogrammatical Factors in Oral and Written Discourse by Skilled Communicators," *Speech Monographs* 33 (March 1966): 73–76. DeVito's "Style and Stylistics: An Attempt at Definition," *Quarterly Journal of Speech* 53 (October 1967): 248–255 is, incidentally, a useful bibliographic guide to research in stylistics through 1966.

[19] Statements 6 and 7 are broadly supported by evidence such as that reported by John Waite Bowers in "Language Intensity, Social Introversion, and Attitude Change," *Speech Monographs* 30 (November 1963): 345–352, and by R. Samuel Mehrley and James C. McCroskey, "Opinionated Statements and Attitude Intensity as Predictors of Attitude Change and Source Credibility," *Speech Monographs* 37 (March 1970): 47–52.

[20] Helen H. Franzwa's "Psychological Factors Influencing Use of 'Evaluative-Dynamic' Language," *Speech Monographs* 36 (June 1969): 103–109 summarizes the evidence concerning this "pollyanna set." It is not established that this "set" exists for all age groups, socioeconomic classes, and subject matters. However, critics may certainly reason that it is not hurtful and may be of some advantage for speakers to adopt "affirmative" rather than "negative" styles.

[21] Two studies by Charles R. Gruner encourage the conclusion that satire (hence probably irony) does not predictably alter the direction of existing opinion. See Gruner, "An Experimental Study of Satire as Persuasion," *Speech Monographs* 32 (June 1965): 149–153, and "A Further Experimental Study of Satire as Persuasion," *Speech Monographs* 33 (June 1966): 184–185.

[22] There is empirical evidence in support of this generalization in studies of the effects of dialectal differences. These studies will be summarized in chapter IX.

[23] Few experimental studies have asked and clearly answered what stylistic strategies generate within listeners. One contribution has been made by John Waite Bowers and Michael M. Osborn's "Attitudinal Effects of Selected Types of Concluding Metaphors in Persuasive Speeches," *Speech Monographs 33* (June 1966): 147–155. This research clearly indicates that *sustained* metaphors alluding to death and sex significantly alter listeners' attitudes toward a topic. However, there are as yet no experiments predicting the *directions* of such attitudinal changes or the rhetorical situations in which these changes are easily evoked and controlled.

Chapter IX

Nonverbal Aspects of Delivery

In the preceding three chapters a few nonverbal features of oral presentation were discussed in relation to aspects of verbal style. No doubt there are hundreds, if not thousands, of additional nonverbal behaviors which evoke meanings when mingled with verbal elements of speaking, but just what those patterns are and how they affect the impact of rhetorical speech in rhetorical situations no one knows fully. Therefore, it is difficult to find appropriate norms by which to interpret and evaluate nonverbal aspects of delivery.

The counsels of traditional rhetorical theory are cluttered with judgments based on individual tastes and cultural preferences, so few normative conceptualizations can be drawn from those sources. Modern study of nonverbal communication is in its infancy and as yet provides chiefly descriptive rather than normative information. The state of knowledge is fairly represented by the following two statements, both of which have clear, empirical support.

In summary: (1) visible action does not harm communication and perhaps helps; (2) certain deficiencies in the audible code, though listeners consider them unpleasant, do not affect comprehension. The conclusion to draw from the second point is not that speakers should cease striving for excellence, for clearly good delivery does no harm. The meaning rather is that in the whole complex of content, style, arrangement, and delivery no one presentational element, such as fluency or voice quality, is likely to affect the outcome significantly.[1]

Albert Mehrabian expresses far more confidence, but only when writing *about circumstances where verbal and nonverbal messages are inconsistent* with each other:

Our studies have produced an answer for most cases in the form of a simple linear model . . . :

Total liking = 7% verbal liking + 38% vocal liking + 55% facial liking.

Thus, in the case of an inconsistency, facial expressions are the most dominant, the vocal component ranks second, and words are the least significant.[2]

There is no real conflict between these statements. It has not been demonstrated that the behaviors experimenters have called "good delivery" markedly improve listeners' comprehension or recall of information. Research does suggest that there are a few behaviors that can become so distracting or unpleasant that they interfere with listeners' comprehension. On the other hand, it seems equally true that when listeners become perplexed about speakers' "real" meanings they *do* look to nonverbal behaviors for data to settle their uncertainty. Taken as a whole, traditional and modern evidence suggests that criticism of nonverbal aspects of delivery ought to develop from these two basic assumptions:

1. Any listener in any rhetorical situation is capable of developing feelings about a speaker's *credibility* in consequence of perceiving nonverbal cues.
2. The nonverbal aspects of speaking will probably affect listeners' responses very little unless verbal and nonverbal behaviors *seem* inconsistent or mutually reinforcing to an unusual degree.[3]

The first of these two statements is the more important for it emphasizes that nonverbal behaviors seem chiefly to affect attitudes and feelings toward speakers as persons.

Virtually all evidence argues that speech critics should look upon purely presentational aspects of speech as phenomena likely to affect speakers' *ethos*. To that extent Pearce and Brommel seem on sound ground when they write:

> Case studies of speeches or speakers which do not include some form of analysis of the delivery as well as of the text must be judged as tentative at best. A written message is not the same as the same words spoken aloud, particularly if the speaker uses a distinctive style.[4]

Given these obligations, the aspects of delivery which comprehensive speech criticism ought to notice are: (1) rhythmical, (2) vocal, (3) dialectal, and (4) gestural. Study of these behaviors ought to note whatever seems unique in presentation and in situational conditions that might cause listeners to be specially attentive to nonverbal aspects of speaking.

RHYTHMIC AND VOCALIC FEATURES OF DELIVERY

In an excellent, brief summary of modern research on vocal aspects of delivery Pearce and Conklin have pointed to three types of investigations that have provided normative information. Of a first class of investigations these authors say, "some studies have demonstrated that 'good' delivery is better than 'poor' delivery as a vehicle for verbal messages." [5] The authors hasten to add that what "good" and "poor" deliveries are remains unclear because the physical attributes of "good" and "poor" deliveries were not standard in these studies. Nonetheless, this class of studies has shown that such behaviors as nonfluency, mispronunciation, grammatical error, and "distracting" physical mannerisms *can* interfere with serious oral communication if they become prominent features of delivery. On the other hand, none of these mannerisms seems to change attitudes significantly when the behavior occurs only occasionally.

Another set of studies has established that "untrained audiences consistently and sometimes accurately identified the emotional state of a speaker from vocal cues alone." It is on the basis of this research that critics gain their firmest grounds for interpreting nonverbal cues, as I shall indicate later.

A third body of investigation has clearly established that listeners consistently *but often inaccurately* ascribe personality traits to speakers on the basis of vocal behaviors the listeners hear or think they hear. The studies show that the listeners are often wrong in these ascriptions, but they make inferences about speakers' credibility nonetheless.

As Pearce and Conklin point out, "nonverbal voice sounds constitute an independent channel of information about the speaker." [6] The research suggests, but does not prove it will be invariably the case, that a speaker's credibility *can* be affected by his style of delivery. On the basis of empirical evidence, then, it is defensible to repeat that the basic importance of exploring vocalic aspects of oral rhetoric is that listeners *may* infer "facts" about speakers' *ethos* from vocal behaviors.

RHYTHMICAL FEATURES

It ought to be clear to anyone who has listened to preachers, auctioneers, certain political speakers and public lecturers, oral readers of literature and has observed religious and other rituals that rhythmical features of utterance can affect listeners' responses. A speech critic ought to try to learn whether compelling rhythmical "beats" reinforced or altered meanings in the speech he studies.

Prominent rhythmical patterns are not always present in oral rhetoric. If they are not, a critic merely notes that there is nothing "special" about rhythmical structures and goes on to other matters. This would be an appropriate critical judgment if one were exploring the rhetoric of Leon Zellner (pp. 337–340) or Jonathan Smith (pp. 385–387). It would certainly not be appropriate to pass over the role of rhythmical patterns if one were criticizing John F. Kennedy's inaugural address (pp. 312–315) or Stokely Carmichael's speech at Morgan State (pp. 343–355). One cannot read Kennedy's address aloud without some sensation that rhythmically paralleled phrasings carry one along through series of ideas, but one seldom gets such a sensation from reading Zellner's speech aloud.

In ways not yet understood, we can be "lifted" or "carried" by rhythmical patterns, provided the patterns are not so prominent as to become obvious. This seems to be the case in most languages. Classical Greek was a language quite different from English in rhythmical structure, yet Aristotle could say:

> The form of a prose composition should be neither metrical nor destitute of rhythm. The metrical form destroys the hearer's trust by its artificial appearance, and at the same time it diverts his attention, making him watch for metrical recurrences. . . . On the other hand, unrhythmical language is too unlimited; we do not want the limita-

tions of metre, but some limitation we must have, or the effect will be vague and unsatisfactory.[7]

Most would agree that Aristotle's observation applies equally to English prose. We, too, sense that some speaking gains impact because rhythm defines, structures, and limits; other speech lacks this particular kind of affective functioning. You can easily sense such differences if you compare the two passages below.

The first excerpt asserts and manages perceptions rhythmically as well as semantically; the second depends almost wholly on semantic meaning for its force. Read the excerpts aloud to sense how the "beats" move you toward adherence to what is said in the first passage while semantic meaning alone must carry you along toward your conclusions in the second. The first speaker "lifts" and makes you sense meanings and emphases that go beyond the words; the second relies on the assertive force of things explicitly said to command your adherence.

> Let every nation know,/ whether it wishes us well or ill,/ that we shall pay any price,/ bear any burden,/ meet any hardship,/ support any friend,/ oppose any foe/ in order to assure the survival and success of liberty./ This much we pledge/—and more./ [8]

The second example:

> I feel the best way to make my point for you is to take two of the proofs that are most generally used/ and show you exactly what's wrong with them./ The first of these proofs is called argument from design./ People who use this type of reasoning about God generally choose some complex kind of natural mechanism and prove/—or at least they assume they prove/—that the mechanism must have been planned./ Thereby, they imply the existence of a Planner./ [9]

Mr. Zellner's speaking is not necessarily inferior to Mr. Kennedy's. It is simply different. Kennedy appeals beyond his words for endorsement of his pledges. Once the "beat" is begun with "Let every nation know,/ whether it wishes us well or ill,/ that we shall pay any price,/" more pledges must follow. The rhythmical structure begun would be incomplete without further repetition, or near repetition, of the structure of several unaccented syllables succeeded by a stressed syllable. The first three rhythmical units set this pattern in motion, though they are of different lengths. What will come next? We expect more unstressed syllables preceding a specially stressed one. And we get "bear any burden," which continues the weak-weak-stress pattern (followed here by a final weak syllable). Now, we expect still further parallels, and Kennedy provides them. Try reading the excerpt as though it ended with "bear any burden." You will be dissatisfied. How many repetitions do you want? Probably at least one more, preferably two. Kennedy gave four—not exactly alike, lest he become metrical. They were similar enough so that listeners could respond to the basic rhythmical structures. In this way he propelled his hearers through his series of pledges, making the pledges seem inevitable because they were *rhythmically* inevitable. There is nothing of this in our passage from Zellner. No thought unit repeats the rhythmical structure of another. Listeners must rely on the basic, semantic and grammatical data for the meaning of what is said.

Recurring rhythmical patterns are not necessarily "better" than unrhythmical patterns like Zellner's. The point of this discussion is a simple one. A competent critic of oral rhetoric must be able to notice that the speaking in these two cases worked on listeners with different forces. Meaning *and feeling* were forwarded through the "music" of prose rhythm when Kennedy spoke; little extra feeling was generated by Zellner's explanation of what he planned to do in his speech, nor does there seem to have been great need of it. Noting these differences in the speakers' styles, we can sensibly assert that Mr. Kennedy roused feelings on behalf of his pledges; whereas, Mr. Zellner depended on the merits of his ideas alone to move his listeners' thoughts along. These observations might explain something else about Kennedy. If a critic remembered that it was common to call Kennedy a "vigorous" and "inspiring" speaker, he might be inclined to think that rhythmical evocations of feelings could have something to do with Kennedy's power to exact such descriptions. A close look at all of Kennedy's speaking would show that it was common for him to introduce rhythmical "beats" that could "carry people along." Perhaps that was a reason he was thought of as "inspiring."

With so little known about how rhythmical structures enhance the meanings of oral prose, a critic is forced to reason chiefly from speculative theory; he has little empirical data on which to base his critical thinking. If, as Ohmann and Perelman and Olbrechts-Tyteca contend, a verbal device such as a series enlarges the significance of the items named and argues that those items are truly similar, we ought to say that adding rhythmical similarity to utterance of the elements of a series would make those elements still more inclusive and, seemingly, more alike. If so, Kennedy implied *both* verbally and rhythmically that none of his pledges could be withheld from the whole policy he spoke of without breaking up the overall policy itself. On this reasoning we would be judging that verbal strategy plus rhythmical strategy made his policy claim more irrefutable than it would have been had either or both types of strategy been omitted.

By turning to the functions of vocal variety in oral rhetoric we shall see additional ways that rhythm works rhetorically.

VOCAL VARIETY

For centuries variety has been alleged to be a rhetorical virtue. But of what does "variety" consist? Research findings show clearly that listeners will respond fully to what they hear only if the pitch, rate, and rhythmical patterns of utterance vary considerably. On the other hand, there is no basis for saying that differentiating these patterns in just any way will prove "varied" and "pleasing." About all we know is that the opposites of vocal "variety" are "monotone" and "monorate." These have deadening effects on listeners' responses. For example, Glasgow studied listeners' comprehension of materials (1) delivered with "good intonation" (varied pitches, stresses, and rates) and (2) delivered in "monotone" (apparently with both monotone and monorate). He found that the listeners comprehended about 10 percent less of the material when they heard it presented in "monotone."[10] In other research narrowness of pitch range (tendency toward monotone) has been found generally associated with psychological disorders involving depression.[11] On these grounds it seems justifiable for a speech critic to reason that wherever rhetorical speech can be fairly described as tending toward monotony in pitch and/or rate, that speech should be judged less communicative and less effective than it could have been.

There are also certain patterns of pitch-duration-inflection that seem to be heard by listeners as evidences of specific emotional states. An important series of studies by Fairbanks, Pronovost, and Hoaglin showed that people think speech sounds "angry" or "fearful" when it has high pitch levels, wide pitch ranges, short phonations, short pauses, and is generally rapid in rate. Speech which sounds "angry" differs from speech that sounds "fearful" chiefly in that "angry" speech has wider pitch ranges and more rapid pitch changes than "fearful" speech. Another finding in these studies is especially important to speech critics. Speech that sounds "indifferent" (the opposite of "emotional") has inflectional features almost the opposite of "angry" or "fearful" speech. Speech which listeners called "indifferent" had a low pitch level, a very narrow pitch range (tending toward monotone), but was not characterized by monorate. In other respects there was not much difference among "indifferent," "angry," and "fearful" speech.[12] These findings suggest that it is monotony of *pitch* that listeners take as a sign of indifference toward what is said and, probably, toward themselves.

There is, then, fairly clear evidence concerning which vocal patterns are particularly inimical to effective rhetorical communication. If high pitch and wide, rapid pitch changes are characteristic of speech which listeners associate with strong emotions and if low pitch with narrow pitch changes produces a sense that the speaker is "indifferent," we might reason that speech with the desirable qualities of "variety," "conversationality," or whatever we call the rhetorically "normal" ought to have vocal characteristics somewhere between the agitated patterns of strong emotion and the deadly patterns of "indifference." On this reasoning we would expect generally "desirable" speech for rhetorical communication to have such vocal-durational-inflectional characteristics as: low to moderate pitch level, moderately wide pitch ranges without strikingly wide sweeps of rising and falling pitches, phonations with clearly varied lengths separated by pauses of varied lengths, and overall rate of utterance varying within the general range of 125–200 words per minute. This is an inferred description of what "good," "direct," "conversational" speech is acoustically. The description cannot be backed up with direct acoustical and phonetic evidence, but no available evidence contradicts the description. It is, then, as good a normative statement as we can create about "ideal" vocal qualities of speech.

The description above is loosely supported by what has been found in experiments comparing listeners' responses to kinds of delivery grossly described as "conversational" and "dynamic." The acoustic properties of these styles of delivery have not been specified in the experiments, but the researchers seem to have tested what they believed was especially "energetic," "hard sell" speech against what they considered "good" conversational style.[13] The reports suggest that the "conversational" deliveries were somewhat like the delivery described above as "direct" and "conversational." The "dynamic" deliveries seem to have had a faster overall rate, wider variations in pitch and pause, and in some cases greater than normal changes of volume. Virtually all these experiments have indicated that speakers using the "conversational" patterns earned higher credibility ratings from listeners than the "dynamic" speakers.[14] Just what dimensions of credibility are sacrificed by "dynamic" delivery and how the sacrifice occurs are not clear, but in one way or another the speaking labeled "dynamic" has generally generated reservations about the *ethos* of speakers using that style.[15]

The findings of this group of investigations further reinforce our supposition that vocal "variety" which is both pleasing and taken as evidence that a speaker is being direct and conversational falls within a range of behaviors bounded on one side by "emotional" patterns and by "indifferent" monotony on the other. A useful critical question therefore becomes: Will the vocal-rhythmical variations in this speaking be likely to convey impressions of "emotionalism," "indifference," or be heard as "good variety" having inflectional patterns lying between these extremes? If it seems vocal-rhythmical patterns are apt to suggest "excitement," a critic ought to ask: Will *these* listeners approve of that excitement?

In some situations a display of excitement—or even of indifference—is appropriate. If listeners are "angry" about something, they are apt to approve speakers who sound "angry" about it.[16] It is equally possible that sounding "indifferent" toward an idea or person is precisely what is required where listeners need to know that their speaker has the "right" sense of values and is willing to ignore what they would ignore. In short, a critic ought to note whether speech does or does not express the "right" emotions for the situation.

When speech is vocally and rhythmically "normal," it can lend supplementary affective power to the forces of content and verbal style. We have observed this kind of reinforcement in an excerpt from Kennedy's inaugural address. For another instance, look at lines 8–11 in the text of George Miller's speech (p. 55). At this point Miller seems to create a rhythmical "beat" without having wholly satisfactory words with which to fill the rhythmical "measures." I am willing to argue that the vocal-rhythmical patterns of Miller's "this will" series were so prominent that they could give listeners a sense that there was much distasteful expediency-mongering on the civil rights issue. Rhythmical parallelism matched verbal parallelism in Miller's delivery here, and I believe the vocal rhythms would "cover" the rather vague and colloquial language Miller used. Working in another way, the paralleled "beats" of Churchill's "He is now but a lackey and serf" and "the merest utensil of his master's will" must, when coupled through Churchillian delivery, have made the metaphors of disdain for Mussolini still more disdainful.

These examples suggest that rhythmical structures coupled with persuasive verbal structures can reinforce other work of the verbal language. When this happens, it seems reasonable to believe that dimensions of feeling are added to semantic meanings. It is even possible, I believe, that as in Miller's lines 8-11 rhythmical structures can achieve what the words cannot.[17]

Where apparently significant forces are vocally stressed, critics ought to describe the phenomena as clearly as possible, consider how those phenomena relate to other rhetorical forces, and comment on the probable significance of the interplay among those elements. There is no reason to believe that vocalic patterns do much more than *modify* what content and verbal style supply as basic stimuli, but vocalic-rhythmical modifications deserve notice because they are so often *affectively* important. The general critical question in this connection is: What, if anything, was *added* rhetorically through vocalization? Speech critics are not interested in vocal-rhythmical patterns in and for themselves as phoneticians might be. But speech critics do need to give more attention than they have usually given to how vocal-rhythmical patterns modify what rhetorical content, structure, and verbal style supply as "raw material" to be voiced.

Dialectal Features

Some critical judgments relating to dialectal and other in-group patterns of speech were discussed in chapter VIII, but something remains to be said about the effects of "strange" and "familiar" dialects.

As I shall use the term, a "dialect" is any language pattern peculiar to people living in a particular geographical region or belonging to an identifiable class or social group. For purposes of rhetorical criticism there is no need to enter the endless debates about whether dialects are "substandard," "culturally equivalent," etc. A speech critic is interested in how dialects *work* in rhetorical situations. Approaching rhetoric couched in dialectal patterns, such a critic wants to know: (1) When do listeners perceive speakers as using "dialects"? and (2) What happens when those listeners decide they are hearing a "dialect"?

Numerous investigations have focused on what happens when a speaker is a *stranger* and uses a dialect different from that used by his listeners. The findings are that the listeners will infer that the speaker has those qualities their stereotypes tell them are characteristic of people who use that particular "alien" dialect. The report of one recent study is particularly explicit:

[The] results clearly show dialect to be a cue principally to a region-relevant stereotype encompassing the user's probable identification with the particular region and its prevalent attitudes and values. The Midwestern listeners . . . used relatively few constructs relating to specific character and dispositional [the speaker's personal disposition] qualities . . . when he [the speaker] used a Southern or New England dialect. Rather, it was as if the speaker was being positioned sociologically in terms of regional background, status, and probable attitudes.[18]

Drawing on his own data and data from other studies, Delia further asserts:

When a stranger is perceived on the basis of his dialect to be a member of the same general group or class as that of the subject, there is a concomitant assumption that he [the speaker] will be liked, enjoyable to converse with, and easy to work with in communication situations. These results are, of course, in no way startling when read in conjunction with the long tradition of research dealing with stereotyping and attraction toward in-group and out-group members.[19]

Another of Delia's findings, also supported by other research, is especially important to speech critics:

The results on all the measures of attraction toward the speaker and anticipations of communication with him show the stereotype based on regional dialect to be quite tentative and subject to accommodation to new information. Hence, the effects introduced by presenting the subjects with specific information concerning the speaker's character produced negative shifts in both the evaluation of the speaker and in the assessments of anticipated communication. These shifts were, of course, most dramatic where the subjects initially heard the General American dialect which was similar to their own. . . . Stereotypes based on regional dialects thus appear to provide tentative guidelines concerning the background and attitudes of the other, but they are not so rigid as to prevent accommodation to new information.[20]

Most research having to do with the impact of dialectal speech, including Delia's, deals with how dialects affect listeners' *first impressions* of *initially unknown* speakers. This research suggests a useful critical question: What are the stereotypes this audience will draw upon in forming *initial* impressions of relatively unfamiliar speakers whose dialects differ from theirs? If a critic can explore the attitudes an audience has toward the locales and groups from which speakers come, he may be able to estimate how those listeners will think about rhetors identified with those locales or groups. Then the critic can consider how these stereotypic impressions will index the listeners' responses to what is said by a given speaker. Clearly critics will be most interested in the "indexing" effects rather than enduring effects of dialects. Delia's evidence makes clear that dialectally induced judgments are rather easily changed.

When listeners' and speaker's dialects are the same, a critic can assume that if nothing else interferes, the speaker will begin with a helpful degree of identification between himself and the listeners. It is when dialects differ that speakers begin with special "burdens" and "blessings" imposed by listeners' stereotypes.

Dialectal influences are probably less significant if a speaker is well known to his audience, though we have little research on the point. The general assumption of rhetorical theory is that prior reputation—initial *ethos*—is more important than dialectal or other incidental forces in defining a known speaker's status. It was surely Winston Churchill's reputation, more than his British English dialect, that determined his initial relationship with the Congress when he addressed it. Stokely Carmichael's reputation as a black activist and as a leader of the Student Nonviolent Coordinating Committee doubtless had more to do with his initial relations with his Morgan State audience than the facts that he could move in and out among Caribbean English, General American speech, Southern American speech, and Black English. The latter facts were probably assets, but they must have constituted modest influences compared to Carmichael's reputation, content, and verbal style.

Dialectal similarities and differences between listeners and speakers are not unimportant rhetorical factors, but critics ought to remember that all speakers have a vast array of means by which to alter dialectally generated first impressions. Dialectal identifications and difference can *modify* rhetorical impact, it appears, but there is no evidence that an intelligible dialect ever dominates in determining listeners' responses to speech during extended discussion or conversation. Sooner or later, even among strangers, content and what Aristotle called *ethos* "created by the speech itself" will contribute most heavily to listeners' judgments of credibility.

VOCAL BEHAVIOR AND ATTRIBUTION OF PERSONALITY TRAITS

If listeners have nothing "better" to go on, they are likely to make judgments about speakers' personalities and credibility on the basis of what vocal quality seems to tell them. Of course, listeners in ordinary rhetorical situations have far more than vocal behavior to judge by. Nevertheless, it is well established that listeners attribute traits of personality to speakers on the basis of vocal qualities. It is equally well established that listeners are *wrong* as often as not in these attributions.[21]

If critics have reasons to suspect that vocal behavior is influencing listeners' perceptions in significant ways, it is useful to know in what directions people's interpretations are likely to move when they interpret personality by observing vocal qualities. A few normative statements can be made, but all must be prefaced by the phrase, "other things being equal":

1. Judgments of *competency* seem especially susceptible to change as vocal qualities change. "Normal" voice quality combined with relatively slow rate seems the behavioral pattern commonly associated with "good" competency.

2. What laymen and experts are apt to designate as "normal" vocal quality (for the individual, of course) tends to elicit impressions of high credibility.

3. Nasality, denasality, tenseness, and throatiness are vocal qualities that tend to cause lowered estimations of speakers' credibility whether the speakers are male or female.

4. Listeners appear to associate the vocal quality called "breathiness" with immaturity, whether the speaker is male or female.

5. Harshness and hoarseness are judged unpleasant in male or female voices. Attributions of associated personality

traits are exceedingly variable, but none is flattering to the speaker.

6. As pitch variations diminish toward monotone, the perceived credibility of both male and female speakers tends to diminish.[22]

These generalizations tend to reaffirm what has already been said in several different connections: the "normal" speech that keeps listeners from making judgments disadvantageous to speakers is speech that is in no obvious way unusual. What the data add to a critic's fund of normative information is chiefly that nasality, denasality, hoarseness, harshness, or breathiness are particularly likely to cause judgments inimical to a speaker's credibility.

INTELLIGIBILITY

Obviously speech must be heard clearly and easily if it is to be effective. Several elemental facts about the nature of spoken English and the difficulties of speech perception deserve to be in all speech critics' collections of normative information.

To be easily understood speech needs to be heard in a frequency range of about 100–3000 cycles per second. Perception of frequencies up to 5000 cycles per second is desirable but not imperative. Full intelligibility of spoken English does not require that all the frequencies produced by male and female voices be heard. Roughly speaking, speech ought to be received by listeners' ears as signals having approximately the fidelity that is delivered by an ordinary telephone. If this will not be the case for all hearers in a rhetorical situation, a critic ought to be aware of the shortcoming, account for it if possible, and calculate the consequences to communicative effectiveness.

Related to the general intelligibility of spoken English is an obvious but often disregarded fact about the language; the intelligibility of spoken English depends heavily upon a listener's ability to discern *consonants*. Ironically, English consonants tend to be the sounds of highest frequency and least amplitude or volume! Consider what is involved in hearing that a speaker said "influence" and not "effluence," or that he said "fret" and not "fresh," "French," or "freckle." Accurate understanding depends significantly upon distinguishing such *weak* consonants as "n" from "f" and on perceiving that "t" was said and not "sh" or "nch" or "ckle." This feature of the English language is one reason that Southern American speech and Black English give trouble to speakers of General American English. Southern and Black English dialects "drop off" many consonants on which speakers of General American English learn to depend for understanding. Also, in Southern and Black English speech vowels, which contribute minimally to word discrimination, often are prolonged.

These same facts about spoken English help to explain why speech needs to be slowed and carefully articulated for the aged and, especially, for the partially deaf. English consonants are for the most part high frequency sounds, and the hearing losses of the aged are often in those higher ranges. Anyone partially deaf across the frequencies of ordinary speech finds it that much harder to hear the language's weak consonants.

Also, echoes and other acoustical phenomena sometimes operate to intensify already prominent vowel sounds and mask the weak consonants.

There are, then, acoustic, linguistic, situational, and physiological factors of which speech critics must at least sometimes take account if they are to describe and judge what goes on in speech situations. It is always fair to ask whether a speaker did as much as he or she could to achieve intelligibility despite the constraints of the language and whatever interfering forces may have existed in the setting.

Any or all rhythmic and vocalic features of delivery can modify listeners' perceptions of content and, especially, of speakers' *ethos*. It is seldom that any of these features dominate perceptions of oral communication, but they deserve review in comprehensive speech criticism. When there are reasons to believe these aspects of delivery could have created special perceptions of *ethos* or uniquely reinforced content of verbalization, critics ought to specify the phenomena they observe, weigh their findings against such norms as have been identified in this section, and include in the total account of the speaking whatever inferences seem justifiable.

ROLES OF GESTURAL SPEECH BEHAVIORS

Abne M. Eisenberg and Ralph R. Smith, Jr. have expressed clearly the facets of nonverbal behavior that chiefly concern speech critics:

> The behaviors which should be included in a discussion of nonverbal communication are those which act as messages on a receiver. Using

this criterion, *the function,* rather than the motivation for an act, is emphasized. This standard is the only one which provides an objective measurement. One can never be certain of a sender's state of awareness, but whether a receiver responds or not can, conceivably, be measured.[23]

These observations are pertinent to all nonverbal behaviors insofar as critics of oral rhetoric are concerned. They have special relevance to criticism of gestural behavior, considered as any visible behavior that may convey rhetorical meaning. In partial answer to a critic's interest in what gestural communication can *say,* one pair of researchers has suggested that gestural behavior can have the following kinds of communicative functions:

1. To substitute (express in another medium) what might be expressed by a word or phrase; e.g., a beckoning gesture may substitute for or reexpress, "Come here!"
2. To illustrate or emphasize the meaning of verbal expression; e.g., pushing a fist into the palm of the other hand could illustrate such a phrase as, "Exert all possible force."
3. To regulate the flow of communication by encouraging, speeding up, interrupting, as with nods, frowns, holding up one's hand, etc.
4. To serve general, adaptive, and perhaps releasing functions. These are behaviors that have become parts of an individual's social pattern and may be peripheral to direct communicative intent; e.g., grooming actions, manipulating objects, or doodling.[24]

These four categories provide convenient means by which any speech critic can identify and describe to others whatever gestural actions seem rhetorically significant. They do not, however, provide a basis for evaluating the effectiveness of gestural communication. For this purpose another category system can be used in combination with Ekman and Friesen's descriptive system.

On the basis of considerable research, Albert Mehrabian has proposed that the *meanings* of gestural (and other nonverbal) cues can be seen as falling within three general classes of interpersonal understandings.

1. There is an array of behaviors which communicate and are perceived as communicating liking and disliking. These include actions that achieve or express desire for more or

less distance between communicants. Behaviors which achieve or express desire for closeness imply liking, and those directed toward increasing distance imply disliking, according to Mehrabian and his colleagues.

2. There is also an array of behaviors that are indicators of "potency and status." They express in metaphorical fashion such interpersonal conditions as relative strength and weakness, relaxation and tension. Among such behaviors, standing upright can communicate strength and bowing, weakness; expansive movement may express strength and relaxation while small, constrained movements are apt to communicate weakness and tension.

3. The third class of communications Mehrabian posits are behaviors that express "responsiveness" or lack of it. These include reactive facial (and vocal) movements that signal response, as in communication of anger or joy.[25]

Though it extends use of Ekman and Friesen's and Mehrabian's proposals beyond the authors' intentions, it seems possible to combine the two category systems to create a method of describing and interpreting gestural behaviors. If we see a speaker leaning forward, looking intently at his listeners in what Ekman and Friesen would call "illustrative" behavior, Ekman and Friesen's label gives us a way of describing. Then, using Mehrabian's categories, we can point to the further fact that the actions illustrate an apparent desire to reduce distance. If Mehrabian's theories are right, our speaker would be communicating "liking." If we think a "liking" behavior fits the content and situation, we would be able to infer and to explain the nonverbal behavior's potentiality to increase listeners' adherence to what the speaker said. Simply by applying the two classification systems we derive intelligible description and criteria for interpreting the nonverbal phenomena. Furthermore, general norms of speaking tell us that whatever identifies a speaker's interests with an audience's interests is apt to enhance the speaker's credibility. Hence, if illustrative leaning and looking movements mean "liking" and thereby communicate some degree of identification, we achieve premises on which to conclude that the actions we are studying probably were constructive rather than distractive in overall communication.

Consider a more complex problem. If we are studying the oral rhetoric in an interview or small-group discussion, we will want to understand who exercised what control in the rhetorical situation.

Following Ekman and Friesen, we would watch, among other things, behaviors that function as "regulators." If we see behaviors that encourage or speed up or otherwise affect the flow of communication, reference to Mehrabian's categories would remind us that we have noted communications of "potency and status" and, perhaps, of "responsiveness." Again, general knowledge of the rhetorical situation would provide information on the basis of which to judge whether these exercises of strength and weakness, influence and responsiveness, were likely to advance or interfere with resolving rhetorical exigences. This kind of analysis and criticism is often important in describing and evaluating the rhetorical events of news conferences, question-and-answer sessions following speeches, and the rhetoric of classrooms. In such situations it is especially important to discover who is exercising control and how. Since much control is exercised nonverbally, the Ekman-Friesen and the Mehrabian categories can give us help in identifying, describing, and interpreting nonverbal acts aimed at control.

The "adaptive behaviors" Ekman and Friesen identify are usually para-rhetorical. For the most part they are actions extraneous to the rhetorical goals of communicative engagements. In most rhetorical situations such actions are present but fail to fit any of Mehrabian's classifications of nonverbal *meaning*. If a speaker doodles or scratches his earlobe as he talks, we shall find it difficult to assert that liking, status, or responsiveness are communicative "contents" of the behavior. We shall have found something extraneous to the rhetorical thrust of the engagement. The only critical question becomes: Would the "extraneous" behavior *interfere?* Again, knowledge of the situation and of the ideational *content* of the rhetorical communication would provide the data from which we could build a reasoned answer to the question.

My suggestion is that a speech critic who classifies notable nonverbal behaviors in *both* Ekman and Friesen's way and Mehrabian's way will be directing his critical thought through (1) systematic, discussable description allowing (2) a statement about the behavior's probable communicative significance. With probable effect (or rhetorical irrelevance) stipulated, the critic is in a position to (3) estimate whether the behavior's communicative meaning was constructive or otherwise in the particular rhetorical engagement.

What recent research on nonverbal communication has chiefly given to speech critics are *ways of talking about* gestural and other nonverbal communication. Unfortunately the state of knowledge about gestural *communication* is much as Ellsworth and Ludwig recently said:

> Research on visual behavior, like almost all research on nonverbal "communication," has so far avoided a question which to us seems central: what cues influence the perceiver and to what cues does he attribute meaning? . . . It [research] tells us that a vast number of discriminable behaviors are constantly occurring, but it does not tell us which of these actually are discriminated by the interacting perceiver.[26]

Since the emergence of the "elocutionary movement" in the late eighteenth century, there has been a widespread notion that there exist discoverable *codes* of physical communication not unlike our linguistic codes. If such codes exist, we still lack knowledge of their lexicons and their grammars, though significant research is being devoted to these matters. We also lack knowledge of the psychological principles that govern perceptions, interpretations, and responses to nonverbal, gestural actions associated with rhetorical speech. In the present state of knowledge a critic of oral rhetoric can only tell what he observed, define its communicative significance by the best categorical systems available to him, and infer how the observed behavior may have modified reception of the verbal components of oral rhetoric.

CONCLUSION

If we recall the body of evidence that suggests delivery has only limited, modifying rhetorical influence except when verbal and nonverbal messages are inconsistent, it seems fair to ask whether critics of oral rhetoric should worry about nonverbal communication at all. They should—at least sometimes. When (1) there is reason to think there is conflict between what is communicated in the verbal and nonverbal channels and (2) when there is reason to think nonverbal forces may *uniquely* reinforce verbal meanings, there seems reason to take the force of nonverbal communication most seriously. Considerable support has developed for Mehrabian's assertion that:

> The general rule for understanding the effects of . . . inconsistent messages is that, when actions contradict words, people rely more

heavily on actions to infer another's *feelings*. In other words, it appears that less-controllable behaviors are assigned greater weights.[27]

Evidence uniformly asserts that rhythmical, vocal, and gestural behaviors are, indeed, searched by listeners when they think they need to penetrate the "real" feelings and intentions of speakers. There is little empirical evidence relating to the assertion that nonverbal phenomena can significantly *reinforce* verbal meaning, but surely all experience with poetry and with markedly rhythmical speeches such as Kennedy's inaugural address argues that reinforcement is very possible.

It seems to me a speech critic's chief job in reference to nonverbal elements of communication is to watch for moments of inconsistency and for moments of unique reinforcement. No carefully developed evidence supports Demosthenes's alleged claim that delivery has prime importance in oral rhetoric. But delivery does attain importance when it contradicts verbal communication. It may have important modifying influence when it specially reinforces words. Vocal and other actions speak as loudly as words—sometimes.

NOTES

[1] Wayne N. Thompson, *Quantitative Research in Public Address and Communication* (New York: Random House, 1967), p. 92.

[2] Albèrt Mehrabian, *Nonverbal Communication* (Chicago: Aldine-Atherton, Inc., 1972), p. 182.

[3] These general statements seem supported by research done by Mehrabian and others and by data developed in studies of the effects of vocalic aspects of oral communication. However, I inserted the phrase "mutually reinforcing to an unusual degree" in Statement 2 without any supporting evidence. The potentialities of nonverbal reinforcement of verbal structure and form have not been studied directly. Reasons for believing such reinforcement is possible will be given later in this chapter.

[4] W. Barnett Pearce and Bernard J. Brommel, "Vocalic Communication in Persuasion," *Quarterly Journal of Speech* 58 (October 1972): 305.

[5] W. Barnett Pearce and Forrest Conklin, "Nonverbal Vocalic Communication and Perceptions of a Speaker," *Speech Monographs* 38 (August 1971): 235–241.

[6] *Ibid.*, p. 236.

[7] *Oxford Translation of Aristotle*, 1408^b, by permission of The Clarendon Press, Oxford; or see *Aristotle's Rhetoric and Poetics*, p. 180.

[8] John F. Kennedy, "Inaugural Address," p. 312.

[9] Leon R. Zellner, "What Can We Prove about God?" p. 337.

[10] George M. Glasgow, "A Semantic Index of Vocal Pitch," *Speech Monographs* 19 (March 1952): 64–68.

[11] Jon Eisenson, J. Jeffery Auer, and John V. Irwin, *The Psychology of Communication* (New York: Appleton-Century-Crofts, 1963), p. 78.

[12] The studies referred to contain additional detail. See Grant Fairbanks and Wilbert Pronovost, "An Experimental Study of the Pitch Characteristics of the Voice during the Expression of Emotions," *Speech Monographs* 6 (1939):

87–104; Grant Fairbanks and LeMar W. Hoaglin, "An Experimental Study of the Durational Characteristics of the Voice during the Expression of Emotion," *Speech Monographs* 8 (1941): 85–90. A summary of the findings of these and related studies can also be found in Eisenson, Auer, and Irwin, *Psychology of Communication,* p. 79.

[13] These studies are conveniently summarized and evaluated in Pearce and Brommel, "Vocalic Communication in Persuasion."

[14] Representative of these studies are: John E. Dietrich, "The Relative Effectiveness of Two Modes of Radio Delivery in Influencing Attitudes," *Speech Monographs* 13 (March 1946): 58–65; John Waite Bowers, "The Influence of Delivery on Attitudes toward Concepts and Speakers," *Speech Monographs* 32 (June 1965): 154–158; Pearce and Conklin, "Nonverbal Vocalic Communication"; Pearce and Brommel, "Vocalic Communication in Persuasion."

[15] It does not follow that *what* the speaker said was doubted. In several experiments the persuasiveness of content remained largely unchanged though confidence in the "dynamic" speaker sagged.

[16] As George Miller concluded his short address to his fellow convention delegates his vocal patterns took on most of the features Fairbanks et al. found in "angry" utterance. This was almost surely appropriate in the situation, for Miller's listeners were politically liberal and generally disapproved of adopting a weak civil rights plank. So did Miller. It seems unlikely that he could have roused these listeners as he wished, much less fulfilled his own goal "to express myself," had he not sounded angry about treating this "moral question" lightly.

[17] In several styles of preaching it is commonplace in the latter portions of sermons to generate rhythmical patterns which make use of previously established refrains and key terms in ways that are not necessarily semantically or syntactically meaningful; nonetheless, the rhythmically vocalized phrases evoke strong degrees of emotion in listeners. Several studies of "old time" Southern preaching have drawn special attention to this evocative process.

[18] Jesse G. Delia, "Dialects and the Effects of Stereotypes on Interpersonal Attraction and Cognitive Processes in Impression Formation," *Quarterly Journal of Speech* 58 (October 1972): 289. The full study is reported on pp. 285–297. Subjects were speakers of General American English, hence Southern and New England dialects were "other" dialects for them.

[19] *Ibid.,* p. 294.

[20] *Ibid.,* p. 295. In one phase of his investigation Delia gave his subjects three positive and three negative statements about the speaker they had heard. These were provided *after* the subjects had made evaluative responses based exclusively on vocal and articulatory evidence. After receiving the added information, subjects reevaluated the speaker. The impressions they had formed exclusively from hearing dialectal speech were altered by the new information.

[21] It deserves notice that virtually all research on these points was carried out using unseen, recorded speakers who uttered brief, uniform passages or nonsense syllables. We do not know how or whether listeners project personality traits on speakers whom they can see and who discuss ideas of their own.

[22] These generalizations are drawn from the strongest findings of David W. Addington, "The Relationship of Selected Vocal Characteristics to Personality Perception," *Speech Monographs* 35 (November 1968): 492–503; Addington, "The Effect of Vocal Variations on Ratings of Source Credibility," *Speech Monographs* 38 (August 1971): 242–247; and LeRoy A. Pavés, "Voice and Characterization for the Actor: A Study," *Express* 7 (February 1970): 9–14.

[23] Abne M. Eisenberg and Ralph R. Smith, Jr., *Nonverbal Communication* (Indianapolis: The Bobbs-Merrill Company, Inc., 1971), pp. 31–32. My italics.

[24] These categories are four of five classes presented in Paul Ekman and Wallace Friesen, "The Repertoire of Nonverbal Behavior: Categories, Origins, Usage, and Coding," *Semiotica* 1 (1969): 49–98. The categories are also listed

and succinctly explained in Eisenberg and Smith, pp. 25–27. I omit the class, "emblems."

[25] See Mehrabian, *Nonverbal Communication,* especially chapter 10, pp. 178–190.

[26] Phoebe C. Ellsworth and Linda M. Ludwig, "Visual Behavior in Social Interaction," *Journal of Communication* 22 (December 1972): 399.

[27] Albert Mehrabian, *Silent Messages* (Belmont: Wadsworth Publishing Company, Inc., 1971), p. 56. My italics.

Chapter X

Special Problems in Speech Criticism

The preceding chapters have treated basic procedures critics can use when seeking to understand how oral rhetoric functions. In the main, they presupposed that the rhetoric examined was continuous, face-to-face speaking. But not all significant, rhetorical speaking occurs uninterruptedly. It occurs as interrupted discourse in interviews, discussions, plays, and elsewhere. Nor need speaker and audience be within each other's view, as any significant radio speech or telephone call illustrates. Furthermore, much important rhetoric is more significant for its long-ranged consequences than for its immediate effects.[1]

Other matters which have gone undiscussed in earlier chapters include the historiographical problems speech critics face when they study important speaking of the past, the perennially troublesome question of how criticism of ethics and criticism of rhetoric are related, and presenting criticism to others. This concluding chapter is devoted to these matters.

THE PROBLEMS OF NONCONSECUTIVE DISCOURSE

Nonconsecutive speech of significance occurs in interviews, news conferences, panel discussion, informal conversation. It also occurs

239

in places we do not always think of as habitats of speech amenable to rhetorical criticism. In almost any play by George Bernard Shaw, any agit-prop skit from communist countries, or any "new left" or "counterculture" play from the 1960s there is significant, oral *rhetoric*. Involve people in serious, dyadic discussion, and rhetoric amenable to criticism is likely to occur. Create a learning unit, and seek to teach it in a classroom, and the the events will constitute a blend of instructional rhetoric and rhetoric-to-the-self, all intended to alter the perceptions of students. Indeed, a committee of scholars not long ago formulated this statement:

> The effort should be made to expand the scope of rhetorical criticism to include subjects which have not traditionally fallen within the critic's purview: the non-discursive as well as the discursive, the non-verbal as well as the verbal, the event or transaction which is unintentionally as well as intentionally suasive. The rhetorical critic has the freedom to pursue his study of subjects with suasory potential or persuasive effects in whatever setting he may find them, ranging from rock music and put-ons, to architecture and public forums, to ballet and international politics. Though the subjects of his investigations should be expanded, his identity need not be lost.[2]

Some of these kinds of rhetoric fall outside our present concern, but this committee's emphasis on the omnipresence of examinable rhetoric is a reminder that influential rhetoric does not exist only in formal public speaking and that a speech critic ought to be prepared to comment on oral rhetoric wherever it occurs. To do this the critic must resolve four analytical problems.

What Is the Rhetorical Situation?

Critics of oral rhetoric need always to ask what characteristics are peculiar to the rhetorical situations they are inspecting, but to ask about the situations of nonconsecutive discourse may require looking for situation in a new way. Particularly in dialogue, it is important to discover the rhetorical situations that are created *within* and *by* talk itself. Put differently, in dialogues rhetorical situations are frequently shaped by the dialogue.

In a recent piece of critical research an investigator asked herself, "What are the rhetorical dimensions, if any, of dyadic, husband-wife conversations conducted in semiprivacy?" She had as raw material several hours of relatively intimate, taped conversations. To know whether there was rhetoric in the conversations, she needed to know whether there were any rhetorical situations that *could* be addressed by either participant. A way of approaching this problem in conversations, most interviews, some press conferences, and other nonconsecutive discourse can be illustrated by considering a single segment of communication found in Ms. Glaser's tapes.[3]

The conversation in question was touching on the couple's efforts to "restore our marriage." The husband created a special rhetorical situation by remarking that he was glad his wife had returned to school for it made her more interesting to live with. Now the wife *had to* say something. She could accept the compliment, promise something more, or in some other way respond to her husband's expressed satisfaction; she could *not* sit silently without endangering her communicative relationship with her husband and perhaps her marriage. From within the flow of the conversation the husband had created a situation containing distinctive constraints and exigences. He had established himself as an audience, and he had defined his own exigences for the moment. The dimensions of a rhetorical situation were present, and the wife's next remarks proved open to rhetorical criticism by substantially the same methods one uses on brief speeches like Congressman George Miller's address to fellow delegates.

Later in the same husband-wife conversation, the wife observed that her husband seemed aloof from neighbors and from some of her other friends. Again, a rhetorical situation was created from within the ongoing conversation. The husband *had to* address an exigence. Within the context of conversation about "restoring our marriage," a defense or other explanation was imperative. The wife waited for her newly created exigence to be met and, of course, the husband began to defend his behavior. Therewith, a new "unit" of oral rhetoric emerged and became open to critical examination in standard ways.

The moments of husband-wife conversation are different only in detail from rhetorical "units" within the play *Othello*. Across a series of carefully managed rhetorical situations Iago moves Othello from suspicion to raging jealousy. Iago's strategies are credible to playgoers because Shakespeare lets them know that Othello is suspicious by nature. Doubt seems necessary to him, and this is the basic, situational "imperfection" with which Iago works. The audience watches Iago slowly modify the "imperfection" by feeding Othello's exigence, his need to doubt. The scenes seem credible because spectators know intuitively that rhetorical situations are constantly created and influenced in conversations.

In short, a speech critic can define "units" of oral rhetoric by looking for the constituents of rhetorical situations *within* non-consecutive discourse. The play, the conversation, the interview, the panel discussion is not always open to rhetorical criticism as a *whole,* but its internal "units" of rhetoric are. Distinctive *rhetorical situations* define those "units." Rhetorical situations created within discourse by strategies of discourse demand "fitting response" no less than any other situations. How well rhetorical responses "fit" these situations is precisely the domain of rhetorical critics. If the responses are oral, they are the domain of critics of oral rhetoric.

A "unit" of rhetoric in nonconsecutive discourse is not always the comment-response unit just considered. Observations need to be made to discover whether other segments deserve to have the tools of speech criticism applied to them.

Finding the Larger "Units"

Sometimes rhetorical maneuvers are aimed at evoking responses from people more or less outside the direct engagement. An obvious case occurs when a lawyer cross-examines a witness. The lawyer knows that his "real" audience is not the witness, but the judge and jury. He knows, too, that he, the witness, the judge, and the jury function within a set of legal constraints and opportunities that define the allowances of a communicative system larger than the one he and the witness are maintaining. Accordingly the lawyer asks questions in a planned way, hoping to elicit statements that will make suasory points within the larger communicative system. If he is reluctant, the witness may follow a counter-strategy, answering according to a different plan and hoping to make different points within the larger system. This kind of "address" can occur intermittently across the entirety of a body of talk, as it is apt to do during a cross-examination. Then, the "thread" of the address "to the outside" must be extracted and viewed as a rhetorical "unit."

A "threadlike unit" of oral rhetoric sometimes develops in press conferences and interviews. In a press conference newsmen and interviewee may have different views of what is important. Newsmen may raise questions about topic X at every opportunity while the interviewee struggles to get story Y at the "top of the news." Such tugs-of-war occur as participants vie for control of subject matter and for the privilege of structuring the conference in order to influence "outside" rhetorical situations (through the day's news).

Where "control of address" is at issue in nonconsecutive discourse it is possible to look upon each party's "thread" of effort as a unit of rhetoric and, perhaps, at the "contest" as a rhetorical debate. If the "sides" can be identified, the rhetoric of each can be considered in much the same way as one would consider a formal speech. The rhetorical situations for the "debate" will be both internal and external. Within the communicative system occupied by the conversants, the exigence is *control of the shape of discourse*. How well each party maneuvers to gain and maintain control *with the other party as audience* will interest a critic. But the rhetorical situation of the *larger* system, to which the tugging parties are trying also to communicate messages, will need study. Its exigences and constraints will have to be explored, and the rhetoric directed to it, through the struggle for control, will also be treated as a "unit" of discourse finally addressed to that larger system and situation.

A different kind of problem arises when a critic tries to study a great mass of rhetorical activity. What, then, shall be the "unit" or "units" on which he concentrates? Suppose the object of criticism is an advertising campaign, the seven Lincoln-Douglas debates, Lord Ashley's eleven-year effort to get the House of Commons to reduce the working day in factories, or some long-ranged educational program. From one point of view each of these can be looked at as a major, coherent, rhetorical effort, but each can also be seen legitimately as a series of specific efforts. If a critic cannot describe, interpret, and evaluate the whole body of rhetoric in a single project, he may choose to confine his immediate coverage to a subunit, perhaps planning to study other subunits later, and possibly anticipating that, when all subunits have been studied, a major, critical synthesis will be possible. Whatever the ultimate goal, experience in criticism suggests that it is wiser to study situational units of discourse than to explore arbitrary units determined by topics, figures involved, years, and so on.

A critical strategy of this general sort is suggested in Leland M. Griffin's "The Rhetorical Structure of the Antimasonic Movement." [4] Bruce Gronbeck applies a similar method to make comprehensible the rhetorical activities of the Black Action Movement and the University of Michigan during a three-month period in 1970. After arranging each side's acts and messages in chronological order, Gronbeck looked for major alterations in the situations within each group and in the "outside system" both groups were also addressing. He also noted changes in the strategies of each group, including the strategy of making no response. By these processes he found himself able to conceptualize the three-month sequence of events as a four-stage controversy.[5] In his study of persuasion by social groups and movements, Herbert W. Simons put succinctly the point illustrated by Griffin's and Gronbeck's critical strategies:

> . . . it should be quite clear that the leader of a social movement must thread his way through an intricate web of conflicting demands. How he adapts strategies to demands constitutes a primary basis for evaluating his rhetorical output.[6]

Whether the speaking we study comes from a general movement such as the Antimasonic movement or the Black Action movement or from individual leaders such as those Simons was writing of, demands and allowances "out there" tend to define how ongoing rhetorical activity ought to change.[7]

The immediacy of oral engagements makes oral rhetoric especially responsive to changes in rhetorical situations. A "unit" of speaking open to critical analysis probably can be better identified by looking for rhetorical situations than by depending on such arbitrary "dividers" as time, printers' discriminations, historical periods, or the like. Critics can also be unduly slavish toward verbal structures that only seem to assert what rhetorical "units" are. The body of utterance that needs critical attention may not be *a* speech, for "*a* speech" may in fact address more than one rhetorical situation and so constitute more than one critical "unit."[8] A campaign of speaking must address a number of different situations; accordingly, it, too, may be open to more efficient criticism if it is conceived as a series of relatively discrete rhetorical "phases." Criticism can then be addressed to these "phases" which the conceivers of the campaign may very well have conceptualized as "units" designed to meet changes in rhetorical situations.

THE INTERPLAY OF MANY RHETORS

There is speaking in which it is difficult to decide *whose* rhetoric to discuss, and how. In every election year hundreds of candidates make broadcasts and appear on other public platforms in the company of their opponents or their party colleagues. All get to talk within the framework of a single rhetorical event. For example, how shall we understand and evaluate the medley of speaking when five candidates for Mayor of New York City appear on a single telecast program and make opening and closing statements, answer questions from interviewers, and comment on each other's comments? To extract each speaker's comment from the melange makes no sense because the statements cannot be reasonably judged apart from their contexts. But we have no clear critical norms for judging five-man-free-flowing-interview-plus-argument formats even if we could comprehend them in full. Yet something like what is expressed by that hyphenated description is the rhetorical "form" before us. Or we may confront another multi-rhetor form. In 1972, President Richard Nixon's campaign speaking was largely planned and done for him by "surrogate speakers"—Cabinet and other officials spoke on his behalf in order to leave him free to conduct international negotiations. What was *this* top-level, pro-Nixon, oral campaign? It was something like Nixon-Agnew-Morton-Laird-Rogers-Richardson-and-company address. We could learn something from inspecting each "surrogate's" speaking, but if we accounted for all individual speeches, we would still not have answered the interesting question: What happened when "surrogate speaking" was addressed to an extended rhetorical situation? Even an examination of successive situational "units" would not give us a competent criticism of the *composite* rhetoric of the surrogate system.

When a critic must explore multi-speaker communications there is wisdom in adopting as critical tools the familiar Gestalt concepts of *figure* and *ground*. Whether the critical "object" is a platform full of speakers, a group of surrogate speakers, or some other collection of rhetors, each speaker is supposed to function as a *figure* presenting himself against the *ground* of all related rhetoric that has occurred and is occurring around him. If an individual speaker fulfills his possibilities in such a setting, he makes use of the *ground* against which he will be perceived. Ideally he will create the best personal and ideational image that is conceivable for him, given his own purposes and the background and purposes of other rhetoric. In our examples each mayoral candidate must strive to *stand out* as a potential leader, above the rhetorical *ground* created by his competitors and by interlocutors who preside over the program. The surrogate speakers must represent their *principal* and his administration. To do so, each should offer himself and his ideas as a worthy part of the collective image that must be created. Each surrogate is *figure* when he speaks, but each must also incorporate himself into a *ground* against which a *foremost figure* can be projected. In 1972, the surrogate campaigners functioned as secondary figures speaking on behalf of a foremost figure, President Nixon. The arrangement was not unique. The speeches at many corporate stockholders' meetings, the pronouncements of a politbureau, the utterances of a group of school principals meeting with parents, and dozens of other collective presentations exist for similar purposes: to offer a series of individual attempts by secondary *figures* to create ideal *ground* against which listeners will perceive a superior, personal or institutional "foremost *figure*." Once the shifting *figure-ground* possibilities of the rhetoric are identified, detailed criticism can proceed in usual ways. The first tasks are to specify who is *figure*, who is *ground*, when, and in what degree.

Without further exemplification it can be said that all critics must decide what "units" of rhetoric they will attend to. Frequently the conceptualization that *a* speaker makes *a* speech in *a* rhetorical situation inadequately describes actual rhetorical events. Then, the critical strategy of searching for the loci of successive rhetorical situations, exigences, and constraints may answer the question: What shall I treat as a "unit" of discourse? Sometimes rhetorical situations rise, decay, and rise again in modified forms. Then "phases" or "periods" of oral rhetoric may constitute the "units" of speech to which critics can most profitably apply their critical methods, subordinating attention to individual speakers and speeches. The rhetoric of social movements seems particularly amenable to this kind of critical study. The late Herbert A. Wichelns was wont to say in his seminars: "Many things are possible; even that speaking may be more important than speakers!" Especially when many speakers associate with one another in rhetorical ventures, the *collective* character of the speaking may be more important than any individual's speaking. It is even likely that the silences occurring between utterances or the days of apparent inactivity between bursts of speaking are not "definers" of "units" of rhetoric but are strategic behaviors occurring within other, situational "units."

THE ROLES OF MEDIA

There are a number of ways by which critics can safely informalize the traditional paradigm that oral rhetoric occurs when *an* orator *formally* addresses *an* audience. The paradigm I have argued for is one asserting that oral rhetoric occurs whenever there is speaking in response to a discernible rhetorical situation having exigences, constraints, and allowances. But even this expanded paradigm leaves out of consideration what media add to or subtract from situational speaking.

In a book on basic methods of speech criticism it would be inappropriate to raise the technical and even metaphysical questions about media and messages concerning which the name of Marshall McLuhan has become a suggestive symbol,[9] but two practical questions need to be raised: (1) How do media affect the reception of rhetorical elements in messages? and (2) How do the media through which a critic possesses messages affect opportunities for effective criticism?

Audiences watch and listen to televised speech without direct interaction with the speakers. People hear faceless voices via radio and telephones. People hear and respond to prerecorded speech on television, radio, and telephones. Obviously these different kinds of receivers do not hear-see precisely the same kinds of communications. Therein lies difficulty for critics. They must recognize that different channels allow audiences to perceive different constituents of what speakers create, yet there is little "hard" evidence concerning what filtering effects different communicative channels have. A radio audience cannot *see* the charm or oafishness that charms or offends a television audience, and so on. Surely, too, it is a mistake to assume that those who "saw it on television" received all of the stimuli received by those who were actually present. So, despite the difficulties, critics must think as carefully as they can about how media modify the basic potentialities of oral rhetoric.

It would be helpful if we had clear, empirical evidence concerning what distinctive things happen when audiences (a) see and hear oral messages in face-to-face situations, (b) hear but do not see the same presentations, (c) see but do not hear the messages "well," (d) see and hear the messages via television or film, (e) hear the messages via telephones with restricted acoustic characteristics, and (f) read messages originally presented orally. Unfortunately only a few bases for such comparisons exist, and we have even fewer generalizations. We lack precise distinctions between listening *as an act* and reading *as an act,* though both philosophically and empirically the two behaviors seem markedly different as processes and in their consequences. In a summary statement drawing on empirical evidence available to 1971, Carl H. Weaver said:

Scholars have found that when large batteries of tests are administered to groups of people and a factor analysis made, the listening and reading tests produce two different factors, not heavily loaded on each other. That is, they do not overlap, as might be expected. Both factors depend on intelligence and probably on some other variables. But when several tests of reading and of listening are administered, the reading tests correlate highly with each other but not with the listening tests; and the listening tests correlate highly with each other but not with the reading tests; this simply means that the tests tap different skills.

Finally, one study demonstrated that when we read a story and when we hear it, we mark different items correctly on a test. No one knows quite why this is so, but it implies different processes for the two kinds of behavior—reading and listening.[10]

Scholarship and everyday thinking have been bound for so long to the concept that print is our "significant" means of communication that it is still commonplace to find scholars, journalists, and others using the term *speech* as a synonym for *language* and vice versa. For reasons Weaver summarizes, as well as for philosophical reasons presented in chapters I and II, speech critics dare not forget that they deal with what is or was *spoken*. They are not dealing with substance created for communication through some other medium. This means that they must be alert to the special potentialities of speech as a medium.

The following four sets of considerations are discussed only summarily. Behind each lies a body of specialized literature, some or all of which you may wish to study firsthand.

1. Numerous studies conducted in very different ways confirm that no medium of communication excels the face-to-face, speaker-listener relationship for (a) achieving efficient communication of meanings—especially the affective; (b) effecting attitudinal changes in the persons involved; and (c) achieving favorable rapport between communicators and respondents. In general, the more opportunity there is for personalized interaction during oral communication, the greater will be the possibility that the communicators' messages will be accurately understood, favorably received, and acted upon.

From such findings, all empirically supported, there emerges a clear, explicit critical norm: If oral communication is occurring in a situation that does not allow face-to-face, interactive relationship between listeners and speakers, the influence is *less* than it might be. When directness and interaction are possible, the *opportunity* for influence through communication is maximized. Of course, what speakers and listeners do in such an optimal situation is a matter to be judged by other critical norms.

2. It is more likely that something said will be understood if it is heard (or overheard) than if the speaker is seen but not heard or not heard well. Since evidences of a speaker's feelings and his attitudes toward what he is saying are picked up better from vocal communication than from only seeing him or reading what he said, *it is affective meaning* that is especially impaired when audition is interfered with.

On the basis of these generalizations critics can infer that affective meanings will be fairly well perceived by audiences who hear speakers via radio, over public address systems that carry speech to areas removed from the sites of speaking, and by listeners who can hear clearly even though at a distance from speakers. Moreover, it can probably be inferred that affective meanings will be adequately caught when the medium of transmission is telephonic, for most important vocal clues to feelings are conveyed within the amplitude and frequency ranges of standard telephonic communication. Obviously, however, the fullest apprehension of meanings will occur when listeners can easily hear and see speakers.

3. It is very difficult to capture the content of oral communication when one can only *see* the speaker. *Some* affective meaning will be perceived but by no means as much as when speech can be heard or both heard and seen.[11]

On this basis critics need to be concerned with whether a speaker "speaks loudly enough," but they should also concern themselves with whether the transmission systems were faithful enough and free enough of interference to carry all necessary acoustic meanings.

4. Insofar as comprehension and retention of *information* are concerned, televised speaking seems no better and no worse than ordinary speech making. Listeners seem to take in and remember about the same amounts of information through both media. But most tests of these media have

used educational materials presented in educational settings, and retention of material has usually been measured
as retention useful for answering multiple-choice questions! Moreover, the relation between listeners' interest in
material and their comprehension and retention of it
has been minimally considered in studies of "live" versus
televised or filmic presentations.

A good deal of caution needs to be exercised in thinking about
the efficacy of televised and filmed speech. We know almost nothing about listeners' absorption of the affective forces communicated
by these kinds of oral communication. Despite all the public hearings and theorizing about how the media of mass communication affect listeners, it is not at all clear whether, how, or in what
degree televised or filmed communications affect listener-viewers'
values. That televised and filmed speaking can change attitudes
is clear. What roles, if any, the media as such play in effecting those
changes is almost entirely a matter of speculation. So, speech
critics who evaluate televised or filmed speaking are left with
norms no more firm than the following. If speaking was televised
or filmed, that fact probably did not interfere with listener-viewers'
understandings of the ideational content. Whether the suggestive
content of the speaking was stronger, weaker, or the same as it
would have been in a face-to-face, minimally interactive situation
is simply not known. For the time being, critics can do little more
than assume that the medium made little difference—unless special, situational facts indicate otherwise.

Another unanswered question about televised and filmed speech
is whether listeners react differently when speech is transmitted
"live" and when it is videotaped or filmed for later presentation.
Did it matter that Leonid Brezhnev's address to the American
people on June 24, 1973, was taped several days earlier (a fact
widely reported in the news media) and "played" on a Sunday
evening? There are no general criteria by which we can make
inferences about this. So, if a critic is to offer inferences about the
effects of "delayed broadcasts," those inferences must be based
on specific evidence drawn from the details of the specific rhetorical
situation.

Lecturers, political speakers, interviewers, interviewees, and
others can often profit from the fact that in a studio they will
have special graphic and sound equipment, artistic talent capable
of producing especially effective reinforcing materials, and expert
advice on personal presentation. In short, speaking can often be

"stage managed" from studios (sometimes in the worst sense, unfortunately) as is not possible when speakers meet their audiences face-to-face. It makes sense, then, to ask about any televised or filmed speaking whether the *full* resources of studio presentation were actually used, for there is clear evidence that a speech astutely reinforced by studio resources can be more effective than the same, unreinforced speech given in a face-to-face setting.

On balance, a summary statement by Joseph T. Klapper, written while he was Director of the Office of Social Research, Columbia Broadcasting System, is probably as good a guide to criticism of the modifying power of media as speech critics can presently have. Said Klapper:

> (1) *All other conditions being equal, as they are in the laboratory,* face-to-face contact is more efficiently persuasive than radio, which, in turn, is more efficient than print. TV and films probably rank between face-to-face contact and radio, but this latter point has not been empirically demonstrated [relative to persuasion].
>
> (2) *All other conditions are, however, rarely equal outside of the laboratory.* . . . Some topics . . . may be susceptible to better presentation by visual rather than oral means, or by print rather than by film, while for other topics no such differences exist. The relative persuasive power of the several media is thus, in real-life situations, likely to vary from one topic to another. Personal influence, however, appears to be generally more persuasive than any of the mass media.[12]

THE PROBLEMS OF HISTORY

All study of speaking is historical study unless it is done by machinery. A spectrograph or properly rigged computer may "study" speaking as it occurs, analyzing utterance virtually instantaneously, but speaking is "over" before a human mind can interpret it, much less describe and evaluate it. Thus, *re*discovering *past* contexts, *past* meanings, *past* responses, and the implications of *past* events are invariably among every speech critic's tasks. All speech critics are therefore historians in part, and the study of history is fundamentally the same whether the "historic event" occurred yesterday or a thousand years ago. Of yesterday's speaking or of Cicero addressing the Roman Senate, every critic must admit with Patrick Gardiner that,

> We are not able to confirm a hypothesis that a given event occurred as the outcome of another specified event, or set of events, by making

an experiment under laboratory conditions. (This restriction is not, of course, confined to history: it characterizes, for example, geology or philology.) We cannot reproduce what we believe to have been the conditions . . . and then watch for the consequences, in the fashion in which we can combine certain chemicals and then see whether the result agrees or disagrees with a prediction of the result of such a combination. And this, so it seems to me, points to a genuinely distinctive feature of the subject-matter and consequently the methodology of the historian as compared to that of certain of the natural sciences, a feature that is at least *connected* with the pastness of historical events.

> . . .

History is about what happened on particular occasions. It is not about what usually happens or what always happens under certain circumstances; for this we go to science. It is about what did actually happen at a clearly specified period of time, in all its detail and in the context of what preceded it and of what succeeded it. . . . And this interest in events for and in themselves is regarded as a distinguishing feature of historical writing.[13]

In each of Gardiner's senses you must become a historian of sorts if you are to criticize speaking. Speech is action. It cannot be preserved in any true sense. As quickly as it is finished, it can be *re*viewed only by reconstruction. That is historical work. To render a critique on an act of speaking, you must, like every historian, reconstruct actions and interactive forces, knowing from the beginning you can never totally recover them. The task is to do one's best in reconstructing "what did actually happen at a clearly specified period" in a "context of what preceded it and of what succeeded it." You are a historian in the sense of Raymond Aron's definition of history: "History is the *retrospective grasp of a human development, that is, it is at once both social and spiritual.*" [14]

Of course, your tasks do not end when you have grasped the "human development" of another moment. You must go on to apply the norms of rhetoric and of orality to your reconstruction of the event and its surroundings. But as a *describer* of rhetorical situations and of orality you confront the historian's basic problems of description and judgment.

Many chapters and many volumes have been written about "doing history." Sound and informative essays specifically concerned with speech critics' problems as historians are also available.[15] For general advice on basic problems of historical investigation and reporting you can scarcely do better than to turn first to Jacques Barzun and Henry F. Graff's often amusing and always sound *The Modern Researcher.*[16]

"The historian . . . arrives at truth through probability," say Barzun and Graff,[17] and a task in which speech critics constantly face historical difficulties arises when they try to verify their records of what was. This problem in "doing history" can be illustrated by looking at the different degrees of historical difficulty you would face in trying to establish the reliability of the records of the speeches whose texts are printed in full in this book. Suppose you planned to make a thorough critique of each. What historical problems would you face and how might they be solved in each case?

John F. Kennedy's inaugural address of 1961 presents fewest problems. You can establish a very strong probability that the text and other records you use in criticism are authentic. First, the text printed here is that published by the United States Government Printing Office. It conforms closely to a tape recording made as the inauguration was telecast. You can easily secure other sound transcriptions of the speech on commercially sold albums and tapes. It would be easy and inexpensive to confirm this text against an audio source. At somewhat more expense and inconvenience you might arrange to see a film or video tape of the address. The event was fully recorded by governmental and private agencies. In short, you can form many firsthand judgments about nonverbal and virtually all verbal elements in the message-that-was. Were it important enough to you, you could probably find and interview people who attended the inaugural, and there are many written accounts of the event. So, as the probabilities of history go, a present day speech critic is exceedingly fortunate in the resources available for reconstructing Kennedy's speaking in 1961. One reason for this is that audio and video technology was sophisticated by the 1960s. Another reason is that Kennedy's speech was a major, ceremonial, state event for the like of which society always makes and keeps detailed records.

Former Vice President Spiro T. Agnew's address on the management of news presents slightly more difficulty. It was not foreseen as a major state event of historic importance. Hence, records are slightly less plentiful. The text offered here is Ms. Joyce Williamson's transcription from a sound recording which I made as Agnew's speech was being telecast. Since Ms. Williamson and I have some special interest in criticism of spoken rhetoric, you might reason that we would be careful in recording the speech, but you cannot *know* that. Because the speech was suddenly announced, sound recordings of it are not widely available through commercial and governmental channels. It would cost several hundred dollars to purchase a duplicate of the video tapes that the major television networks possess. For somewhat more than a hundred dollars you could arrange to view such a tape at a network headquarters. At less cost you could buy a sound recording from a broadcasting station. Were you to go to the printed texts that appeared in newspapers and such magazines as *Vital Speeches of the Day,* you would fina some significant differences between those texts and Ms. Williamson's. You face the historian's problem about differing testimony: Who is the most reliable reporter?" Unless you locate an audio recording, you ought to rely on Ms. Williamson, though it would still be true that your verification is less dependable than for Kennedy's inaugural address. Your critical reasonings would have to be a bit more tentative than for Kennedy.

George Miller's speech to his fellow California delegates presents additional historical problems. The text I offer is from a tape recording I made as Miller's speech was being telecast from the Democratic National Convention in 1956. Congressman Miller lives in Alameda, California, but it is unlikely he has a record of his speech. And not many of the forty-some delegates or the people who watched television that day are likely to remember the fifty-five seconds during which Miller spoke nearly twenty years ago. Doubtless there are sound recordings and possibly "kinescope" recordings of the 1956 Democratic Convention, but only a few archives, if any, will have preserved every moment telecast from this convention. If you found such a record, you would have to search it for *a single minute* of a convention that lasted several days. The practical fact is that were my accuracy as a reporter of crucial importance to you, the easiest line of verification open to you might well be to come and listen to my tape. (I am not authorized to distribute the speech except in printed form.) On the whole, then, Miller's is one of the many cases in which speech critics are dependent upon a single source for the data from which all their critical reasoning begins. Jonathan Smith's speech is another such case; so is Stokely Carmichael's. All texts of these speeches stem from a single text, and the historical issue becomes: "How reliable was the source?"

Leon R. Zellner's speech illustrates another type of problem critics and historians face even when dealing with events occurring in an era when the technology of record keeping is excellent. *The primary evidence is lost—forever.* There was a sound recording of this speech. It was accidentally erased! I made the recording as Mr. Zellner spoke in a classroom in Chambers Building, University Park, Pennsylvania. I can assure you that I personally typed out the printed transcript from that tape. I believe I rechecked the text against the tape at least once. Through an accident, the tape was erased soon after the typed transcript was made. There was never any other record of the speech, for Mr. Zellner spoke extemporaneously. Eighteen undergraduates, two graduate students, and I heard the speech when it was delivered. It would be difficult to locate Mr. Zellner's whereabouts. To reach him and the actual audience would require extended research, and it is doubtful that any could help us perfect our text if we found them.

This kind of problem in verification occurs often, even for modern speaking of fame and importance. A classic instance is a speech the late Senator Joseph McCarthy made in Wheeling, West Virginia, on February 9, 1950. There, for the first time, he allegedly charged that there were 205 Communists working in the State Department of the United States. What number he actually gave and how he qualified it soon became major political issues, but verification had become impossible. The speech was given to a Lincoln Day meeting of Wheeling Republicans. The only known sound recording was made by a Wheeling radio station—and erased before the speech became the focus of contention in the press and in the United States Senate. The "official" text remains one which Senator McCarthy himself placed in the *Congressional Record* weeks after the event. Though it was the "kickoff" of the so-called "McCarthy Era" in American history, the speech remains a matter of difficulty to historians and critics alike. Reading what journalists, historians, and rhetorical critics have written about it will show you how variously they have reconstructed the "truth" of what was said in Wheeling.[18]

Stokely Carmichael's speech at Morgan State College presents problems of historical verification that are different from those offered by Zellner's speech. Again, we are dependent on a single source for the text, and the original sound recording may or may not be lost. But we have additional means of verification which we do not have for George Miller or Zellner. No specific issue about the speech requires that we have *exact* reproduction of the speaker's words, as is necessary to settle the main issue concerning McCarthy's speech.

The text of Mr. Carmichael's speech was issued by the Student Nonviolent Coordinating Committee of which Mr. Carmichael was National Chairman when the speech was made. It was published as a transcription from a tape recording. The releasing group no longer exists. Who transcribed it and under what circumstances were not reported. It would take extended research to discover whether or not the original recording still exists. Another text substantially like that reproduced here appeared on page 12 of the *Afro-American* (Philadelphia Edition) for the week of January 28, 1967. The source of that text was not given. The two texts could be compared, but the assertion that the text printed in this book is a transcription from a sound recording gives it the stronger claim to credibility should discrepancies be found.

On the other hand, certain other kinds of verification are possible. If you were undertaking a critique of this speech, you ought to note that though Carmichael was a prominent and controversial figure in 1967, no one has challenged the accuracy of this report of what he said. And since there are some sound recordings of Mr. Carmichael's other speaking, you could study them at firsthand to find out whether the text from Morgan State has the general, verbal features of his other speaking. You could even make tests of whether the Morgan State text has the rhythms you find in audio recordings of his other speaking. You could, in short, make a kind of verification that is standard in historical and literary research; you could test the Morgan State text for *representativeness,* using Carmichael's other speaking as normative.

Critics do not invariably try to make definitive statements; their goal is sometimes to understand *approximately* what happened. That would not be a sufficient goal if McCarthy's Wheeling speech were your critical object or if you were using your criticism in a definitive biography of Carmichael, but it would be a sufficient goal if Mr. Carmichael's *general* civil rights speaking were what you wanted to understand and account for.

Turning to Winston Churchill's "Address to Congress," we begin to meet historical problems that arise just because the critical object lies additional years away. There may exist in the archives of the United States or British governments, or among the Churchill family's papers, the text from which Churchill read when he delivered this speech. It is also probable that a disk recording of the speech was made and that the original or dubbings from it exist.[19] The printed text on pp. 301–308 comes from the *Congressional Record, Senate* (December 26, 1941), pp. 10117–10119. We do not know how this text was secured—whether from stenographic recording, an "advance text," or a "reading copy" supplied after the speech. We know that Congressmen have the privilege of "editing" their remarks before their publication in the *Record*. It is reasonable to think Churchill would be given the same courtesy if he or his staff wished it. So, without a sound recording (which research *might* turn up) the task of verification has to be carried out largely through written accounts.

Assume for the time being that you are preparing to do a critique of this speech and cannot locate a sound recording of it. What is open to you? The speaker was famous and the occasion a ceremony of state. That means many news agencies covered the event. You could examine how American and British wire services and major newspaper syndicates covered the occasion. You might find out whether an "advance text" was ever issued. If none was, one source of mis-reporting speech texts would be eliminated. Sometimes news services make their own stenographic records of speaking—even when "advance texts" are available. Should you find such a text you could compare it with the text from the *Record*. Which source should you prefer in case discrepancies appear? The stenographic record *always* because most speakers alter their plans during speaking. Indeed, a complete stenographic record from a generally reliable news agency usually has greater claim to accuracy than a "reading text," from which the speaker may have deviated. Without a stenographic record, you could still make the kinds of checks for representativeness which were mentioned in reference to Carmichael. There are easily available recordings of some of Churchill's speaking.

In trying to verify the text of Churchill's speech you would be entering what might be called the "last years of the world of print." Because sound recording was technologically primitive and preservation of audio-recordings awkward, your expectations of being able to verify printed records against the actual sounds of speaking must necessarily be lower. Since you must verify chiefly through written records, you ought to expect errors in your sources for speech records. You probably must content youself with close approximations of what was actually said because every rehandling of type provides new opportunity for errors to creep in, even when reporting is careful—which it often is not.[20]

Theodore Roosevelt's "The Man with the Muck-Rake" belongs to a time in which it is barely possible to reconstruct the sounds and sights of speech. Phonographic recording was in its infancy in 1906, so there was no instantaneous sound recording of it. If a "reading copy" of the speech exists, no one has so far published a facsimile of it. Intensive historical research would be needed to find and authenticate that text, if it exists. The text printed here comes from Roosevelt's *Works* published in 1926; it comes, in turn, from *Presidential Addresses and State Papers* (New York: The Review of Reviews Co., 1910), vol. 5. Other texts exist, as I have indicated on p. 290. There is, then, an interesting trail to follow in testing the authenticity of the text I have chosen, but in order that you may make your own discoveries I shall pursue it no farther here. The immediate point is that you have before you a "standard" text which has become *the* historic version but which research will show is almost certainly at least slightly different from what Roosevelt actually uttered.

To verify this or any like text you must engage in considerable historical research which, in this instance, will produce some grounds for doubt if your research is thorough. But even after such research you will be left in the not uncommon position of using an approximate record or drawing no critical inferences at all. That is not wholly disabling. Research will show that Roosevelt surely said most of what our text reports. And it will show that this text and others much like it have created the historical image of what Roosevelt addressed to his audience and the nation. At the very least, you can examine the "historical Roosevelt" as I have done at points in earlier chapters.

Because Roosevelt's speech was given during the infancy of sound recording it constitutes an interesting, borderline case in historical-critical research in speech. A sensitive critic will wonder what Roosevelt really sounded like. There are ample *written* descriptions of how he sounded and looked. Because he lived at the opening of the twentieth century, we can actually *hear* him— after a fashion. He made several sound recordings on cylindrical phonograph records, and reproductions of these recordings are available in albums of famous speakers' voices. The quality of the sound is poor, and the recordings were made in studios without live audiences. Nonetheless, we can "know" Roosevelt slightly "through the ear," as we can other major speakers who lived at the beginning of the twentieth century. By reading listeners' descriptions of Roosevelt's speaking and blending what they say with our own inferences from hearing fragmentary, primitive, sound recordings, we can get critical data that are not all secondhand. Our knowledge will not be as dependable as when we study Kennedy, Agnew, Carmichael, or Churchill, but we can reconstruct Roosevelt's "The Man with the Muck-Rake"—as *speech*— better than we can reconstruct any speaking that occurred before the twentieth century.

When we go back into the nineteenth century and earlier to study speaking, we enter "the world of print" totally. Then, *all* criticism is at secondhand in the sense that we are dependent on other reporters and describers for all that we know as "the record." I have introduced Jonathan Smith's speech into this book to illustrate some of the harder problems critics face when the written record is scant. I have tried to show in critical discussion of Smith's speech (pp. 376–384) that even in such circumstances, where knowledge of the event is severely limited, criticism can still yield findings of benefit to both general and historical understanding.

Almost nothing is known about Jonathan Smith. Nothing at all is known of his manner of speaking, except what can be inferred from the speech text that has come down to us. Of the text a historian wrote:

> Some of the art of this speech may perhaps be credited to George Richards Minot, the historian of Shays' Rebellion, who was secretary of the Massachusetts convention. But there was no disguising the blunt eloquence of the solid farmer who could see beyond his township in the Berkshire hills.[21]

Mr. Van Doren casts suspicion on the text, but neither he nor anyone else has given reasons why the record of what Smith said in the Massachusetts Convention should be more or less accurate than the rest of the Convention's record, presumably prepared by the secretary, Mr. Minot.

Whether we accept Van Doren's suspicion at face value depends entirely on our reasoned assessment of *his* reasoning. We know we can have only an approximate record of what Smith said, but shall we believe there is more of George Richards Minot in the Smith text than there is, say, in the speech by Mr. Amos Singletary who spoke just before Smith? In the absence of "hard" evidence, we can only consider Van Doren's *way of thinking* about the text, for Van Doren contradicts himself in leveling the suspicion. If Smith's "art" was supplied by Minot, or someone else, how can Van Doren know Smith had any "blunt eloquence" at all? Would not whatever Smith really said be necessarily "disguised" if a pseudoauthor added "art"? Van Doren appears to have thought carelessly.

This is the kind of historical evaluation critics must make—and stand on—where there is uncertainty about what was said and how. You must make your own judgment in deciding what faith you place in the single record we have of what Jonathan

Smith said in 1788. The criticism I have supplied on pp. 376–384 assumes that the record is *approximately* reliable because I can find no strong reason for thinking otherwise.

The kind of historical-critical judgment the Smith text demands of us is not at all unusual. We also face it respecting Pericles's "Funeral Oration." Thucydides reports the speech, but he did not hear it nor does he claim to have seen a text of it. In fact, Thucydides seems usually to have written what he thought *ought* to have been said. Is the eloquence then that of Pericles, of Thucydides, or of both? We cannot be sure. Nor is the problem faced only with old speeches. Equally unconfirmable records have been left of twentieth-century speaking.[22] It has already been noted that anyone seeking to know what an American Congressman said in Congress is in an uncertain position. Since Congressmen can edit their speeches before they appear in the *Congressional Record,* one must reason out the degree of confidence those records deserve each time the *Record* provides the only source available.[23] The important point is that even unreliable records allow useful criticism. Only texts that are false to what people understood to be true do not. Even with records about which we are decidedly suspicious, it is possible to extract useful information by applying critical methods peculiar to critics of oral rhetoric. One might ask any or all of the following questions.

1. Do features that we *can* trust tell us anything significant about the speaker, his art, his conception of his audience, or the processes of communication themselves? What does what we *can* trust tell us the audience must have been like if they approved or disapproved the message?
2. If the record is extensively suspect but was circulated widely as a representation of real speech, what did it do to the speaker's status among those exposed to the faulty record? Why?
3. If we know *how* the suspect record came into being (as we know William Wirt wrote Patrick Henry's "Give Me Liberty or Give Me Death" speech by consulting witnesses after the fact), what does the making of the record tell us about the rhetorical purposes of those who created it? How well did they succeed, and with what effects? Why, for example, are the suspect "Funeral Oration" and the "Give Me Liberty or Give Me Death" speech still in circulation?

4. If the suspect record was *thought* to be true, what rhetorical work did it do among those who believed it, and why?
5. Whether suspect or not, how well does the record *fit* the known rhetorical situation? Why? Does that tell us anything about the rhetoric, sociology, and history of the period?

These questions can yield important historical, sociological, cultural, and rhetorical information, but to get useful answers one must understand the workings of rhetoric in general and of oral rhetoric in particular.

Thoroughly verifiable records of speaking are needed for ideal criticism of oral rhetoric, but even fragments and doubtful records circulate *as though* they were remnants of genuine speech. In that sense they never cease to be "true" shades of oral rhetoric. To many Westerners the speech Shakespeare wrote for his Mark Antony to deliver over the body of Caesar *is* a critical event in Rome's civil conflicts. It is therefore an utterance whose criticism falls peculiarly within the province of rhetorical critics even though there is no evidence that the real Mark Antony ever spoke such words as Shakespeare gave him. *Alleged* speech can influence. Accurately recorded speech can influence. Speech heard at firsthand can influence. One must understand speech and rhetorical processes to explain any of these influences, and those are the understandings speech critics must be able to claim if they are to claim competence.

STUDYING AUDIENCES

Sooner or later every critic of oral rhetoric faces the question: How did the speaking affect the listeners? If critics can make no comment on this question, their work seems no more than antiquarianism, whether "antiquity" was five minutes ago or three thousand years ago. Yet firm statements about rhetorical effects are virtually impossible to come by.

The televised Kennedy-Nixon debates in 1960 were perhaps the most intensively studied speaking events in history. Summing up the mass of research carried out by social scientists, journalists, rhetorical scholars, and others, Katz and Feldman wrote:

Did the debates really affect the final outcome? Apart from strengthening Democratic convictions about their candidate, it is very difficult to say conclusively.

But if you *ask* people whether the debates influenced their voting decision, they say yes. . . . This is more true for Democrats than for Republicans, as has already been pointed out. But consider the 6 per cent in the national Roper study . . . who say that the debates "made them decide" or the 39 per cent in the Bruskin study . . . who mention the debates in answer to a very different question concerning "the one most important thing" that led to Kennedy's victory. Even these people, almost certainly, were reinforced by the debates in their prior inclinations rather than converted. On the one hand, who is to say that the doubts and reservations which existed among Democrats regarding Kennedy might not have been dispelled at all if it had not been for the debates? [24]

Never before or since have the resources of social science and rhetoric been brought so systematically to bear in trying to discover what televised speaking *does* to audiences and how. That the findings allow no firm declaration of *the* truth about rhetorical effects simply illustrates that any study of causes in communication (outside a laboratory) is historical study and yields statements about *probabilities* and *potentialities* but never about indisputable causes and effects. Whether such investigation uses the tools of social science or those of general inference, it is always investigation of *social history*.

When he deals with speaking and its consequences, then, a speech critic will be rigorous and realistic only if he is guided by the basic principle of all sound historical investigation. Barzun and Graff have put that principle well:

> The commandment about furnishing evidence that is decisive leads us . . . to a . . . fundamental rule: in history, as in life critically considered, *truth rests not on possibility nor on plausibility but on Probability*.
>
> Probability is used here in a strict sense. It means the balance of chances that, given such and such evidence, the event it records happened in a certain way; or, in other cases, that a supposed event did not in fact take place. . . . The grounds on which he [a historian] passes judgment are, again, the common grounds derived from life: general truths, personal and vicarious experience (which includes a knowledge of previous history), and any other kind of special or particular knowledge that proves relevant.
>
> At many points the estimate of probability made by the student will coincide with that of an ordinary man; but there is this difference, that the scholar will not have reached it offhand—it will not be a correct snap judgment, but a correct *critical* judgment.[25]

The major reasons that speech critics of scientific or descriptive turns of mind can only pursue probabilities were suggested by the late Hugh Dalziel Duncan, a sociologist and student of human communication:

> A description of communicative means must . . . involve a description of audiences reached by those means, and this description must be based on the *forms of relationships* between speaker and audience. The speaker's status longings and position, his class interests, his style of life, his sexual habits, his religious affiliations, are of interest in communicative theory only insofar as they serve as clues on how the forms of communication affect conduct.
>
> . . .
>
> Different audiences must be addressed in different ways. If we could isolate audiences according to class, status, party, or ethnic derivation, and control the situation, the act, the roles, the means, and the purpose of our speech, bending audiences would become a simple matter of rhetorical technique.
>
> . . .
>
> [But] the small homogeneous audience, familiar to Aristotle and to modern anthropologists, no longer exists in the public life of modern times. We do not believe, as Greek orators did, that Athenian reason is universal reason. Nor can we assume that appeals directed only to elites will decide action. The voice of the people is no longer the voice of God, but it is still the voice of profit, of mass armies, and of the ballot box. And in democratic society, where differential status prevails, elites in one role are "the people" in another.[26]

As Duncan points out, there is more "going on" in a communicative situation than utterance of words and decoding by hearers functioning like telephone receivers. Hundreds of interrelated forces shape the impact of any oral communication in any moment: prior and evolving *ethos* of the speaker, the human relationships that evolve between speaker and listeners, listeners' responses to the channels of communication, the extent to which reasons and sensory experiences can be shared by speaker and listeners, the audience's conceptions of itself and society's conceptions of the audience (e.g.: Does the audience think itself an "elite"? Is it *acknowledged* to be an "elite"? Etc.). Under these circumstances anyone—scientist or critic—who seeks unambiguous, "valid" statements about cause and effect in oral engagements has missed the complexity of the phenomena being studied. But to say this is not to say that reasoning *about* causality is absurd. Speech critics and social scientists do have general norms by which to distinguish generally "well chosen," "well framed," "well presented" oral communication from the generally "ill chosen," "ill framed," and "ill presented." Many of these norms have been discussed in previous chapters of this book. These and others derive from scientific study and from the evidence of criticism. They are the premises from which you can reason to what is *potentially* causative in rhetorical situations but not to what is certainly so.

To analyze audiences in rhetorical situations you need some topics of inquiry to serve as guides for getting data from which to reason with the aid of rhetorical norms. Without implying that anyone can answer all of them or that they exhaust what a critic might ask about audiences, I suggest that the following lines of inquiry are likely to produce useful data about the audience's "side" of rhetorical engagements, especially where speech is the means of communication.

1. *What strong and what dormant attitudes does this audience have relative to the subject matter under consideration?* Everyone has "positions" on a wide variety of matters. Many positions are contradictory to one another, and some are more strongly held than others. At a given moment, some attitudes are more salient than others. By altering patterns of strong and dormant attitudes as subject matters and circumstances change, we maintain a sense of internal, attitudinal consistency. Consequently communicative strategies aim at intensifying attitudes already at the forefront of listeners' consciousness, at bringing dormant attitudes to the fore, or at causing suppression of formerly dominant positions. If a critic can make out the attitudes that are salient within an audience and the attitudes that are capable of being *made* salient, he has grounds from which to reason about the *probable* effects of rhetorical strategies.

For example, in July 1973, both the so-called "Watergate scandal" and commodity price increases were matters very much in the public eye. Opinion polls indicated that there were widespread, negative attitudes toward both the scandal and increasing prices. But the polls also suggested that concern over prices was becoming stronger than concern over the scandal and its ramifications. If this seeming change in the salience of the two sets of attitudes were confirmed by careful research, a thoughtful critic of the rhetoric of the "Watergate Hearings" ought to conclude that those on the attack in the hearings probably were beginning to face what Bitzer calls a "decaying" rhetorical situation. He could infer, too, that rhetoric about inflation and price changes faced a "maturing" set of exigences at the same time. If data about attitudes proved strong, the critic could infer that "Watergate rhetoric" needed to be given *special* rhetorical potency in order to sustain public attention, but rhetoric about prices would have received increasingly ready attention and increasing support insofar as it made pricing problems seem less penalizing, either immediately or in the near future.

2. *What anxieties, conflicts, and latitudes of acceptance and rejection account for the attitudes found in the audience?* To the extent that a critic can judge what lies behind attitudinal patterns, he can reason about what discourses and presentations will *probably* secure adherence or dissent. In the example already used, suppose evidence were found that (a) economic anxieties were becoming intense, (b) consumers had a sense of conflict about whether to spend before prices went higher or hoard money until prices declined, (c) citizens were becoming bored by talk about "dirty tricks" and "hankypanky" in government, and (d) a near majority of citizens were made "edgy" by *any* upward price movements. From such data a critic could make a very credible argument that any rhetoric promising price controls would *probably* have drawn public opinion and interest away from the "Watergate scandal" and reduced the scandal as a factor in the public's general political judgments. Linking such information with knowledge about how rhetoricians can handle audiences' tensions (see chapter IV), our critic could work out an informed judgment of how well this or that speaker or group actually handled the anxieties, conflicts, and latitudes of acceptance and rejection *which the audience presented as psychological forces to be worked with.*

3. *In what direction is the audience already tending respecting the topic of discussion?* As Ms. Williamson's critique of former Vice President Agnew's speech shows, an answer to this question is crucial if a critic is to account for the response which Agnew's speech immediately evoked. The national audience was *already* unfavorable toward many parts of the news media. There was a strong tendency toward adopting Mr. Agnew's conclusions *before* he spoke. From his point of view, then, the task was to organize and articulate existing views, to intensify and give expression to a tendency. The probable reason his speech received the great approval it did is that he focused already mounting suspicions; he had little need to argue that those suspicions were justified.

In 1973, the Nixon administration faced an opposite tendency in public attitudes. Apparently as a result of the Watergate revelations and of rising prices, public endorsement of Mr. Nixon and his policies sagged to a historic low point (below 30 percent approval). Obviously any speaker representing the Nixon administration needed to hunt for facts, arguments, promises, and other materials strong enough to allay or reverse a trend of opinion running against the administration. Knowing this much, a critic could inspect the administration's rhetoric of, say, late 1973, asking whether the administration's strategies were "strong enough" to have a prospect of reversing the negative trend. And a critic inspecting Democratic rhetoric in the same year ought to ask whether spokesmen from that side took full advantage of a trend then running in their favor.

4. *What are known factors of resistance against influence such as the speaker seeks to exert?* Jonathan Smith's speech on the Federal Constitution illustrates speaking which we cannot understand unless we also understand specific doubts that a number of convention delegates had about the Constitution. For example, no critic will see the astuteness of Smith's analogy concerning farmers' relations with "rich men" unless he knows that among a number of the delegates there was a suspicion that the rich would dominate any centralized government. This was a major reason a good many farmers feared the Constitution. Historical records are few concerning this rhetorical situation; nonetheless this particular factor of resistance can be identified by reading the history of the period. Once the ground of resistance is discovered, the special rhetorical function of Smith's analogy immediately becomes clear.

What factors of resistance stood in the way of John F. Kennedy's "unity theme" in his inaugural address? A bit of research will remind a critic that Kennedy had won election over Richard Nixon by a very narrow margin, that there were unsettled charges of "vote steals" in Illinois and elsewhere, and that a good many other kinds of anti-Kennedy, anti-Democratic feelings remained after the intense campaign and close election. *Partisanship,* in short, was a resistive force Kennedy *had to* work against as astutely as possible. And, of course, he did—in his very first words and by shifting thought to the shared heritage of the American Revolution (paragraphs 1–3). By asking what resistance existed, we discover that his opening words were not just ceremonially proper; they could have the effect of easing a kind of resistance that was likely to be a problem to the new administration.

5. *Do any available lines of thought have inherent or "built-in" attractiveness for an audience with the attitudes and tendencies already located?* This question will remind a critic of the various

arguments and suggestions available to a speaker in his situation. From these possibilities the critic can judge the extent to which the speaker drew upon available rhetorical resources. The question is not very important in judging Agnew's speech because only rein- forcement of an existing set of attitudes was necessary. But know- ing what the audience was specially ready to hear is imperative in weighing Jonathan Smith's rhetorical effectiveness. The farmers he could best address were men who measured political matters by the standards of rural life and by standards favorable to per- sonal independence. Historians have established this much. What does that tell a critic about *inherently* attractive lines of rhetorical thought? Whatever would show that personal independence would be preserved under the Constitution would be a "wise" line of thought for Smith. Whatever would show that the new government would run like local government and be responsive to local opinion would be inherently attractive to Smith's fellow "ploughjoggers."

Reasoning *from* (a) what we can learn about an audience's attitudes, *to* (b) what would be especially advantageous rhe- torically, and then *to* (c) what the speaker actually did can be a method of analysis wherever the attitudes of an audience can be described even in general terms. We can even know enough about the Massachusetts farmers of 1788 to predict *probably* effective rhetorical strategies. A look at Smith's speech shows that he made extensive use of inherently attractive lines of argument. On that count, then, we can say he was probably as effective as it was possible for him to be.

6. *Does anything known about the audience's attitudes imply that some sources of ideas will evoke stronger and more favorable attitudes than others?* This question is especially important when critics deal with organized campaigns of speaking like those in advertising, in politics, and public movements of promotion or protest. *"Who can most effectively say this to whom?"* is a question campaign managers constantly ask themselves; hence, a critic dealing with a campaign must ask that question, too. If we were studying the "surrogate campaigners" who spoke on Mr. Nixon's behalf in the 1972 presidential campaign, it would be imperative to consider whether the attitudes of specific audiences made it wiser for the Secretary of State or the Secretary of the Interior to make a given pro-Nixon statement in a given place.

The same line of inquiry helps a critic to understand specific situations. It requires such an inquiry to catch what Lincoln and Douglas were doing when they debated at Alton, Illinois in

1858. Consider this excerpt from one of Lincoln's speeches at Alton. It shows that he recognized the importance of our present question and that he and Judge Douglas had adopted special strategies because they knew that Henry Clay was a favored source among southern Illinoisans. Said Lincoln:

> He [Judge Douglas] brings forward part of a speech from Henry Clay—*the* part of *the* speech of Henry Clay which I used to bring forward to prove precisely the contrary. I guess we are surrounded to some extent to-day, by the old friends of Mr. Clay, and they will be glad to hear anything from that authority. . . . I have before me an extract from that speech which constitutes the evidence this pretended "Old Line Whig" at Chicago brought forward to show that Mr. Clay didn't suppose the negro was included in the Declaration of Independence. Hear what Mr. Clay said. . . .[27]

As critics, Lincoln and Douglas had asked themselves whom the political attitudes of southern Illinoisans made "best sources" on constitutional questions. Apparently each concluded that this audience would respond more favorably to Henry Clay as a source than to either of them. So Douglas spent a large portion of his first speech at Alton aligning himself with opinions Clay had propounded; Lincoln, not to be outdone, contended that *his* views were more like Clay's than Douglas's. For critics studying the debate, it is crucial to learn to the fullest extent possible what attitudes did exist regarding Clay as a source and regarding "Old Line Whiggism" as a system of political positions. If we cannot learn these things, we cannot know whether Douglas and Lincoln were approaching "effectiveness" or wasting their time.

In a time when there are diverse media of communication, the question of attitudes toward sources arises in another way. Various groups of people seem to prefer some channels of communication over others for specific kinds of information. If speaking occurs over radio or television, it may be useful for a critic to know whether that medium is "trusted" as a source of information of the sort offered. It appears that radio messages about public issues are somewhat more readily believed than televised messages, and that many people rely heavily on specific radio stations for information about art, politics, consumers' information, and so on. It is also the case that different groups' confidence in various newspapers and news magazines differs from topic to topic. Thus, if a speech is supposed to have influence beyond its immediate hearers, it is important for a critic to discover what sources had special credibility and with whom, on the subject discussed. It is impossible to generalize in advance on these matters because preferences for and confidence in sources change, but it remains important to ask regularly about each audience's attitudes toward different sources and media of information. To do so will always draw a critic's attention to aspects of credibility which might otherwise be overlooked.

Advantages of pursuing the lines of inquiry just enumerated are that you will collect valuable information concerning listeners and will also build up your image of what could be done rhetorically. By inferring what was possible with an audience you create an image of an "ideal" way of reaching that audience. You can then compare that ideal with what was actually done. If X was possible and would probably have achieved the most favorable responses from the listeners addressed and if the speaker(s) did Y which fell short of X, less than the possible was achieved. But if the speaker(s) did X, all that seems possible appears to have been done—whatever the ultimate outcome. This is the kind of critical reasoning you will find in the two critiques printed in this book.

Ms. Williamson infers from data about the national audience's attitudes that all major beliefs former Vice President Agnew wanted accepted were already present in the minds of a large segment of the audience. Therefore, she reasons, Agnew's task was only to make listeners focus on the beliefs that were within them. From examining Agnew's methods, she further infers that Agnew's rhetoric had the potentiality to focus and reinforce those attitudes. She concludes that Mr. Agnew did very nearly all that was rhetorically necessary on behalf of his purpose.

The critique of Jonathan Smith's speech is reasoned in the same way. The critic decides that in the Massachusetts Convention it was the western farmers whom Smith needed most to address. Their attitudes toward the Constitution and the people supporting it are explored. What might win the votes of western farmers is conceptualized, and what Smith actually said is compared to that "ideal." The critic finds that, save for the ambiguous opening, Smith's choices of arguments fit the "ideal." The conclusion is, therefore, that Smith's choices of lines of arguments were almost ideal; he probably influenced the farmers as much as was possible for *him* in *that* rhetorical situation.

By analyzing attitudes, possible lines of argument, and speakers' choices in these ways critics produce reasoned, discussable evaluations of argumentative strategies. They do not allege the impossible—that a speaker's rhetoric *did* this or that. Except in unusual circumstances, no critic can know exactly how lines of thought worked within the minds of listeners; but if critics make reasonable assessments of listeners' attitudes, they can make cogent assertions about *probabilities* of rhetoric as cause and about response as effect. In the language of Barzun and Graff, they will sensibly calculate "the balance of chances that, given . . . [the] evidence, the event . . . happened in a certain way." Their knowledge "will not be a . . . snap judgment, but a . . . correct *critical* judgment." [28]

Speech critics often want to know more about probable effects than a study of *immediate* probabilities will tell them. A critic may want to know how a speech or a group of speeches worked over a fairly long period of time. Insofar as studying audiences is a part of such criticism, the method of critical thinking need not differ from that just outlined. The attitudes of audiences are studied *over the period of time the critic is interested in.* The rhetorical possibilities for dealing with those audiences are imagined. The resemblance between these rhetorical possibilities and the actualities is noted, and a judgment is rendered in light of the comparison. This is substantially what Griffin did in his study of the rhetoric of the Antimasonic movement. An excerpt from his conclusions will suggest the path of his analysis:

Certainly it must be said that the Antimasonic rhetoricians were effective in their efforts to generate a flood of argument and appeal. Many lines of argument, based generally on political, social, and religious reasons for objecting to secret societies, were developed. The rhetoricians were successful, evidently, in establishing the credibility of the seceding Masons and in building a fund of testimony by the technique of soliciting testimonials. . . . While the pro-Mason rhetoricians based their defense principally on the sanction of authority, on the appeal of the "great names" of the Masonic fraternity, the aggressor rhetoricians evoked the sanctions of Justice and Equality; and they did so in an age when men, as rarely before, were scornful of authority and in search of equality and justice. It must be said, too, that the Antimasonic rhetoricians displayed remarkable facility in their employment of available channels of propagation. Their success in enlisting the aid of the clergy; their use of the lecture platform; their development of free presses; their organization for rhetorical purposes . . . of a political Party; their extensive use . . . of almanacs as a propaganda medium . . . were important factors in bringing their persuasion to the people.

And yet the Antimasonic rhetoricians made errors, perhaps fatal ones, which resulted in the development of unfavorable opinion and were factors contributing to the dissolution of the movement. . . . The conscious neglect of the citizens of the southern states as an audience . . . was an unexplainable error. The policy of attacking the neutral elements of the public . . . was undoubtedly an error.

. . .

In their eagerness to flood the public with a multiplicity of discourse, the aggressor rhetoricians did not stop at the proper point. On the one hand, through the use of arguments and appeals which grossly exaggerated any possible dangers inherent in Freemasonry, they offended just and reasonable men. . . . On the other hand, through the incessant din of their discourse, they became in time, merely tiresome and repellent.[29]

Griffin then cites examples of writings of the time which show that at least some people in the national audience were expressing the view that the Antimasons were becoming "tiresome" fairly early in their campaign of rhetoric against Masonic Lodges and their members.[29] As a good critic making his report to others, Griffin does not "parade" his data on the attitudinal changes that took place over the years of the Antimasonic movement's campaign. The raw data collected from dozens of historical sources are illustrated in his critical report, but Griffin had collected much more information about the attitudes of various audiences. As the excerpt shows, he calculated what the Antimasons *could* do, and he drew critical inferences about which of their rhetorical choices were in accord with the possibilities of the rhetorical situation and which were not. If you study the excerpt carefully, you will notice that Griffin's conclusions show he has asked himself each of the six questions presented earlier in this section, and his answers to each have been used in arriving at his final, critical judgment of the Antimasons' rhetorical astuteness and limitations.

To study oral rhetoric as influence across long or short periods of time requires a standard method in dealing with audiences. Always, a critic must know what the audience(s) possessed as active and dormant attitudes, as anxieties and senses of conflict, as resistant opinions, and as attitudes toward rhetorical sources and media. Knowing these things and their tendencies, the critic can reason out what lines of thought were inherently or conceivably potent, given the speakers' purposes. Final critical judgments on the wisdom of chosen lines of thought come from comparing the "ideal" mix of thought and strategy with the actual mix. Whether one audience or many, one generation or several, are conceived as audience-within-situation, audience analysis follows the same fundamental pathway if it is reasonable about the probabilities of rhetorical causation.

THE PROBLEM OF ETHICS

Since rhetoric was first perceived as a social art, the relationships among ethical propriety, rhetorical behavior, and rhetorical criticism have been subjects for debate and polemic. The reason can be stated simply. A standard definition of *ethics* is: "the principles of morality, including both the science of the good and the nature of the right." [30] By this or any other usual definition of *ethics,* any human action toward another human is bound to have *ethical* significance. Human interactions always affect someone's "good" or "rightness." Speaking is always a personalized action that involves others in making judgments about "good" and "bad" ideas and actions. Thus, "principles of morality" are never absent from rhetorical situations. Someone's "good" or "bad" is always at issue because it is the very nature of a rhetorical situation that things change within it by virtue of human *choice.* And no one can *choose* without creating distinctions among "goods."

We cannot, then, have rhetorical experiences without having ethical experience. Naturally, the problem of whether a critique of rhetorical action and a critique of ethics are one and the same arises out of this intertwining of ethical and rhetorical experience. The issue is ancient as well as modern. Plato saw the matter thus:

> ... it is gods he [the ideal speaker] must think of. He must strive to gain the capacity to speak what *they* favor, to conduct himself in a manner favored by *them*—and this to the utmost extent of his powers. Wiser men than we are, Tisias, tell us that the man who has intelligence should not set as the goal of his training the gratification of his fellow slaves—though this may be an incidental result—but that of good and noble masters. [31]

Here and throughout his writings Plato makes clear that his kind of critique would *first* ask whether a speaker served the gods and "good and noble masters." If the speaking did *that,* it might then be worthwhile to explore its rhetorical strategies to discover how the speaking served those laudable ends.

Aristotle expressed a counterview:

> ... things that are true and things that are better are, by their nature, practically always easier to prove and easier to believe in. .... And if it be objected that one who uses such power of speech unjustly might do great harm, *that* is a charge which may be made in common against all good things except virtue, and above all against the things that are most useful, as strength, health, wealth, generalship. A man can confer the greatest of benefits by a right use of these, and inflict the greatest of injuries by using them wrongly.[32]

For Aristotle, as is clear here and elsewhere, a critique of *artistic* excellence and a critique of *moral* excellence were separable but related. It is significant that Aristotle chose to write one book on rhetoric and *another* on ethics. The two "arts"—rhetoric and the art of the good life—derived from separate sets of *principles,* in Aristotle's view. By contrast, Plato invariably discussed the arts of communication as *evidences of* the presence or absence of goodness.

Arguments can be made for either view. They have been. As in other domains, so in speech criticism: the world seems divided into Platonists and Aristotelians. The issue between these schools of thought seems more an issue about how to *do* criticism than about what constitutes "good" in life.

An "Aristotelian" tends to say: "When making an ethical critique of communication, you must state your canons of ethics, then measure the intentions and ends of communicators against those principles or canons. When you make a rhetorical criticism, you must state your norms of excellence in communication, then measure the visible strategies of communicating against possibilities those norms show are fitting in the given case." This position says, in effect, that *ethical* critiques and *rhetorical* critiques have to be made separately because principles of ethics and principles of effective communication are different (though ultimately interrelated). Ethical principles are principles according to which moral "goods" and "bads" are measured; rhetorical and speech norms are propositions that identify possibilities achievable within particular kinds of communicative interactions.

It does not follow from this reasoning that an ethicist dare not judge communicative strategies. It does follow that as long as he remains an ethicist he will judge by principles which assert what is good and what is not good. He will not judge by rhetorical principles.

It does not follow that a speech critic may not comment on ethical dimensions of communicative acts. It does follow that *if* he does, he must be prepared to defend as fitting the *ethical* principles he has "borrowed" for the purpose. Finally, it does not follow that we can completely understand communicative experience without *both* ethical and rhetorical critique. "Goods" *and* "social possibilities" need to be understood if we are to see rhetorical acts whole. But rhetorical norms do not identify ethical norms, nor is the reverse possible. What is "good" in a rhetorical sense is not the same as what is "good" in a moral sense. The *rhetorically* possible encompasses what is possible for "evil" purposes as well as for morally "good" purposes.

Because human acts, including rhetorical acts, always have ethical dimensions, it is altogether too easy for speech critics to slip into the role of the ethical critic *without doing their homework in preparation for ethical judgment.* There is not, and apparently never has been, just one set of ethical principles to which everyone in the world agrees. Ethical systems are many, and they conflict with one another in most societies. Consider just four basic tenets of differing ethical systems that compete for adherence in our own day, in the United States:

1. "By the good is meant that which contributes to the well-being and happiness of men." [33] (The standard here is ordinarily called "utilitarian.")

2. "But the principal result of existential psychoanalysis must be to make us repudiate the *spirit of seriousness.* The spirit of seriousness has two characteristics: it considers values as transcendent givens independent of human subjectivity, and it transfers the quality of the "desirable" from the ontological structure of things to their simple material constitution." [34]

3. "And may we not say that the man whose activity is of the intellect and who cultivates that and keeps it in the best condition is also the man whom the gods love above all others?" [35]

4. "You shall love the Lord your God with all your heart, and with all your soul, and with all your mind. This is the great and first commandment. And a second is like it. You shall love your neighbor as yourself." [36]

One could cite additionally the basic ethical tenets of Marxism, hedonism, nihilism, and a dozen other -isms which assert different principles from which to reason about the nature of "the good." All these furnish premises from which at least some Americans reason about moral questions and, therefore, about the ethical dimensions of speech acts.

With so many competing ethical systems available, does it not behoove a critic wishing to comment on the ethics of an oral communication to specify *which* ethical premises he is using? If he expects to make sense to any person who holds ethical premises even slightly different from his own, he must, else he cannot offer reasoned criticism.

What would a defensible, reasoned ethical critique of a rhetorical act be like? In a beginners' book on ethics, William K. Frankena gives the specifications succinctly:

> The institution of morality contains a number of factors: (1) certain *forms of judgment* in which *particular* objects are said to have or not to have a certain moral quality, obligation, or responsibility; (2) the implication that it is appropriate and possible to give *reasons* for these judgments; (3) some *rules, principles, ideals,* and *virtues* which can be expressed in more *general judgments* and which form the background against which particular judgments are made and reasons given for them; (4) certain characteristic natural or acquired *ways of feeling* which accompany these judgments, rules, and ideals, and help to move us to act in accordance with them; (5) certain *sanctions* or additional sources of motivation which are also often expressed in verbal judgments, namely, holding responsible, praising, and blaming; (6) a *point of view* which is taken in all this judging, reasoning, and feeling, and which is somehow different from those taken in prudence, art, and the like.[37]

I suggest that every ethical critique of a rhetorical act ought to be rendered defensible on all six counts which Professor Frankena enumerates. If it cannot be so defended, the judgment must stand as a personal opinion, having no more status in criticism than any other expression of unsupported opinion, bias, or prejudice. An ethical *critique* of speech acts will make clear:

1. *Why* this *form* of judgment is appropriate in this particular case (Frankena's points 1 and 2).
2. *Why* the rules, principles, ideals, and virtues being demanded in the particular case are *generally* appropriate in all cases of this sort (Frankena's point 3).
3. *Why* we *ought* to feel favorably toward *any* and *all* speech acts that are consistent with the principles being applied

here, and *why* we *ought* to feel less favorably toward *any*
speech acts which fail to live up to the principles (Frankena's
point 4).

4. *Why* the "sanctions" of praise or blame assigned here are
   earned by the speech behavior in question (Frankena's
   point 5).

5. *Why* the "sanctions" applied here are not merely practical or self-serving but transcend the particular case being
   sanctioned (Frankena's point 6).

A critical judgment of rhetorical speaking which fulfills this
bill of particulars is an ethical critique deserving respect for its
clarity and forthrightness.

Very little ethical criticism of oral rhetoric fulfills these
specifications for critique, yet the specifications are no more
rigorous than the specifications we impose on a competent critique
of the *art* of a speaker. In both cases we ask for: a defense of norms
applied, an explanation of their appropriateness in the case at issue,
reasons for admiring achievement of the possible and for regret-
ting any shortcoming, a defense of one's evaluation in light of
the data and the "ideal," and inferences concerning whether the
critical judgment can be generalized to all like cases.

When we get ethical criticisms of speaking which fill these
specifications, we know we are in the presence of reasoned
judgment, just as we know it when we hear or read similarly
comprehensive critiques of rhetorical art. The pervasive danger
in speech criticism is that critics of the *art* tend to mistake their
opinions on moral questions for "reasoned judgments." Then we
get "criticism" like Richard H. Rovere's "criticism" of General
Douglas MacArthur's "Address to Congress" delivered on
April 19, 1951:

> . . . to me there is rather a fetid air about it. It does not leave me with
> the impression that a cool and candid mind has been at work on diffi-
> cult matters of universal concern. Instead, it leaves me with the im-
> pression that a closed and in a sense a rather frantic mind has been at
> work to the end of making an appeal to history—not neglecting to use
> any of the rule-book hints on how to do it. I think not of history but of
> second-rate historian as I read the speech.[38]

Mr. Rovere, a journalist of note, sweepingly indicts MacArthur's
intelligence and his ethics—without defending any of the norms
he applies, without arguing their appropriateness in this case,

without justifying his derogation of MacArthur's allegedly in-artistic choices, without defending his apportionment of blame, and without contending that comparable practices would de-serve comparable blame in situations other than that of April 19, 1951. The result is, we learn a good deal about Mr. Rovere's likes and dislikes but almost nothing about General MacArthur's ethical achievement or nonachievement—or about his rhetoric. Mr. Rovere did not provide a *critique* of either the ethical or rhetorical dimensions of MacArthur's address.

How different was former Vice President Hubert H. Humphrey's ethical critique!

> The issues represented by General MacArthur's speech, however, are far more important than the personality questions involved and more significant than the techniques of speech he has so artistically developed. It is to those issues I enter my dissent.
>
> In my judgment, the basic issue involved in the controversy is one of civilian versus military control over our foreign policy. In a democ-racy, the elected representatives of the people are responsible for de-termining foreign policy, and this responsibility is not vested in the military leaders. [The *form* of judgment appropriate and the "rule" appropriate to this and all other like cases are stated.] . . . In dismiss-ing General MacArthur, President Truman, as Commander in Chief under our Constitution, had no choice. The General—a brilliant and able military leader—disagreed with our government's foreign policy and with the recommendations of General Marshall and the Joint Chiefs of Staff. No government can exist so divided in policy since no government can be guided by two inconsistent foreign programs. [Why we *ought* to feel unfavorably toward the General's insistent dissent from the government's policy and why praise and blame *must* be distributed according to previously stipulated principles.] General MacArthur, as an individual, has a perfect right to disagree with our government's foreign policy but he has no right and no pre-rogative as a military commander to formulate his own policy in opposition to policy established by our government. [The "sanction" of blame is justified because MacArthur overstepped the political-moral constraints binding on *any* "military commander."] [39]

Perhaps as briefly as clarity allows, we have in Humphrey's statement the main elements of an ethical-political critique presented as a part, but as a separate part, of a general critique of a rhetorical event.

What I have called "the problem of ethics" in criticism ceases to be a problem whenever critics recognize that a critique of rhetoric per se grows out of the *rhetorical* principles appropriate to a case, whereas a critique of the ethics of rhetorical behavior grows out of *ethical* principles demonstrably applicable to the case. Speech critics are free to undertake speech criticism or ethical criticism or both. But each kind of criticism, if completely done, begins by identifying and defending the appropriateness of the specific principles being applied to the work under study. Rhetorical principles are not ethical principles nor, I would argue, are ethical principles rhetorical principles. Rhetorical critiques can be rendered on rhetorical speaking. Ethical critiques can be rendered on rhetorical speaking. The findings of both may be blended in a critic's ultimate exposition, but separate credentials and separate defenses of the criticisms are due in any circumstance.

This being a book on rhetorical criticism of rhetorical speech, I have chosen to leave discussion of ethical criticism—a quite different art—to others, except in this section.

COMMUNICATING CRITICISM

Communicating criticism, once a critic's investigative work is completed, is a rhetorical act. What shall be communicated, and how, depends on who the audience will be and how they will want to use the criticism given them. One thing is certain, only a lover can bear to hear the full tale of any careful critic's labors. And even a lover lends only ears; the mind goes to other, more interesting matters.

What a consumer of criticism really wants to know are three things: (1) what your judgment is; (2) what support you have for your judgment; and (3) what should be done with your judgment now that you have rendered it.

Who are the real consumers of speech criticism? Chiefly people whose daily lives involve the making of oral rhetoric—in classrooms, in politics, in religious work, in education, in public relations programs and advertising, in the media of mass communication, and so on. For important reasons workers in health delivery systems, in business and industry, in labor unions, and in other practical enterprises also display interest in speech criticism *if it is presented in ways that are rhetorically appropriate to them.* And, of course, scholars interested in communication, history, sociology, literature, philosophy and other students of social experience show interest in good criticism of speaking if it is tailored to *their* interests. These are not generalizations without foundation. Names and references could easily be given identifying specific contributions speech critics (not always under that name) have made to each kind of consumer just named. Educational systems, political groups, religious groups, public relations and advertising firms, hospitals and medical associations, industries and labor unions *pay* for the services of speech critics— when they find good ones. A "good" speech critic by the definition of such groups is one who can reconstruct his or her findings for practical, immediate use by the organization being served.

The first practical principle of presenting speech criticism is to present findings in a form adapted to the consumer's needs. This is what critics demand that other speakers and writers do, but too few speech critics follow their own principles. Failure to make criticism useful to others and succumbing to the temptation to tell all of one's critical experience seem the chief reasons that speech criticism appears to many people a strange, inbred, self-serving enterprise that is interesting chiefly to esoteric souls called speech critics. I know only one set of guidelines for presenting speech criticism usefully, hence successfully.

Once the laborious processes of testing rhetorical speech in first one manner and then another has ended, a critic usually knows more than he can handle about the speaking and its rhetorical situation. This is a time for pause, for refreshment by other means. Pulling away from the critical details increases the likelihood that upon your return those details can be seen as patterned phenomena allowing general interpretations. Years of psychological study devoted to "creative thinking" have given us few explanations of that process, but one of the clearest findings is that drawing one's self away from the details of work (without forgetting the work) is a condition that usually precedes that mysterious event of discovery called "insight" or sometimes even more ambiguously, "synthesis." Pulling away—if only briefly— seems an essential step of good criticism.[40]

When you return to your critical data after a short respite, ask yourself: "What am I willing to claim were the *main* and the *most significant* features of this speaking?" The time you have spent in analyzing situation, content, form, language, and presentation will not have been spent in data gathering only; consciously and subconsciously your critical perceptions will have been flowing together—connecting with one another. The act of asking what all you know "adds up to" will produce some "headings" of critical communication if you have done your analyses thoughtfully. Whether your criticism is to be given orally to a friend, a class, a client, or is to be written out as a consultant might do for his employer, you need to find your "main heads." You are no different in this respect from any other communicator.

My own mental "central idea" for the criticism of Jonathan Smith's speech (pp. 376–384) was simple but exceedingly useful in getting the criticism organized for communication. It was just this: "Smith's speech 'fit' the situation splendidly, except at one spot; and Smith 'fit' the task as a speaker." With that much in mind, I could proceed to the next phase of organizing the critical data. I needed to say to myself, "Very well. What is the 'proof'?" With that challenge I could begin to build the "case" I have presented, pulling from my array of critical observations those that fit together so that you could see the chief reasons for my judgment. Had I just heard some speaking in a classroom, the process would have been much the same though quicker and using a slightly different initial question because the task of classroom criticism is to *teach* as well as judge. The initial question (after a few moments of thought about the general goals of my teaching) would be something like: "What ought I to point to as the main features of this speaking *if I want to help this speaker to move from where he is toward better speaking?*" Criticism rendered as part of teaching does not reveal all the critic has perceived; it presents what the client needs to know *now* in order to plan next steps toward fuller development. This is even true when a critic evaluates a mass of speaking as he might respecting a group's promotional effort. If you were counseling a group of religious speakers or a sales staff, your focus would be the same. Effective critical evaluation would present precisely as much of your observations and judgments as the group could take advantage of at the moment of criticism.

Whether your audience is ready for your total judgment or for only a part of it, your task always is fundamentally the same: You have to find your overall conclusion and then find the general headings under which you can assemble whatever portions of your data are needed for clear expression and reasonable defense.

The general task of a speech critic has been well described by Lawrence W. Rosenfield:

. . . among the formal aspects which unite speech criticism with other varieties of critical discourse is the expert-spectator posture assumed by all critics. Another feature common to all criticism and setting it apart from the bulk of public discourse is its reliance upon forensic reasons-in-support-of-verdicts as its primary method for advancing contentions.[41]

To paraphrase Aristotle, you state your case (conclusions) and you prove it. If teaching is a further function of the criticism, you state pertinent portions of your conclusions, you prove them, and you offer a third thing: suggestions on *how* the criticism is to be used. In either case the *basic* structure is: state conclusions and give "reasons-in-support-of-verdicts."

In the paragraphs above I have emphasized practical rather than "scholarly" criticism. Most discussions of speech criticism emphasize "scholarly" criticism over practical. The position I wish to insist upon is that even "scholarly" criticism ought always to be practical—directed to someone's needs. Historians can and do use the expertise of qualified speech critics. So do literary scholars. So do educational systems (though they call criticism a part of "improvement of teaching"). If your criticism is to be used by historians or literary scholars, it will need the rhetorical attributes we normally call "academic scholarship." You will need to cite data and sources carefully, for academic scholarship is an enterprise of connecting detailed bits of information and of reviewing other people's interpretations of data. If scholars are your audience, follow the forms of academic scholarship; but you will serve best by observing also the characteristic form of criticism: stating your verdicts and proving them as reasonably and fully as you can.

If educators are your audience, the characteristic form of criticism does not change, though *applications-for-the-future* ought to be highlighted as a third part of comprehensive presentation. A school system (or governmental agency or religious group) will be interested in your criticism only if the receivers can understand what to *do* with it once you have presented it to them. They are not much interested in "scholarly" appurtenances, but they are interested in the arguments that justify your conclusions and in your proposals for perfecting their communicative enterprises.

Once you know your conclusions and the reasons for them, you, as critic, now become rhetorician! How shall you present what you have found out? That depends on *your* rhetorical situation. You study it. You devise presentational strategies suited to making yourself understood and influentially useful within that situation. The ultimate form of your critical rhetoric must be a response to the exigences of your communicative purposes and the rhetorical situation. There is only one constant: You state your case and you support it.

We end where we began. Criticism is argument based on judicious application of norms to the record of human experience. Criticism of oral rhetoric is argument based on the judicious application of the norms of effective oral rhetoric to the historical records of serious speech.

NOTES

[1] Edwin Black makes this point especially well in his *Rhetorical Criticism: A Study of Method.*

[2] "Report of the Committee on the Advancement and Refinement of Rhetorical Criticism," in Lloyd F. Bitzer and Edwin Black, eds., *The Prospect of Rhetoric* (Englewood Cliffs, N.J.: Prentice-Hall, Inc., 1971), p. 221.

[3] This account is based on a critical study by Ms. Susan Glaser, a graduate student at The Pennsylvania State University. The study is being expanded in a Master's thesis.

[4] Reprinted from Donald Bryant: *The Rhetorical Idiom: Essays in Rhetoric, Oratory, Language, and Drama.* © 1958 by Cornell University. Used by permission of Cornell University Press. By noting characteristics of situational factors and developments within the Antimasonic movement's rhetoric, Griffin feels he saw rhetoric develop through "a period of inception, a period of rhetorical crisis, and a period of consummation" (p. 146). By noting what social settings demanded and comparing these to the rhetoric's changing thrusts toward these demands, Griffin was able to perceive the total rhetorical movement as a series of "units" which he could criticize separately and, finally, collectively.

[5] See Gronbeck's "The Rhetoric of Social-Institutional Change: Black Action at Michigan" in Mohrmann, Stewart, and Ochs, *Explorations in Rhetorical Criticism,* pp. 96–123, esp. pp. 118–121.

[6] "Requirements, Problems, and Strategies: A Theory of Persuasion for Social Movements," *Quarterly Journal of Speech* 56 (February 1970): 7. The essay has been reprinted in Douglas Ehninger, *Contemporary Rhetoric* (Glenview: Scott, Foresman and Co., Inc., 1972), pp. 190–198.

[7] Unless, of course, communication is not really intended to address an "outside" situation, as when its chief function is to serve the egos of speakers and their own kind. In that case it is the personal or in-group rhetorical situations that need most attention in order to discover where discourse ought to change. See Richard B. Gregg, "The Ego-Function of the Rhetoric of Protest."

[8] I suggest that Churchill's "Address to the Congress of the United States" can legitimately be conceived as addressing two rhetorical situations, each deserving special attention in criticism.

[9] An article which summarizes better than most the basic issues McLuhan and others have raised is James W. Cary, "Harold Adams Innis and Marshall McLuhan." This essay originally appeared in *The Antioch Review,* vol. 27 and is now conveniently available in Douglas Ehninger, *Contemporary*

Rhetoric, pp. 305–327. Since I do not see how McLuhan's notions enhance the processes of rhetorical critique, his writings are little referred to in this book.

¹⁰ Carl H. Weaver, *Human Listening: Processes and Behavior* (Indianapolis: The Bobbs-Merrill Company, Inc., 1972), p. 12.

¹¹ This observation in no way contradicts what has been said earlier (pp. 231–235) concerning listeners' reliance upon nonverbal aspects of speech when there is *conflict* between what is said and what is implied by nonverbal behavior.

¹² Joseph T. Klapper, *The Effects of Mass Communication* (New York: The Free Press, 1960), pp. 108–109. Italics in the original source.

¹³ Patrick Gardiner, *The Nature of Historical Explanation,* 1961 Oxford University Press, pp. 39–41. By permission of The Clarendon Press, Oxford.

¹⁴ Raymond Aron, *Introduction to the Philosophy of History,* trans. George J. Irwin (Boston: Beacon Press, 1962), p. 79. Italics in the original.

¹⁵ Among those directly helpful to critics who explore oral rhetoric are the following: J. Jeffery Auer, *An Introduction to Research in Speech* (New York: Harper & Brothers, Publishers, 1959), chap. 5, "The Historical Method," pp. 118–146; A. Craig Baird, *American Public Addresses, 1740–1952* (New York: McGraw-Hill Book Co., Inc., 1956), "Introduction: The Study of Speeches," pp. 1–14; William B. Hesseltine, "Speech and History," *Central States Speech Journal* 12 (Spring 1961): 176–181; Marie K. Hochmuth (Nichols), "The Criticism of Rhetoric," *A History and Criticism of American Public Address,* III, 1–23; Marie Hochmuth Nichols, *Rhetoric and Criticism* (Baton Rouge: The Louisiana State University Press, 1963), chap. 2, "Rhetoric, Public Address, and History," pp. 19–33; Charles W. Lomas, "Rhetorical Criticism and Historical Perspective," *Western Speech Journal* 32 (Summer 1968): 191–203; Robert W. Smith, "The 'Second' Inaugural Address of Lyndon Baines Johnson: A Definitive Text," *Speech Monographs* 34 (March 1967): 102–108; Lester Thonssen, A. Craig Baird, and Waldo W. Braden, *Speech Criticism,* 2nd ed., Part IV, "Preliminary Aspects of Rhetorical Criticism," pp. 305–384.

¹⁶ Jacques Barzun and Henry F. Graff, *The Modern Researcher* (New York: Harcourt, Brace & World, Inc., 1970), rev. ed.

¹⁷ *Ibid.,* p. 109.

¹⁸ A reconstruction of this speech, based on all available sources, appears in Robert Dean Brooks, "Senator Joseph R. McCarthy's Lincoln Day 1950 Communications on Communism and Subversion," unpublished M. A. thesis (Ithaca, Cornell University, 1961), pp. 38–60. This is probably the most carefully researched text of the speech in existence; but since no printed text was ever made of the speech while the sound recording existed, Brooks's text remains considerably less reliable than the text of Mr. Zellner's speech.

¹⁹ In 1941 neither videotaping nor audiotaping processes were in use. Television broadcasting had been authorized in the United States only six months before Churchill spoke. Filmed "news reels" were the nearest approximations to what we now think of as "television coverage." Radio coverage existed, of course.

²⁰ Read Robert W. Smith's "The 'Second' Inaugural Address of Lyndon Baines Johnson" (see note 15 above for full reference) to get an understanding of the numbers of errors in official and wire-service texts of what even the most important officials say.

²¹ Carl Van Doren, *The Great Rehearsal* (New York: Viking Press, Compass Books, 1961), p. 200.

²² See Donald C. Bryant et al., *An Historical Anthology of Select British Speeches* (New York: The Ronald Press Company, 1967), "G. B. Shaw, G. K. Chesterton, and Hilaire Belloc," pp. 474–490 for the *probable* text of a modern, public debate entitled "Do We Agree?"

[23] Many details of past Congressional reporting are discussed in Zon Robinson, "Are Speeches in Congress Reported Accurately?" *Quarterly Journal of Speech* 28 (February 1942): 8–12, and in Elizabeth Gregory McPherson, "Reporting the Debates of Congress," *Quarterly Journal of Speech* 28 (April 1942): 141–148. More recently the subject has been discussed by J. A. Hendrix in "A New Look at Textual Authenticity of Speeches in the *Congressional Record*," *Southern Speech Journal* 31 (Winter 1965): 153–159; and by Walter W. Stevens in "Inaccuracies in the Texts of Congressional Speeches," *Central States Speech Journal* 15 (August 1964): 183–188. A good, brief discussion of problems of producing accurate texts of speaking carried on broadcasting media is Theodore Clevenger, Jr., Donald W. Parson, and Jerome B. Polisky, "The Problem of Textual Accuracy," in Sidney Kraus ed., *The Great Debates*, pp. 341–347. This essay deals with problems of constructing accurate texts of the 1960 Kennedy-Nixon debates. The best general discussion of textual problems is chapter 9, "Establishing the Authenticity of Texts," in Thonssen, Baird, and Braden, *Speech Criticism*, pp. 323–346. A useful essay giving some attention to textual accuracy in British speaking is Richard Murphy, "Problems in Speech Texts," in D. C. Bryant ed., *Papers in Rhetoric and Poetic*," pp. 70–86.

[24] Elihu Katz and Jacob J. Feldman, "The Debates in the Light of Research: A Survey of Surveys," in Kraus, ed., *The Great Debates*, pp. 211 and 213. The authors cite twenty-one different studies by social scientists and refer incidentally to a considerable number of theoretical conceptualizations that could be used in interpreting the "effects" of these debates. The article appears on pp. 173–223 of the work cited.

[25] Barzun and Graff, *The Modern Researcher*, p. 155. Any serious critic ought to read thoughtfully the entirety of Barzun and Graff's chapters 7 and 8, "Truth and Causation" and "Pattern, Bias, and the Great System," pp. 146–173 and 174–195, respectively.

[26] Hugh D. Duncan, "The Need for Clarification in Social Models of Rhetoric," in Lloyd F. Bitzer and Edwin Black, eds., *The Prospect of Rhetoric*, pp. 144–145.

[27] *The Illinois Political Campaign of 1858*, p. 201.

[28] See p. 262.

[29] Leland M. Griffin, "The Antimasonic Movement." Reprinted from Donald Bryant: *The Rhetorical Idiom: Essays in Rhetoric, Oratory, Language, and Drama.* © 1958 by Cornell University. Pp. 157–159. Used by permission of Cornell University Press.

[30] *The American College Dictionary* (New York: Random House, 1964).

[31] *Phaedrus*, trans. W. C. Helmbold and W. G. Rabinowitz (New York: The Liberal Arts Press, 1956), 273–274; p. 67.

[32] *Oxford Translation of Aristotle*, 1355^a–1355^b, by permission of The Clarendon Press, Oxford; or see *Aristotle's Rhetoric and Poetics*, p. 23.

[33] Thomas R. Nilsen, *Ethics of Speech Communication* (Indianapolis: The Bobbs-Merrill Company, Inc., 1966), p. 10.

[34] Jean-Paul Sartre, *Existentialism and Human Emotions* (New York: Philosophical Library, 1957), p. 92. The passage appeared originally in Sartre's *Being and Nothingness*, Hazel E. Barnes trans.

[35] Aristotle, *Nichomachean Ethics*, from J. A. K. Thomson, *The Ethics of Aristotle* (Baltimore: Penguin Books, Inc., 1955), p. 309.

[36] Jesus. Matthew, 22:37–39. Revised Standard Version.

[37] William K. Frankena, *Ethics* (Englewood Cliffs, N.J.: Prentice-Hall, Inc., 1963), p. 8. Italics in the original.

[38] A solicited criticism of MacArthur's speech published in Frederick W. Haberman, "General MacArthur's Speech: A Symposium of Critical Comment," *Quarterly Journal of Speech* 37 (October 1951): 325.

[39] *Ibid.*, p. 323.

⁴⁰ A good many speech teachers reflect the same view when they report that they "need some time" before giving a critique of a classroom speech, debate, group discussion, or other effort at speaking. "Instant analysis," to borrow Mr. Agnew's phrase, seems less than ideal in a classroom or elsewhere.

⁴¹ Lawrence W. Rosenfield, "The Anatomy of Critical Discourse," *Speech Monographs* 35 (March 1968): 69.

Appendix A

Speeches for Reference and Analysis

In this Appendix are the texts of six speeches delivered in the United States between 1906 and 1967. Portions of them have been extensively used as illustrative matter in the chapters of this book. None of the speeches has been analyzed fully. Each speech is therefore a potential object for comprehensive criticism.

As a group, the speeches illustrate very different kinds of oral rhetoric. Three were presented by statesmen on different kinds of occasions. One is a lecture-demonstration originally presented on television. One is a student's speech in response to a typical public speaking assignment. One is the speech of a black civil rights leader addressing black students. Collectively the speeches illustrate different rhetorical styles, methods of presentation, and distinctive problems in developing information concerning rhetorical situations.

An introduction is provided for each speech. Each introduction gives basic information concerning the speaker and his rhetorical situation, but no introduction is complete in the sense that it provides all available background. Additional information of significance exists in each case, and numerous clues to especially interesting lines of critical research are embedded in the introductions, as well as in the chapters that have preceded. My object has been to provide enough introductory and suggestive material to allow profitable classroom criticism but to leave enough unsaid so that a good many discoveries will be made by anyone who undertakes comprehensive critical analysis of any speech.

In short, here and in the preceding chapters *some* critical work has been done on each of the six speeches but none has been fully described, interpreted, and evaluated. The texts and introductions will, I hope, serve as interesting "raw materials" for critical discussion and as inviting starting points for major projects in original criticism.

THE MAN WITH THE MUCK-RAKE

Theodore Roosevelt

On September 14, 1901, Theodore Roosevelt (1858–1919) became the twenty-fifth President of the United States [1] following the death of William McKinley under whom he had served as Vice President from the beginning of McKinley's second term. After graduating from Harvard College in 1880, Roosevelt entered public life by winning election to the New York State Assembly in 1882. Because he was a "reformer" he was not well received by some of his fellow Republicans; for this and personal reasons he briefly abandoned politics (1882–1886) for ranch life in Dakota Territory. Upon returning to New York he made an unsuccessful bid for Mayor of New York City and in succeeding years enhanced his reputation as a reformer while serving as a member of the United States Civil Service Commission and as head of the New York City police board. Later, while serving as Assistant Secretary of the Navy, Roosevelt resigned his office to organize and share leadership of the "Rough Riders" whose exploits in the Spanish American War were widely publicized. It was, in the main, his war service that brought Roosevelt to national attention.

Following the Spanish American War, Roosevelt served as Governor of New York for two years and was nominated and elected Vice President in 1900. After McKinley's assassination, Roosevelt completed that term and was reelected President in 1904. He retired in 1909 but reentered politics in 1912 as the Progressive Party's candidate for the presidency. Woodrow Wilson won the election of 1912, and Roosevelt again retired from active political life, this time for his remaining years. By the time of his death he had established significant reputations as a naturalist, a historian, a general writer, a political leader, and a popular public speaker.

In a sense Roosevelt's entire public life was rhetorical action. Harold Zyskind says of him:

> Everyone recognizes what Roosevelt repeatedly said his method was: to assimilate theory to practice, the ideal to the real, altruism to success. In broad terms applicable to thought and action alike, this is an operational rhetoric: a rhetoric because the end is to do and say what has impact on the minds of men, and operational because the "what" is conceived in terms of effect achieved by altering or adjusting to actual circumstances. [2]

On the speaker's platform Roosevelt was energetic, enthusiastic, and eager to mold opinion. He "incessantly extolled some gospel, and in a manner distinctly homiletical," says one speech critic. [3] The same critic calls "The

---

This text is from Theodore Roosevelt, *Works*, vol. 16, *American Problems* (New York: Charles Scribner's Sons, 1926), 415–424.

[1] He was the twenty-sixth man to be elected or to succeed to the presidency, Grover Cleveland having been elected to separated terms.

[2] Harold Zyskind, "A Case Study in Philosophical Rhetoric: Theodore Roosevelt," *Philosophy and Rhetoric* 1 (Fall 1968): 230.

Man with the Muck-Rake" the Rooseveltian speech "most attuned to the times and having the greatest impact on the culture of the period." [4]

In March 1906, Roosevelt had given an informal, unreported talk on journalistic responsibility to the Washington Gridiron Club (an association of newspaper men). The press understood that he would later speak formally on the same subject. "The Man with the Muck-Rake" was that somewhat uneasily awaited speech.

Roosevelt used the ceremony of laying the cornerstone for a new House of Representatives Office Building as the occasion for his address. In his speech he tried to define the responsibilities and risks of journalistic critics, and by accident or design he also dropped indications that he favored federal taxes on incomes and inheritances and federal regulation of interstate businesses (see paragraphs 15 and 16).[5] This portion of the speech received more immediate attention in the press than what Roosevelt said about journalism, but four days after the speech the great San Francisco earthquake occurred and drove discussion of taxes and muckraking from the newspapers' pages. Afterward, "The Man with the Muck-Rake" came to stand in history as one of the famous American critiques of journalism and as an early critique of the social significance of mass media of communication. Except among scholars, the "tax issue" and the "regulation issue" have been all but forgotten as features of what Roosevelt said on April 14, 1906.

The rhetorical situation for "The Man with the Muck-Rake" cannot be fully understood without some knowledge of journalistic "muckraking" at the beginning of the twentieth century. The American historian, Henry Steele Commager, provides good leads toward this understanding:

> What was new was the appearance of editors who appreciated its value— men like S. S. McClure, John Brisben Walker, and John O'Hara Cosgrave— and of a remarkable group of journalists able and eager to exploit it: Lincoln Steffens, Ida Tarbell, Burton J. Hendrick, Mark Sullivan, Charles E. Russell, and others. These managed, in the few years in which they had a free hand, to stir public opinion as it had never been stirred before by journalism and to increase the circulation of their magazines by the hundred thousands.

> The picture of American life which the muckraking magazines drew was almost as one sided as that which had been painted by the sedate monthlies. If the earlier journals reflected the age of confidence, the new mirrored the age of doubt.[6]

---

[3] Richard Murphy, "Theodore Roosevelt," p. 347. Speech Association of America. *A History and Criticism of American Public Address* Vol. III, Edited by Marie Kathryn Hochmuth |Copyright 1955| New York: Russell & Russell, 1965.

[4] *Ibid.,* p. 359.

[5] Stephen E. Lucas has made a cogent case that this section of the speech was of major importance in Roosevelt's planning for this rhetorical situation. See Lucas's "Theodore Roosevelt's 'The Man with the Muck-Rake': A Reinterpretation," *Quarterly Journal of Speech* 59 (December 1973): 452–462.

[6] Henry Steele Commager, *The American Mind* (New Haven: Yale University Press, 1950), p. 76.

To diagnose the rhetorical situation for the fiscal portion of the speech requires broader research that reconstructs the general economic attitudes of the period, the popular view of "big business," and the political relations between business and governmental institutions.

Estimating the reliability of this speech text is an interesting and not very difficult task. Some clues may be found by looking at:

> *Putnam's Monthly* 1 (October 1906): 42–47.
> *The Outlook* 82 (April 21, 1906): 883–887.

The text from Roosevelt's *Works* follows.[7]

---

[7] Portions of this introduction first appeared in Carroll C. Arnold, Douglas Ehninger, John C. Gerber, *The Speaker's Resource Book,* 2nd ed. (Chicago: Scott, Foresman and Co., 1966), pp. 101–102. Used by permission of the publisher.

THE MAN WITH THE MUCK-RAKE

Theodore Roosevelt

Over a century ago Washington laid the corner-stone of the Capitol in what was then little more than a tract of wooded wilderness here beside the Potomac. We now find it necessary to provide by great additional buildings for the business of the government. This growth in the need for the housing of the government is but a proof and example of the way in which the nation has grown and the sphere of action of the National Government has grown. We now administer the affairs of a nation in which the extraordinary growth of population has been outstripped by the growth of wealth and the growth in complex interests. The material problems that face us to-day are not such as they were in Washington's time, but the underlying facts of human nature are the same now as they were then. Under altered external form we war with the same tendencies toward evil that were evident in Washington's time, and are helped by the same tendencies for good. It is about some of these that I wish to say a word to-day. /1/

In Bunyan's "Pilgrim's Progress" you may recall the description of the Man with the Muck-rake, the man who could look no way but downward, with the muck-rake in his hand; who was offered a celestial crown for his muck-rake, but who would neither look up nor regard the crown he was offered, but continued to rake to himself the filth of the floor. /2/

In "Pilgrim's Progress" the Man with the Muck-rake is set forth as the example of him whose vision is fixed on carnal instead of on spiritual things. Yet he also typifies the man who in this life consistently refuses to see aught that is lofty, and fixes his eyes with solemn intentness only on that which is vile and debasing. Now, it is very necessary that we should not flinch from seeing what is vile and debasing. There is filth on the floor, and it must be scraped up with the muck-rake; and there are times and places where this service is the most needed of all the services that can be performed. But the man who never does anything else, who never thinks or speaks or writes, save of his feats with the muck-rake, speedily becomes, not a help to society, not an incitement to good, but one of the most potent forces for evil. /3/

There are, in the body politic, economic and social, many and grave evils, and there is urgent necessity for the sternest war upon them. There should be relentless exposure of and attack upon every evil man whether politician or business man, every evil practice, whether in politics, in business, or in social life. I hail as a benefactor every writer or speaker, every man who, on the platform, or in book, magazine, or newspaper, with merciless severity makes such attack, provided always that he in his turn remembers that the attack is of use only if it is absolutely truthful. The liar is no whit better than the thief, and if his mendacity takes the form of slander, he may be worse than most thieves. It puts a premium upon knavery untruthfully to attack an honest man, or even with hysterical exaggeration to assail a bad man with untruth. An epidemic of indiscriminate assault upon character does not good, but very great harm. The soul of every scoundrel is gladdened whenever an honest man is assailed, or even when a scoundrel is untruthfully assailed. /4/

Now, it is easy to twist out of shape what I have just said, easy to affect to misunderstand it, and, if it is slurred over in repetition, not difficult really to misunderstand it. Some persons are sincerely incapable of understanding that to denounce mud-slinging does not mean the indorsement of whitewashing; and both the interested individuals who need whitewashing, and those others who practise mud-slinging, like to encourage such confusion of ideas. One of the chief counts against those who make indiscriminate assault upon men in business or men in public life, is that they invite a reaction which is sure to tell powerfully in favor of the unscrupulous scoundrel who really ought to be attacked, who ought to be exposed, who ought, if possible, to be put in the penitentiary. If Aristides is praised overmuch as just, people get tired of hearing it; and overcensure of the unjust finally and from similar reasons results in their favor. /5/

Any excess is almost sure to invite a reaction; and, unfortunately, the reaction, instead of taking the form of punishment of those guilty of the excess, is very apt to take the form either of punishment of the unoffending or of giving immunity, and even strength, to offenders. The effort to make financial or political profit out of the destruction of character can only result in public calamity. Gross and reckless assaults on character, whether on the stump or in newspaper, magazine, or book, create a morbid and vicious public sentiment, and at the same time act as a profound deterrent to able men of normal sensitiveness and tend to prevent them from entering the public service at any price. As an instance in point, I may mention that one serious difficulty encountered in getting the right type of men to dig the Panama Canal is the certainty that they will be exposed, both without, and, I am sorry to say, sometimes within, Congress, to utterly reckless assaults on their character and capacity. /6/

At the risk of repetition let me say again that my plea is, not for immunity to but for the most unsparing exposure of the politician who betrays his trust, of the big business man who makes or spends his fortune in illegitimate or corrupt ways. There should be a resolute effort to hunt every such man out of the position he has disgraced. Expose the crime, and hunt down the criminal; but remember that even in the case of crime, if it is attacked in sensational, lurid, and untruthful fashion, the attack may do more damage to the public mind than the crime itself. It is because I feel that there should be no rest in the endless war against the forces of evil that I ask that the war be conducted with sanity as well as with resolution. The men with the muck-rakes are often indispensible to the well-being of society; but only if they know when to stop raking the muck, and to look upward to the celestial crown above them, to the crown of worthy endeavor. There are beautiful things above and roundabout them; and if they gradually grow to feel that the whole world is nothing but muck, their power of usefulness is gone. If the whole picture is painted black there remains no hue whereby to single out the rascals for distinction from their fellows. Such painting finally induces a kind of moral color-blindness; and people affected by it come to the conclusion that no man is really black, and no man really white, but they are all gray. In other words, they neither believe in the truth of the attack, nor in the honesty of the man who is attacked; they grow as suspicious of the accusation as of the offense; it becomes well-nigh hopeless to stir them either to wrath against wrong-doing or to enthusiasm for what is right; and such a mental attitude in the public gives hope to every knave, and is the despair of honest men. /7/

To assail the great and admitted evils of our political and industrial life with such crude and sweeping generalizations as to include decent men in the general condemnation means the searing of the public conscience. There results a general attitude either of cynical belief in and indifference to public corruption or else of a distrustful inability to discriminate between the good and the bad. Either attitude is fraught with untold damage to the country as a whole. The fool who has not sense to discriminate between what is good and what is bad is well-nigh as dangerous as the man who does discriminate and yet chooses the bad. There is nothing more distressing to every good patriot, to every good American, than the hard, scoffing spirit which treats the allegation of dishonesty in a public man as a cause for laughter. Such laughter is worse than the crackling of thorns under a pot, for it denotes not merely the vacant mind, but the heart in which high emotions have been choked before they could grow to fruition. /8/

There is any amount of good in the world, and there never was a time when loftier and more disinterested work for the betterment of mankind was being done than now. The forces that tend for evil are great and terrible, but the forces of truth and love and courage and honesty and generosity and sympathy are also stronger than ever before. It is a foolish and timid, no less than a wicked, thing to blink the fact that the forces of evil are strong, but it is even worse to fail to take into account the strength of the forces that tell for good. Hysterical sensationalism is the very poorest weapon wherewith to fight for lasting righteousness. The men who with stern sobriety and truth assail the many evils of our time, whether in the public press, or in magazines, or in books, are the leaders and allies of all engaged in the work for social and political betterment. But if they give good reason for distrust of what they say, if they chill the ardor of those who demand truth as a primary virtue, they thereby betray the good cause, and play into the hands of the very men against whom they are nominally at war. /9/

In his "Ecclesiastical Polity" that fine old Elizabethan divine, Bishop Hooker, wrote:

"He that goeth about to persuade a multitude that they are not so well governed as they ought to be, shall never want attentive and favorable hearers; because they know the manifold defects whereunto every kind of regimen is subject, but the secret lets and difficulties, which in public proceedings are innumerable and inevitable, they have not ordinarily the judgment to consider." /10/

This truth should be kept constantly in mind by every free people desiring to preserve the sanity and poise indispensable to the permanent success of self-government. Yet, on the other hand, it is vital not to permit this spirit of sanity and self-command to degenerate into mere mental stagnation. Bad though a state of hysterical excitement is, and evil though the results are which come from the violent oscillations such excitement invariably produces, yet a sodden acquiescence in evil is even worse. At this moment we are passing through a period of great unrest—social, political, and industrial unrest. It is of the utmost importance for our future that this should prove to be not the unrest of mere rebelliousness against life, of mere dissatisfaction with the inevitable inequality of conditions, but the unrest of a resolute and eager ambition to secure the betterment of the individual and the nation. So far as this movement of agitation throughout the country takes the form of a fierce discontent with evil, of a determination to punish the authors of evil, whether in industry or politics, the feeling is to be heartily welcomed as a sign of healthy life. /11/

If, on the other hand, it turns into a mere crusade of appetite against appetite, of a contest between the brutal greed of the "have-nots" and the brutal greed of the "haves," then it has no significance for good, but only for evil. If it seeks to establish a line of cleavage, not along the line which divides good men from bad, but along that other line, running at right angles thereto, which divides those who are well off from those who are less well off, then it will be fraught with immeasurable harm to the body politic. /12/

We can no more and no less afford to condone evil in the man of capital than evil in the man of no capital. The wealthy man who exults because there is a failure of justice in the effort to bring some trust magnate to an account for his misdeeds is as bad as, and no worse than, the so-called labor leader who clamorously strives to excite a foul class feeling on behalf of some other labor leader who is implicated in murder. One attitude is as bad as the other, and no worse; in each case the accused is entitled to exact justice; and in neither case is there need of action by others which can be construed into an expression of sympathy for crime. /13/

It is a prime necessity that if the present unrest is to result in permanent good the emotion shall be translated into action, and that the action shall be marked by honesty, sanity, and self-restraint. There is mighty little good in a mere spasm of reform. The reform that counts is that which comes through steady, continuous growth; violent emotionalism leads to exhaustion. /14/

It is important to this people to grapple with the problems connected with the amassing of enormous fortunes, and the use of those fortunes, both corporate and individual, in business. We should discriminate in the sharpest way between fortunes well-won and fortunes ill-won; between those gained as an incident to performing great services to the community as a whole, and those gained in evil fashion by keeping just within the limits of mere law-honesty. Of course no amount of charity in spending such fortunes in any way compensates for misconduct in making them. As a matter of personal conviction, and without pretending to discuss the details or formulate the system, I feel that we shall ultimately have to consider the adoption of some such scheme as that of a progressive tax on all fortunes, beyond a certain amount either given in life or devised or bequeathed upon death to any individual—a tax so framed as to put it out of the power of the owner of one of these enormous fortunes to hand on more than a certain amount to any one individual; the tax, of course, to be imposed by the National and not the State Government. Such taxation should, of course, be aimed merely at the inheritance or transmission in their entirety of those fortunes swollen beyond all healthy limits. /15/

Again, the National Government must in some form exercise supervision over corporations engaged in interstate business—and all large corporations are engaged in interstate business—whether by license or otherwise, so as to permit us to deal with the far-reaching evils of overcapitalization. This year we are making a beginning in the direction of serious effort to settle some of these economic problems by the railway-rate legislation. Such legislation, if so framed, as I am sure it will be, as to secure definite and tangible results, will amount to something of itself; and it will amount to a great deal more in so far as it is taken as a first step in the direction of a policy of superintendence and control over corporate wealth engaged in interstate commerce, this superintendence and control not to be exercised in a spirit of malevolence toward the men who have created the wealth, but with the firm purpose both to do justice to them and to see that they in their turn do justice to the public at large. /16/

The first requisite in the public servants who are to deal in this shape with corporations, whether as legislators or as executives, is honesty. This honesty can be no respecter of persons. There can be no such thing as unilateral honesty. The danger is not really from corrupt corporations; it springs from the corruption itself, whether exercised for or against corporations. /17/

The eighth commandment reads: "Thou shalt not steal." It does not read: "Thou shalt not steal from the rich man." It does not read: "Thou shalt not steal from the poor man." It reads simply and plainly: "Thou shalt not steal." No good whatever will come from that warped and mock morality which denounces the misdeeds of men of wealth and forgets the misdeeds practised at their expense; which denounces bribery, but blinds itself to blackmail; which foams with rage if a corporation secures favors by improper methods, and merely leers with hideous mirth if the corporation is itself wronged. The only public servant who can be trusted honestly to protect the rights of the public against the misdeed of a corporation is that public man who will just as surely protect the corporation itself from wrongful aggression. If a public man is willing to yield to popular clamor and do wrong to the men of wealth or to rich corporations, it may be set down as certain that if the opportunity comes he will secretly and furtively do wrong to the public in the interest of a corporation. /18/

But, in addition to honesty, we need sanity. No honesty will make a public man useful if that man is timid or foolish, if he is a hot-headed zealot or an impracticable visionary. As we strive for reform we find that it is not at all merely the case of a long up-hill pull. On the contrary, there is almost as much of breeching work as of collar work; to depend only on traces means that there will soon be a runaway and an upset. The men of wealth who to-day are trying to prevent the regulation and control of their business in the interest of the public by the proper government authorities will not succeed, in my judgment, in checking the progress of the movement. But if they did succeed they would find that they had sown the wind and would surely reap the whirlwind, for they would ultimately provoke the violent excesses which accompany a reform coming by convulsion instead of by steady and natural growth. /19/

On the other hand, the wild preachers of unrest and discontent, the wild agitators against the entire existing order, the men who act crookedly, whether because of sinister design or from mere puzzle-headedness, the men who preach destruction without proposing any substitute for what they intend to destroy, or who propose a substitute which would be far worse than the existing evils—all these men are the most dangerous opponents of real reform. If they get their way they will lead the people into a deeper pit than any into which they could fall under the present system. If they fail to get their way they will still do incalculable harm by provoking the kind of reaction which, in its revolt against the senseless evil of their teaching, would enthrone more securely than ever the very evils which their misguided followers believe they are attacking. /20/

More important than aught else is the development of the broadest sympathy of man for man. The welfare of the wage-worker, the welfare of the tiller of the soil, upon these depend the welfare of the entire country; their good is not to be sought in pulling down others; but their good must be the prime object of all our statesmanship. /21/

Materially we must strive to secure a broader economic opportunity for all men, so that each shall have a better chance to show the stuff of which he is made. Spiritually and ethically we must strive to bring about clean living and right thinking. We appreciate that the things of the body are important; but we appreciate also that the things of the soul are immeasurably more important. The foundation-stone of national life is, and ever must be, the high individual character of the average citizen. /22/

ADDRESS TO THE CONGRESS

Winston Spencer Churchill

Behind the moments of this address lay Winston Churchill's colorful life, the early years of World War II, and his leadership as Prime Minister of Great Britain. Immediately behind lay the United States' effort to remain uninvolved in the war and the shattering of that hope by the Japanese attack on Pearl Harbor in Hawaii, slightly less than three weeks before Churchill addressed a joint session of the United States Congress. Resources for filling out the background of the rhetorical situation of December 26, 1941, are plentiful; this introduction points up only unique features.

Churchill made clear in his *The Grand Alliance* [1] that his speech to the Congress on the day after Christmas was a strategically secondary, but emotionally important, part of his activities during a momentous visit to the United States to consult on strategies for the further conduct of the war. He had begun arranging for this series of conferences on the day after Japanese planes struck Pearl Harbor. He had at least two special concerns, as he later pointed out. He feared the Americans might not see that defeat of the Axis powers depended on winning in Europe first and then concentrating on the Japanese forces. The Americans might be too ready to reverse those priorities, he thought. A less immediate but enduring concern was to lay groundwork for a postwar alliance of "English-speaking peoples." These seem to have been the major ideas he came to Washington to promote—the first with governmental officials and the second, in a long-ranged way, with the American people.

Because it was the Christmas season, many Congressmen and other officials were away from Washington during Churchill's visit. The New York *Times* reported that Congressional leaders decided for this reason that the occasion of Churchill's appearance before a joint session of Congress should be kept "informal" and that the setting should be the Senate Chamber rather than the larger House Chamber where such sessions were usually held. [2]

Churchill wrote that he approached this speech with special feelings. It was the first time he had ever addressed a legislature other than Parliament. But "it was possible to feel a blood-right to speak" to the American Congress because his ancestry on his mother's side could be traced in

The text presented here is that which appears in the *Congressional Record*, 77th Congress, First Session, vol. 87, part 9, pp. 10117–10119; December 26, 1941.

[1] Copyright 1950, by Houghton Mifflin Company. References here are to the Bantam Book edition (New York: Bantam Books, 1962).
[2] New York *Times,* December 26, 1941, p. 1. Interestingly no mention was made of this unusual arrangement in reports published in *The Times* (London).

America to "a lieutenant who served in George Washington's army." [3] Doubtless, too, he knew that among foreign political figures he was a special favorite with many Americans. And he recognized the specialness of Christmas for British and American citizens.

He found the Senate Chamber crowded and "impressive" as he looked through "the grille of microphones." [4] All three major radio networks (NBC, CBS, and Mutual) carried the speech in North America, and it was broadcast by shortwave to the rest of the world. *The Times* (London) later reported that "millions" had heard the speech in Britain, a prospect of which Churchill was surely aware as he spoke.

In Churchill's view and in the views of American and British news re- porters the speech was an enormous success. Churchill recalled that he had received full attention from the Congressmen, Senators, Cabinet officers, and others who were in the Senate Chamber. "I got my laughter and ap- plause just where I expected them," he wrote.[5] A headline in the New York *Times* read: "Congress Thrilled. Prime Minister Warns of Dark Days but Holds Victory Certain. Urges Cooperation. U.S. and Britain Must Prevent Future Wars—He Gets Ovation." [6] *The Times'* (London) correspondent reported to his paper that Churchill gave a "stirring speech" to a "roar of cheers" and "held the audience from the first word to the last." Editorially *The Times* said, "The occasion was unique, and it was significant in the history of Anglo-American relations." [7] In a later issue *The Times* com- mented with satisfaction on the great number of "messages of friendship and acclaim" that began to "reach him in the White House" almost as the speech was concluded. This was the more remarkable, thought *The Times'* editorial writer because Churchill was a "man who . . . had stood before the Senate and House and had in fact proposed that the alliance of the English-speaking peoples in war should be continued over into the days of peace in order to make the peace real." [8] This observation clearly reflected the writer's sensitivity to previous American isolationism, "America First- ism," "neutralism," and other pre-Pearl Harbor forces of public opinion which had restrained American assistance to the embattled Allies and, before that, counseled noninvolvement in all foreign affairs outside the Western Hemisphere.

In the United States and abroad, Churchill's speech was almost univer- sally acclaimed as an outstandingly successful effort. There is little doubt that the speaker's established reputation as a foe of totalitarian powers, as a powerful war-time orator, as an impressive war leader, and as "half an American" gave him initial advantages in his rhetorical situation. And probably the "strange Christmas" season, as Churchill had called it,

---

[3] Churchill, *The Grand Alliance,* p. 565.
[4] *Ibid.,* p. 566.
[5] *Ibid.*
[6] New York *Times,* December 27, 1941, p. 1.
[7] *The Times* (London), December 27, 1941, p. 4 and p. 5.
[8] *The Times* (London), December 29, 1941, p. 4.

conditioned Americans for the kind of address he gave. Churchill had said at President Roosevelt's annual Christmas tree-lighting ceremony on Christmas Eve: "Let us grown-ups share to the full in their [children's] unstinted pleasures before we turn again to the stern task and the formidable years that lie before us. . . ." [9]

On the day after Christmas, as newspaper headlines announced the imminent loss of the Philippines and Wake Island, Churchill turned thoughts to "the stern task" with striking expressions of determination and assurance. Of course, the fact that the United States was in the first, excited stages of gearing up for war must also have influenced the situation in which his American listeners found themselves.

There is more to learn about the situation in which Churchill spoke to the world from the United States Senate Chamber. These observations only begin the story. Here is the text of his speech as it appears in the *Congressional Record.*

---

[9] *The Grand Alliance,* p. 565.

ADDRESS TO THE CONGRESS
Winston Spencer Churchill

At 12 o'clock and 30 minutes, p. m., Rt. Hon. Winston Churchill, escorted by the committees of the two Houses, and accompanied by his personal assistant, Commander C. R. Thompson, R. N.; J. M. Martin, Esq., private secretary; Sir Charles Wilson, president of the Royal College of Physicians of London, England; and Capt. F. D. W. Brown, private secretary, entered the Chamber, and was escorted to a seat on the rostrum in front of the Vice President and the Speaker pro tempore of the House of Representatives.

The VICE PRESIDENT. Members of the Senate and guests of the Senate, the Prime Minister of Great Britain, the Right Honorable Winston Churchill. [Prolonged applause.]

Mr. CHURCHILL. Members of the Senate and of the House of Representatives of the United States, I feel greatly honored that you should have invited me to enter the United States Senate Chamber and address the representatives of both branches of Congress. /1/

The fact that my American forebears have for so many generations played their part in the life of the United States, and that here I am, an Englishman, welcomed in your midst, makes this experience one of the most moving and thrilling in my life, which is already long and has not been entirely uneventful. [Laughter.] /2/

I wish indeed that my mother, whose memory I cherish across the vale of years, could have been here to see. By the way, I cannot help reflecting that if my father had been American and my mother British, instead of the other way round, I might have got here on my own. [Laughter and applause.] In that case, this would not have been the first time you would have heard my voice. In that case, I should not have needed any invitation; but, if I had, it is hardly likely that it would have been unanimous. [Laughter.] So perhaps things are better as they are. /3/

I may confess, however, that I do not feel quite like a fish out of water in a legislative assembly where English is spoken. I am a child of the House of Commons. I was brought up in my father's house to believe in democracy. "Trust the people"—that was his message. I used to see him cheered at meetings and in the streets by crowds of workingmen away back in those aristocratic Victorian days when, as Disraeli said, the world was for the few, and for the very few. Therefore I have been in full harmony all my life with the tides which have flowed on both sides of the Atlantic against privilege and monopoly and have steered confidently toward the Gettysburg ideal of "government of the people, by the people, for the people." [Applause.] /4/

I owe my advancement entirely to the House of Commons, whose servant I am. In my country, as in yours, public men are proud to be the servants of the state, and would be ashamed to be its masters. On any day, if they thought the people wanted it, the House of Commons could by a simple vote remove me from my office. But I am not worrying about it at all. [Laughter.] As a matter of fact, I am sure they will approve very highly of my journey here—for which I obtained the King's permission—in order to meet the President of the United States [applause] and to arrange with him for all that mapping out of our military plans, and for all those intimate meetings of the high officers of the armed services of both countries which are indispensable to the successful prosecution of the war. /5/

I should like to say, first of all, how much I have been impressed and encouraged by the breadth of view and sense of proportion which I have found in all quarters over here to which I have had access. Anyone who did not understand the size and solidarity of the foundations of the United States might easily have expected to find an excited, disturbed, self-centered atmosphere, with all minds fixed upon the novel, startling, and painful episodes of sudden war as they hit America. After all, the United States has been attacked and set upon by three most powerfully armed dictator states, the greatest military power in Europe, and the greatest military power in Asia. Japan, Germany, and Italy have all declared and are making war upon you, and a quarrel is opened which can only end in their overthrow or yours. But here in Washington, in these memorable days, I have found an Olympian fortitude which, far from being based upon complacency, is only the mask of an inflexible purpose and the proof of a sure and well-grounded confidence in the final outcome. [Applause.] We in Britain had the same feeling in our darkest days. We, too, were sure that in the end all would be well. /6/

You do not, I am certain, underrate the severity of the ordeal to which you and we have still to be subjected. The forces ranged against us are enormous; they are bitter; they are ruthless. The wicked men and their factions who have launched their peoples on the path of war and conquest know that they will be called to terrible account if they can not beat down by force of arms the peoples they have assailed. They will stop at nothing. They have a vast accumulation of war weapons of all kinds; they have highly-trained and disciplined armies, navies, and air services; they have plans and designs which have long been contrived and matured; they will stop at nothing that violence or treachery can suggest. /7/

It is quite true that on our side our resources in manpower and in materials are far greater than theirs; but only a portion of your resources are as yet mobilized and developed, and we have both of us much to learn in the cruel art of war. We have, therefore, without doubt, a time of tribulation before us. In this time some ground will be lost which it will be hard and costly to regain. Many disappointments and unpleasant surprises await us. Many of them will afflict us before the full marshalling of our latent and total power can be accomplished. /8/

For the best part of 20 years the youth of Britain and America have been taught that war was evil, which is true, and that it would never come again, which has been proved false. /9/

For the best part of 20 years the youth of Germany, Japan, and Italy have been taught that aggressive war is the noblest duty of the citizen, and that it should be begun as soon as the necessary weapons and organization have been made. We have performed the duties and tasks of peace. They have plotted and planned for war. This naturally has placed us in Britain, and now places you in the United States, at a disadvantage which only time, courage, and straining, untiring exertions can correct. /10/

We have, indeed, to be thankful that so much time has been granted to us. If Germany had tried to invade the British Isles after the French collapse in June 1940, and if Japan had declared war on the British Empire and the United States at about the same date, no one can say what disasters and agonies might not have been our lot. But now, at the end of December 1941, our transformation from easygoing peace to total-war efficiency has made very great progress. The broad flow of munitions in Great Britain has already begun. Immense strides have been made in the conversion of American industry to military purposes, and now that the United States is at war, it is possible for orders to be given every day which a year or 18 months hence will produce results in war power beyond anything which has yet been seen or foreseen in the dictator states. Provided that every effort is made, that nothing is kept back, that the whole manpower, brainpower, virility, valour, and civic virtue of the English-speaking world, with all its galaxy of loyal, friendly, or associated communities and states, are bent unremittingly to the simple but supreme task, I think it would be reasonable to hope that the end of 1942 will see us quite definitely in a better position than we are now [applause], and that the year 1943 will enable us to assume the initiative upon an ample scale. [Applause.] /11/

Some people may be startled or momentarily depressed when, like your President, I speak of a long and a hard war. Our peoples would rather know the truth, sombre though it be; and, after all, when we are doing the noblest work in the world, not only defending our hearths and homes but the cause of freedom in every land, the question of whether deliverance comes in 1942, or 1943, or 1944, falls into its proper place in the grand proportions of human history. [Applause.] Sure I am that this day, now, we are the masters of our fate; that the task which has been set for us is not above our strength, and that its pangs and toils are not beyond our endurance. As long as we have faith in our cause and unconquerable will power, salvation will not be denied us. In the words of the Psalmist:

He shall not be afraid of evil tidings: his heart is fixed,
trusting in the Lord. /12/

Not all the tidings will be evil. On the contrary, mighty strokes of war have already been dealt against the enemy. The glorious defense of their native soil by the Russian Armies and people have inflicted wounds upon the Nazi tyranny and system which have bitten deep, and will fester and inflame not only in the Nazi body but in the Nazi mind. [Applause.] /13/

The boastful Mussolini [laughter] has crumpled already. He is now but a lackey and serf, the merest utensil of his master's will. [Laughter and applause.] He has inflicted great suffering and wrong upon his own industrious people. He has been stripped of all his African empire. Abyssinia has been liberated. Our armies of the east, which were so weak and ill equipped at the moment of French desertion, now control all the regions from Teheran to Benghazi, and from Aleppo to Cyprus and the sources of the Nile. [Applause.] /14/

For many months we devoted ourselves to preparing to take the offensive in Libya. The very considerable battle which has been proceeding for the last 6 weeks in the desert has been most fiercely fought on both sides. Owing to the difficulties of supply on the desert flank we were never able to bring numerically equal forces to bear upon the enemy. Therefore we had to rely upon a superiority in the numbers and quality of tanks and aircraft, British and American. Aided by these, for the first time we have fought the enemy with equal weapons. For the first time we have made the Hun feel the sharp edge of those tools with which he has enslaved Europe. The armed force of the enemy in Cyrenaica amounted to 150,000 men, of whom about a third were Germans. General Auchinleck set out to destroy totally that armed force; and I have every reason to believe that his aim will be fully accomplished. [Applause.] /15/

I am so glad to be able to place before you, Members of the Senate and of the House of Representatives, at this moment when you are entering the war, proof that, with proper weapons and proper organization, we are able to beat the life out of the savage Nazi. [Applause.] What Hitler is suffering in Libya is only a sample and a foretaste of what we must give him and his accomplices wherever this war shall lead us, in every quarter of the globe. /16/

There are good tidings also from blue water. The life line of supplies which joins our two nations across the ocean, without which all might fall, is flowing steadily and freely, in spite of all the enemy can do. It is a fact that the British Empire, which many thought 18 months ago was broken and ruined, is now incomparably stronger and is growing stronger with every month. [Applause.] /17/

Lastly, if you will forgive me for saying it, to me the best tiding of all, the United States—united as never before—has drawn the sword for Freedom, and cast away the scabbard. [Applause.] /18/

All these tremendous facts have led the subjugated peoples of Europe to lift up their heads again in hope. They have put aside forever the shameful temptation of resigning themselves to the conqueror's will. Hope has returned to the hearts of scores of millions of men and women, and with that hope there burns the flame of anger against the brutal, corrupt invader, and still more fiercely burn the fires of hatred and contempt for the filthy Quislings whom he has suborned. In a dozen famous ancient states, now prostrate under the Nazi yoke, the masses of the people, all classes and creeds, await the hour of liberation, when they, too, will be able once again to play their part and strike their blows like men. That hour will strike, and its solemn peal will proclaim that the night is passed and that the dawn has come. /19/

The onslaught upon us, so long and so secretly planned by Japan, has presented both our countries with grievous problems for which we could not be fully prepared. If people ask me, as they have a right to ask me in England, "Why is it that you have not got ample equipment of modern aircraft and army weapons of all kinds in

Malaya and in the East Indies" I can only point to the victories
General Auchinleck has gained in the Libyan campaign. Had we
diverted and dispersed our gradually growing resources between
Libya and Malaya, we should have been found wanting in both
theatres. If the United States has been found at a disadvantage at
various points in the Pacific Ocean, we know well that it is to no
small extent because of the aid which you have been giving to us
in munitions for the defense of the British Isles and for the Libyan
campaign, and, above all, because of your help in the battle of
the Atlantic, upon which all depends, and which has in consequence
been successfully and prosperously maintained. /20/

Of course, it would have been much better, I freely admit, if we
had had enough resources of all kinds to be at full strength at all
threatened points; but, considering how slowly and reluctantly we
brought ourselves to large-scale preparations, and how long such
preparations take, we had no right to expect to be in such a fortunate position. The choice of how to dispose of our hitherto
limited resources had to be made by Britain in time of war, and by
the United States in time of peace; and I believe that history will
pronounce that upon the whole—and it is upon the whole that these
matters must be judged—the choice made was right. /21/

Now that we are together, now that we are linked in a righteous
comradeship of arms, now that our two considerable nations, each
in perfect unity, have joined all their life energies in a common
resolve, a new scene opens upon which a steady light will glow
and brighten. /22/

Many people have been astonished that Japan should, in a single
day, have plunged into war against the United States and the
British Empire. We all wonder why, if this dark design, with all
its labourious and intricate preparations, had been so long filling
their secret minds, they did not choose our moment of weakness
18 months ago. Viewed quite dispassionately, in spite of the losses
we have suffered and the further punishment we shall have to take,
it certainly appears to be an irrational act. It is, of course, only
prudent to assume that they have made very careful calculation
and think they see their way through. Nevertheless, there may be
another explanation. /23/

We know that for many years past the policy of Japan has been
dominated by secret societies of subaltern and junior officers of
the Army and Navy who have enforced their will upon successive
Japanese cabinets and parliaments by the assassination of any
Japanese statesman who opposed or who did not sufficiently

further their aggressive policy. It may be that these societies, dazzled and dizzy with their own schemes of aggression and the prospect of early victories, have forced their country, against its better judgment, into war. They have certainly embarked upon a very considerable undertaking [laughter]; for, after the outrages they have committed upon us at Pearl Harbor, in the Pacific islands, in the Philippines, in Malaya, and the Dutch East Indies, they must now know that the stakes for which they have decided to play are mortal. When we consider the resources of the United States and the British Empire, compared to those of Japan, when we remember those of China, which has so long and valiantly withstood invasion [great applause], and when also we observe the Russian menace which hangs over Japan, it becomes still more difficult to reconcile Japanese action with prudence, or even with sanity. What kind of people do they think we are? Is it possible they do not realize that we shall never cease to persevere against them until they have been taught a lesson which they and the world will never forget? [Prolonged applause.] /24/

Members of the Senate and Members of the House of Representatives, I turn for one moment more from the turmoil and convulsions of the present to the broader spaces of the future. /25/

Here we are together, facing a group of mighty foes who seek our ruin. Here we are together, defending all that to free men is dear. Twice in a single generation the catastrophe of world war has fallen upon us; twice in our lifetimes has the long arm of Fate reached out across the oceans to bring the United States into the forefront of the battle. If we had kept together after the last war; if we had taken common measures for our safety, this renewal of the curse need never have fallen upon us. [Applause.] Do we not owe it to ourselves, to our children, to tormented mankind, to make sure that these catastrophes do not engulf us for the third time? /26/

It has been proved that pestilences may break out in the Old World which carry their destructive ravages into the New World, from which, once they are afoot, the New World cannot by any means escape. Duty and prudence alike command, first, that the germ centres of hatred and revenge should be constantly and vigilantly surveyed and treated in good time; and, secondly, that an adequate organization should be set up to make sure that the pestilence can be controlled at its earliest beginnings before it spreads and rages throughout the entire earth. [Applause.] /27/

Five or six years ago it would have been easy, without shedding a drop of blood, for the United States and Great Britain to have insisted on fulfillment of the disarmament clauses of the treaties which Germany signed after the Great War. That also would have been the opportunity for assuring to Germans those raw materials which we declared in the Atlantic Charter should not be denied to any nation, victor or vanquished. /28/

Prodigious hammer strokes have been needed to bring us together today; or, if you will allow me to use other language, I will say that he must, indeed, have a blind soul who cannot see that some great purpose and design is being worked out here below, of which we have the honour to be the faithful servants. /29/

It is not given to us to peer into the mysteries of the future; still I avow my hope and faith, sure and inviolate, that in days to come, the British and American peoples will for their own safety and for the good of all, walk together side by side in majesty, in justice, and in peace. /30/

[Prolonged applause, the Members of the Senate and their guests rising.]

ADJOURNMENT TO TUESDAY

At the conclusion of Mr. Churchill's address, the distinguished guests having retired from the Chamber the Senate (at 1 o'clock and 5 minutes p. m.), under the order previously entered stood in adjournment until Tuesday, December 30, 1941, at 12 o'clock meridian.

INAUGURAL ADDRESS
John F. Kennedy

John F. Kennedy became the thirty-fourth President of the United States on January 20, 1961, as he took the oath of office moments before beginning the speech printed below. He had been born in Brookline, Massachusetts in 1917, graduated from Harvard University in 1940, wounded in naval service during World World II, elected to Congress in 1946 and to the Senate in 1952. In 1960 he was nominated for the presidency by the Democratic party's National Convention, and in November he defeated Richard M. Nixon in one of the closest presidential elections in American history. His administration of two years, ten months, and two days ended when he was assassinated in Dallas, Texas on November 22, 1963.

Among the slogans of Kennedy's campaign for the presidency were, "Let's get this country moving again," "We can do better," and "the New Frontier." [1] These forecast the tone of Kennedy's inaugural address. The speech was a call to unity, action, and to a national exercise of power to defend and expand liberal political forces at home and abroad. The two most frequently quoted lines from the speech became: ". . . ask not what your country can do for you—ask what you can do for your country," and ". . . we shall pay any price, bear any burden, meet any hardship, support any friend, oppose any foe to assure the survival and success of liberty." They are lines whose repetition indicated that Kennedy's calls for an energetic foreign policy and for public service at home were grasped by the public.

When the speech had ended, both Republicans and Democrats called it "superb," "brilliant," "inspiring." Diplomats told reporters they were gratified by Kennedy's challenge to Communist nations "to negotiate in good faith." Most who responded negatively to the speech were content to charge that it was laden with generalities and constituted "mood music." Among the few to express specific reservations immediately was Senator Everett Dirksen (Republican) of Illinois. His remark to the press reads today as almost prophetic of the grounds on which Mr. Kennedy's brief administration would be criticized by some a decade later. Dirksen called the speech "all-encompassing" and suggested that "it set huge goals" he was not sure Americans were willing to carry out in full.[2] It is, in any case, a reflection of the initial rhetorical power of the speech that its language and its "real" meanings became items of controversy in later debates on how far the United States' commitments ought to reach beyond its borders.

---

[1] Several points made in this introduction are drawn from the introduction to the same speech which appears in Arnold, Ehninger, and Gerber, *The Speaker's Resource Book,* 2nd ed., published by Scott, Foresman and Company and used by their permission. Douglas Ehninger was primary author of that introduction and analysis.

[2] New York *Herald Tribune,* January 21, 1961, p. 1.

Mr. Kennedy delivered his speech from the steps of the Capitol, the traditional setting for presidential inaugurations. The day was unusually cold, and heavy snow during the preceding forty-eight hours prevented some from attending the ceremonies. Nonetheless, attendance was good and, of course, the speech was televised nationally and broadcast to the world by radio.

The term "charismatic" has frequently been applied to John Kennedy, and with good reason. He had relative youth, good looks, visible energy, and he radiated optimism, confidence, and determination. For these reasons no printed text of his inaugural address can convey its full force. No punctuation can truly reflect his careful phrasing; only audio or audio-visual records can reveal the assurance Kennedy gave by utterance and pacing to his calls for action. The balances and antitheses with which the prose is studded were expertly "sounded," deliberately but energetically. Further force was added by what later became known as "the Kennedy chop"—a quick, downward thrust of his right forearm and hand, punctuating virtually every point he wanted to emphasize. Sometimes, at his most emphatic, he rapped his knuckles on the reading desk or punched his fist against it. At first his voice was somewhat high pitched and strained, but he soon modulated it and for most of the speech sounded fully controlled and assured. His New England dialectal pattern was prominent but expected. Eccentricity in delivery would be noticed, if at all, in unusual downward inflections as he posed his rhetorical questions. By pauses and inflectional changes he rendered major thought units distinct; all but one of the shifts of thought indicated by paragraphs in the text were clearly emphasized in delivery. (The exception occurred between paragraphs 21 and 22.)

Theodore Sorenson, who assisted in the writing of Kennedy's inaugural address, later reported that Mr. Kennedy directed him to study Abraham Lincoln's speeches with care. Perhaps this is why the rhythms of Lincoln's "Second Inaugural" appear at a number of points in Kennedy's inaugural.

The text presented here comes from *Public Papers of the Presidents of the United States: John F. Kennedy, 1961*.[3] Sound recordings of the speech show that the text is a verbatim report of what Kennedy said.[4]

As is usual in inaugural speeches, Kennedy's inaugural address was general; courses of action were suggested rather than contended for. From linguistic and logical points of view it can be charged that the speech contains many generalities, near clichés, vague and unsupported promises, and reflected theories of historical and social causation that are highly

---

[3] (Washington, D. C.: United States Government Printing Office, 1962.) These documents are published by the Office of the Federal Register, National Archives and Records Service and are sold by the Superintendent of Documents, U.S. Government Printing Office.

[4] Here and there I have inserted commas that do not appear in the official text. These give additional hints of how Kennedy phrased his lines; even so punctuated, the text cannot show the actual oral phrasings.

debatable. Yet the fact is that these phrases and their sounds were applauded internationally and accepted as guidelines for action by millions of Americans. Indeed, a strong case can be made that "Kennedy's close allies" were right when they said that this address successfully claimed "a clear mandate to act, and cut short the doubts cast by some Republicans on the validity of his election." [5]

The first question facing speech critics is: *How* did these words, as delivered, achieve so much in the rhetorical situation of January 20, 1961?

---

[5] New York *Herald Tribune,* January 21, 1961, p. 1.

INAUGURAL ADDRESS

John F. Kennedy

Vice President Johnson, Mr. Speaker, Mr. Chief Justice, President Eisenhower, Vice President Nixon, President Truman, Reverend Clergy, fellow citizens:

We observe today not a victory of party, but a celebration of freedom—symbolizing an end as well as a beginning—signifying renewal as well as change. For I have sworn before you and Almighty God the same solemn oath our forebears prescribed nearly a century and three quarters ago. /1/

The world is very different now. For man holds in his mortal hands the power to abolish all forms of human poverty and all forms of human life. And yet the same, revolutionary beliefs for which our forebears fought are still at issue around the globe— the belief that the rights of man come not from the generosity of the state but from the hand of God. /2/

We dare not forget today that we are the heirs of that first revolution. Let the word go forth from this time and place, to friend and foe alike, that the torch has been passed to a new generation of Americans—born in this century, tempered by war, disciplined by a hard and bitter peace, proud of our ancient heritage—and unwilling to witness or permit the slow undoing of those human rights to which this nation has always been committed, and to which we are committed today at home and around the world. /3/

Let every nation know, whether it wishes us well or ill, that we shall pay any price, bear any burden, meet any hardship, support any friend, oppose any foe to assure the survival and the success of liberty. /4/

This much we pledge—and more. /5/

To those old allies, whose cultural and spiritual origins we share, we pledge the loyalty of faithful friends. United, there is little we cannot do in a host of cooperative ventures. Divided, there is little we can do—for we dare not meet a powerful challenge at odds and split asunder. /6/

To those new states whom we welcome to the ranks of the free, we pledge our word that one form of colonial control shall not have passed away merely to be replaced by a far more iron tyranny. We shall not always expect to find them supporting our view. But we shall always hope to find them strongly supporting their own freedom—and to remember that, in the past, those who foolishly sought power by riding the back of the tiger ended up inside. /7/

To those peoples in the huts and villages of half the globe, struggling to break the bonds of mass misery, we pledge our best efforts to help them help themselves, for whatever period is required—not because the communists may be doing it, but because it is right. If a free society cannot help the many who are poor, it cannot save the few who are rich. /8/

To our sister republics south of our border, we offer a special pledge—to convert our good words into good deeds—in a new alliance for progress—to assist free men and free governments in casting off the chains of poverty. But this peaceful revolution of hope cannot become the prey of hostile powers. Let all our neighbors know that we shall join with them to oppose aggression or subversion anywhere in the Americas. And let every other power know that this Hemisphere intends to remain the master of its own house. /9/

To that world assembly of sovereign states, the United Nations, our last best hope in an age where the instruments of war have far outpaced the instruments of peace, we renew our pledge of support—to prevent it from becoming merely a forum for invective —to strengthen its shield of the new and the weak—and to enlarge the area in which its writ may run. /10/

Finally, to those nations, who would make themselves our adversary, we offer not a pledge but a request: that both sides begin anew the quest for peace, before the dark powers of destruction unleashed by science engulf all humanity in planned or accidental self-destruction. /11/

We dare not tempt them with weakness. For only when our arms are sufficient beyond doubt can we be certain beyond doubt that they will never be employed. /12/

But neither can two great and powerful groups of nations take comfort from our present course—both sides overburdened by the cost of modern weapons, both rightly alarmed by the steady spread of the deadly atom, yet both racing to alter that uncertain balance of terror that stays the hand of mankind's final war. /13/

So let us begin anew—remembering on both sides that civility is not a sign of weakness, and sincerity is always subject to proof. Let us never negotiate out of fear. But let us never fear to negotiate. /14/

Let both sides explore what problems unite us instead of belaboring those problems which divide us. /15/

Let both sides, for the first time, formulate serious and precise proposals for the inspection and control of arms—and bring the absolute power to destroy other nations under the absolute control of all nations. /16/

Let both sides seek to invoke the wonders of science instead of its terrors. Together let us explore the stars, conquer the deserts, eradicate disease, tap the ocean depths and encourage the arts and commerce. /17/

Let both sides unite to heed in all corners of the earth the command of Isaiah—to "undo the heavy burdens . . . (and) let the oppressed go free." /18/

And, if a beach-head of cooperation may push back the jungle of suspicion, let both sides join in creating a new endeavor, not a new balance of power, but a new world of law, where the strong are just and the weak secure, and the peace preserved. /19/

All this will not be finished in the first one hundred days. Nor will it be finished in the first one thousand days, nor in the life of this Administration, nor even perhaps in our lifetime on this planet. But let us begin. /20/

In your hands, my fellow citizens, more than mine, will rest the final success or failure of our course. Since this country was founded, each generation of Americans has been summoned to give testimony to its national loyalty. The graves of young Americans, who answered the call to service surround the globe. /21/

Now the trumpet summons us again—not as a call to bear arms, though arms we need—not as a call to battle, though embattled we are—but a call to bear the burden of a long twilight struggle, year in and year out, "rejoicing in hope, patient in tribulation"—a struggle against the common enemies of man: tyranny, poverty, disease, and war itself. /22/

Can we forge against these enemies a grand and global alliance, North and South, East and West, that can assure a more fruitful life for all mankind? Will you join in that historic effort? /23/

In the long history of the world, only a few generations have been granted the role of defending freedom in its hour of maximum danger. I do not shrink from this responsibility—I welcome it. I do not believe that any of us would exchange places with any other people or any other generation. The energy, the faith, the devotion which we bring to this endeavor will light our country and all who serve it—and the glow from that fire can truly light the world. /24/

And so, my fellow Americans: ask not what your country can do for you—ask what you can do for your country. /25/

My fellow citizens of the world: ask not what America will do for you, but what together we can do for the freedom of man. /26/

Finally, whether you are citizens of America or citizens of the world, ask of us here the same high standards of strength and sacrifice which we ask of you. With a good conscience our only sure reward, with history the final judge of our deeds, let us go forth to lead the land we love, asking His blessing and His help, but knowing that here on earth God's work must truly be our own. /27/

NOTE: The President spoke at 12:52 p.m. from a platform erected at the east front of the Capitol. Immediately before the address the oath of office was administered by Chief Justice Warren.

The President's opening words "Reverend Clergy" referred to His Eminence Richard Cardinal Cushing, Archbishop of Boston; His Eminence Archbishop Iakovos, head of the Greek Archdiocese of North and South America; the Reverend Dr. John Barclay, pastor of the Central Christian Church, Austin, Tex.; and Rabbi Dr. Nelson Glueck, President of the Hebrew Union College, Cincinnati, Ohio.

THE WORLD OF JAZZ

Leonard Bernstein

An astute speaker creating rhetoric for listeners searches his or her mind and the world "out there" for data and ideas that have power to alter exigences in foreseen rhetorical situations. Such speaker-planners usually find more content than they can purposefully use. Then the question arises: What shall I *choose* for my rhetorical purpose? Almost never will everything available "properly address a mediating audience." [1]

Leonard Bernstein is an expert lecturer who has coped expertly with the problems of choosing right rhetorical materials from among a wealth of resources not inherently rhetorical. The world of music is filled with content that Aristotle would have called *rhetorically* "inartistic proofs." There are musical scores, music played, instruments, attitudes and feelings about music, players of music, the history of music and music makers, and so on. For the most part rhetorical purposes have nothing to do with the existence of these things, but a speaker may have rhetorical *use* for some or all of them. Leonard Bernstein often does. As a man who loves music deeply, he sometimes decides he wants to make others feel and understand the "joy of music." Then, he wants not only to create music but to make rhetoric on behalf of music. To act on this impulse he must find ways of converting rhetorically "inartistic" content into rhetorically *artistic* content, and he must interweave that content with fundamentally rhetorical materials.

Bernstein's famous *Omnibus* lectures admirably exemplify how speakers need to think and work when they reach into nonrhetorical data and ideas for proofs that will meet the requirements of specific rhetorical situations. Bernstein's principles of achieving this kind of adaptation constitute guidelines for converting any rhetorically "inartistic" content into content treated with rhetorical art. What he says about music and musical materials in the passage below can as well be said about numbers, documents, special testimonies, graphical data, architecture, or mathematics. Substitute any of those terms for "music" and its cognates, and the passage will still retain its rhetorical wisdom.

> If we are to try to "explain" music, we must explain the *music,* not the whole array of appreciators' extramusical notions which have grown like parasites around it.
>
> . . . Obviously we can't use musical terminology exclusively, or we will simply drive the victim |laymen| away. We must have intermittent recourse to certain extra-musical ideas, like religion, or social factors, or historical forces, which may have influenced music. We don't ever want to talk down; but how *up* can we talk without losing contact? There is a happy medium somewhere between the music-appreciation racket and purely technical discussion; it is hard to find, but it can be found.

[1] Bitzer, "The Rhetorical Situation," p. 13.

It is with this certainty that it can be found that I have made so bold as to discuss music on television, on records, and in public lectures. Whenever I feel that I have done it successfully, it is because I may have found the happy medium. And finding it is impossible without the conviction that the public is *not* a great beast, but an intelligent organism, more often than not longing for insight and knowledge. So that, wherever possible, I try to talk about music—the *notes* of music; and wherever extra-musical concepts are needed for referential or clarifying purposes, I try to choose concepts that are musically relevant, such as nationalistic tendencies, or spiritual development, which may even have been part of the composer's own thinking. For example, in explaining jazz, I have avoided the usual pseudo-historical discussions (up-the-river-from-New Orleans) and concentrated on those aspects of melody, harmony, rhythm, etc., which make jazz different from all other music. . . . The extra-musical kind of reference can be useful if it is put in the service of explaining the notes; and the road-map variety can also be serviceable if it functions along with some central idea that can engage the intelligence of the listener. Therein lies the happy medium, which I humbly hope to have achieved. . . .[2]

A speaker wishing to speak of graphics, architecture, mathematics, or the like might need to change "notes" to "forms" or "notations"; he would then have from Bernstein's formula sound guidance for converting *his* rhetorically inartistic content into influential rhetorical substance.

The *Omnibus* television programs of the 1950s are, themselves, significant objects for criticism. They were experiments in popular education conducted within the framework of American commercial broadcasting. The *Omnibus* series began in 1952 with subsidies from the Ford Foundation and with additional support from commercial sponsors. From its beginning through 1955–1956, the series was presented from 5:00–6:30 P.M. (Eastern Time) on the Columbia Broadcasting System's television network.[3] The goal of the series was to offer varied, "mature entertainment," professionally conceived and artistically presented. Drama, music, documentaries, and lecture-demonstrations were its staples. Most presentations were conceived and produced exclusively for the *Omnibus* series. Among these special presentations were Bernstein's lectures on: "Beethoven's Fifth Symphony," November 14, 1954; "The World of Jazz," October 16, 1955; "The Art of Conducting," December 4, 1955; "The American Musical Comedy," October 7, 1956; "An Introduction to Modern Music," January 13, 1957; "The Music of Johann Sebastian Bach," March 31, 1957; and "What Makes Opera Grand?" March 23, 1958.[4]

---

[2] Leonard Bernstein, *The Joy of Music* (New York: Simon and Schuster, 1959), pp. 16–17. Copyright © 1954, 1955, 1956, 1957, 1958, 1959, by Leonard Bernstein. Reprinted by permission of Simon and Schuster, Inc.

[3] The program shifted to the American Broadcasting System and to evening hours beginning with the 1956–1957 series.

[4] The scripts of these seven programs appear, complete with musical scores and "business" directions, in Bernstein's *The Joy of Music.*

Bernstein's advancement in his professions as conductor, composer, and educator was undoubtedly assured without benefit of his televised lectures, but Robert Saudek, Producer of the *Omnibus* series, could rightly say,

> One of the wonders of TV is that it can take an articulate man like Bernstein, unknown to all but a special few on the frontiers of culture, and make him known to every household in the country.[5]

Bernstein was not widely known as a lecturer prior to his appearances on *Omnibus* (of which "The World of Jazz" was his second). He was a faculty member of the Berkshire Music Center and Professor of Music at Brandeis University. He had also been Assistant Conductor of the New York Philharmonic Symphony and Conductor of the New York City Symphony. By 1957, he had become co-conductor of the New York Philharmonic, and in 1958 he began his eleven-year tenure as Music Director of the Philharmonic.

Several critical approaches to Bernstein's "The World of Jazz" can contribute to one's understanding of effective oral communication. Some have been begun in chapters of this book. One might also explore in detail the means by which Bernstein achieved or failed to achieve his goal of keeping the nature of music—the "notes"—in the forefront of his listeners' attention. Something can also be learned from examining the rhetorical invention he exercised in finding "extra-musical references" that would clarify his exposition without suggesting irrelevant ideas.

Bernstein's use of the resources of television is suggested by the script as published in *The Joy of Music*. In addition to the usual special resources of well-equipped television studios Mr. Bernstein had an orchestra, musical instruments, his admittedly inferior singing voice, and, of course, all the musical compositions he knew. His wealth of resources beyond those of ordinary speech could have been employed in ways that would obscure "those aspects . . . which make jazz different from other music." But he chose among them and managed them to serve "some central idea that can engage the intelligence of a listener." In his choices there are important lessons concerning wise rhetorical use of television as a medium of communication.

Larger lines of critical investigation also open up *through* study of "The World of Jazz." By referring to the scripts of the six other lectures published in *The Joy of Music,* one might compare Bernstein's rhetorical methods of treating popular music with his methods of discussing classical music. Moreover, one could evolve a significant set of rhetorical principles for educating mass audiences from a study of Leonard Bernstein's educational rhetoric.

---

[5] From an interview with Patrick D. Hazard, *"Omnibus:* Easy as ABC," *Scholastic Teacher* edition of *Senior Scholastic* 69 (October 4, 1956): 15T.

No reader will have failed to notice the unqualified enthusiasm of this introductory essay. My critical opinion is that Leonard Bernstein's *Omnibus* lectures are the most rhetorically perfect expositions presented on American television. Some of my reasons have been given in earlier chapters, but completion—or refutation—of so complimentary a judgment is work for other critics.

Here is the script for "The World of Jazz" as Bernstein published it in *The Joy of Music* (pp. 94–119).[6]

---

[6] Copyright 1954, 1955, 1956, 1957, 1958, 1959, by Leonard Bernstein. Reprinted by permission of Simon and Schuster, Inc.

THE WORLD OF JAZZ

Leonard Bernstein

TELECAST: OCTOBER 16, 1955

[Program opens with jazz band playing. Fades down.]

Leonard Bernstein:

Now, anyone hearing this music, anyone on any civilized part of this earth, east or west, pole to pole, would immediately say: That is jazz. We are going to try to investigate jazz, not through the usual historical approach which has become all too familiar, but through approaching the music itself. We are going to examine the musical "innards" of jazz to find out once and for all what it is that sets it apart from all other music. /1/

Jazz is a very big word; it covers a multitude of sounds, all the way from the earliest Blues to Dixieland bands, to Charleston bands, to Swing bands, to Boogie-Woogie, to crazy Bop, to cool Bop, to Mambo—and much more.* It is all jazz, and I love it because it is an original kind of emotional expression, in that it is never wholly sad or wholly happy. Even the Blues has a robustness and hard-boiled quality that never lets it become sticky-sentimental, no matter how self-pitying the words are. /2/

[Blues singer sings a verse of J. C. Johnson's "Empty Bed Blues" to illustrate plaintive words set to vigorous music.]

And, on the other hand, the gayest, wildest jazz always seems to have some hint of pain in it. Listen to this trumpet, and see what I mean:

---

  * For those who wish to follow examples of the foregoing terms, these recordings are recommended:
  Leadbelly: "Good Morning Blues," in *Take This Hammer*, Vol. 1, 10" Folkways, FA 2004
  King Oliver, Jelly-Roll Morton, etc.: "Back o' Town," 12" Riverside 12-130
  Red Nichols, Dorsey Bros.: "Charleston," in *Jazz of the Roaring Twenties*, 12" Riverside 12–801
  Benny Goodman: 1938 *Carnegie Hall Jazz Concert*, 2 12" Col. OSL-160
  Meade Lux Lewis, Albert Ammons, etc.: *Giants of Boogie-Woogie*, 12" Riverside 12-106
  Charlie Parker: *The Immortal Charlie Parker*, 12" Savoy 12001
  Lee Konitz: *Lee Konitz with Warne Marsh*, 12" Atlantic 1217
  Perez Prado: *Mambo Mania*, 12" Victor LPM-1075

[*Trumpet player using a harsh mute and "wah-wah" effects begins playing W. C. Handy's "Ole Miss."*]

That is what intrigues me about jazz; it is unique, a form of expression all its own. /3/

I love it also for its humor. It really plays with notes. We always speak of "playing" music: we play Brahms or we play Bach—a term perhaps more properly applied to tennis. But jazz is real play. It "fools around" with notes, so to speak, and has fun with them. It is, therefore, entertainment in the truest sense. /4/

But I find I have to defend jazz to those who say it is low-class. As a matter of fact, all music has low-class origins, since it comes from folk music, which is necessarily earthy. After all, Haydn minuets are only a refinement of simple, rustic German dances, and so are Beethoven scherzos. An aria from a Verdi opera can often be traced back to the simplest Neapolitan fisherman. Besides, there has always been a certain shadow of indignity around music, particularly around the players of music. /5/

I suppose it is due to the fact that historically *players* of music seem to lack the dignity of *composers* of music. But this is especially true of jazz, which is almost completely a player's art, depending as it does on improvisation rather than on composition. But this also means that the player of jazz is himself the real composer, which gives him a creative, and therefore *more* dignified, status. /6/

Then there are those who argue that jazz is loud. But so are Sousa marches, and we don't hear complaints about them. Besides, it's not always loud. It is very often extremely delicate, in fact. Perhaps this objection stems from the irremediable situation of what is after all a kind of brass band playing in a room too small for it. But that is not the fault of jazz itself. /7/

However, the main argument against jazz has always been that it is not art. I think it *is* art, and a very special art. And before we can argue about whether it is or not, we must know *what* it is; and so I propose to share with you some of the things I know and love about jazz. /8/

Let's take that Blues we heard before and find out what it's made of:

[*Jazz band plays four bars of "Empty Bed Blues."*]

Now what are the elements that make that jazz? /9/

First of all there is the element of melody. Western music in general is based, melodically speaking, on scales, like the major scale you all practiced as kids:

L. B. plays piano:

But there is a special one for jazz, which is a variation of that regular major scale. In jazz, this scale gets modified three different times. The third note gets lowered from this:

to this:

The fifth from this:

to this:

And the seventh from this:

to this:

Those three changed notes are called "blue notes."

So instead of a phrase which would ordinarily go something like this:

which is not particularly jazzy—we would get, using blue notes, this phrase:

—which begins to show a jazz quality. /10/

But this so-called "jazz scale" is used only melodically. In the harmony underneath we still use our old unflatted notes, and that causes dissonances to happen between that tune and the chords:

L. B. plays piano:

But these very dissonances have a true jazz sound. For example, jazz pianists are always using these two dissonant notes together:

* Actually, these blue notes are most commonly used in terms of the descending scale:

—and there is a reason for it. They are really searching for a note that isn't there at all, but one which lies somewhere between the two notes—between this:

and this:

—and the note is called a quarter-tone. /11/

The quarter-tone comes straight from Africa, which is the cradle of jazz and where quarter-tones are everyday stuff. We can produce one on a wind instrument or a stringed instrument or with the voice, but on the piano we have to approximate it by playing together the two notes on each side of it:

The real note is somewhere in there, in that crack between them. /12/

Let's see if I can sing you that quarter-tone, if you will forgive my horrid voice. Here is an African Swahili tune I once heard. The last note of it is a quarter-tone:

L. B. sings:

Sounds as if I'm singing terribly out of tune, but actually I am singing a real note in another musical language. In jazz it is right at home.

L. B. plays piano:

Now, just to show you how important these so-called "blue notes" are to jazz, let's hear that same Blues played without them, using only the plain white notes of the scale:

[*Clarinet plays passage from "Empty Bed Blues" using only whole notes.*]

There is something missing, isn't there? It just isn't jazz. /13/

But even more important than melody in jazz is the element of rhythm. Rhythm is the first thing you associate with the word *jazz,* after all. There are two aspects to this point. The first is the beat. This is what you hear when the drummer's foot is beating the drum:

[*Bass drummer begins regular foot-beat.*]

or when the bass player is plucking his bass:

[*Bass player begins plucking strings of his instrument, to the drummer's beat.*]

or even when the pianist is kicking the pedal with his foot:

[*Piano player joins by kicking his foot pedal to the drummer's rhythm.*]

All this is elementary. The beats go on from beginning to end of a number, two or four of them to a measure, never changing in tempo or in meter. This is the heartbeat, so to speak, of jazz. /14/

But more involved, and more interesting, is the rhythm going on *over* the beat—rhythmic figures which depend on something called "syncopation," a word you have certainly heard but maybe were never quite sure of. A good way to understand syncopation might be to think of a heartbeat that goes along steadily and, at a moment of shock, misses a beat. It is that much of a physical reaction. /15/

Technically, syncopation means either the removal of an accent where you expect one, or the placing of an accent where you least expect one. In either case, there is the element of surprise and shock. The body responds to this shock, either by compensating for the missing accent or by reacting to the unexpected one. /16/

Now where do we expect accents? Always on the first beat of a bar, on the downbeat. If there are two beats in a bar, *one* is going to be strong, *two* is going to be weak—exactly as in marching: *right,* left, *right,* left. Even if there are four beats in a bar, it is still like marching. Although we all have only two legs, the sergeant still counts out in four: *hup,* 2, 3, 4, *hup,* 2, 3, 4. There is always that natural accent on *one.* Take it away, and there is a simple syncopation:

L. B. gasps during missing first beat:

$$(!) \, 2, 3, 4 \qquad (!) \, 2, 3, 4 \text{ etc.}$$

You see that that missing accent on the first beat evokes a body response. /17/

Now, the other way to make syncopation is exactly the reverse: put an accent on a weak beat, the second or the fourth, where it doesn't belong. Like this:

One, *TWO,* three, *FOUR*
One, *TWO,* three, *FOUR*

This is what we all do, listening to jazz, when we clap our hands or snap our fingers on the offbeat. /18/

Those are the basic facts of syncopation; and now we can understand its subtler aspects. Between one beat and another there lie shorter and even weaker beats; and when these get accents the shock is correspondingly greater, since the weaker the beat you accentuate, the greater the surprise. Let's take eight of those fast beats in a bar: 1 2 3 4 5 6 7 8. The normal accents would fall on one and five: 1! 2 3 4 5! 6 7 8. Now, instead, let's put a big accent on a real weak one, the fourth:

1 2 3 4! 5 6 7 8

[*Drum takes up from count, then claves, trumpet, etc.*]

As you see, we get a pure rhumba rhythm.

Of course, the strongest syncopation of all would obviously be obtained by doing both things at once: putting an accent on a weak beat and taking away the accent from the strong. So now we will do this double operation: put a wallop on the weak fourth, and remove the strong fifth beat entirely; and we get:

1 2 3 4!——6 7 8

[*Percussion instruments take up the beat.*]

It begins to sound like the Congo, doesn't it? /19/

Trumpet adds melody:

Now that you've heard what syncopation is like, let's see what that same Blues we heard before would sound like without it. I think you'll miss that essential element, the very life of jazz:

[*Saxophone player repeats sixteen bars of "Empty Bed Blues," playing it "square," using no vibrato.*]

Sounds "square," doesn't it? /20/

Well, that takes care of two very important elements: melody and rhythm. But jazz could not be jazz without its special tonal colors, the actual sound values you hear. These colors are many, but they mostly stem from the quality of the Negro singing voice. For instance, when Louis Armstrong plays his trumpet, he is only doing another version of his own voice. Listen to an Armstrong record, like "I Can't Give You Anything but Love," and compare the trumpet solo with the vocal solo. You can't miss the fact that they're by the same fellow.* But the Negro voice has engendered other imitations. The saxophone is in itself a kind of imitation of it—breathy, a little hoarse, with a vibrato, or tremor, in it.

[*Here a saxophone plays a passage first with and then without vibrato*]

Then there are all the different growls and rasps we get by putting mutes on the horns. Here, for example, is a trumpet with a cup mute:

[*As Bernstein mentions each successive instrument it is played in the fashion he alludes to.*]

and a wah-wah mute:

* Louis Armstrong: "I Can't Give You Anything but Love," *Armstrong Favorites,* Columbia.

And a trombone with a plunger mute:

There are other tonal colors that derive from Afro-Cuban sources:
Bongo drums:

maracas:

the Cuban cowbell:

and all the others. /21/

Then there are the colors that have an Oriental flavor:
the vibraphone:

the various cymbals:

and so on. /22/

These special colorations make their contribution to the total quality of jazz. You have certainly all heard jazz tunes played "straight" by non-jazz orchestras and wondered what was missing. There certainly is something missing—the coloration. /23/

There is one more jazz element which may surprise some of you who think jazz is not an art. I refer to form. Did you know, for example, that the Blues is a classical form? Most people use the word *Blues* to mean any song that is "blue" or torchy or low-down or breast-beating—like "Stormy Weather," for example. But "Stormy Weather" is not a Blues, and neither is "Moanin' Low," nor "The Man I Love," or even "The Birth of the Blues." They are all popular songs. /24/

The blues is basically a strict poetic form combined with music. It is based on a rhymed couplet, with the first line repeated. For example, Billie Holiday sings:

> *"My man don't love me, treats me awful mean;* *
> *Oh, he's the lowest man I've ever seen."*

But when she sings it, she repeats the first line—so it goes:

> *"My man don't love me, treats me awful mean;*
> *I said, my man don't love me, treats me awful mean;*
> *Oh, he's the lowest man I've ever seen."*

That is one stanza of Blues. A full Blues is nothing more than a succession of such stanzas for as long as the singer wishes. /25/

Did you notice that the Blues couplet is, of all things, in iambic pentameter?

* © Copyright Edward B. Marks Music Corporation. Used by permission.

˘ — ˘ ˘ — ˘ — ˘ — ˘ —
"*My man/don't love/me, treats/me aw/ful mean*"

This is about as classic as one can get it. It means that you can take any rhymed couplet in iambic pentameter—from Shakespeare, for example—and make a perfect *Macbeth* Blues:

"*I will not be afraid of death and bane,*
Till Birnam forest come to Dunsinane."

It makes a lovely Blues:

[*Bernstein sings the* Macbeth *couplet to the same music as* "*My man don't love me . . .*"]

Now if you've noticed, each of these three lines got four bars apiece, making it all a twelve-bar stanza. But the voice itself sang only about half of each four-bar line, and the rest is supposed to be filled up by the accompaniment. This filling-up is called a "break." And here in the break we have the origin of the instrument imitating the voice, the very soil in which jazz grows. Perhaps the essential sound of jazz is Louis Armstrong improvising the breaks in a Blues sung by Bessie Smith. From this kind of voice imitation all instrumental improvising has since developed.* /26/

Did you notice the instrument that has been accompanying our singers today? It is a harmonium, that wheezy little excuse for an organ which we all associate with hymn tunes. But far from being out of place in the Blues, this instrument is especially appropriate, since the chords in the Blues must always be exactly the same three chords we all know from hymn tunes:

L. B. plays on harmonium:

These chords must always remain in a strict classical pattern, pure and simple. Try to vary them, and the Blues quality flies out the window. /27/

Well, there you have it: melody, rhythm, tone color, form, harmony. In each department there are special features that make *jazz,* instead of just music. Let's now put them all together, and hear a full-blown, all-out happy Blues. Oh, did you know that Blues could be happy? Just listen.

* Bessie Smith and Louis Armstrong: "Reckless Blues," *The Bessie Smith Story,* Vol. I, Columbia LP LM 4807.

[*Jazz band plays a Blues arrangement of "King Porter Stomp,"
Dixieland style*]

By this time I've probably given you the impression that jazz
is nothing but Blues. Not at all. I've used the Blues to investigate
jazz only because it embodies the various elements of jazz in so
clear and pure a way. But the rest of jazz is concerned with applying these same elements to something called the popular song.
The popular song, too, is a form; and it has certain strict patterns.
Popular songs are in either two-part or three-part form. By
far the most numerous are in the three-part. You all know this
form, of course, from hearing it so much. It is as simple as pie.
Anyone can write one. /28/

Take "Sweet Sue," for instance. All you need is the first eight
bars, really—which in the trade are called the front strain:

[*Bernstein plays first eight bars on the piano.*]

Now the song is practically written, since the whole thing
will be only thirty-two bars long—four groups of eight bars
apiece. The second eight is the same exactly as the first:

[*Bernstein plays second eight bars on piano.*]

Sixteen bars, and we're already half finished. Now the next
eight bars, which are called the release, or bridge, or just simply
"the middle part," must be different music. But it doesn't matter
if it's very good or not, since most people don't remember it too
well anyway:

[*Plays third line.*]

And then the same old front strain all over again:

[*Plays the final line.*]

and its finished. Thirty-two bars, and a classic forever. Easy,
isn't it? /29/

But "sweet Sue" is still not jazz. A popular song doesn't become
jazz until it is improvised on, and there you have the real core of
all jazz: improvisation. Remember, I said that jazz was a
player's art rather than a composer's. Well, this is the key to the

whole problem. It is the player who, by improvising, makes jazz. He uses the popular song as a kind of dummy to hang his notes on. He dresses it up in his own way, and it comes out an original. So the pop tune, in acquiring a new dress, changes its personality completely, like many people who behave one way in blue jeans and a wholly different way in dinner clothes. Some of you may object to this dressing-up. You say, "Let me hear the melody, not all this embroidery." But until you accept this principal [*sic*] of improvisation, you will never accept or understand jazz itself. /30/

What does improvising mean? It means that you take a tune, keep it in mind with its harmony and all, and then, as they used to say, just "go to town," or make it up as you go along. You go to town by adding ornaments and figurations, or by making real old-fashioned variations just as Mozart and Beethoven did. Let me show you a little of how Mozart did it, and then you may understand how Erroll Garner does it. Mozart took a well-known nursery rhyme, which we know as *"Ah, Vous Dirai-je Maman,"* and which we know as "Twinkle, Twinkle Little Star" or as a way of singing the alphabet:

[*Bernstein plays the piano and sings: "Twinkle, twinkle, little star/ How I wonder what you are."*] /31/

[*As his next words suggest, Bernstein here presents initial portions of four different compositions by Mozart.*]

Now Mozart makes a series of variations. One of them begins:
   Then another:
   Another:
   And another:
They are all different pieces, yet they are all in one way or another that same original tune. /32/

The jazz musician does exactly the same thing. There are infinite possible versions of "Sweet Sue," for example. The clarinet might improvise one chorus of it this way:

[*Clarinetist begins "Sweet Sue."*]

Now he could have done that in any number of ways; and if I asked him to do it again tomorrow morning, it would come out a whole other piece. But it would still be "Sweet Sue," and it would still be jazz. /33/

Now we come to the most exciting part of jazz, for me at any rate: simultaneous improvising. This happens when two or more musicians improvise on the same tune at the same time. Neither one knows exactly what the other is going to do; but they listen to each other, and pick up phrases from each other, and sort of talk together. What ties them together is the chords, the harmony, of "Sweet Sue." Over this harmony, they play two different melodic lines at the same time, which, in musical terms, makes a kind of accidental counterpoint. This is the germ of what is called the "jam session." Now the trumpet is going to join with the clarinet in a double improvisation on "Sweet Sue." See if you can distinguish the two melodic lines:

[*Trumpet and clarinet begin to improvise on "Sweet Sue."*]

You see how exciting this can be? This business of improvising together gave rise to the style called Dixieland, which is constantly having a big revival. One of the most exhilarating sounds in all music is that of a Dixieland band blaring out its final chorus, all stops out, with everyone improvising together.* /34/

But jazz is not all improvization, not by a long shot. Much of it gets written down, and then it is called an arrangement. The great days of the arrangements were the Thirties, when big, startling swing arrangements were showing off the virtuosity of the great bands—like Casa Loma, Benny Goodman, Artie Shaw, the Dorsey brothers, and so on. Now jazz is hard to write down. There is no way of notating exactly those quarter-tones we talked about, nor the various smears and growls and subtle intonations. Even the rhythms can only be approximated in notation, so that much of the jazz quality is left to the instincts of the player who is reading the music. Still, it does work, because the instincts of these players are so deep and genuine. /35/

Let's listen to a good, solid swing arrangement of a chorus of "Sweet Sue" as we might have heard it back in 1938.** /36/

Now remember, this arrangement was for dancing. In 1938 we were all dancing; and that brings up the most important

---

* Bix Beiderbecke: "Sweet Sue," *The Bix Beiderbecke Story,* Vol. 3, Columbia LP ML 4813.
** Benny Goodman: "Sweet Sue," *This Is Benny Goodman,* Victor LP M 1239.

point of all. Nobody seems to dance to jazz very much any more, except for mambo lovers, and they are limited to those who are athletic enough to do it. What has happened to dancing? We used to have a new dance practically every month: the Lindy Hop, the Shag, the Peabody, the Big Apple, Boogie, Susie-Q. Now we have only dances you have to take lessons to do. /37/

What does this mean? Simply that the emphasis is on listening, these days, instead of on singing and dancing. This change had to happen. For one thing, the tremendous development of the recording industry has taught us to listen in a way we never did before. But even more significant, with the advent of more complicated swing and jazz like Boogie-Woogie and Bop, our interest has shifted to the music itself and to the virtuosity of its performance. That is, we are interested in what notes are being played, how well, how fast, and with what originality. You can't listen to Bop intelligently and dance too, murmuring sweet nothings into your partner's ear. You have to listen as hard as you can to hear what's happening. /38/

So in a way, jazz has begun to be a kind of chamber music, an advanced sophisticated art mainly for listening, full of influences of Bartók and Stravinsky, and very, very serious. Let's listen for a moment to this kind of arrangement of our old friend "Sweet Sue."

[*Band plays "Sweet Sue" in the "cool" style of the 1950s.*]

Whether you call this kind of weird piece "cool" or "crazy" or "futuristic" or "modernistic" or whatever, the fact is that it is bordering on serious concert music. The arrangement begins to be a *composition*. Take away the beat, and you might not even know it's jazz at all. It would be just a concert piece. And why is it jazz? Because it is played by jazz men, on jazz instruments, and because it has its roots in the soil of jazz and not of Bach. /39/

I think the key word to all this is the word *cool*. It means what it implies. Jazz used to advertise itself as "hot"; now the heat is off. The jazz player has become a highly serious person. He may even be an intellectual. He tends to wear Ivy League clothes, have a crew cut, or wear horn-rimmed glasses. He may have studied music at a conservatory or a university. This was unthinkable in the old days. Our new jazz man plays more quietly, with greater concentration on musical values, on tone quality, technique. He knows Bartók and Stravinsky, and his music shows it. He tends to avoid big, flashy endings. The music just stops when it is over. /40/

As he has become cool, so have his listeners. They don't dance; they listen respectfully, as if to chamber music, and applaud politely at the end. At jazz clubs all over the world you find audiences who do not necessarily have a drink in their hands and who do not beat out the rhythm and carry on as we did when I was a boy. It is all rather cool and surprisingly controlled, considering that jazz is essentially an emotional experience. /41/

Where does this lead us in our investigation? To some pretty startling conclusions. There are those who conclude from all this that here, in the new jazz, is the real beginning of serious American music, that at last the American composer has his own expression. Of course when they say this they are intimating that all American symphonic works up to now are nothing but personalized imitations of the European symphonic tradition from Mozart to Mahler. Sometimes, I must say, I think they have a point. At any rate, we can be sure of one thing: that the line between serious music and jazz grows less and less clear. We have serious composers writing in the jazz idiom, and we have jazz musicians becoming serious composers. Perhaps we've stumbled on a theory. /42/

But theory or no theory, jazz goes on finding new paths, sometimes reviving old styles, but, in either case, looking for freshness. In any art that is really vital and searching, splits are bound to develop; arguments arise and factions form. Just as in painting the non-objectivists are at sword's point with the representationalists, and in poetry the imagists declaim against the surrealists, so in jazz music we have a major battle between the traditionalists and the progressives. /43/

These latter are the ones who are trying hardest to get away from the patterns of half a century, experimenting with new sonorities, using note relationships that are not common to the old jazz, and, in general, trying to keep jazz alive and interesting by broadening its scope. Jazz is a fresh, vital art in the present tense, with a solid past and an exciting future. /44/

WHAT CAN WE PROVE ABOUT GOD?

Leon R. Zellner

Leon R. Zellner's classroom speech exemplifies oral rhetoric that depends heavily on close reasoning for its effects. The text below is therefore an excellent one on which to experiment with the critical methods and principles discussed in chapter III, "Explicitly Argued Content." The text also serves as an illustration of the fact that close reasoning seldom occurs apart from suggestive and stylistic appeal if the rhetoric is strong. Partial analyses which have already been presented make it clear that full analysis of this speech would probably reveal points of strength and of deficiency in style and structure. Since this speech was given in anticipation of criticism, as most classroom speeches are, the text invites criticism that culminates in advice concerning the speaker's further development as a communicator.

At the time he gave this talk, Mr. Zellner was a junior majoring in business administration at The Pennsylvania State University. He spoke on March 7, 1965, in the speech class in which he was enrolled. The assignment for the speech read as follows: "Deliver extemporaneously a ten- to twelve-minute talk in which you develop your personal views on any aspect of the following topics: politics, religion, sex, social relations, the arts, or your personal philosophy of life. Your objective may be to explain, to persuade, or to aim at inducing your audience to engage with you in further inquiry into a problem you present." Other talks in response to this assignment had been presented on three preceding days and several speakers had touched on aspects of religion, as Mr. Zellner indicates. Zellner thus had the advantage of speaking to an audience at least somewhat prepared to hear about his chosen subject.

Zellner's rhetorical situation was like that which exists in most speech classes composed of alert students enrolled in a required course in which grades are given. However, in this class the standard that "good" speaking is not "performing" but is *communicating efficiently and interestingly* had been firmly set. In addition, Zellner had been negatively criticized by some colleagues and by his instructor on grounds that his earlier speaking had often been too wordy to make points clearly and to have full emotional impact on his listeners. It was therefore a peculiarity of the rhetorical situation that some of the audience—certainly his instructor—would watch language and structure with special care, without diminishing the general expectation that he should influence the attitudes of his audience. Under these circumstances it was significant that Zellner gave his listeners a clear proof that he was not "reciting" but was "thinking on his feet." During his talk a few snowflakes began to fall out of doors, and he astutely incorporated that fact into his argument (see paragraph 7).

The audience for the speech consisted of eighteen undergraduate students, the classroom instructor, and two teacher-interns, both women graduate students. Seven of the undergraduates were women and eleven were men; most were in their sophomore or junior years. Among the eighteen there were students majoring in education, business administration, engineering, argiculture, hotel administration, the sciences, and the liberal arts.

There was nothing unusual about the classroom or general setting. Both a lectern and a desk were available at the front of the room, and speakers chose to use either or neither. Zellner used neither and spoke without notes of any sort. All speeches in this series were unobtrusively tape recorded.

The text that follows was transcribed from the tape by Mr. Zellner's permission. It is probably a very close record of what Zellner said, but it is not entirely certain that the typed text was rechecked against the tape before the tape was accidently erased.

WHAT CAN WE PROVE ABOUT GOD?
Leon R. Zellner

Many people have made their expressed purpose in life that of either proving or disproving the existence of God by the use of scientific data. Let me point out immediately that what I'm going to do today is neither of these. What I'm going to try to show is that man's scientific arguments, by which I mean arguments drawn from any natural phenomenon, cannot possibly prove or disprove the existence of God. /1/

Several other speakers in the past three days have made speeches of religious content, and for this reason I feel I should define exactly what I mean when I use the word *God* in this talk. In what I say I'll take God to mean not only the God of the Judeo-Christian faiths, but the supreme being lying at the zenith of any religion whatever. One other point of clarification I feel is necessary before I go farther. That is the meaning of the word *prove*. To prove something means to demonstrate that thing to be a fact. So, what I'm trying to show you is that it is impossible for man through scientific reasoning and logic to prove that the existence of God is a fact or not a fact. Today, I'll deal primarily with the first of these proofs—that is, the proofs that say God *must* exist. However, I'd like you to keep always in mind that the refutations of these proofs can also be used to refute arguments that try to prove the nonexistence of God. /2/

I feel the best way to make my point for you is to take two of the proofs that are most generally used and show you exactly what's wrong with them. The first of these proofs is called argument from design. People who use this type of reasoning about God generally choose some complex kind of natural mechanism and prove—or at least they assume they prove—that the mechanism must have been planned. Thereby, they imply the existence of a Planner. One of these complex systems often used is the solar system which we know—the rotation of earth around the sun, the moon around the earth, and so forth. Another mechanism used is the eye, wherein you have the retina. Were it a little differently shaped, we wouldn't be able to see. Or, there are various other mechanisms of the eye which, if changed, would cause the loss of sight. One other mechanism used is the existence of the protein molecule, which is, indeed, the basis for all life. Had the atoms within this molecule been arranged in any degree differently, life as we know it could not possibly exist. /3/

To refute any one of these arguments from design is actually the equivalent of refuting them all, since they all follow the same basic lines of logic. Therefore, I'll deal primarily with the solar system because we know it better. The followers of this train of thought, of which Sir Isaac Newton was one, say that because the earth and the sun and all the other planets have specific masses and specific velocities, they follow a specific course. They also argue that these courses could not possibly have been selected through the forces of chance. They say these particular orbits were predesigned by some super-being which they call God. /4/

Let me illustrate. Suppose, for example, that this line

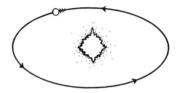

represents the orbit of the earth around the sun. These people argue that for the earth to take this course by chance is infinitely improbable. Basically, they argue this because in the vastness of what we call space, there's so much room that this earth could have as easily spiraled into the sun, gone straight out into nowhere, or followed a parabolic or hyperbolic curve. But this orbit is the path it chose. Since that path is infinitely improbable, it must have been predesigned. That's the argument. /5/

Now, suppose the earth, rather than following its orbital path, had instead followed this one:

What are the chances that the second path might have been taken? They are equally infinitely impossible. Therefore, the arguers are actually not proving anything, since they are saying, in fact, that all possible courses are infinitely impossible. They aren't proving anything by saying just one of them was chosen. The probabilities for any one path are equal. /6/

This line of thought brings up an idea which may seem a bit curious. It is that no matter what happens in nature, it is infinitely improbable. This is to say if we try to figure out the probabilities for the fact that it's now snowing here at this moment, it can be proved that it's infinitely improbable that it would snow here today. It is necessary for a whole complex chain of events to occur before it can possibly snow in State College. If the earth weren't rotating at its particular speed, we wouldn't be here with the snow. If the earth were not revolving around the sun as it is, perhaps the climate would be warmer and it would be impossible for it to snow here. If the masses of air had any other set of molecules than they have at this instant, it would be impossible for it to snow. This kind of argument can be applied to anything in nature. Take the existence of a flower in a particular spot. There are an infinite number of places where that flower could grow. So, for a flower you don't plant but which just happens to grow, it is infinitely improbable that that flower could grow where it does. /7/

There are two basic fallacies in all this arguing. The first is that you cannot explain, just by the complexity of a situation, that the complex had to be planned by some all-knowing mind. The second fallacy here is one that is more or less implied rather than expressed. Anyone who reads a great deal on the subject or explores a number of these "proofs" finds that the proponents of the "proofs" are always proving the existence of God by means of things which man considers noble, advantageous, beautiful, or virtuous. Men make this argument under the assumption that if a God does exist, by our definitions of God he must necessarily produce good and virtuous things. Their next step is to reverse this logic and say that since virtuous things do exist, they must have been produced by God. This is a fallacy as old as logic itself. Because we know that lightning can cause a house to burn, we're not justified, when we see a house burning, to conclude that the cause of that fire was lightning. You *can* argue from cause to effect, but you cannot argue *necessarily* in the reverse direction. /8/

The second proof often used for the existence of God is that there are miracles. A miracle, as you know, is some breach of a natural law. In one of the articles I've been reading the author cites the fact that as soon as you mention miracles those you talk to tend to think, "What about people who have regained sight or have been able to walk after years without being able to use their legs?" These events prove nothing. They may, indeed, be miracles. They may be the intervention of some power, affecting what *we* call natural laws. However, they may as easily be the results of natural laws we don't yet know. The only time we can ever be sure some extraordinary event is a miracle is when we are one hundred percent sure that we know every natural law that exists. Since this is a condition we'll never attain, because we can never know there is a natural law we don't know, it is impossible to say that "miracles" are or aren't breaches of natural law. /9/

So what have I shown you? Have I shown that God does not exist? Certainly not. I've shown only one thing—that to believe in a God requires, not some type of scientific proof, but rather a faith. Imagine a small child trying to "prove" Einstein's theory of relativity. He may, if he is highly intelligent, be able to understand something of this and take it on faith. He may think, "I know Einstein was supposed to be an important man, so I'll accept what he said as true." Now, I'm saying to you that man, trying to prove the existence of God, is like a small child trying to prove a theory far more complex and far greater than Einstein's theory of relativity. /10/

If we could *prove* the existence of God, if we could take him down and put him in this chair and compile statistics that state his IQ is 130, his height such-and-such and his weight so much, and assert that he has specific personality traits—if we could do that, we'd have taken away the fact that he is a *god*. If I can take any one of you and prove *anything* about you—that you do exist, that I can see you are six feet two, or that your weight is 130— when I can start taking you apart, dissecting you and looking into your character, you cannot possibly be a god. /11/

In the Book of Proverbs, in the Bible, chapter 3, verse 5, there is a line which says, "Trust in the Lord with all thine heart; and lean not unto thine own understanding." To me, what this means is this: "Trust" is the equivalent of faith—to believe. Believe in the Lord, have faith that he exists, but when you're trying to believe this, don't depend on your understanding. Don't try to *prove* it, because that's impossible. By the very definitions which we apply to a god, he's omnipotent, he's perfect goodness, perfect righteousness; a god is unattainable to man. This is the point that's really important: a god is something unattainable to man. This is what makes him a god. If we could pinpoint God and say what he is, he would be no god because he wouldn't be all-powerful. So I'd like to repeat again that any proof of God comes through faith and believing; it is not something for which we find proof or disproof through the usages of science, logic, or reason. /12/

SPEECH AT MORGAN STATE COLLEGE

Stokely Carmichael

Stokely Carmichael was born in Port-of-Spain, Trindad, British West Indies, in 1941. He came to the United States with his parents in 1952. He graduated from Howard University in Washington, D.C. in 1964 and promptly became a full-time worker on behalf of civil rights for black people. In May 1966, he became National Chairman of the Student Nonviolent Coordinating Committee (SNCC) and extensively reorganized this civil rights group in an attempt to make it an agency promoting his "Black Power" philosophy. The article in *The New York Review of Books,* to which he refers in the speech that follows, was a major exposition of the policies and goals he was recommending to "the movement" when he used the phrase, "Black Power."

Carmichael's speech at Morgan State College was made at a time when within the civil rights movement and among black citizens generally there were clear exigences calling for rediscovery or reinterpretation of the goals and methods of action on behalf of racial equality. In general, Carmichael was insisting that black people must "do things for themselves"; they must gain control of the agencies of power and of the money that affected their daily lives. As National Chairman of SNCC since May 1966, he had acted on this philosophy by redistributing authority in the organization so that it resided primarily with black members.

The "Black Power" concept was seen as threateningly militant by many whites and was unfavorably received by a number of black leaders. It was perhaps for these reasons that much of Carmichael's speaking and writing in 1966 and 1967 was devoted to clarifying the directions toward which he was urging the civil rights activists. In fact, the civil rights movement seemed at this time to lack clear direction. It would probably be fair to say that Mr. Carmichael was trying to fill what seemed a void in leadership.

Only recently, Floyd McKissick, National Director of the Congress of Racial Equality, had said the civil rights movement was "dead." The historian, C. Vann Woodward, had agreed.[1] Dr. Martin Luther King had recently left a civil rights program he had undertaken in Chicago. Budget cuts were reducing the amounts of federal money available for "Great Society" programs of special interest to black people. War in Vietnam drew attention away from racial issues, and some black leaders were moving from racial advocacy into the antiwar movement. All these factors and more caused a good many people to wonder where the equal-rights movement was and ought to be headed. In sum, January of 1967 was a time in which there was genuine want of clarity about how the ideal of equal rights ought to be pursued in the United States.

---

[1] Robert E. Baker, "News Analysis: The Civil Rights Movement," *The Washington Post,* January 16, 1967, pp. A1 and A4.

In January, Stokely Carmichael was on a lecture tour presenting his answers to the exigences troubling advocates of equal rights for all citizens. Just before coming East, he had been in Chicago. On January 14, a television interview he had given in Chicago was made public. In it Carmichael announced that he would not seek reelection to the chairmanship of SNCC when his term expired in May 1967. This, of course, aroused widespread interest in his future plans. When he came to Washington, D.C. on Sunday, January 15, he spoke to an overflow audience at the Church of the Redeemer (Presbyterian). In the course of this speech he said that when his term as Chairman of SNCC was ended, he would "return to field organizing in the South." [2] He also reiterated the importance of implementing his "Black Power" philosophy. "We must take over our own community," he said.[3] White journalists, in Washington at least, were still rather confused about Carmichael's immediate and long-ranged plans.

On the 16th of January, Mr. Carmichael moved on to Baltimore, Maryland, where he delivered two speeches: one at Morgan State College during the day and an evening address at Metropolitan Methodist Church. At Morgan State he was the guest of a group of campus activists calling themselves DISSENT, and at the Methodist church he was sponsored by a group called U-JOIN, a "grass-roots direct-action group" in the community. About 1,400 listeners heard him at Morgan State and more than 1,600 at Metropolitan Methodist Church.[4]

Neither of Mr. Carmichael's Baltimore speeches was widely covered in the press. *The Afro-American,* a news weekly with main editorial offices in Baltimore, covered both speeches and published a full text of the Morgan State College speech.[5] On the other hand, *The Pittsburgh Courier* of January 28th published a long article on Carmichael's refusal to seek reelection in SNCC but said nothing of his recent speeches and interviews in Chicago, Washington, and Baltimore.[6] Neither of Carmichael's Baltimore speeches received coverage in *The Washington Post* or the New York *Times.*

The text that follows is that which appears in Haig A. Bosmajian and Hamida Bosmajian, *The Rhetoric of the Civil Rights Movement.*[7] It is a text released by SNCC and is reportedly a printed version of a taped transcription of the address.

---

[2] *Washington Post,* January 16, 1967, p. A4.

[3] *Ibid.*

[4] Most facts in this paragraph are taken from *The Afro-American,* Philadelphia Edition, week of January 28, 1967, p. 5.

[5] The speech appears on p. 12 of the paper's Philadelphia Edition for the week of January 28.

[6] The *Courier* is a national news weekly devoted to affairs of black people. The article on Carmichael's announcement appeared on p. 1 of the January 28, 1967 issue.

[7] Haig A. Bosmajian and Hamida Bosmajian, *The Rhetoric of the Civil Rights Movement* (New York: Random House, Inc., 1969), pp. 109–125. Random House, Inc. was Mr. Carmichael's publisher during the 1960s.

SPEECH AT MORGAN STATE COLLEGE

Stokely Carmichael

JANUARY 16, 1967

Good afternoon. It is good to be back here at Morgan. I used to party here when I was at school—after we sat in in Baltimore on Route 40. /1/

I would hope that some of the people who have been disagreeing with the concept of black power would be here today. I would suggest that they read two articles—one which I wrote for *The New York Review of Books* in September and one that appeared in the *Massachusetts Review* in the fourth quarter of 1966. They explain the theoretical concept of black power, they criticize the exponents of the coalition theory and those who say that integration is the only route to solving the racial problem in this country. /2/

I would think that at a black university it would be absurd for me to talk about black power, but rather to talk to black students about what their role is to be in the coming struggle. And so my remarks today would be addressed to you, black students of Morgan, to give you a chance to hear some of the things that you never hear about. You need to stop being ashamed of being black and come on home. /3/

So that while there are many members of the press here, you should pay them no mind because they will not be able to understand what we are talking about. As to the criticism we have been receiving from the press, I was reading George Bernard Shaw the other night and I came across a sentence which I thought was quite apropos. He said that all criticism is in fact autobiography. So the press ought to dig them some Mr. Shaw. /4/

We want to level, before we begin, against several people at this university who, in October, when we were supposed to speak, canceled the speech. Now we understand there were all sorts of bureaucratic tie-ups for canceling the speech. We know that elections were close at hand in Maryland and there was a feeling that—on my part, I am not saying that anyone really said this— that the people were scared, and so they canceled the speech. They were scared that if I spoke here, Mahoney would win. Now one of the reasons I want to talk about that is that I think it is important to understand what that means. What I think the country is trying to do is to kill the free speech of the Student Nonviolent Coordinating Committee. /5/

So that in the beginning I would like to read from one of my favorite men—Frederick Douglass—I hope he is yours. You know Baltimore was his home spot, where he spent his early age. It was from Baltimore that he escaped to freedom. I want to read it because I think it is crystal clear in our minds what we must do in this generation to move for black power. Our mothers scrubbed floors. Our fathers were Uncle Toms. They didn't do that so we could scrub floors and be Uncle Toms. They did it so that this generation can fight for black power and that is what we are about to do and that is what you ought to understand. Mr. Douglass said,

> Those who profess to favor freedom yet deprecate agitation are men who want crops without plowing up the ground; they want rain without thunder and lightning. They want the ocean without the awful roar of its many waters. . . . Power concedes nothing without demand. It never did and it never will. Find out just what any people will quietly submit to and you have found out the exact measure of injustice and wrong which will be imposed upon them, and these will continue till they are resisted with either words or blows, or with both. The limits of tyrants are prescribed by the endurance of those whom they oppress.

Following in Mr. Douglass's footsteps, we intend to strike our first blow for our liberation, and we will let the chips fall where they may. We do not wish to earn the good will of anybody who is oppressing us. They should rather try to earn our good will since they have been oppressing us. /6/

Now we ought to then outline the points we want to discuss. We want to talk about what this country has been able to do to black people. What it has been able to do is to make us ashamed of being black. And that is one of the first recognitions of a free people. That we recognize that we must be united as a people, that we understand the concept of peoplehood and not be ashamed of ourselves. That means that we must stop imitating white society and begin to create for ourselves and our own and begin to embody our own cultural patterns so that we will be holding dear to those things which we have created. /7/

For example, it is nonsensical for black people to have debutante balls. It is nonsensical because you are imitating that which white society has given to you and which you know nothing about. Wouldn't it be better to take that $500 and give it to Morgan so that you could begin to develop a good black institution? /8/

Now imitation runs deep in the black community in this country. It runs very deep. You know when we first got people to go to college and they went to the first white university in this country, there were things called fraternities and sororities. We are going to talk about it. /9/

Now what happened was that our black brothers and sisters could not get into these fraternities. They kept them out because of the color of their skin. So what did our brothers do—they turned around and formed something called Kappas, and only light-skinned Negroes could get in. Our black sisters, not to be outdone, formed AKA for only bluebloods. So the other dark-skinned brothers, not to be outdone, set up Omega and Alpha. And then, of course, we had the counterparts, the Deltas. Now, wouldn't it have been far better if those people, instead of imitating a society which had been built on excluding them, had turned around and built a fraternity which would have included everybody? Perhaps that is the greatest problem which you as black students face. You are never asked to create, only to imitate. /10/

The philosophers [Albert] Camus and [Jean Paul] Sartre raised the question of self-condemnation in most of their writings. Camus, you know, is an existentialist. He wrote *The Rebel, The Stranger*. You ought to read them. What Camus says is that self-condemnation is impossible. And we in SNCC agree with that. Self-condemnation is impossible. /11/

There are examples of that. For example, there were Nazi prisoners during World War II. Those who were captured. If they admitted that they had killed six million Jews, they had to commit suicide. They must commit suicide. The ones who were able to live were the ones who had said, "We did not kill six million human beings—they were subhuman, they were inhuman, they were inferior." Or, "We were just following law and order." Does that sound familiar? So it is crystal clear that self-condemnation is impossible. /12/

And so it is with white America as a whole community. White America is incapable of condemning that which it has done to black people as a total community inside this country. Therefore we must do it, we must condemn. And after having condemned we do not try to imitate, but begin to create. And you must understand that very, very clearly in your mind. /13/

Sartre writes the introduction to Mr. [Frantz] Fanon's book, *The Wretched of the Earth*—he happens to be a black pragmatist, existentialist. And Fanon says, in *The Wretched of the Earth,* of course self-condemnation is impossible. Neither of us can condemn ourselves and then stay alive. If we do, we become our own executioner and we must take our lives. That becomes even more important for us here in America. /14/

Now then we come to the question of definitions. We will talk about that for a while. It is very, very important because I believe that people who can define are masters. /15/

I want to read a quote. It is one of my favorite quotes. It comes from *Alice in Wonderland* [by] Lewis Carroll. You ought to read him. Just like you ought to read *Winnie the Pooh* and *Huckleberry Finn.* Twain is my favorite author. He has got a subtlety that no other American author has been able to reach. The quote: "When I use a word," Humpty Dumpty said in a rather scornful tone, "it means just what I choose it to mean, neither more or less." "The question is," said Alice, "whether you can make words mean so many different things." "The question is," said Humpty Dumpty, "who is to be master." /16/

That is all. That is all. Understand that. You remember a couple of years ago when our black leaders would talk about integration. They would say, "We want to integrate." They would be talking about good houses, good schools, good neighborhoods. White people would say, "You want to marry my daughter." Now you have got to understand this concept very, very clearly, because what they were doing was defining integration for these black leaders, and these black leaders allowed them to. I used to see these black leaders say, "We want to integrate." The white man would say, "You want to marry my daughter." They would say, "No, I don't want to marry your daughter. We just want to be your brother, we don't want to be your brother-in-law." Or, "We want to live next door to you, we don't want to live in your bedroom." By the time this cat finished reacting to a definition by a white man, he was out the window. And by the time he came back to be aggressive, the black community said "later" for the cat. He allowed white people to define his reaction. /17/

Now when we get asked that question in SNCC, you know what we say. The white woman is not the queen of the world, she is not the Virgin Mary, she can be made like any other woman. Let's move on, let's move on. /18/

Now then, that is very, very important because the same things happen. Now, I say, "black power" and someone says "You mean violence." And they expect me to say, "No, no. I don't mean violence,

I don't mean that." Later for you; I am master of my own term. If black power means violence to you, that is your problem, as is my marrying your daughter. I know what it means in my mind. I will stand clear and you must understand that because the first need of a free people is to be able to define their own terms and have those terms recognized by their oppressors. It is also the first need that all oppressors must suspend. /19/

Camus says that when a slave says "No" he begins to exist. You see, you define to contain. That's all you do. I define this as yellow. It means that this is yellow. This is not yellow. So that when I speak of yellow you know what I am talking about. I have contained this. And so for white people to be allowed to define us by calling us Negroes, which means apathetic, lazy, stupid, and all those other things, it is for us to accept those definitions. We must define what we are and move from our definitions and tell them to recognize what we say we are. /20/

Now you watch cowboy movies all the time. We all do. And you know there would be a fight and there would be Indians and they would be coming from the hills and Chief Crazy Horse would have a million Indians and they would be yelling, "wha, wha, wha," and they would be killing the good white women. And at last here comes the cavalry. They would come riding in and they would get out their guns and shoot up everybody—men, forward march, forward, shoot. "Look out, that one on the right." Boom, we have got him," he's dead. They would come back and they would say, "We had a victory today. We killed the Indians." Now the next time, the Indians would beat the hell out of the white man and they would say, "Those dirty Indians—they massacred us." See what they were doing. In a victory, you shoot people and you kill them that way, but in a massacre you kill them with a knife and everybody knows that's foul. Now the Indians had victories too. That we must begin to recognize. That's very important. /21/

You ever listen to the news? Every day now, "Viet Cong terrorists today bombed and killed fifty women and children," what a shame. In the meantime, our jet bombers have been flying heavily over Hanoi, dropping bombs. /22/

And the power to define is the most important power that we have. He is master who can define. That was made clear in the McCarthy period. If McCarthy said you were a Communist, you had to get up and say, "No, I am not a Communist." He had the power to define. It is the same thing. My fellow Americans, the Communists, the slanted-eye Viet Cong are our enemy. You must go kill them. You don't have the right to define whether or not that cat is your enemy. The master has defined it for you. And when he says "Jump," you say, "How high, boss?" So then we must begin to define our own terms and certainly our own concept of ourselves and let those who are not capable of following us fall by the wayside. /23/

Now we want to talk a little about Vietnam. We think it is drastically important. You must begin to understand the nature of this country called America, which exploits all other nonwhite countries. Now you know we are fighting for freedom, democracy, for peace. Nobody questions it. Yes, we are going to kill for freedom, democracy, and peace. Those little Chinese, Vietnamese yellow people ain't got sense enough to know they want their democracy; we are going to fight for them, give it to them because Santa Claus is still alive. /24/

I want to read a quote made August 4, 1954, before the United States governors in Seattle. Incidentally, I highly recommend this book. It is called *Vietnam, Vietnam,* by Felix Greene. (Incidentally, I think the trouble with our black students is that they just don't read too much. If we could get the bougaloo like we could books, we would be up tight.) "Now let us assume," the quote says, "that we lost Indo-China." Now that is in 1953; we were not fighting the war, the French were fighting it for us. We were just giving them the money. "Now let us assume we lost Indo-China. The tin and other items we so greatly value [from that area] would cease coming." So that when the United States votes $400 million dollars to help that war, we are not voting a give-away program. /25/

"We are after the cheapest way to prevent the occurrence of something terrible—the loss of our ability to get what we want from the riches of the Indo-Chinese territory and from Southeast Asia." That quote was made by President Dwight D. Eisenhower. /26/

Now we may say that Dwight wasn't too smart. In our neighborhood, because he talked so well, we used to call him the white Joe Louis. But that was in 1953. So, well, we figure, you know Dwight wasn't too smart and that was a long time ago and we have become more civilized. /27/

I want to read you a statement now, by Henry Cabot Lodge. He's the good-looking one, you know, tall, blond hair, blue eyes. His quote a year ago:

Geographically, Vietnam stands at the hub of a vast area of the world, Southeast Asia. An area with a population of 249 million persons. He who holds or has influence in Vietnam can affect the future of the Philippines and Formosa to the east, Thailand and Burma with their huge rice surpluses to the west, and Malaysia and Indonesia with their rubber, ore, and tin to the south. Vietnam, thus, does not exist in a geographical vacuum from its large storehouses of wealth and the population can be influenced and undermined.

He is absolutely right. Because that's what that war is all about. And that's why we are not going. Those, then, are the words of the ambassador to Saigon. They are not my words. And he outlines very clearly what the war is being fought for. /28/

If you understood anything about this country, you would know that 75 percent of this budget is spent on war materials. That means that for this country to survive it must always be at war. You will not get a victory for this country if you win in Vietnam. That's no victory. The country must keep fighting. You do not invent things that have no use. You invent them so that they have a use. And every time you invent a better bomb, you must drop it. So you invent another bomb. That is correct and that is why this country keeps going at the breakneck speed it is going in terms of its military might. And we have to understand that. Because we are told in this country that we are civilized—another word to define. /29/

You know Rudyard Kipling defined civilization for us. He talked about the white man's burden. Pick up your whiteness and go to Africa and cultivate the savages and illiterates. So they got all these nice, white people of good will who wanted to do well. They got in their little black robes and they went to Africa and they saw these little black savages, man, running around with no shirts on. "Why, you dirty man, cover up yourself. You are getting me excited." They were going to civilize us because we were uncivilized, because we were illiterate. So they came to Africa with the Bible and we had the land. When they left, they had the land and we still got the Bible. And that was civilization for them. They were civilizing us. /30/

Indeed what is civilization? To be able to drop bombs on Hiroshima? Is that civilization? To be able to drop bombs on Hanoi? Is that civilization? Is it? Do we want to be civilized too? This country has said that civilization is at stake and there is no other solution except that of war. So what they do is, they train us in ROTC. You dig it? All they do in ROTC is teach you how to kill. You may try to justify it all you want, but your job is to kill. The job of the Army is to kill. That is the reason why it is there. Not to teach you how to become anything. If you want to be taught something, build a school in my neighborhood and let me go there. Don't tell me about going to Vietnam to learn nothing. /31/

Now then, I have to be appalled at the president of the university who stands up and says that black power is about violence while at this very campus he encourages institutionalized violence by compulsory ROTC and does not speak about that. Who does he think he is kidding? There is nothing wrong with violence. It is just who is able to control it. That's what counts. Everybody knows that. You have institutionalized violence on your campus. You have to dress up in a monkey suit and train how to kill once a week. And what is your response to that, as black students coming to a university where they are supposed to teach you civilization? Is that civilization too? That one was killed? Is that what you are imitating? Is it for you not to reason why at a university, but to do and die? Do you not have the guts to say, "hell no"? Do you not have the guts to say: "I will not allow anyone to make me a hired killer. When I decide to kill, since it is the greatest crime that man can make, I will make that decision. And I will not only decide to kill, I will decide whom to kill." /32/

So that you are now at a vast black university where they have already incorporated in your thinking, violence. And here you are marching around every Friday, or Thursday, or Wednesday, or whatever it is, with your shoes spit-shined 'til three o'clock in the morning, marching with a gun in your hand, learning all about how to shoot. Over in Vietnam they put you on a front line and you are shooting. But that is not violence, because you can't define for yourself. You ought to tell the school that if you wanted to learn how to kill, you would go to West Point. They turn them out there. You came here to learn how to help your people of Baltimore in the ghettos, upon whom you turn your backs as soon as you get a chance. /33/

And what can you tell a black man in Baltimore who lives in the ghettos about killing? Hasn't he been subjected to it all of his life? What is your analysis about the rebellions that have been occurring all around the state? Are you like everybody else? Are you against violence? Do you analyze? Do you recognize what it means? Let me explain. /34/

The reason why they say we expound violence isn't because we expound violence, but because we refuse to condemn black people who throw rocks and bottles at policemen. That is why, and I say that is the only reason why. Because I look at all the other Negro leaders—so-called leaders—every time there is a riot. "We deplore violence, we avoid use of violence, it is very, very bad, there is only a small group of vagabonds, they don't represent our community, and violence never accomplishes anything. Yes, we are training our boys to go to Vietnam. We think it is a good thing to send them to Vietnam but violence never accomplishes anything at all." /35/

Now you have got to understand this very clearly. If you know anything about the ghetto, you would know that on any given Friday or Saturday night there is more violence inside the ghetto than any place else in any given city. You know that we cut and butcher and shoot each other. And do you also know that in any given ghetto there is more police power, that is, in terms of numbers, there are more police per block, per square inch than in any other area of the city? /36/

What does that mean to you? It means that, on Friday night, while there are more police, there is more violence among black people. So obviously they don't give a damn about the violence among black people. . . . But one black boy throws one rock at some filthy grocery store and the whole damned National Guard comes into our ghetto. Why is that? Because property rights mean more than human rights and in the ghetto we do not own the property. If we get robbed, you can call the policemen 'til you turn white. He ain't coming. But just hit a grocery store. Just throw a molotov cocktail through a window and see how quick they come in. They deplore violence. They can't stand the violence that goes on in the street. It's all right on Friday and Saturday night when we cut each other in the street and no one black man ever talks about it. We need nonviolence in the black community. That's where we need it. /37/

We have to learn to love and respect ourselves. That's where it should begin. That's where it must begin. Because if we don't love us, ain't nobody going to love us. /38/

Now what happens then is that the people who have power in our ghettos are the property owners. So that when their stores are touched, they call the National Guard. But to analyze that one step further, everybody in our ghettos knows that we are charged higher prices for rotten meat. Everybody knows that, but nobody says, "We deplore the high prices they charge the Negro for rotten meat." They don't say that. Nobody moves to readjust the problems black people are facing in the ghetto—the slum-lord machinery setup. And if they try to, they find out that the people who own the property are the people who make the laws. /39/

Property rights, property rights is what the United States Constitution is based on. You should know that. . . . Property rights. People who didn't own property could not vote when this country was first founded. Not until years afterwards such people were able to vote. So the analysis is the question of property versus propertyless people. That's what it's all about. /40/

That's what those rebellions are about. Nothing else, nothing less. And what appalls me about the black leaders is they do not have the guts to condemn the grocery-store owner. Now I will say anytime a man has been charging us all that money for fifteen years, his store should have been bombed five years ago. Should have been out of the neighborhood five years ago. And if nobody wants to do it, then you can't blame people when they move to do it for themselves. If you want to stop rebellion, then eradicate the cause. /41/

You are college students, you should think. Now then we want to talk finally about the responsibility of youth. That's black students. It is time for you to stop running away from being black. It is time for you to understand that you, as the growing intellectual, the black intellectuals of this country, must begin to define beauty for black people. /42/

Beauty in this society is defined by someone with a narrow nose, thin lips, white skin. You ain't got none of that. So now what you try to do when you pick a homecoming queen, you look for the brightest thing that looks light, bright, and damn near white. And you have your mothers sending you up here. . . . "Be sure to pick a nice-looking fellow with curly hair when you get married, dear." Or if your lips are thick, bite them in. Hold your nose; don't drink coffee because you are black. /43/

Everybody knows black is bad. Can you begin to get the guts to develop a criteria for beauty for black people? That your nose is boss; your lips are thick, you are black, and you are beautiful? Can you begin to do it so that you are not ashamed of your hair and you don't cut it to the scalp so that naps won't show? Girls, are you ready? Obviously it is your responsibility to begin to define the criteria for black people about their beauty. Because you are running around with your Nadinola cream. Your campus, the black campuses of this country, are becoming infested with wigs and Mustangs and you are to blame for it. You are to blame for it. /44/

What is your responsibility to your fellow black brothers? Why are you here? So that you can become a social worker so that you can kick down a door in the middle of the night to look for a pair of shoes? Is that what you come to college for? So that you can keep the kid in the ghetto school, so that you can ride up in a big

Bonneville with [an] ᴀᴋᴀ sign stuck on the back? Is that your responsibility? Is that your responsibility? What is your responsibility to black people of Baltimore who are hungry for the knowledge you are supposed to have? /45/

Is it so that you can just get over? Do you forget that it is not your sweat that put you where you are? Do you not know that your black mothers scrubbed floors so you can get here, and the minute you get out, you turn your back on them? What is your responsibility, black students? What is it? Is it to become a teacher so you can be programed into a ghetto school? So that you can get up and say, "It's a shame how our children are culturally deprived"? What do you know about culturally deprived? What is your definition of culture? Isn't it anything man-made? Is it not anything man-made? How the hell can I be culturally deprived? You deny my very existence, to use that term. Do you question what they tell you at school? Or do you only accept, carry it back, get over, and go out to further stymie black people in the ghetto? /46/

I blame you for the rebellions across the country last summer. And I will blame you again when they increase more this summer. It is your obligation to be back in the ghetto helping out black people who are looking, who are acting, begging, and thinking a way to solve their problems. And you are running out of the ghetto as fast as your sports cars and Mustangs can carry you. /47/

What is your responsibility, black students of Morgan? Do you know about DuBois? Have you read Douglass? Do you know Richard Wright? Can you quote A. J. Rogers? Do you know Claude McKay? Can you understand, can you understand LeRoi Jones? /48/

There is a young man with me now. His name is Eldridge Cleaver. He just spent eight years in jail. He is writing some of the most profound writing that has come out in the country from black men. Do you know of him? Have you read his stuff? Why haven't you read his stuff? Is it because you are too busy trying to find out where the Kappas are partying Friday night? Why is it that you haven't read his stuff? Is it that you are spit-shining your shoes so that you can become a lieutenant colonel to go to Vietnam when you graduate? Why is it that you haven't read his stuff? Is it that you don't want to read anything about being black because you, too, are ashamed of it and are running from it? So you want to run to your debutante ball with your light-skinned girlfriend to be white. So you want to run to your Kappa fraternity ball and forget all else. /49/

When the ghettos rebel you are going to be the buffer, and you are the ones who are going to be caught in the middle. The gate is swinging open. Brothers and sisters, you had better come home. You had better come home early this summer. You had better take what knowledge you have and use it to benefit black people in the ghetto. You had better recognize that individualism is a luxury that black students can no longer afford. You had better understand that. You had better begin to see yourself as a people, and as a group, and therefore you need to help to advance that group. /50/

Can you be aggressive? Can you say that Baltimore is almost 52 percent black and black people should own, run it, lock, stock, and barrel? They do it every place else. Or, are you afraid? /51/

Can you not go out and organize those people to take the political power which they have been denied? Can you not help? Or are you too busy trying to be a doctor and lawyer so that you can get a big car and a big house and talk about your house in the suburbs and "I'm the only one out there"? /52/

Can you begin to say that James Brown is us, that he is a musical genius as much as Bach or Beethoven? Can you say it? Can you understand your culture? Can you make them teach it to you here in college, rather than to teach you Bach and Beethoven which is only one-sided? Why can't you also have James Brown so that you can begin to know that culture is all about? /53/

I want to finish with two quotes. The first is by Bertrand Russell. You know about the war tribunal. You should. Bertrand Russell is calling the war tribunal to judge people of this country. I want to read from what he calls "An Appeal to My Conscience" [*An Appeal to the American Conscience*]. You ought to try to understand it very clearly because what you ought to understand about the war in Vietnam is that it has interest for you not only personally, that is, during your student days, but it is very political for black people. When McNamara says he is going to draft 30 percent black people out of the ghettos, baby, that is nothing but urban removal, that's all it is. And if you don't begin to understand that you are going to be the fellows leading the charges of your 30 percent black people. You don't understand that. Do you have the guts to stand up now and say, "I will not follow law and order, I will follow my own conscience"? /54/

That's what they sent Eichmann to jail for, you know, because he followed law and order. And they said that there is a higher law than the law of government. There is the law of each of us and they are absolutely right. And that is my law, and I will not go to Vietnam, I will not serve in the Army. I will say, hell no. The choices are very clear. They are crystal clear. You either suffer or you inflict suffering. Either you go to Leavenworth or you become a killer. I will not become a killer. I will choose to suffer. I will go to jail. To hell with this country. /55/

Now then the quote by Mr. Russell:

> Just as in the case of Spain, Vietnam is a barbarous rehearsal. It is our intention that neither the bona fides nor the authenticity of this tribunal will be susceptible to challenge from those who have so much to hide.
>
> President Johnson, Dean Rusk, Robert McNamara, Henry Cabot Lodge, General Westmoreland, and their fellow criminals will be brought before a wider justice than they recognize and a more profound condemnation than they are equipped to understand.

That is a profound statement. /56/

Now the last statement that I want to leave you with is by John Donne. You know John Donne is my favorite philosophical poet of the seventeenth century. He said, "The death of any man diminishes me because I am involved in mankind." /57/

Now what this generation has allowed to happen is that we are not involved in mankind. When we began to crawl, they sent six million people to an oven and we blinked our eyes. And when we walked, they sent our uncles to Korea. And we grew up in a cold war to continue their head-wrecking period so that we are immune to humanity. We, this generation, must save the world. We must become involved in mankind. We must not allow them to stage the killing of every and any thing that gets in their way. We must not become part of that machinery. /58/

Now I want to read my favorite quote: "If I am not for myself, who will be? If I am for myself alone, who am I? If not now, when? And if not you, who?" /59/

I want to thank you. /60/

Appendix B

SPIRO T. AGNEW'S SPEECH ON
TELEVISED NEWS

Joyce Conklin Williamson

Published transcripts of the address by Vice President Spiro Agnew to
the Midwest Regional Republican Committee at Des Moines, Iowa on
November 13, 1969 seem generally incomplete. I have compared the texts
printed in *Vital Speeches of the Day* and in the New York *Times* with a
tape recording of the speech as given. Neither printed text contains
Agnew's opening comment concerning the presence of television cameras
nor what were apparently variations from a prepared text. I therefore
supply with this critique an edited text of the address as actually
presented.

An advance text of this speech was released to the press one hour
before the speech was delivered. Presumably this is the text we are
given in most journalistic sources.

When Richard Nixon announced his running mate for the 1968
presidential election, people across the United States had comparable
basic reactions: "Spiro Who?" Few people outside his own state of
Maryland had heard Agnew's name. When the election was won, many
assumed that Agnew would live in the shadow of the President as vice
presidents of the past have done. He did not. The name of Spiro Agnew
does not elicit a passive response today, nor did it in 1969.

Agnew quickly made himself a controversial figure, and his speech
of November 13, 1969 made him especially controversial. It also gave him
influence he had not previously had. Suddenly his picture was on the
covers of *Time* and *Newsweek*. His speeches received reviews on radio
and television. Virtually every weekly magazine found place for an
article about him. Some news commentators attacked him. A few lauded
him. None ignored him. Now he was a frequent guest on television
"talk shows." And Agnew jokes increased in number.

Had all this been planned? Or was it an accident? What had happened?
In order to estimate why Agnew spoke as he did at Des Moines and
what people found in his speech we must examine some events that
preceded.

I. Exigence

To determine what exigence existed for this speech we must look not
just at Spiro Agnew but at the situation within the country and at

---

Ms. Williamson's critical essay on Vice President Agnew's speech was
prepared as a Spring 1972 classroom project in speech criticism at The Pennsylvania State University. Material in the essay is incorporated in an M. A.
thesis on Agnew's speaking, now in preparation. The essay is published by
permission of Ms. Williamson.

President Nixon's position as a political leader. A foremost fact of
the time was the Vietnam War.

In the weeks before Agnew spoke the October 15th "Moratorium" had
recently passed. Protests were still being staged in Washington, chiefly
against the war. The President was trying to exert pressure on Congress
to gain authority to transform the military draft to a lottery and to
strengthen legislation curbing narcotics traffic. He was not having great
success, but a Gallup Poll reported that "58 percent of the American
public supported the President's Vietnam policies." [1] This was the
highest level of endorsement Nixon had received since moving into the
White House.

The President's positions were generally popular, then. And he had
recently made a speech which has great importance to an understanding
of Agnew's speech at Des Moines. President Nixon had announced,
three weeks in advance, that he would make a speech concerning policies
toward Vietnam. The speech occurred on November 3, 1969. In it Nixon
presented a "timetable" for withdrawal of American forces from
Vietnam; he did not accede to demands for "immediate withdrawal."
He would not end the war by surrender, he said; he assured the nation
that the "silent majority" was behind him and neither he nor they would
give in to a "vocal minority."

Agnew addressed himself directly to the aftermath of Nixon's speech.
The network newsmen attacked the President's policy immediately
upon its conclusion. To Agnew it was "instant analysis and querulous
criticism." We find Agnew responding descriptively:

> One commentator [CBS's Marvin Kalb] twice contradicted the President's
> statement about the exchange of correspondence with Ho Chi Minh. An-
> other [ABC's Bill Lawrence] challenged the President's abilities as a
> politician. A third [ABC's Bill Downs] asserted that the President was
> now following the Pentagon line. Others by the expressions on their
> faces, the tone of questions, and the sarcasm of their responses made clear
> their sharp disapproval.

However the press may have treated Nixon's speech on November 3,
the public responded favorably. Telephone calls jammed the White
House switchboard, over 8,000 telegrams were on his desk by 7:00 A.M.
the following morning, virtually all praising his stand on the war; there
were 63,000 communications processed by the weekend, running 11 to
1 in Nixon's favor. A special Gallup telephone survey found 77 percent
of those questioned backing the President. And most importantly for
the administration, nearly 200 Congressmen, from both parties,
subscribed to a resolution supporting the President's conduct of the war.[2]

There was, then—in the public view at least—a conflict of perceptions
concerning the Nixon administration—between those held by a large

---

[1] "Betting on 'The Silent Majority,' " *Newsweek,* 74 (November 17, 1969): 35.
[2] *Ibid.*

section of the public and those apparently held by journalists and commentators appearing on network television. This was the basic fact that created an exigence for the speech Spiro Agnew would give from Des Moines.

II. Constraints

Lloyd Bitzer contends that "every rhetorical situation contains a set of *constraints* made up of persons, events, objects, and relations which are parts of the situation because they have the power to constrain decision and action needed to modify the exigence." [3] Spiro Agnew, himself, and his office were constraints. An article published in *Newsweek* seems to me to summarize very well a number of such constraining forces.

> Ever since John Adams took the first oath of office, Vice Presidents of the United States have occupied themselves in a fitful, and generally unsuccessful, search for something to do. Theodore Roosevelt imagined that the job might afford him an excellent opportunity to complete his studies for the New York bar exam. Richard M. Johnson, understudy to President Martin Van Buren, spent one of his Vice Presidential summers managing an inn. John Tyler retired to his Virginia plantation immediately after being inaugurated and was not seen in Washington again until President William Henry Harrison suddenly died a month later. In more recent times, the suffocating functionlessness of the post reduced Lyndon Johnson's explosive energies to a torpor relieved only by an occasional jaunt with a Pakistani camel driver and condemned the zestful spirit of Hubert Humphrey to four years of soggy obeisance.
>
> Enter Spiro T. Agnew. Barely known before that, he has turned the extraordinary trick of making the Vice Presidency—or at least his own portrayal of it—into one of the most fascinating roles on the Washington stage. Rough of speech and smooth of haberdashery, he commands both attention and controversy in an Administration where both are at a premium. His admirers hail him for talking plainly on issues from which most politicians flinch. His critics reproach him for indulging in rabble-rousing bombast at a time when bitter factionalism is already intense. His behavior is interpreted in the most extravagant—and contradictory— of terms: courageous, Machiavellian, or just plain dumb. But whatever else he may be, Spiro Agnew is a raised voice in a hushed Administration, a flash of color against distinctions, a 'character' in a crowd where personality seems uncommonly subdued. He may or may not be a boon to the Republic, but at least he is a Vice President who has found something to do.
>
> Bloopers: That something, most notably, is to talk—the Veep has delivered more than 70 speeches since taking office. During last year's campaign, he became famous for a series of bloopers: he spoke of a 'fat Jap' and 'Polacks' and called Humphrey 'soft on communism'; he hazarded the opinion that 'if you've seen one city slum, you've seen them all.' And last month he resumed his outspokenness in a far more serious vein. In New Orleans, he charged that the October Vietnam Moratorium had been

---

[3] "The Rhetorical Situation," *Philosophy and Rhetoric* 1 (January 1969): 8.

'encouraged by an effete corps of impudent snobs' (prompting a new doves' lapel button: 'Effete Snobs for Peace'). In Harrisburg, Pa., he denounced politicians who encourage antiwar demonstrations as 'ideological eunuchs,' suggested that a decadent few were misguiding the nation's youth and warned darkly that 'we can afford to separate them from our society—with no more regret than we should feel over discarding rotten apples from a barrel.' [4]

The portrayal seems to me excellent for it emphasizes the traditional and immediate images that must have constituted important events, relations, and personal attributes which would affect decision on any major claim offered by Vice President Spiro T. Agnew. There were, of course, other constraints, and I have earlier touched upon these. Aside from the constraining forces emanating from Agnew's person and his role, we might put the matter thus. Agnew's speech was an attack upon the handling of news by the media, and it was news coverage of the President's speech that immediately led to and gave focus to Agnew's speech. It appears that Agnew envisioned change in news reporting and sought an audience in which to promote that change. In short, this man chose to work through his own image, his role, the popularity of the administration's policies, the specifics of television coverage of the President and of the war, and, of course, the forum given by his Iowa hosts and the television networks themselves. I shall discuss his management of these opportunities and limitations in a later section, but first some data concerning the national audience must be considered.

III. Audience

I used the phrase "sought an audience" above because I contend that Agnew knew what he wanted to talk about, and how. He needed to *find* an immediate audience that would receive him warmly and allow him to make the kind of speech he had in mind. But he needed an audience that would give him broader coverage than any dinner crowd with local associations could provide. He had a speech for a nationwide audience, however appropriate it might also be for a friendly smaller group. My belief is that instead of having an audience and seeking a suitable subject, Agnew's posture was the reverse; he had the speech and sought the audience.

The point needs to be pressed farther. Whom did Agnew really want to affect? Newsmen? The public? We cannot say with certainty for we cannot read his mind; yet there is evidence on the matter which will be investigated when we come to analysis of the content of Agnew's speech. For now I note only some possibilities. He could have wanted to antagonize newsmen, or to create an awareness in the public, or to rouse feelings already in the public, or simply to bring his own personality into brighter

---

[4] "Agnew Finds a Role," *Newsweek,* 74 (November 17, 1969): 38.

light. What the speech had potentiality to do must be looked for when
we explore its rhetorical characteristics.

It is known that the Vice President had not even been invited to
address the Midwest Regional Republican Conference in Des Moines.
The Des Moines *Register,* a morning paper, said the day after the speech
that the Vice President's office had telephoned McDill Boyde, chairman
of the conference, only the preceding Tuesday and asked that Mr. Agnew
be invited to address the conference. It was also admitted that President
Nixon's speech writer, Pat Buchanan, had written the speech and that
it was approved by some officials at the White House. It has not been
divulged whether the speech was discussed with the President.

Turning to national attitudes relative to the subject of Agnew's speech,
certain very important facts emerge. There was widespread dissatisfaction
with the communications media, especially the news divisions. A poll
taken shortly before the speech revealed that 42 percent of a national
sample of voters believed that the television networks did not accurately
report the news. Only 40 percent of the people thought coverage was fair
and another 18 percent weren't sure. There was, then, a very large
audience entirely ready to hear and respond favorably to a speech condemning practices of newscasters. The Vice President, using the special
role he had and had developed, "took advantage of his high office to
criticize." [5]

Did the rhetorical situation, including the immediate and national
audience, invite Agnew's speech on news reporting? I conclude that it
did. And Agnew was the right man to give the speech to the two audiences.
He had established that he had no fear of speaking bluntly. He could say
what the President could not. He, himself, had been the butt of many
gibes from the press, as was well known. He had the reputation, the
personal involvement with the issue, and the administrative standing
to make him the ideal member of the administration to "take on" the
broadcasters. He and his speech fit the situation so well that the newsmen
became immediately concerned about how far Agnew—with the audience
behind him—might go in forcing reforms of the news media.

IV. Content

One must keep in mind while analyzing the content and form of this
speech that Agnew knew he would be speaking to a receptive, cooperative, immediate audience and to generally receptive millions via the
medium he was about to criticize. I judge that he knew beforehand that
he would be accepted by a large majority in both audiences and that he
knew he would be totally rejected by most newsmen and a minority of
the general audience. That the general audience was friendly to his theme
allowed him to say things in ways that would not have worked without

---

[5] David Brinkley on the Huntley-Brinkley Report, November 14, 1969.
Taken from a tape recording of the program.

friendship to his ideas. As I have noted, 42 percent of the general audience was already prepared to have someone assail the newscasters, and another 18 percent was uncertain about the newscasters' fairness.

The attitudes of the audience being what they were, there was no need for Agnew to offer the standard logical supports that a full argument would include. A large segment of the audience possessed its own DATA to support Agnew's CLAIMS. For them and for others he provided added DATA, of course. But he had no need to justify the representativeness of those DATA or to prove with BACKING that his own and his listeners' DATA constituted "unfairness" instead of something else. In short, a majority of Agnew's two audiences had the proofs of his CLAIMS in their own heads. In consequence there is little to be gained from an analysis of the explicit content of this speech. Detailed examination will simply show that again and again Agnew identified well known or new DATA and inferred without warranting and with only a little qualification that the newscasters were engaged in advocacy rather than news reporting.

One learns the real nature of Agnew's speech mainly by examining what the details of the speech *implied* and what the address proved to be as *form*.

What were the simplest interpretations listeners could put upon Agnew's DATA and his CLAIMS? Agnew's broad claim was that the television news departments had too much power, that they controlled the thinking of an entire nation. His supports were only a few, selected examples of instances in which he believed a slanted view of the news had been presented. The primary DATA were subjectively interpreted. He said the treatment of Nixon's November 3rd speech was a total attack on the President and his policy. The majority, which already shared Agnew's jaundiced view of the telecasters, would have little difficulty in accepting his interpretation. I might object that Agnew failed to notice whether any newscaster *was* fair, but I have no reason to think that a majority in Agnew's audiences would pause to demand this kind of QUALIFICATION.

The next body of DATA offered in support of Agnew's general CLAIM came after more than half the speech had been completed. He commented on the coverage of the Democratic National Convention in Chicago. These DATA could broaden his base of accepting listeners. Democrats had suffered from unfair coverage, not just Republicans. Was he thinking of the fact that only a week before a subcommittee of the House Commerce Committee (controlled by Democrats) had issued a "finding" charging televised news with slanted coverage of the Democratic convention? In any case, his claim that the Democrats had suffered unfairness had potential to render his overall charge against newsmen bipartisan.

A third segment of supportive DATA from Agnew's major CLAIM was that more bad news was always reported than good news. Again, this was perhaps a weak base from which to win over the unfriendly among his hearers, but the instances cited were probably "more proof" to the auditors already suspicious of news coverage. Agnew did not link reporting bad news to his charge that the news was being slanted, but one may suppose that by including these DATA *among* DATA alleging bias he made it easy for the suspicious to leap to conclusions that the DATA were *all* related.

Agnew's DATA supporting the CLAIM that television has control over national understanding of events function in an interesting way. The statistics he provided and his comparison of numbers of viewers with numbers of newspaper readers logically support a conclusion that television *could* control thinking, but they do not prove that television newscasters *manipulate* the country as a *whole*. But we must return again to the widespread belief that those running television were *trying* to manipulate. Roughly two-fifths of the nation already believed that, and another fifth seemed to think it might be true. Campaigns had been conducted to take cigarette advertising from television; controversies had raged about what should be presented on television during children's viewing hours; the supposition that manipulation was possible and actual was a cultural commonplace. Therefore, I believe, it was easy for Agnew to gain acceptance of his charge of attempted manipulation, even though his argument, as formal argument, had no great proof-power.

If Agnew's purpose was to make a vast number of people feel that the potential for news manipulation and thought manipulation existed in television, his DATA and the inferential patterns familiar to large numbers of listeners ought to have achieved that purpose.

What solutions did Agnew offer for his listeners' problems and anxieties? He actually offered no solution to the problem he discussed. This was deliberate: "I've made no attempt to suggest the answers. The answers must come from the media men." He was not asking for any sort of censorship agency; he insisted the newsmen were already doing the censoring; that was the trouble. Newsmen reacted by saying Agnew was trying to take away the freedom of the press. Others said he aimed at censorship of news. But I think it would be reasonable to say that many in the general public felt Agnew had done what he could by alerting them to a situation that they must guard against. In any case, to the extent that Agnew's strategy left general listeners frustrated, the rest of the speech clearly identified the target for that frustration—the news media!

Another point becomes clear when one thinks about Agnew's ambiguity concerning solutions. That ambiguity particularly stirred the newsmen. They seemed not to know whether to fear him or not. So they did a thing Agnew and the administration almost certainly wanted; by vigorous and continuing self-defense they *kept alive* the issue of whether they did or did not have integrity! And they are still doing so. Agnew opened the debate on the integrity of news media in such a way that the debate was sure to continue—with the almost certain outcome that suspicions of the press would spread.

If we look at the ways in which Agnew gave ideas special claims to attention through management of their contexts, we begin to see the *form* of the speech. Agnew placed his most direct criticism of the newscasters in the very first part of his speech, when he criticized the handling of Nixon's address. He attacked *first*. Then, he kept the attack prominent throughout. Even when he made a positive statement such as, "The networks have tackled our most difficult social problems . . . ," he always attached a qualifier such as: "But it was also the networks that elevated. . . ." He said, ". . . every American has a right to disagree with the President . . . but the President of the United States has a right to. . . ." Or we hear, "Advocates for the networks have claimed a First Amendment right . . . ," and then, "But the situations are not identical."

There is in the speech a basic pattern of interrelating ideas: the condemnatory constitutes the bulk of what is said, and in any consideration of possibly positive elements the positive is *qualified*. The critical either stands out alone or the critical "surrounds" admissions of merit. I suggest that what emerges from this kind of rhetoric is an *indictment*— but one that has the air of fairness without any moderation of the attack.

I have established, I believe, that the power of Vice President Agnew's speech lay in its suggestive rather than in its formally argumentative elements. This makes it all the more significant to notice that nothing in the speech is incompatible with anything else—from *any* listener's point of view. Agnew indicts and calls for the media to clean their own houses. Everything in the speech serves those two ends—especially the first. But merely to raise the question of whether all rhetorical elements are psychologically compatible is to have one's attention drawn to the fact that even in his *choices of words* Agnew kept the "heat" of indictment and challenge constant. Consider these phrasings from only a small segment of the speech:

> "Are we *demanding* enough. . . ?"
> "His words and policies were subjected to instant analysis and *querulous criticism*."
> "Their *hostility*. . . ."
> "Their minds were made up *in advance*."
> "*Contradicted . . . challenged . . . asserted*."
> "*Sharp* disapproval."
> "To guarantee . . . it would be challenged, one network *trotted* out. . . ."
> "He attacked . . . criticized."
> "He was showing his "heavy *compulsion* to justify his *failure*. . . ."
> "He [Churchill] didn't have to *contend with a gaggle* of commentators. . . ."

Virtually anywhere in the speech one can find the unified thrust of the whole message "held together" tightly by indicting, motive-assigning, evaluative terms. The *negative,* respecting television's newsmen, is sustained at all levels of communication: from selection of main ideas to selection of individual words.

To ask what kinds of judgments Agnew asked from his listeners is
merely to confirm, from another direction, what I have already said. For
the most part Agnew demands assent to "facts" and optative—generally
evaluative—judgments of what those "facts" prove. If my evidence
about the attitudes of the majorities in his audiences is sound, these
demands could not fail. And this characteristic of the speech was fore-
ordained. Agnew designed a speech for people with the kinds of "knowledge" and the kinds of preferences *he* had. I have shown that a majority
of the national audience had or was at least open to Agnew's beliefs about
the media men and about news coverage. What Agnew had to do was say
forcefully: "*We* know these to be 'facts,' don't we? And we disapprove on
grounds of unfairness and undue exercise of power, don't we?" In the portion of the audience in which I believe Agnew was chiefly interested, the
assents were already present to be harvested.

Agnew harvested. He did not hesitate to say what his intention was:
"The purpose of my remarks tonight is to focus your attention on this
little group of men who not only enjoy a right of instant rebuttal to
every Presidential address. . . ." But what did he really *do?*

He did a number of things none of which could be anything but
helpful to Agnew as a public figure and to his announced rhetorical purpose. He roused the news commentators, forcing them to respond and to
keep Agnew and his charges against them in the public eye. He had a
certain "revenge" on them for their many gibes; he and his friends must
have enjoyed that. The public became aware of Agnew as a leading
public figure; he was no longer *just* a Vice President. He reinforced a
general concern about the power of television. And there is some evidence
that newscasting *did* change—if not in direct consequence of Agnew's
speech at Des Moines, in consequence of its aftermath. If, as some
suggested, the speech was intended to establish Agnew as the President's
spokesman, that was achieved.

All the observations I have made in analyzing this speech contribute
toward the conclusion that this was an address that filled not just
one need but served each and all of the purposes I have just mentioned.
And this was a strong rhetorical merit. Any and all of these results
would ultimately benefit the federal administration and benefit Agnew
as a member of it. That the speech was attacked and Agnew was attacked
was a rhetorical "plus." Enough people were on Agnew's side of the
"media question" so that in the short run at least controversy about
the speech could only keep Agnew's "advantage" over the media men
before the eyes of those who applauded that advantage.

V.   Oral Style

I have already touched on the way in which Agnew's careful selection
of evaluative language contributed to the unified form of the address
as a sustained indictment and challenge. My contention is that this is
one of the two important observations to make about how language

functioned from Des Moines. Nothing striking comes from studying
Agnew's grammatical constructions and other traditionally studied
aspects of verbal style. Agnew was simple, clear, direct, and except for
artfully holding the speech together with negatively evaluative terms, he
displayed no linguistic practices we might not find in any clear, competent
speaker of American English. However, the identity of views held by
Agnew and a majority of each of his audiences seems to have given his
style the qualities Roderick P. Hart, Jr. has found associated with what
Hart calls "doctrinality." Given the situation, this is not unexpected,
but to make the point is to summarize the entirety of my critical evaluation
of the address.

Agnew's immediate audience was made up of his fellow Republicans
who had fought to put him and the President in office. Agnew came to
them as a defender of the President, and he came to the nation as a critic
of news coverage about which a large part of the population was already
suspicious. To both audiences he came as one sharing existing views.
His basic rhetorical need was to articulate those shared views—on behalf
of the President and the administration and in criticism of televised news.
It is not surprising but it is clarifying, then, to say that Agnew spoke
as a man who shared philosophical viewpoints with his listeners.

He left it to his listeners to warrant his movements from DATA to
CLAIM. He left his listeners to find what solace (or frustration) they
might in the prospect of self-examination by the news media. He neglected
to identify the sources of his DATA in most instances—treating the
DATA as common knowledge. He was absolute in judgment when he
was not engaged in qualifying judgments favorable to the newsmen. He
asserted; he seldom "proved." Except by way of illustration, he eschewed
details in his "arguments." He intensified tensions already existing in
consequence of beliefs he and his listeners shared. Those against him
were driven still farther away, and they were given "openings" for continuing the debate which Agnew was beginning. Those openings were
made by the casualness of logical inferences and by the fact that specific
details he offered illustrated DATA but did not establish the sufficiency
of his DATA. Agnew confidently and deliberately "pronounced" this
rhetoric of shared ideas—a rhetoric that excluded the unsharing where
it did not directly attack them.

The polls had told Vice President Agnew he had friends on this subject.
With a tightly cohering speech articulating and reinforcing these shared
views he could give shape and self-recognition to a heretofore silent
majority, which resented a minority's "querulous" criticism of administrative policy and who perceived the telecasters as the leading voices of
that minority. When the speech was over, 67 percent of all Americans
endorsed it. Three months later 56 percent still endorsed it. I believe
I have shown the rhetorical reasons that this could happen.

My thesis is that the speech served all the purposes Vice President
Agnew could have had for making it. It had nothing in it that could do

disservice to those purposes. It was a fitting response to an attitudinal situation that had, in Bitzer's language, "matured" to the point at which a strong articulation of the administration's defense and criticism of contemporary journalism could generate resounding approval. With impressive rhetorical efficiency Spiro T. Agnew entered that situation and mediated approving change. Content appropriate to a sharing of views, and emerging indictment and challenge, were essential to that achievement. These Agnew provided in abundance.[6]

---

[6] I have not discussed Agnew's delivery in this critique because I find nothing unique about it. It was deliberate, aggressive, and confident; many speakers could duplicate it. My analyses give me no grounds for saying more.

VICE PRESIDENT AGNEW ON TELEVISED NEWS

November 13, 1969

Des Moines, Iowa

Thank you very much Governor Ray, Governor Ogilvie, Governor Teaman, Mr. Boyde, Miss Peterson, the many distinguished officials of the Republican Party gathered for this Midwest regional meeting. It's indeed a pleasure for me to be here tonight. I had intended to make all three of the regional meetings that have been scheduled thus far, but unfortunately I had to scrub the Western one; Hawaii was a little far at the moment—at that time— but I'm glad to be here tonight and I look forward to attending others. I think it's obvious from the cameras here that I didn't come to discuss the ban on cyclamates or DDT. [Laughter.] /1/

I have a subject I think is of great interest to the American people. Tonight I want to discuss the importance of the television medium to the American people. No nation depends more on the intelligent judgment of its citizens. No medium has a more profound influence over public opinion. Nowhere in our system are there fewer checks on such vast power. So nowhere should there be more conscientious responsibility exercised than by the news media. The question is: Are we demanding enough of our television news presentations? And are the men of this medium demanding enough of themselves? /2/

Monday night a week ago, President Nixon delivered the most important address of his Administration, one of the most important of our decade. His subject was Vietnam. My hope—as his—at that time was to rally the American people to see the conflict through to a lasting and just peace in the Pacific. For thirty-two minutes, he reasoned with a nation that has suffered almost a third of a million casualties in the longest war in its history. /3/

When the President completed his address—an address, incidentally, that he spent weeks in the preparation of—his words and policies were subjected to instant analysis and querulous criticism. The audience of seventy million Americans gathered to hear the President of the United States was inherited by a small band of network commentators, and self-appointed analysts, the majority of whom expressed in one way or another their hostility to what he had to say. /4/

This text was edited from a tape recording and the printed texts appearing in *Vital Speeches of the Day* and The New York *Times*. It was prepared by Joyce Conklin Williamson and is used by her permission.

It was obvious that their minds were made up in advance. Those who recall the fumbling and groping that followed President Johnson's dramatic disclosure of his intention not to seek another term have seen these men in a genuine state of *non*preparedness. This was not it. /5/

One commentator twice contradicted the President's statement about the exchange of correspondence with Ho Chi Minh. Another challenged the President's abilities as a politician. A third asserted that the President was following a Pentagon line. Others, by the expressions on their faces, the tone of their questions, and the sarcasm of their responses made clear their sharp disapproval. /6/

To guarantee *in advance* that the President's plea for national unity would be challenged, one network trotted out Averell Harriman for the occasion. Throughout the President's address, he waited in the wings. When the President concluded, Mr. Harriman recited perfectly. He attacked the Thieu Government as unrepresentative; he criticized the President's speech for various deficiencies; he twice issued a call for the Senate Foreign Relations Committee to debate Vietnam once again; he stated his belief that the Vietcong or North Vietnamese did not really want a military takeover of South Vietnam; and he told a little anecdote about a "very, very responsible" fellow he had met in the Vietnamese delegation. /7/

All in all, Mr. Harriman offered a broad range of gratuitous advice, challenging and contradicting the policies outlined by the President of the United States. Where the President had issued a call for unity, Mr. Harriman was encouraging the country *not* to listen to him. /8/

A word about Mr. Harriman. For ten months, he was America's chief negotiator at the Paris peace talks—a period in which the United States swapped some of the greatest military concessions in the history of warfare for an enemy agreement on the shape of the bargaining table. Like Coleridge's "Ancient Mariner," Mr. Harriman seems to be under some heavy compulsion to justify his failures to anyone who will listen. And the networks have shown themselves willing to give him all the air time he desires. /9/

Now, every American has a right to disagree with the President of the United States and to express publicly that disagreement. But the President of the United States has a right to communicate directly with the people who elected him, and the people of this country have the right to make up their own minds and form their own opinions about a Presidential address, without having a President's words and thoughts characterized through the prejudices of hostile critics before they can even be digested. /10/

When Winston Churchill rallied public opinion to stay the course against Hitler's Germany, he didn't have to contend with a gaggle of commentators raising doubts about whether he was reading public opinion right, or whether Britain had the stamina to see the war through. /11/

When President Kennedy rallied the nation in the Cuban missile crisis, his address to the people was not chewed over by a round-table of critics who disparaged the course of action he'd asked America to follow. /12/

The purpose of my remarks tonight is to focus your attention on this little group of men who not only enjoy a right of instant rebuttal to every Presidential address, but, more importantly, wield a free hand in selecting, presenting, and interpreting the great issues in our nation. /13/

First, let's define that power. At least forty million Americans every night, it's estimated, watch the network news. Seven million of them view ABC, the remainder being divided between NBC and CBS. /14/

According to Harris polls and other studies, for millions of Americans the networks are the sole source of national and world news. In Will Roger's observation, what you knew was in the newspaper. Today, for growing millions of Americans, it's what they see and hear on their television sets. /15/

Now how is this network news determined? A small group of men, numbering perhaps no more than a dozen anchormen, commentators, and executive producers settle upon the twenty minutes or so of film and commentary that's to reach the public. This selection is made from the ninety to 180 minutes that may be available. Their powers of choice are broad. They decide what forty or fifty million Americans will learn of the day's events in the nation and in the world. /16/

We cannot measure this power and influence by the traditional democratic standards, for these men can *create* national issues over night. They can make or break by their coverage and commentary a moratorium on the war. They can elevate men from obscurity to national prominence within a week. They can reward some politicians with national exposure and ignore others. /17/

For millions of Americans the network reporter who covers a continuing issue—like the ABM or civil rights—becomes, in effect, the presiding judge in a national trial by jury. /18/

It must be recognized that the networks have made important contributions to the national knowledge—through news, documentaries, and specials. They have often used their power constructively and creatively to awaken the public conscience to critical problems. The networks made hunger and black lung disease national issues over night. The TV networks have done what no other medium could have done in terms of dramatizing the horrors of war. The networks have tackled our most difficult social problems with a directness and an immediacy that's the gift of their medium. They focused the nation's attention on its environmental abuses—on pollution in the Great Lakes and the threatened ecology of the Everglades. /19/

But it was also the networks that elevated Stokely Carmichael and George Lincoln Rockwell from obscurity to national prominence. /20/

Nor is their power confined to the substantive. A raised eyebrow, an inflection of the voice, a caustic remark dropped in the middle of a broadcast can raise doubts in a million minds about the veracity of a public official or the wisdom of a government policy. /21/

One Federal Communications Commissioner considers the powers of the networks equal that of local, state, and federal governments all combined. Certainly it represents a concentration of power over American public opinion unknown in history. /22/

Now, what do Americans know of the men who wield this power? Of the men who produce and direct the network news, the nation knows practically nothing. Of the commentators, most Americans know little, other than that they reflect an urbane and assured presence, seemingly well informed on every important matter. /23/

We do know that, to a man, these commentators and producers live and work in the geographical and intellectual confines of Washington, D. C., or New York City, the latter of which James Reston terms the "most unrepresentative community in the entire United States." /24/

Both communities bask in their own provincialism, their own parochialism. /25/

We can deduce that these men read the same newspapers. They draw their political and social views from the same sources. Worse, they talk constantly to one another, thereby providing artificial reinforcement to their shared viewpoints. /26/

Do they allow their biases to influence the selection and presentation of the news? David Brinkley states: "Objectivity is impossible to normal human behavior." Rather, he says, we should "strive for fairness." /27/

Another anchorman on a network news show contends, and I quote: "You can't expunge all your private convictions just because you sit in a seat like this and a camera starts to stare at you. I think your program has to reflect what your basic feelings are. I'll plead guilty to that." /28/

Less than a week before the 1968 election, this same commentator charged that President Nixon's campaign commitments were no more durable than campaign balloons. He claimed that, were it not for the fear of hostile reaction, Richard Nixon would be giving in to—and I quote him exactly, "his natural instinct to smash the enemy with a club or go after him with a meat axe." Had this slander been made by one political candidate about another, it would have been dismissed by most commentators as a partisan attack. But this attack emanated from the privileged sanctuary of a network studio and therefore had the apparent dignity of an objective statement. /29/

The American people would rightly not tolerate this concentration of power in government. Is it not fair and relevant to question its concentration in the hands of a tiny, enclosed fraternity of privileged men elected by no one and enjoying a monopoly sanctioned and licensed by government? /30/

The views of the majority of this fraternity do *not*—and I repeat, *not*—represent the views of America. That is why such a great gulf existed between how the nation received the President's address and how the networks reviewed it. /31/

Not only did the country receive the President's address more warmly than the networks, but so also did the Congress of the United States. Yesterday, the President was notified that 300 individual Congressmen and fifty senators, of both parties, had endorsed his efforts for peace. /32/

As with other American institutions, perhaps it is time that the networks were made more responsive to the views of the nation and more responsible to the people they serve. /33/

Now, I want to make myself perfectly clear. I'm *not* asking for government censorship, or any other kind of censorship. I'm asking whether a form of censorship already exists when the news that forty million [applause interrupts]—when the news that forty million Americans receive each night is determined by a handful of men responsible only to their corporate employers and is filtered through a handful of commentators who admit to their own set of biases. /34/

The questions I'm raising here tonight should have been raised by others long ago. They should have been raised by those Americans who have traditionally considered the preservation of freedom of speech and freedom of the press their special provinces of responsibility. They should have been raised by those Americans who share the view of the late Justice Learned Hand that, "Right conclusions are more likely to be gathered out of a multitude of tongues than through any kind of authoritative selection." /35/

Advocates for the networks have claimed a First Amendment right to the same unlimited freedoms held by the great newspapers of America. But the situations are not identical. Where the New York *Times* reaches 800,000 people, NBC reaches twenty times that number on its evening news. /36/

Nor can the tremendous impact of seeing television film and hearing commentary be compared with reading the printed page. /37/

A decade ago, before network news acquired such dominance over public opinion, Walter Lippmann spoke to the issue. He said, "There's an essential and radical difference between television and printing. The three or four competing television stations control virtually all that can be received over the air by ordinary television sets. But, besides the mass circulation dailies, there are weeklies, monthlies, out-of-town newspapers, and books. If a man doesn't like his newspaper, he can read another from out of town, or wait for a weekly news magazine. It's not ideal, but it's infinitely better than the situation in television. There, if a man doesn't like what the networks are showing, all he can do is turn them off and listen to a phonograph." [1] "Networks," he stated, "which are few in number, have a virtual monopoly of a whole medium of communication. The newspapers of mass circulation have no monopoly on the medium of print." [2] /38/

Now a "virtual monopoly of a whole medium of communication" is not something that democratic people should blindly ignore. And we are not going to cut off our television sets and listen to the phonograph just because the airways belong to the networks. They don't. They belong to the people. /39/

As Justice Byron White wrote in his landmark opinion six months ago, it's the right of the viewers and listeners, not the right of the broadcasters, which is paramount. /40/

---

[1] From the delivery it is difficult to tell where quotations end. Inflection suggests this point.
[2] Again, inflection suggests this completes another unit of quotation. Printed texts do not indicate.

Now it's argued that this power presents no danger in the hands of those who have used it responsibly. But, as to whether or not the networks have abused the power they enjoy, let us call as our first witness former Vice President Humphrey and the city of Chicago. According to Theodore White, television's intercutting of the film from the streets of Chicago with the current proceedings on floor of the convention created the "most striking and false political picture of 1968—the nomination of a man for the American presidency by the brutality and violence of merciless police." /41/

If we are to believe a recent report of the House of Representatives' Commerce Committee, then television's presentation of the violence in the streets worked an injustice on the reputation of the Chicago police. According to the Committee findings, one network, in particular, presented, and I quote, "a one-sided picture which, in large measure exonerates the demonstrators and protestors. Film of provocations of police that was available never saw the light of day, while the film of the police response, which the protesters provoked, was shown to millions." /42/

Another network showed virtually the same scene of violence from three separate angles without making clear it was the same scene. And while the full report is reticent in drawing conclusions, it is not a document to inspire confidence in the fairness of the network news. /43/

Our knowledge of the impact of network news on the national mind is far from incomplete,[3] but some early returns are available. Again, we have enough information to raise serious questions about its effect on a democratic society. Several years ago, Fred Friendly, one of the pioneers of network news, wrote that its missing ingredients were, "conviction, controversy, and a point of view." The networks have compensated with a vengeance. /44/

And in the networks' endless pursuit of controversy, we should ask: What is the end value—to enlighten or to profit? What is the end result—to inform or to confuse? How does the ongoing exploration for more action, more excitement, more drama serve our national search for internal peace and stability? /45/

Gresham's Law seems to be operating in the network news. Bad news drives out good news. The irrational is more controversial than the rational. Concurrence can no longer compete with dissent. *One* minute of Eldridge Cleaver is worth *ten* minutes of Roy Wilkins. The labor crisis settled at the negotiating table is *nothing*

---

[3] This is what was said. Doubtless *complete* was meant.

compared to the confrontation that results in a strike—or better yet, violence along the picket lines. /46/

Normality has become the nemesis of the network news, and the upshot of all this controversy is that a narrow and distorted picture of America often emerges from the televised news. A single dramatic piece of the mosaic becomes in the minds of millions the entire picture. The American who relies upon television for his news might conclude that the majority of American students are embittered radicals, that the majority of black Americans feel no regard for their country, that violence and lawlessness are the rule rather than the exception on the American campus. /47/

We know that none of these conclusions is true. /48/

Perhaps the place to start looking for a credibility gap is not in the offices of the government in Washington but in the studios of the networks in New York. /49/

Television may have destroyed the old stereotypes, but has it not created new ones in their places? What has this passionate pursuit of controversy done to the politics of progress through local compromise, essential to the functioning of a democratic society? The members of Congress or the Senate who follow their principles and philosophy quietly, in the spirit of compromise, are unknown to many Americans, while the loudest and most extreme dissenters on every issue are known to every man in the street. /50/

How many marches and demonstrations would we have if the marchers did not know that the ever-faithful TV cameras would be there to record their antics for the next news show? /51/

We've heard demands that Senators and Congressmen and judges make known all their financial connections so that the public will know who and what influences their decisions and their votes. Strong arguments can be made for that view. But when a single commentator or producer, night after night, determines for millions of people how much of each side of a great issue they are going to see and hear, should he not first disclose his personal views on the issue as well? /52/

In this search for excitement and controversy, has more than equal time gone to the minority of Americans who specialize in attacking the United States, its institutions, and its citizens? /53/

Tonight, I've raised questions. I've made no attempt to suggest the answers. The answers must come from the media men. They are challenged to turn their critical powers on themselves—to direct their energy, their talent, and their conviction toward improving the quality and objectivity of news presentation. They are challenged to structure their own civic ethics to relate their great feeling with the responsibilities they hold. /54/

And the people of America are challenged, too—challenged to *press* for responsible news presentations. The people can let the networks know that they want their news straight and objective. The people can register their complaints on bias through mail to the networks and phone calls to local stations. This is one case where the people must defend themselves; where the citizen, not the government, must be the reformer; where the consumer can be the most effective crusader. /55/

By way of conclusion, let me say that every elected leader in the United States depends on these men of the media. Whether what I've said to you tonight will be heard and seen at all by the nation is not my decision. It's not your decision. It's *their* decision. /56/

In tomorrow's edition of the *Des Moines Register* you'll be able to read a news story detailing what I've said tonight. Editorial comment will be reserved for the editorial page, where it belongs. Should not the same wall of separation exist between news and comment on the nation's networks? /57/

Now my friends, we'd never trust such power as I've described, over public opinion, in the hands of an elected government. It's time we questioned it in the hands of a small and unelected elite. /58/

The great networks have dominated America's airwaves for decades. The people are entitled to a full accounting of their stewardship.[4] /59/

---

[4] From beginning to the end of speaking, but including interim applause, Mr. Agnew spoke for approximately twenty-eight minutes.

JONATHAN SMITH ON THE FEDERAL
CONSTITUTION: A CRITIQUE

Several historians of our Constitution have made special note of a
charmingly direct little speech made by Jonathan Smith on January 24
or 25, 1788, in the Massachusetts Convention to ratify the Constitution.
To weigh the rhetorical potentialities of this address can contribute a
footnote to history and illustrate that useful rhetorical criticism is
possible even where historical and biographical information is severely
limited. These are the purposes of this essay.

From studying this speech and related data I conclude that Smith's
short speech very nearly achieved the rhetorical ideal for the situation in
which it was given. It seems a speech that was needed in the Massachusetts
Convention. Jonathan Smith seems the right man to have made it,
and what he said had qualities that could directly serve the cause of the
Constitution in a Convention where the final decision was still in doubt.

The rhetorical situation of the Massachusetts Convention began to
evolve on September 17, 1787. On that date the Constitutional Convention
of the United States heard a reading of its final draft of the Constitution.
The delegates subsequently signed the document and submitted it to
the states for ratification. Conditions for its ratification specified that
decisions should be made by specially elected conventions in the states
and that the Constitution should come into effect when and if nine states
ratified it. State conventions did not have the right to alter the document
submitted to them. They must ratify or reject the Constitution as drawn.

Pennsylvania, New Jersey, Connecticut, Georgia, and Delaware chose
their conventions promptly, and those bodies ratified the Constitution
before the middle of January 1788. The Massachusetts Convention
convened on January 9, 1788, and historians agree that a majority of
the Massachusetts delegates were opposed to or in grave doubt about
the Constitution when they first came together. Even such leaders as
John Hancock and Samuel Adams had to be won over if there was to be
ratification, but the strongest opposition came from farmers and
artisans, particularly those from the western part of the state. As debate
and discussion progressed, the reservations of several eastern leaders
moderated, but representatives of the "little people," especially from the
west, remained fearful of the proposed change. Some uncertain number of
new supporters were still thought needed during the week of January 24.

From speeches made in the convention, from newspaper accounts,
and from personal records historians have now explored, it seems
clear that opponents of the Constitution consistently played upon the
following fears of what might happen if the proposed new government
went into effect:

  1. Congress might become a tyrannical clique disregarding its
     constituents.

2. A federal government with powers to set the times for elections and to tax the people could destroy the people's powers of self-government and could take away individuals' control over their own property.
3. The powers of Congress to regulate trade, create an army, collect duties, etc. would erode the rights of the states and eventually create a federal tyranny.
4. Six-year terms for Senators would make them unresponsive to their constituents' wishes.
5. The new government would find easy ways to clothe its operations in secrecy, thus destroying responsibility to the people.
6. No bill of individual rights existed in the Constitution, making the entire proposal a threat to individual liberty.

We can probably assume that the vocal opponents of the new government expressed concerns like those held by delegates who were merely in doubt or had reached no decision. If so, the fears mentioned above constituted attitudes which pro-Constitution forces needed to change in order to win a victory. I conclude that these concerns identify immediately important aspects of the rhetorical exigence Jonathan Smith addressed.

A further and unique exigence faced a man like Smith. Although he could address rural delegates as a peer, getting farmers and their representatives to support the Constitution was difficult in special ways. Some rural representatives in the Convention, and a good many of their constituents, had a record of opposition to strong government, even in their own state. A few delegates had been directly involved in the famous Shays' Rebellion, a violent movement among farmers and artisans which had closed courts by force in order to prevent imprisonment of debtors and foreclosures on mortgaged property. The rebellion was recent. The first threats had occurred on September 12 and 13, 1786, at Taunton (Bristol County) and at Concord, both in the eastern part of the state. Violence swiftly spread westward. Berkshire County, where Jonathan Smith lived, was caught in the grip of severe anti-government, anti-court, anti-wealth conflict involving raids in which several persons were killed. It was in this northwestern county that there occurred the bizarre event to which Smith refers in his speech: in February 1787, a company of rebels fought government troops on one of the Berkshire roads and, during the skirmish, put their prisoners between themselves and the militiamen while the rebels reloaded their firearms.

To the extent that ratification of the Constitution depended on votes from rural delegates, anti-governmental feelings in this group constituted a serious obstacle to persuasion for any pro-Constitutional speaker. No doubt rural speakers could soften the fears of rural delegates more easily than "rich men" and "learned men," but even rural speakers would find it difficult to establish wide credibility if they supported the new government. They would surely run some danger of seeming to their more radical brethren treacherous to their own kind. Jonathan Smith would thus find his credibility at least somewhat at issue.

As I have indicated, the options before the Convention were limited. All aspects of the Constitution could be discussed but, in the end, the Convention must vote for or against the entire document without changing any part of it. And timing was important. Proponents of change hoped to hurry the Convention along in order to contribute swiftly to the enacting total of nine state ratifications. Conversely, delay was the obvious strategy of opponents. Rejection of the document was their first goal, but failing that, achieving delay could discourage other states from ratifying and so hinder achievement of nine ratifications.

Such was the rhetorical situation Jonathan Smith chose to enter as a pleader for ratification. Unfortunately we know very little about Smith. Were it not for his speech, he would be all but lost to history. He was from Lanesboro, a tiny village in Berkshire County. He had fought in the Revolutionary War, entering service as an ensign and leaving as a captain or a colonel—records conflict on this point. He had held the office of justice of the peace, been a delegate to the convention that framed the Constitution of Massachusetts, and was now the elected convention delegate from his town. He was a farmer, and there are hints in histories of Berkshire County that he had other occupations as well. It appears, then, that Smith had some special standing in his town and county. It also appears that since the Revolution he had been somewhat of an "establishment" man. Moreover, his town of Lanesboro was one of only seven of the twenty-two Berkshire County towns to send pro-Constitution delegates to this Convention in Boston. On balance, it seems Smith would need to speak with care if he were to influence rural delegates not already committed to ratification. His experience might give him some special credit with the genuinely uncertain among his peers, and it would surely gain him a reasonably serious hearing from other delegates experienced in governmental affairs.

This is all we know and can conjecture about Jonathan Smith as a speaker in this Convention. His main advantages were that he was one of the "plain men" and one with a bit of special experience that could specially recommend his judgments.

There was little that was special about the moment at which Jonathan Smith choose to speak. He rose to answer another spokesman for the "little folks." The Secretary's notations concerning the day read in part:

> Friday, January 25.—The 8th section still under debate; but the conversation continued desultory; and much attention was paid to the inquiries of gentlemen on different parts of the Constitution, by those who were in favor of it.
>
> Mr. AMES, in a short discourse, called on those who stood forth in 1775 to stand forth now; . . . .

Hon. Mr. SINGLETARY. |There follows the record of Singletary's short speech contending that excessive exercise of central governmental power was what the Revolution had been against. The speech ended thus.| These lawyers, and men of learning, and moneyed men, that talk so finely, and gloss over matters so smoothly, to make us poor illiterate people swallow down the pill, expect to get into Congress themselves; they expect to be the managers of this Constitution, and get all the power and all the money into their own hands, and then they will swallow up all us little folks, like the great *Leviathan,* Mr. President; yes, just as the whale swallowed up *Jonah.* This is that I am afraid of; but I won't say any more at present, but reserve the rest for another opportunity.[1]

Jonathan Smith rose next to respond, and to extend his arguments beyond Singletary's position to the whole question of rural citizens' interests in the new government.

As a speaker trying to influence undecided and doubting persons ought, Smith undertook to reason with them. His first argument, by analogical example, extends through lines 6–33. It has much suggestive power, as I shall show; but it also is an obvious contention that the DATA of past experience justify the CLAIM that governmental change is needed lest tyranny seem preferable to anarchy another day. Here, as at most other points of evident argumentation (lines 51–55, 66–74, 76–82, and 85–87), the method is analogically inductive. In this instance Smith *says* (lines 14–16) he is proceeding causally, but in fact listeners must grant the accuracy of his "history" and also supply a WARRANT granting that "last winter" is sufficiently representative of how social forces work to predict similar events if no changes are made in government.

The analogical character of other clearly argued points in the speech is more evident. The constituents of delegates are presumably like constituents of prospective Congressmen; Congressmen will be little different from convention delegates. Association with learned men in land-title actions shows how advantageous it is to be associated with them in governmental actions. Compromises on fences illustrate the value of compromises on laws and governmental procedures. Timing in farming and timing in governmental action are similarly matters of maturation.

All such analogies presuppose that those addressed will accept the similarities of instances as particularly significant *in the present case.* In this respect Smith's analogical instances had rhetorical strengths but some weaknesses.

Smith's instances touched rural delegates' own experiences. All these delegates had some experience with Shays' Rebellion and the related

---

[1] These extracts and the text of Smith's speech which follows come from Jonathan Elliot, ed., *The Debates in the Several State Conventions, on the Adoption of the Federal Constitution* (Washington: By the Editor, 1836), pp. 100–104.

conflicts, and all were familiar with problems of clearing titles to land
and evolving neighborly cooperation in building fences. Harvests and
the maxims Smith used at the close of his speech were also familiar
to all. The instances comprising Smith's DATA had such familiarity that
no one was likely to reject them out of hand. The logical problem with
Smith's reasoning lay in the fact that not all listeners would WARRANT
Smith's CLAIMS as he did.

Delegates who had been active in the previous year's rebellion might
not see "last winter" as the "anarchy" Smith found it; and it is doubtful
that delegates uncertain about the Constitution would see the Constitution
as the obvious "answer" Smith claimed it was. Those already against
the Constitution would find little persuasiveness in Smith's implicit assurance that events like those of "last winter" would be forestalled by
ratification of the new government.

It would require a listener either eager for stability or one who reasoned
almost wholly by agrarian analogies to find full satisfaction in Smith's
analogies. But Smith's case does not rest upon analogical WARRANTS
alone. As we shall see, all of these arguments contain telling suggestive
elements supportive of Smith's case. Moreover, Smith's challenge to
Singletary's doubts are buttressed by a telling maxim: "They that are
honest men themselves are not apt to suspect other people." And his
harvest analogy is concluded with an either-or "threat": "If we won't
do it now, I am afraid we never shall have another opportunity."

Both maneuvers have the important potential of placing the burden of
proof on the opponents of the Constitution. If there is reason to suspect
prospective Congressmen, Singletary and his friends must *re*build their
case, or they stand convicted of Smith's charge against their own
integrity. If "harvesting" is to be rejected now, anti-Constitutionalists
must supply alternatives to losing all chances for change. If they do
not, listeners will be left with Smith's ringing either-or formulation—
his final utterance.

The whole question of what alternatives there are to the conditions of
"last winter" is brought into the open by the structure of Smith's
evaluative narration. Smith shrewdly inserts an important summative
and implicitly argumentative unit of thought at the close of his narrative
(lines 34–43). The Constitution is the "cure" for "these disorders." The
entire initial section of Smith's speech (lines 1–33) emerges as a "need
argument." Whoever finds the events of "last winter" disturbing, or has
responded to Smith's suggestively threatening images, must be
ready to hear of solutions. Smith spends his *ethos* as a "plain man" and
as a man experienced in constitutional matters. He has read the new
Constitution "over and over." He has applied what he learned as a framer
of the state Constitution. He has looked for those valued features: checks
and balances. "And I found them all there." Those virtues of the new
Constitution are so evident it requires no lawyer to point them out. Thus
he, a plain man, assures those who are suspicious of "learned men."

By placing this affirming section immediately after his narrative of disturbances Smith creates the possibility that listeners will find themselves in a dilemma from which they can escape *only* by choosing what Smith calls "anarchy" and "tyranny"—or the Constitution in which plain but experienced Mr. Smith has found comforting safeguards. Creating this anarchy *vs.* Constitution dichotomy appears to me the most compelling strategy a rhetorician could address to uncertain members of this Convention. In Massachusetts as elsewhere the great weakness of the anti-Constitutionalists' position was that they could offer no constructive alternative to the Constitution. In the Massachusetts Convention no one argued that all was well under the *status quo*—the Articles of Confederation. Implicitly, if not explicitly, all speakers granted that some improvement of existing conditions was desirable. Constitutionalists offered their document as a desirable instrument of change. Anti-Constitutionalists opposed it but had no design for modifying the *status quo.* Jonathan Smith was wise, I believe, in dramatizing conflict and disorder so recently experienced and in juxtaposing to that lurid picture the safety of the Constitution's "checks and balances of power." Moreover, the strategy "boxed in" the opponents of the Constitution. Unless they denied the picture painted in Smith's first thirty-three lines, they must seem to prefer the risks of disorder to a reasonable alternative. In these ways, it seems to me, Smith's initial unit of argument assumes the form of a dramatized need answered by a safe solution. Psychologically, if not logically, thought development was strongly directive. A listener hesitating to accept Smith's solution was left in this rhetorical situation with nothing to contemplate save yesterday's turmoil.

From line 43 to the end of his speech Smith refutes, reassures, and invites. The *ethos* of his opponents is impugned. Their arguments are turned against them by analogies I have already discussed (lines 43–55). He insists that the machinery of the Constitution will *work* (lines 56–65), and he assures his listeners that the presence of checks and balances in the Constitution will protect them. Finally come inviting and reassuring agrarian analogies and maxims. Where else should a reasonable "plain man" turn save to the Constitution?

The *form* of Smith's suasive effort begins to emerge. The thoughts of attentive listeners have been directed through contemplation of turmoil under the *status quo,* toward safeguards of the Constitution, toward the weaknesses of opponents' motivations and thinking, to ratification of the Constitution as the "natural" way of solving the day's problems and reaping future benefits. In today's terms, the speech is a movement of ideas from "Need" to "Solution" to "Benefits." And this is a form of communication ideally designed to assuage tensions and anxieties.

My analysis seems too neat. It deserves to be rechecked. The same listener-gratifying form in Smith's thought is outlined by asking what types of judgments Smith requests from his listeners. The entirety of lines 1–33 invites listeners to concede that Smith's facts are correct *and*

to deplore those "facts" optatively. A sudden change occurs in lines 34–55.
Now, factual judgments are invited concerning what is in the Constitution and concerning why men suspect each other. Optative responses
of general approval and disapproval are also encouraged. But sprinkled
through this section of the speech are clear invitations to *predict the
future:* the Constitution is a "cure," the presence of checks and balances
is reassuring, even the learned and the monied men are unlikely to abuse
their power under the Constitution (only the jealous would think so);
there is not more to fear from Congressmen than from convention delegates. It seems to me that listeners are repeatedly asked to see the future
under the Constitution as safe and in other ways desirable. As they are
asked to accede to "facts" about the Constitution and about the minds
of its opponents, the judgments, if granted, must be favorable toward
the Constitution and unfavorable toward its critics. It is apparent that
from line 56 to the conclusion of the speech Smith steadily invites his
listeners to peer into a future and to find there the boons of *safe*
representative government, *assistance* from the learned and monied,
the *wisdom* of compromise for the sake of safety, and the *benefits* of
reaping at the appointed "time to reap."

Whether one views the speech as a formal structure or as a series of
requests for adherence, the form of Smith's communication appears the
same. Recognition of problems is evoked, the prospect of a solution is held
forth, and the boons and the security of accepting Smith's solution are
projected into the future.

I emphasize the presence of this structured form because it seems
precisely the form rhetorical theory dictates when the ends of speaking
are to assuage doubts and to assist undecided persons to come to decisions.
Any speaker alert to the constraints of the rhetorical situation at this
Convention should have recognized that the target audience consisted of
those delegates still in a state of conflict concerning the desirability of
the Constitution. To resolve their dissonance required assuaging their
fears of a government possibly dangerous to individual liberty and to local
government. I am convinced that Smith's formal arguments, his general
implications, and the overall form of his address were astutely calculated
to reduce these senses of inner conflict, to salve the fears that seem to
have deterred doubters in this Convention, and to reassure those who
feared for the future of individual liberty and local government.

To discuss the role of language in Smith's suasive effort is to discuss
rhetorical data of which we cannot be sure. As Carl Van Doren has pointed
out, we do not know that Smith's recorded words are his. But neither
do we know this about Mr. Singletary's words, or the words of most
speakers who spoke in the various state ratification conventions of 1787
and 1788. All we know is that the words of the only text we have of Jonathan Smith's short speech are part of the history of how our national
Constitution came into being. Acknowledging that our text may be badly

flawed, I choose to take it seriously. Whatever its accuracy, this bit of American rhetoric is almost a model of what a "plain man" from western Massachusetts should have said on behalf of the Constitution.

 A striking fact about the style of this speech is that the suggestiveness of the language varies systematically through the problem-solution-benefits stages of the communication. The most vivid, active, sensual images and metaphors occur in the first 33 lines. It is in this portion of the speech that such words as these occur: *ploughjogger, black cloud rose, burst, took up arms, musket of death, to your breast, rob, threaten, be on your guard, alarms, prisoners set in front, set up his standard, flocked to it*—and three terms especially potent in eighteenth-century America: *anarchy, monarch,* and *tyrant.* One cannot draw a comparable list of compelling terms from the entire remainder of the speech! However, the final 7 lines contain almost as many metaphors as are found in the first 33 lines, but virtually all now have an agrarian flavor. Sheer numbers help to reflect the subtle shifts in emotional tone achieved through choice of language. In the first 33 lines I identify 10 metaphorical phrasings, all potentially calling sensory experience into play and most conveying some dimension of threat. In the next 49 lines I can find but nine metaphors and three of them are borrowed from Amos Singletary's remarks in order to season suggestions that Singletary is small minded. In the final 7 lines I can see eight metaphors, all but one ("leap in the dark") being agrarian and suggesting processes of growth and harvest. If empirical evidence that sustained metaphors significantly affect the responses of listeners is to be believed, the dangers Smith pictured while presenting "the problem" must have seemed more threatening by virtue of his threatening metaphors and the "normality" of his final appeal for ratification more "natural" by virtue of his agrarian growth metaphors.

 The midsection of Smith's speech is strikingly devoid of most figurative verbal devices. For the most part the section is made up of short, simple or compound statements communicating chiefly through denotative meanings. But the section does contain *seven rhetorical questions.* There are no such questions in the first 33 lines or the final 7. If it is true, as rhetorical theory postulates, that rhetorical questions invite self-persuading answers, it is certainly when discussing solution and benefits that Smith should have resorted to this stylistic structure.

 In sum, through language as well as general ideas Smith made the *status quo* of "last winter" seem directly threatening. By simple grammatical structures, denotative language, and rhetorical questions he made the Constitution seem a simple, obvious solution. And by a concentrated array of figurative, agrarian maxims, metaphors, and claims he made ratification seem a step analogous to an agrarian harvest. At beginning and end he concentrated rhetorical forces likely to evoke what the Greeks called *pathos,* but he spoke in terms a Spartan or

Aristotle's comtemplative man might admire when he presented the
reasonableness of the Constitution as a solution for past turmoil.

Only once did Jonathan Smith speak inexpertly. He was vague concerning his rhetorical purpose when he began. This gave Mr. Widgery
and Mr. Kingsley opportunity to challenge the relevance of what he
said. But the interruptions had the fortunate effect of forcing Smith to
be clear: "I am going, Mr. President, to show you, my brother farmers,
what are the effects of anarchy, that you may see the reasons why I wish
for good government." With the aim of his initial point clear, he led his
hearers undeviatingly through tension-inducing, solution-perceiving,
reassuring stages of experience. And no one in the Convention ever
directly challenged this "plain man's" all but perfect counsel to his
"brothers."

It is a misfortune that none of Smith's contemporaries left an
impression of how Smith sounded as he spoke in Boston—or anywhere
else. I choose to suppose that his manner was as judicious and un-
affected as his rhetorical content, style, and overall form of communication. Indeed, I am tempted to believe that it was Smith's nearly perfect
blending of matter and manner in the service of rhetorical counsel
that led Secretary Minot to accord Jonathan Smith of Lanesboro 75 lines
in a record of debate that dispatched a speech by the famous Fisher Ames
with a four-line summary.[2]

Did Smith win votes? We do not know. He certainly summoned rhetorical
forces that had that potential. That is also why historians and rhetorical
scholars have lingered over his little speech as they have thumbed the
pages of Elliot's *Debates* to learn how our Constitution came to be adopted.

---

[2] The lines referred to are as printed in the 1836 edition of Elliot's *Debates*.

ON THE FEDERAL CONSTITUTION
Jonathan Smith

1   Mr. President, I am a plain man, and get my living by
2   the plough. I am not used to speak in public, but I beg your
3   leave to say a few words to my brother ploughjoggers in
4   this house. I have lived in a part of the country where I have
5   known the worth of good government by the want of it.
6   There was a black cloud that rose in the east last winter and
7   spread out over the west.

[*Here Mr. Widgery, one of the opponents of the Constitution interrupted: "Mr. President, I wish to know what the gentleman means by the east." Mr. Widgery was from New Gloucester and, like some others, was exceedingly sensitive to any blame thrown on his section (now Maine).*]

8   I mean, sir, the county of Bristol; the cloud rose there,
9   and burst upon us, and produced a dreadful effect. It
10   brought on a state of anarchy, and that led to tyranny. I say
11   it brought anarchy. People that used to live peaceably and
12   were before good neighbors, got distracted and took up arms
13   against government.

[*Here Mr. Kingsley interrupted, asking what "the history of last winter" had to do with the Constitution. Several other members, including Samuel Adams, called out that Smith was in order and should "go on in his own way."*]

14   I am going, Mr. President, to show you, my brother farm-
15   ers, what were the effects of anarchy, that you may see the
16   reasons why I wish for good government. People, I say, took
17   up arms; and then, if you went to speak to them, you had
18   the musket of death presented to your breast. They would
19   rob you of your property; threaten to burn your houses;
20   oblige you to be on your guard night and day; alarms spread
21   from town to town; families were broken up. The tender
22   mother would cry, "O, my son is among them! What shall I
23   do for my child!" Some were taken captive, children taken
24   out of their schools, and carried away. Then we would hear
25   of an action, and the poor prisoners were set in the front, to
26   be killed by their own friends. How dreadful, how dis-
27   tressing was this! Our distress was so great that we would
28   have been glad to snatch at anything that looked like a
29   government. Had any person, that was able to protect us,
30   come and set up his standard, we should have flocked to it,

31   even if it had been a monarch; and that monarch might
32   have proved a tyrant; so that you see that anarchy leads to
33   tyranny, and better have one tyrant than so many at once.
34   Now, Mr. President, when I saw this Constitution, I found
35   that it was a cure for these disorders. It was just such a
36   thing as we wanted. I got a copy of it, and read it over and
37   over. I had been a member of the Convention to form our
38   own state Constitution, and had learnt something about
39   the checks and balances of power, and I found them all here.
40   I did not go to any lawyer, to ask his opinion; we have no
41   lawyer in our town, and we do well enough without. I
42   formed my own opinion, and was pleased with this Con-
43   stitution. My honorable old daddy there
          [*points to Mr. Amos Singletary who had spoken in opposition
          to the Constitution just before Smith rose*]
44   won't think that I expect to be a Congressman, and swallow
45   up the liberties of the people. I never had any post, nor do I
46   want one. But I don't think the worse of the Constitution
47   because lawyers, and men of learning, and moneyed men,
48   are fond of it. I don't suspect that they want to get into Con-
49   gress and abuse their power. I am not of such a jealous
50   make. They that are honest men themselves are not apt
51   to suspect other people. I don't know why our constituents
52   have not as good a right to be jealous of us as we seem to be
53   of the Congress; and I think those gentlemen, who are so
54   very suspicious that as soon as a man gets into power he
55   turns rogue, had better look at home.
56   We are, by this Constitution allowed to send ten mem-
57   bers to Congress. Have we not more than that number fit to
58   go? I dare say, if we pick out ten, we shall have another ten
59   left, and I hope ten times ten; and will not these be a check
60   upon those that go? Will they go to Congress, and abuse
61   their power, and do mischief, when they know they must
62   return and look the other ten in the face, and be called to
63   account for their conduct? Some gentlemen think that our
64   liberty and property are not safe in the hands of moneyed
65   men, and men of learning. I am not of that mind.
66   Brother farmers, let us suppose a case, now: Suppose you
67   had a farm of 50 acres, and your title was disputed, and
68   there was a farm of 5000 acres joined to you, that belonged
69   to a man of learning, and his title was involved in the same
70   difficulty; would you not be glad to have him for your friend,

71 rather than stand alone in the dispute? Well, the case is the
72 same. These lawyers, these moneyed men, these men of
73 learning, are all embarked in the same cause with us, and we
74 must all swim or sink together. And shall we throw the Con-
75 stitution overboard because it does not please us alike?
76 Suppose two or three of you had been at pains to break up a
77 piece of rough land, and sow it with wheat; would you let it
78 lie waste because you could not agree what sort of a fence to
79 make? Would it not be better to put a fence that did not
80 please every one's fancy, rather than not fence it at all, or
81 keep disputing about it until the wild beasts came in and de-
82 voured it?
83   Some gentlemen say, "Don't be in a hurry; take time to
84 consider"; and "Don't take a leap in the dark." I say, "Take
85 things in time; gather fruit when it is ripe." There is a time
86 to sow and a time to reap; we sowed our seed when we sent
87 men to the Federal Convention; now is the harvest. Now is
88 the time to reap the fruit of our labor. And if we won't do it
89 now, I am afraid we never shall have another opportunity.

Index